Market, Class, and Employment

Market, Class, and Employment

Patrick McGovern, Stephen Hill, Colin Mills,
and Michael White

OXFORD
UNIVERSITY PRESS

OXFORD
UNIVERSITY PRESS

Great Clarendon Street, Oxford OX2 6DP

Oxford University Press is a department of the University of Oxford.
It furthers the University's objective of excellence in research, scholarship,
and education by publishing worldwide in

Oxford New York

Auckland Cape Town Dar es Salaam Hong Kong Karachi
Kuala Lumpur Madrid Melbourne Mexico City Nairobi
New Delhi Shanghai Taipei Toronto

With offices in

Argentina Austria Brazil Chile Czech Republic France Greece
Guatemala Hungary Italy Japan Poland Portugal Singapore
South Korea Switzerland Thailand Turkey Ukraine Vietnam

Oxford is a registered trademark of Oxford University Press
in the UK and in certain other countries

Published in the United States
by Oxford University Press Inc., New York

British Library Cataloguing in Publication Data

Data available

Library of Congress Cataloging in Publication Data

Market, class, and employment / Patrick McGovern . . . [et al.].
    p. cm.
  Includes bibliographical references and index.
  ISBN-13: 978-0-19-921338-2
  ISBN-13: 978-0-19-921337-5
  1. Industrial relations–Great Britain.   2. Work–Great Britain.
I. McGovern, Patrick, 1966–
  HD8388.M37 2008
  331.0941–dc22   2007033470

Typeset by SPI Publisher Services, Pondicherry, India
Printed in Great Britain
on acid-free paper by
Biddles Ltd., King's Lynn, Norfolk

ISBN 978–0–19–921337–5
ISBN 978–0–19–921338–2 (Pbk.)

1 3 5 7 9 10 8 6 4 2

Acknowledgements

For the idea of researching change in the employment relationship, and the example of how to do so in practice, the authors owe their chief debt to Duncan Gallie, who also gave helpful advice and encouragement at various points.

Deborah Smeaton, of the Policy Studies Institute, was a member of the original research team and made substantial contributions to the research ideas, fieldwork, and analysis. We are most grateful to her for these, and for being an excellent colleague.

The research was funded by a major grant from the Economic and Social Research Council's *Future of Work* Programme (L212252037) with additional support from the Work Foundation. The authors have also drawn on a further ESRC-funded study under the same programme, the main results from which (together with full acknowledgements) have been reported in White et al. (2004). Patrick McGovern, Colin Mills, and Stephen Hill benefited from the support of the Suntory and Toyota International Centre for Economics and Related Disciplines (STICERD) at the LSE, while Michael White received additional support from the Regent Street Polytechnic Trust. Colin Mills wishes to thank the Sociology Department of the University of Oxford for special leave during the 2005–6 session and Professors Jan Hoem (Rostock) and Jan O. Jonsson (Stockholm) for being such gracious hosts at the Max Planck Institute for Demographic Research and the Swedish Institute for Social Research. Special thanks should also go to Professor Katherine Newman and the Department of Sociology at Princeton University for hosting Pat McGovern while this book was being completed. Pat would also like to acknowledge the support of the Leverhulme Foundation during this phase.

We are specially grateful to Peter Nolan, Director of the *Future of Work* Programme, for his most valuable practical help and staunch encouragement throughout. The programme provided many opportunities for researchers working on a wide range of research projects to meet, discuss, and comment upon each others' working papers. Through this, we

v

received help from colleagues on the programme, too numerous to name. We set up an Advisory Group to our project with members drawn from practitioners in private, public, and voluntary sector organizations. We thank them for giving their time to help us and for their high quality advice which proved most valuable to the design of our inquiry.

As part of the research, a national interview survey of British employees, 'Working in Britain in the Year 2000', was carried out on behalf of the research team by System Three Social Research, under the direction of Bruce Hayward and Stuart Robinson. We are grateful to them and their team of interviewers for the dedication with which they completed this demanding task. The present book also draws frequently on an earlier survey of employees, 'Employment in Britain': full acknowledgements for that survey can be found in Gallie et al. (1998).

Many others contributed advice and help at various stages. These included Nick Abercrombie, Alex Bryson, Tak Wing Chan, Jackie Coyle-Shapiro, Shirley Dex, Geoffrey Evans, Alan Felstead, David Firth, John Goldthorpe, Francis Green, Jon Jackson, Jouni Kuha, Matt Mulford, Michael Rose, Jim Skea, Robert Taylor, Sally Walters, and Stephen Wood. Additionally, findings and preliminary ideas from our research have been presented at about 30 seminars, workshops, and conferences. We are grateful for the comments that participants gave us at all these events. We also thank the anonymous referees of Oxford University Press who provided us with stimulating comments and suggestions.

A book with four authors can become something like a horse with four riders, a beast confused about the direction in which it should go. Whether we have managed to avoid this, we will leave it to the reader to decide for himself or herself. The other three co-authors wish to record their gratitude to Patrick McGovern, who kept us all to the task, firmly chided us when we were at our most delinquent and kept the flame alive when it seemed possible that it might flicker and die. We should also like to acknowledge the support of our partners and families during the many twists and turns of this epic journey. All of the authors have contributed to every chapter, but primary responsibility for chapter content has been devolved as follows: Patrick McGovern, Chapters 2 and 4; Stephen Hill, Chapter 1; Colin Mills, Chapter 8; Michael White, Chapters 5, 6, and 7. Chapter 3 is a collaboration between Mills, McGovern, and Hill while Chapter 9 was co-authored by McGovern and White.

PMcG, SH, CM, MW

May 2007

Contents

List of Figures

List of Tables

Glossary of Acronyms

AIC	Akaike's Information Criterion
BIC	Bayes' Information Criterion
BSA	British Social Attitudes
CEPS	Change in Employer Practices Survey of 2002
CFA	Confirmatory Factor Analysis
CV	curriculum vitae (career resume)
EiB	Employment in Britain Survey of 1992
EPOS	electronic point-of-sales (systems)
ESRC	Economic and Social Research Council
EU	European Union
EUROSTAT	statistical service of the EU
HPWS	high performance work systems (configuration of HRM below)
HRM	human resource management
ICT	information and communications technology
IJD	index of job desirability
LFS	Labour Force Survey(s); see also QLFS below
MAR	missing at random
NS-SEC	National Statistics Socio-Economic Classification
OLS	Ordinary least squares (linear regression analysis)
ONS	Office for National Statistics
POSAIJD	Predicted Occupational Shrunken Average Index of Job Desirability
QLFS	Quarterly Labour Force Survey(s)
SCMB	Social Class in Modern Britain
SEG	Socio-economic group (classification)
SOC	Standard occupational classification
SOR	Stereotyped ordered regression

UK   United Kingdom of Great Britain and Northern Ireland

US   United States—usually as adjective

USA   United States of America

WiB   Working in Britain in the Year 2000 Survey

WIRS/WERS   Workplace Industrial Relations Survey (until 1990)/Workplace Employment Relations Survey Series (1998 and 2004)

1

The changing economy of work

Over the past twenty-five years and especially at the onset of the new century, there has grown a widespread belief that working lives in Britain have changed in significant ways, and not always for the better. Economic restructuring at the macro and firm levels, political ideology, and social change appear, so it is claimed, to have combined to alter the nature of work and employment in important respects.

Many commentators are convinced that a new type of global economy is emerging. This differs radically from the one that developed, matured, and strengthened after the Second World War. Ulrich Beck (2000) discusses the apparent transition from the First to the Second Modernity, that is, from a work to a knowledge society, and towards a new political economy of insecurity. He refers to the 'Brazilianization' of employment in the West, which he believes is now marked by flexibility, insecurity, and discontinuity. Manuel Castells (2000) argues that, over the last thirty years or so, a new economic system has begun to develop, which is informational, global, and networked. This, he believes, has immense potential for both good and ill. Richard Sennett (2006) charts the decline of what he calls social capitalism and the rise of a new form of capitalism which is global, driven by short-term profit-seeking behaviour, and revolutionized by new informational and communication technologies. While it is mainly confined at present to large companies in particular economic sectors, he predicts that the new capitalism will spread more widely in the future. Bennett Harrison (1997) identifies globalization and network forms of inter-organizational relationships and relations of production as the key features of the emerging world economy. However, he argues against Castells and others that, while the new technologies of distributed information processing and telecommunications enable global coordination, they are not essential to economic transformation.

In summary, these commentaries and interpretations suggest that a new economy may be developing, which at present is unevenly distributed across economic sectors. The authors generally accept, moreover, that it takes different forms across different societies which have their own cultural and institutional contexts. For these reasons, all their predictions about its future shape and the associated patterns of employment and work organization must remain speculative. But the analysis is on somewhat firmer ground when considering the erosion of the older patterns, particularly the forms typically found in the liberal market economies of the USA and Britain, and among the coordinated market economies of continental Europe.[1] There is substantial evidence on this score, much of which has become so familiar as to obtain the status of stylized fact. The erosion of the 'golden' post-war age—*Les Trentes Glorieuses* (Fourastié 1979)—is used by these authors to draw inferences about what they regard as the current and future deterioration of working life, and its causes.

1.1. The Old Order

The notion of a new economic order, and especially the inferences drawn about changes in working lives and employment relationships, can be fully understood only when contrasted with what might be called the 'old order'. Karl Polanyi (1957)[2] described how 'organized capitalism' had developed as an economic system that restrained its own potential because, without restraints, it would tear society to pieces. The restraints included the supranational and national control of money, the formation of business monopolies and cartels, protective trade agreements or barriers of various types, and associative institutions such as employers' federations and trade unions that curbed opportunism. Sennett (2006: 15–82) has revisited Max Weber's account of the Prussian or Bismarkian model of capitalism, in order to show how bureaucratic, social capitalism was developed as a solution to the dangers of unregulated capitalism and came to dominate large organizations in the twentieth century.

Relations between employers and employees became progressively more regulated over time under Western industrial capitalism. Philip Selznick (1969) showed how even in the especially liberal society of the USA there had been a gradual development of individual employment rights and protections through case law and new legislation, and also by the diffusion of norms of employer conduct. For Britain, an important part was played by the growth of the union movement and the development of collective bargaining institutions, which have been charted by eminent scholars from Sidney and Beatrice Webb (1894) to Allan Flanders and Hugh Clegg (1954). In addition, and perhaps no less important in the long run, there is a long tradition of paternalist relations between employer and employee, surveyed by Alice Russell (1991). She illustrated how pre-industrial paternalism first survived in isolated pockets of the early industrial revolution, and much later was developed more systematically by large British employers, including the public services, into welfare benefits that would attract and motivate the labour they wanted. For employees, therefore, there appeared to be a long trajectory of improving work conditions, even if the process was slow and punctuated by industrial conflicts. This was complemented by the growth of welfare provisions, especially in the immediate post-war period, in every country of the West that gave some protection against the adverse financial consequences of sickness, injury, job loss, and old age. Germany had pioneered social insurance in the late-nineteenth century, and Britain and the Scandinavian countries systematically developed the welfare state after the end of the war. The Beveridge Plan and the founding of the National Health Service were the crucial developments in Britain (Beveridge 1942, 1944; Bevan 1952; Marshall 1965).

These economic, social, and political tendencies, it is argued, combined after the Second World War with the full maturity of Fordist production techniques that had been instituted in the interwar period. This fusion created an era of relatively full employment and security through most of the Western nations, coupled with improving working conditions and pay, and higher standards of living through the widening availability of affordable consumer durables. A compelling account of the era was rendered by Jean Fourastié (1979) on the eve of its demise.

1.2. The Forces of Change

The issue is how these economic, social, and political tendencies, which were often benign for employees, were questioned by the new order that began to emerge after 1980, following the crisis of the 1970s with its 'oil shocks', rampant inflation, and stagnant productivity. For many commentators, the intensification of market competition in the new order is of considerable importance. The incorporation of national economies into a more international economic system, often but not necessarily referred to as 'globalization', has intensified the competitive pressures that companies face, in Britain as elsewhere.

Much of the early evidence on this score concerned manufacturing. In their review of the US material, Bennett Harrison and Barry Bluestone (1988) pointed to a decline of profits in manufacturing, falling output of home-produced goods as imports gained ground, and the rise of Japan as a major exporting nation. All these developments were under way in the 1970s. Similar evidence was assembled in the UK, including early indications that global manufacturing capacity was outstripping demand across many product sectors (Armstrong, Glyn, and Harrison 1984). The standard indicator of international competition has subsequently become the proportion of internationally traded goods relative to GDP, or in global terms, the ratio of world trade to world output (Ladipo and Wilkinson 2002a: 11–15). This indicator has been rising for many years for most industrialized countries and for the world economy. During 1990–2002, which is the focal period of this book, Britain's spending on imports rose by 79 per cent and receipts from exports rose by 80 per cent; over the same period, GDP increased by 66 per cent.[3] There is no question that this trend is set to continue. Great political and diplomatic investments have been made, and continue to be made, in dismantling trade barriers, although protections for US and EU agriculture now form a significant obstacle to further change.

A more recent development has been the advent of newly industrializing countries, which are dependent on exports for their growth. The rise of China as a major manufacturer, destined before long to become the world's largest,[4] is very well known. Several other countries, including Brazil, India, Indonesia, and South Korea, now maintain rates of increase in manufacturing and external trade that are well ahead of Western economies. The collapse of the Soviet communist bloc around 1990 has also been followed by the progressive assimilation of East European countries, and of Russia itself, into the international capitalist economy, which adds further to the world's economic integration and its competitive activity.

Competition in services is less easy to identify clearly, and one has to rely more on qualitative indications of increasing pressures. In particular, deregulation and/or the removal of State monopolies from the 1980s onwards, policies in which Britain appeared to follow the lead of the USA, have opened some important kinds of service to more competition: notably financial and legal services, travel and transport, and communications. Similarly, many public services, especially in local government, have been opened to competition from profit-making firms through privatization and the compulsory competitive tendering of service provision, policies which were introduced by the Thatcher government. Overall, employment in the public sector fell by nearly one-third between 1979 and 1997, partly through this process of transfer to the private sector (Morgan, Allington, and Heery 2000). A transformation of Britain's high streets has also taken place as chain-outlet businesses have supplanted independent firms. This has occurred not only in retailing but also in food and drink outlets and in many other consumer services: when one excludes the smallest outlets with less than five employees, four in five of consumer service businesses are now part of multi-site operations.[5] Whether this represents more or less competition is not clear, but it does suggest that the type of competition may have changed towards the efficiency-based system of manufacturing. This was predicted by Theodore Levitt (1972).

The 'service economy model' now characterizes Britain, the USA, and Canada (Castells 2000: 245). These are the three G8 countries where the proportion of manufacturing employment declined and service employment increased most markedly in the final three decades of the twentieth century.[6] Castells interprets these decisive shifts in employment and occupational structures as a corollary of the rise of 'informationalism', where the service sector is geared more to capital management than producer services, social services such as health care and education grow, and the managerial section of the employed population expands significantly.

Even when market services are sheltered from competition, they remain exposed to the threat of hostile takeover if performance weakens, as are manufacturing companies. This reflects a change in financial markets that is as important as increasing competition in product markets. This is strongly argued in Britain's case by Will Hutton (1995), and by David Ladipo and Frank Wilkinson (2002a). Capital markets have changed considerably over the last four decades, notably through the growing and now very substantial role of financial institutions in the markets for equity investments and loans, the continuing expansion of alternative investment opportunities around the world, and the emergence of major new sources of international investment capital. Many restrictions on the international movement of capital were removed in the 1980s, and there has been a continuing tendency towards deregulation coupled with reduced transaction costs from new technology. This is generally believed to have favoured a more innovative and dynamic financial environment

(Buckle and Thompson 2004). The increased globalization of financial markets has significantly changed the international economy (Castells 2000: 101–6). These circumstances help to explain the persisting force of the 'shareholder value' revolution that came to prominence in the 1980s, and the pressures that it exerts on senior executives (Hutton 1995; Sennett 2006). Shareholders display a new assertiveness in demanding appropriate rates of return on their investments and in their willingness to discipline those management teams who fail to perform in the short term.

Alongside the changes in the competitive and institutional context, the internal technology of production has also changed considerably and eroded the Fordist production methodology with its emphasis on continuity and integration. The 'knowledge' strand of the contemporary economic system is thought to be growing stronger in what is often referred to as the 'knowledge' economy, which Daniel Bell (1974) called 'post-industrial' and Castells (2000) has labelled 'informational'. The knowledge economy is thought to have several characteristics: goods and services embody more technical knowledge in their design and production than at any time in the past; knowledge as a commodity has value even in the absence of a physical embodiment (*vide* the activities of financial analysts); highly educated, knowledge workers are the fastest growing and best remunerated section of the labour force, while the less skilled face a more precarious situation; and intellectual property is the stock in trade of many organizations. Changes observed within the British labour force are consistent with this, including fewer manual jobs and a substantial increase in technical, professional, and managerial jobs.[7]

1.3. The Response of Employers and Consequences for Employees

What are the implications of intensified and universalized competition, of increasingly powerful financial systems and of a transition to an economy of services and of knowledge, for employers and employees in Britain and similar post-industrial economies? We here consider some of the general interpretations that have been advanced. A more detailed discussion of employers' responses and their consequences for employees (especially recent British contributions to this debate) will be found in Chapter 2.

In broad terms, the effects of the trends on people in work are often thought to include a more rigorous treatment by employers who have to promote shareholder value in a harsher environment, with disruptive shifts in the aggregate demand for labour because of greater volatility in the international economy.

The simplest interpretation, as well as one of the earliest, is that of Harrison and Bluestone (1988). For them, the key factor in the response of US employers to changing competitive conditions was falling profits. Employers reacted to restore profits by 'zapping labour' (Harrison and Bluestone 1988: 21–52). In essence, the aim was to force labour costs down, in part by abandoning previous policies that provided security and internal career structures. This resulted in a set of adverse consequences for employees that have been widely reported. The pressure to reduce costs while responding more rapidly to changing markets led large firms into substantial internal restructuring. They have cut the number of people they employ ('downsizing') and the number of vertical levels within the organization ('delayering' or 'flattening'), in order to cut staff costs and remove organizational inertia in the face of change. In place of vertically integrated organizations, companies have begun to introduce decentralized and more flexible structures that are coordinated by internal markets and information networks. Harrison and Bluestone (1988: 13) label the overall effect as 'vertical disintegration'.[8] At the same time, a new form of work organization was developed: one based on self-managing teams, which required more highly skilled and responsible employees (Hirschhorn 1984: 115–16, 1985).

Another interpretation of the response of employers to the new circumstances has emphasized the progressive abandonment of the widespread 'standard' employment contract. Standard employment has been defined by Arne Kalleberg, Barbara Reskin, and Ken Hudson (2000: 258) as

The exchange of a worker's labor for monetary compensation from an employer . . . with work done on a fixed schedule—usually full-time—at the employer's place of business, under the employer's control, and with the mutual expectation of continued employment.

Employment that is usually full time, permanent, eligible for occupational benefits, and embedded in a career structure is thought to have been in part replaced by temporary or marginal forms of employment, and by non-standard forms of part-time employment. This uses ideas from the traditional analysis of labour market segmentation and dual economy theory (Kerr 1950, 1954; Doeringer and Piore 1971; Edwards 1979; Althauser and Kalleberg 1981). Labour markets, according to this view, were segmented and standard employment was more common in the major, capital-intensive companies which dominated the primary sector of the US economy, often with oligopolistic product markets. In the secondary sector, where primitive market competition continued, companies were likely to base employment more on market principles, offering less secure and more contingent jobs, less predictable wages, poorer welfare benefits, and more part-time work. Even within large primary companies, there were some employees who were not included in the full benefits of standard employment and were located in secondary labour market segments on the periphery of the core system. Gender and ethnicity could be a source of differentiation, with women and certain ethnic minorities being less likely to experience standard employment.[9]

If the standard model is assumed to apply widely, it is natural to infer that as competition erodes protections, more of the 'primary' jobs will disappear while poor-quality 'secondary' jobs expand. Thus, Beck (1992, 2000) sees a future where most or all jobs will be of a 'destandardized' type. Less extreme views suggest that non-standard forms of employment will not become dominant but will be increasingly important for employers seeking flexibility. Organizations may retain their core functions and capabilities while abandoning more peripheral activities (such as internal cleaning, catering, printing, and payroll services) and contracting for these with outsiders (Ackroyd and Procter 1998; Purcell and Purcell 1998; Cully et al. 1999: 34–8; White et al. 2004; Kersley et al. 2006: 54, 103–7). This 'outsourcing', and the use of staff on short term, temporary contracts, allows companies to adjust their numbers more easily. The same policies also facilitate restructuring, since they reduce the costs of terminating jobs, such as redundancy pay in Britain. Thus, more flexible external labour markets and more flexible internal organization may go hand in hand.[10]

There are also more general accounts of these changes, which are couched in terms of 'internalized' employment arrangements giving way to 'externalized' or market-based arrangements. The contention is that the typical form of standard employment was based more on internalized organizational arrangements than market forces (Cappelli 1995; Harrison 1997: 258–61; Baron and Kreps 1999: 167–88). In the USA, the frequent development of several features in combination, namely relatively high employment security, internal labour markets (which are organizational procedures for assigning staff to hierarchical positions), internal career ladders (which might give some reward to seniority as well as performance), company welfare benefits, and pension plans for full-time employees, constituted the full norm of standard employment. It is precisely this norm that is said to be giving way to an increasingly externalized, market-based approach by employers, as organizations move along the continuum between the extremes of complete internalization and complete market determination. Peter Cappelli (1999a, 1999b), a well-known advocate of this view, reports that many large employers in the USA have cut back their internalized systems to become more responsive to market circumstances. Significantly, this change did not apply solely, or even particularly, to peripheral or lower-level jobs in the organization. Rather, employers wanted speedily to acquire skilled and talented individuals as required, and also to divest themselves of such people when market opportunities were altered. The internalized systems, which tied employers to employees and vice versa, were seen as barriers to this type of business flexibility in the use of talent. In reality, senior employees were unlikely to have been completely dependent on a single employer in the past: while many companies might have offered individuals long-term employment, even jobs for life, senior, higher-grade managerial and professional employees were likely to possess transferable competencies and a proportion would choose to use their market power to move among companies (Doeringer and Piore 1971: 2–4; Piore 1975). In Cappelli's account, the market-based, externalized response by employers takes account of the shift towards knowledge-based competition as well as the general increase in competitive intensity. It is thought to give rise to different forms of careers, where individuals rather than employers have to take the lead, constructing their own 'portfolio' careers with moves across companies and sometimes across occupations (Handy 1996: 23–31).

A central feature of the change from the established features of standard employment has been the search for cheaper, more efficient, and more effective ways of using staff. These are believed to have taken several forms. A reduction in the costs of employment can be achieved immediately by cutting the number of people on the payroll. Downsizing can be a strategy to retain indispensable employees, who have knowledge and skills that cannot be easily found on external labour markets, while dispensing with permanent staff whose services can be accessed at lower cost in other ways. These include contracting out work to cheaper suppliers, which are located in lower cost areas and have less favourable terms and conditions of employment. Relocation can include transferring jobs to the informal economy in the home country and exporting them to other companies (or to overseas branches of the home organization) in lower cost economies. An alternative is to increase the proportion of contingent staff in the organization, notably by hiring people on a temporary basis, on fixed-term contracts, or as contingent part-time employees.

New technology provides another path to reduce staffing costs. The history of the application of mechanization and then automation in organizations suggests that the easier that it becomes to standardize routine and repetitive tasks and make these programmable, the simpler it is to replace people by machines or information technology. This was the experience of manufacturing during the twentieth century, from the days of the Scientific Management of mechanized assembly lines to contemporary, computer-controlled, flexible manufacturing systems. It was also the pattern of the organization of office work after the 1960s: the development and commercial application of computing, from the early mainframes through more recent microcomputers and telecommunications, have been used to standardize tasks and reduce the size of the back office function. Fewer employees are required and should organizations choose people as well as information technology, then standardized and simplified white-collar tasks can be performed in-house by contingent staff or, as an alternative, they can be relocated elsewhere and outsourced to contractors.

There is a very different argument, however, that new technology can enhance the human skills required by organizations, as well as eliminate or relocate the unskilled and partly skilled aspects of production and office work (Hirschhorn 1984: 114–51, 1985; Castells 2000: 255–81). British research using nationally representative samples of employers (Daniel 1987) and of employees (Gallie et al. 1998) has found that new technology is on balance associated with increases in skills, although such research is plagued by the difficulty of defining skill. Castells suggests that the emerging informational economy may be accompanied by occupational upgrading, because, as the nature of work changes, certain jobs now require more intelligence, education, and the ability to make decisions. But he believes that the realization of this potential is likely to be hindered by the choices that companies make to restructure work processes and employment in particular ways, in response to unconstrained competition (Castells 2000: 266, 280).

The changing relationship between employer and employee has also been explained in terms of risk shifting. Unfortunately, this term is often used in a loosely defined way to refer to the whole array of uncertainties that individuals face and, when used like this, it has little analytical value. Some authors, however, deploy the concept more precisely and argue that risk shifting represents a specific change in employers' labour policies, which is part of a wider restructuring of social relations. Thus, Richard Breen (1997) begins with a general problem, which he describes as a long-term decline in those institutions that once acted to hedge against market risk.[11] He argues that in Britain, until recently, the welfare state, the nuclear family, and capitalist enterprises all acted to offset market risk by placing it in the context of a 'generalized (or quasi-generalized) reciprocity' (Breen 1997: 473). In other words, the parties were committed to each other's welfare, and life chances were somewhat buffered against market forces. However, Breen claims that those who enjoy greater social power have sought to recast these institutions so that 'they establish option-like relationships' with the less powerful (Breen 1997: 475). This decline in the arrangements that hedged against market-based risks brings about a process of recommodification. Underlying this argument is an assumption of powerlessness on the part of recommodified labour (otherwise employees would resist the change), and it is important to note that Breen distinguishes carefully between the classes that are exposed and those that are not exposed to this process. Employees in the higher occupations, for instance, generally continue to enjoy reciprocity in their employment relationships. This is clearly a very different conceptualization from the 'market externalization' thesis.

The common element in these interpretations of the responses of employers to changing conditions is a reduced commitment by employers to at least some of their employees, who can readily be removed in the search for short-term results. There are, however, different views of the policies of employers in the current era. Indeed, the first set of new ideas about the employment relationship, as the crisis of the 1970s developed, emphasized the need for an improved internal management of people. According to US business school theorists like Richard Walton (1972, 1985, 1987; see also Beer et al. 1984), organizations needed to move 'from control to commitment' by means of the systematic development of individual employees and increased opportunities for participation and voice. These attributes were discerned in leading Japanese multinationals and regarded as essential if US companies were to compete in terms of innovation and productivity. In short, the response to greater competition was seen to be a better use of human resources: the model came to be known as human resource management (HRM). In the USA, subsequent development has shifted towards the identification of sets of organizational practices that, in combination, raise individual and team performance: these are the 'high performance work systems' (HPWS) that are described and evaluated in studies such as that by Eileen Appelbaum and her colleagues (Appelbaum et al. 2000). In this model, competitive pressures are to be met by higher productivity from existing employees

11

rather than by cutting labour costs. Furthermore, the acquisition of skills and talent in a knowledge economy should be ensured by internal development rather than through the external job market.

The extensive use of HRM policies and practices in Britain (Wood and de Menezes 1998; Forth and Millward 2004; White et al. 2004) points to the adherence of many employers to 'internalized' rather than 'externalized' or 'marketized' models of the employment relationship. However, policies to cut labour costs, such as downsizing and delayering, are likely to be found when extensive HRM practices are both present and absent (White et al. 2004: 140–1; see also Kalleberg 2003 and Wood, de Menezes, and Lasaosa 2003 for discussions of mixed approaches). This appears to question the idea that there are two mutually exclusive models of the employment relationship, with the internalized model based on reciprocity while the externalized or marketized model involves commodified relations. It seems more likely that employers will tend to maintain the internalized and reciprocal form of relationship, while allowing some flexibility to cope with intensified market pressures. An important question is whether this flexibility is confined to the treatment of peripheral workers, or whether it also involves some modification of the internalized relationship of core employees.[12]

1.4. Contracts and Employment Relationships

We have now completed our review of current ideas about the supposed emergence of a new economy of work. A closer understanding of internalized and marketized employment relations requires a more formal conceptualization. We use the concept of employment contract at many points in our analysis. This has now become a point of common ground among economists, sociologists, and organizational psychologists who wish to explain different patterns of employment relations.[13] Sociologists have in the past preferred 'employment relationship', in recognition of the fact that the formal, contractual elements of employment are one part, and usually a relatively small part, of the totality of rights, obligations, formal and informal social relationships which employment creates between employers and employees. A standard sociological criticism of the traditional focus of economists on formal contracts was that economists ignored what was not explicitly required, but may still have been legitimately expected or done, by the contracting parties. Sociologists, by contrast, emphasized the social institutions, de facto norms, and emergent properties that underpin contractual relationships. However, the attention now paid by economists to incomplete contracts and their implicit provisions, which are socially determined, has effectively removed these points of difference. As John Goldthorpe (2000*a*) notes, the systematic analysis of contractual relations by economists has created a language and set of concepts that provide sociologists with powerful tools to pursue their own traditional interests.

1.4.1. *The Incompleteness of Employment Contracts*

It is widely accepted that employment contracts usually differ from other contracts in their incompleteness and consequential lack of precision. This was pointed out by Karl Marx among others, who reminded us that employers buy only the labour power of employees and not their actual labour. The latter has to be extracted within the workplace, the 'hidden abode' where labour is realized. In the most common form of employment contract, employers and employees enter open-ended relationships, the details of which may emerge only with the passage of time and may be implicit as well as explicit. 'Relational' employment contracts contain formal contractual terms that are supplemented by implicit or informal understandings. The latter embody tradition and custom and practice (Baron and Kreps 1999: 62–3), and they may display emergent properties and change over time as a result of the interactions between employers and employees. The employee often possesses potentially valuable knowledge that is not available to the employer, who will seek ways of ensuring that the employee uses it to the advantage of the organization. At the same time, incomplete contracts are prone to moral hazard, shirking, and opportunism, reflecting a divergence in the interests of each party to the employment relation. Employers and employees must find ways of containing these relational stresses if the contract is to be mutually beneficial.

This contractual framework helps to explain the choices made by organizations in determining how they get people to do the required work. A basic division is between contracting with suppliers via the external market, which is an arms-length relation, and offering employment contracts within the organization, where the producers of goods and services become employees who are subject to the governance structure of a managerial hierarchy. The long-run tendency has been for work to be internalized within organizations, that is, for organizations to become employers rather than coordinators of contracts with outside entities. It is assumed that the choice of managerial governance rather than arms-length contracting is due to the greater efficiency of the former over the latter for the types of transactions involved in employment. For Max Weber, the internalized form, which he called 'bureaucracy',[14] arose from the problems of coordination in organizations of large size, including the modern business corporation, and is the only efficient form for these circumstances (see Weber 1947: 329–40). The contractual relation places the employee at the command of superiors, so that the hierarchy comes to exercise 'imperative coordination'.

An economic foundation for the choice between internalized and externalized contracts has been provided by transaction cost analysis (Williamson 1981, 1985). Different forms of contractual relation involve different transactions costs, for instance in framing contracts and in monitoring their performance. Employment rather than contracting on the external market is typically the preferred arrangement when the level of uncertainty is such that it is difficult to draft completely explicit contracts and monitor supplier performance. The incompleteness of the information available to the employer and the likelihood of opportunism by the suppliers of services are both factors here. However, as noted earlier, there has probably been some return towards externalization, through outsourcing, over recent years. Relevant factors here would include the standardization of some services, such as the production of a payroll, which makes it easier to specify the contract, and the advance of information and communications technology (ICT) networks, which makes monitoring easier and cheaper. Nonetheless most of the work of most organizations continues to be carried out by their own employees.

Most employees in most organizations are on permanent contracts and have substantial periods of job tenure, even in the USA (Jacoby 1999a). An important feature of employment as a relational contract is that even in the contemporary economy it provides employees with a degree of protection against various risks. First, in open-ended relationships, employees are sheltered against the risks of the external labour market. A comparison with the spot market for labour illustrates this point. In spot markets, contracts are of fixed and often short duration, because individuals are hired for a specific period of time or quantity of output. Individuals are then obliged to re-enter the labour market and compete for the next contract. In relational contracts, employees enter the external labour market less often and, when they do, are likely to do so as much out of choice as of necessity. Second, employees are protected against business risks that arise out of fluctuations in product and capital markets, because employers shoulder these fluctuations, at least for a period of time. It is claimed that employees tend to be risk averse while, if their portfolio is diversified, the owners of capital will be risk neutral (Milgrom and Roberts 1992: 187). In relational employment contracts, employers generally prefer to retain experienced staff and normally bear the cost of providing secure employment and secure wages during fluctuations in the business environment.

1.4.2. *The Problem of Motivation*

A significant issue is why employers appear to persist with permanent contracts under increasingly competitive conditions. One possible explanation is the following. When work becomes an employment contract that is controlled by the authority relations of management, a familiar set of problems emerges. Employers are faced by the need to recruit and retain employees, and to induce them to exert effort on their behalf as well (Tilly and Tilly 1998: 200–13). The latter issue of control and motivation is the least tractable. Moreover, the solutions that are often adopted may also help to resolve the issues of recruitment and retention. The area of control and motivation is part of the explanation of the continuation of permanent contracts.

Economists and sociologists recognize that employment contracts give employers access to the time and potential productivity of their employees but not a determinate amount of effort or output. Drawing on the language of Marx, sociologists have encapsulated this as the problem of turning 'labour power' into 'labour'. For economists, the issue is the moral hazard associated with the relationship between a principal and an agent. However it is expressed, the problem is the same.[15] Employment contracts are inevitably incomplete. Indeed, the impossibility of drawing up a complete contract is a major reason for adopting an employment arrangement rather than contracting on the outside market in the first place. Contracts will contain some explicit provisions that detail certain employee obligations, but most elements have to remain implicit. Thus, employees place themselves under the command of employers, who then have to find ways to ensure that they pursue their interests. But employers typically have incomplete information about the nature of jobs and the capabilities of employees, how well they have worked, and whether they have been honest. Employees have the information but have an interest in concealing it from their employers. Incomplete and implicit contracts under conditions of information asymmetry matter, because employees cannot be relied upon to promote employers' interests and vice versa.

Both parties to the employment relationship have different interests and therefore employment relationships, and while they involve cooperative activity, are also potentially adversarial.

The issue for employers in all forms of employment relationship, therefore, is to get employees to pursue employers' interests. One way is the exercise of managerial authority, although this has its limits as noted above. Monitoring reduces the information problem that is central to moral hazard, but can be expensive and may not be fully effective in many situations. Richard Edwards (1979) developed a typology of managerial control that included 'simple' or personal control, that is, the direct monitoring of employees by a supervisor who has relevant knowledge of the task and what an employee might be expected to achieve. Appropriate where tasks and work organization are simple, it is less effective where tasks are skilled and complex and require considerable tacit or private knowledge, and work organization is more complex. Hence, it is of little use in a knowledge business or with knowledge workers. Technical control, which involves the machine pacing of work, is appropriate for inducing effort in certain technologies: for example, assembly-line production or telephone call centres. However, sociologists generally now see more mileage for employers in controls that work at the normative level and motivate employees. Persuading employees to internalize the objectives of employers is more effective than mere obedience to commands. Patrice Rosenthal, Stephen Hill, and Riccardo Peccei (1997) have discussed the various conceptualizations of normative commitment and control, which stretch from Edwards' notion of bureaucratic control (Edwards 1979) through organizational culture, ideology, and discourse. All forms of normative commitment and control rely upon a continuing, long-term relationship between employer and employee to be effective, as norms have to be learned and internalized.

Economists have mainly taken a different tack and concentrated on how employer and employee interests may be aligned and rendered compatible by means of incentives, with or without monitoring.[16] Yet the conclusion is remarkably similar. The economics position may be summarized briefly. The issue is to make implicit contracts become self-enforcing, that is to structure their provisions so that both parties have incentives and are motivated to honour them, and neither would gain by cheating (Milgrom and Roberts 1992: 332–3). Individual incentive payments (such as piece rates and commission) are the simplest approach, but they require measurable outputs and do not fit complex divisions of labour where the individual's contribution is difficult to pinpoint.

Group incentives, which are based on the performance of a team, are also often appropriate because they complement the communal nature of some forms of work. James Baron and David Kreps (1999: 261–8) suggest that, under certain conditions, group incentive schemes work very effectively and, moreover, fit well with high-commitment HRM. They also believe that profit-sharing and employment stock ownership schemes in the USA, which give employees a share in the performance of the whole organization, can enhance both performance and motivation (Baron and Kreps 1999: 5, 264).[17]

The economic view of incentives, however, is wider than these forms. Of special importance is the competition for promotion, giving access to those who succeed to higher pay and added privilege (Lazear 1998; Tilly and Tilly 1998: 216–23). Promotion serves as a means of aligning objectives. It does so by rewarding good behaviour and penalizing bad. One aspect of the rising career wages that have commonly been found in the professions and in internal labour markets for managerial employees is the increase of wages with seniority. Thus, the lower pay of younger employees may be viewed as deferred pay, which will be recouped in later life. People who are judged to have cheated or fallen short on the contract are not promoted and therefore 'forfeit their deposit' of deferred pay. Even in the absence of systematic monitoring, the individual will be wary about behaving in a way that jeopardizes these long-run returns. Furthermore, it can be argued that over time individuals tend to find employment niches that suit their own preferences and provide them with 'rents'. These are better rewards than they could expect to get on the open job market, which may in part reflect the firm-specific knowledge and skills that they have accumulated and that have less value elsewhere. So long-term employment tends to generate its own incentives for employees, which are also good for employers. In the exposition of Baron and Kreps (1999: 65–6), by staying together the employer and the employee develop 'relation-specific assets' that both can enjoy.

Whether approaching the issue via theories of control and commitment or via theories of incentive, it is clear that open-ended and long-term employment can help to solve the motivational problem of incomplete contracting. Internalized employment policies may have advantages when high levels of employee performance are demanded. Yet this conclusion remains vulnerable to the problems of uncertainty and insecurity which are created by volatile markets and technologies that can alter conditions during a long-term relationship. Certainly, credible commitments remain an important issue. Employers and employees are

17

both opportunistic and have incomplete information; therefore, one may question why the parties to an employment exchange can be confident that each side is likely to honour the formal and informal commitments that they have entered, when they agree to an open-ended and relational contract. Credible commitments appear to be particularly problematic when restructuring and downsizing have become more common features of corporate behaviour.

1.4.3. *Employees' Power*

Baron and Kreps (1999: 66–7) suggest that the balance of power between employers and employees, and their concern for their reputations, constrain the opportunism of both parties.[18] The balance of power is generally regarded by sociologists of work and employment as asymmetrical, with employers being considerably more powerful than employees. But the preceding analysis indicates that in situations where employees possess a high degree of specialized competence (often referred to as 'asset specificity'), the cost to the employer of losing these assets is sufficiently high that a balance of power may make sense. The dependence of employers on the specialized competencies of employees will certainly promote a relationship where power is distributed less asymmetrically than where asset specificity is low. Furthermore, even where there is no collective representation of employees, the employer must take account of the reactions of employees as a whole and not just of an individual who is being poorly treated. In the insider–outsider theory (Lindbeck and Snower 1988), employers' wage and employment decisions are affected by recruitment costs and by the ability of employees to increase these costs by withholding cooperation from new recruits. In other words, employees have the power to impose added costs on employers either by quitting or by creating barriers to cooperation.

1.4.4. *The Importance of Reputation*

Reputation is important to employers, because they need to be known to keep their formal and informal commitments to employees if they are to recruit successfully in future. Therefore, the requirement to maintain a public reputation for honouring agreements with employees is an important constraint on the behaviour of employers. Reputation also works in the other direction, of course, because their own reputations for honouring explicit and implicit contractual obligations will be important to employees should they wish to look for alternative employment. Against this, US employers did in practice appear to set aside many of their promises to employees during the 1980s and 1990s when market conditions turned against them (Harrison and Bluestone 1988; Cappelli 1999a). However, people may of course make some allowance for changing circumstances when they appraise the reputation of others. In this case, employees may still consider that an employer has a worthwhile reputation if, when confronting market imperatives, it deviates reluctantly from its commitments and tries to mitigate the effects. When downsizing, for example, an employer may consult with staff and provide practical help to those made redundant. Indeed, appraisals of reputation may be relative rather than absolute. In a period when many employers cut jobs, an employer that does so in moderation may still enjoy a favourable reputation.[19]

To summarize, internalized employment regimes have several advantages over externalized ones. Internalized regimes foster long-term relational contracting, which in turn does much to solve the problems of high transaction costs, incomplete and asymmetrical information, and weak motivation that are manifest in externalized regimes. The difficulty for an internalized regime is to achieve sufficient flexibility in adapting to new conditions, without destroying the confidence of employees in the relational contract, and without tarnishing the employer's own reputation. This will require a continual re-balancing of policies and practices, and risks inconsistency and incoherence. Whether British employers in practice achieve this balance, what difficulties they encounter, and how employees react are ultimately empirical issues which will be investigated in this book.

1.5. Contracts, Class, and Inequality

The discussion has considered employees and the employment relationship in general terms so far. However, the growth of a different economic order also raises questions about the distribution of rewards and life chances between groups in Britain, and about their relative positions in the structure of employment. Does the new order with its tougher competitive conditions presage increased inequality, and if so who will be the winners and who the losers? Will existing distinctions of class continue to apply or will there be new axes of differentiation? Will the privileged form of employment relationship that was traditionally enjoyed by the higher occupations, notably managers and professionals, be eroded by greater pressure for performance?

Growing inequality in earnings and family incomes in the long-established capitalist economies has been emphasized in various accounts of the emergence of a new economy, including those by Harrison and Bluestone (1988), Castells (2000), and Beck, who also speaks of an 'erosion of the middle class' (Beck 2000: 113–14). Inequalities in earnings have increased since 1980 in many countries, and especially in the USA and Britain. A common explanation is that this results from 'skill biased technical change'. The argument, which is closely connected with the idea of a knowledge economy, is that new technologies, especially ICT, and the business opportunities which they create, now require greater numbers of highly educated or technically competent individuals. Because there is a lag in the production of such individuals, supply and demand are poorly matched and higher earnings result for those with capabilities that are in short supply (Krueger 1993; Machin and van Reenen 1998; see also DiNardo and Pischke 1997 for a critique). Meanwhile, those people who have relatively low educational levels and lack the skills to handle 'informational' tasks find it harder to obtain reasonably paid jobs, because a greater proportion of jobs include such tasks. However, this explanation does not in itself imply a long-term rise in inequality, since an imbalance between supply and demand can be corrected by education and learning.

Another account of inequality is more structural in nature. One of the features of the recent period, in both the USA and Britain, has been a weakening of trade unions, which have been important in the past in reducing earnings differentials. Econometric analyses (DiNardo, Fortin, and Lemieux 1996; DiNardo and Lemieux 1997; Gosling and Lemieux 2001) have shown for the USA, Canada, and Britain that inequality is systematically related to the levels of unionization at different times, and is also affected by the setting of national minimum wages. Therefore, if weak unions are believed to accompany the new, more competitive economic conditions, greater inequality is also likely in the absence of more regulation by public policy. A reasoned case for governmental regulation is made by Ladipo and Wilkinson (2002*b*).

Inequality should be viewed not only in terms of financial outcomes but also with regard to differences in the power and privilege of the social classes that occupy different positions in the hierarchy of employment. Whether these differences are growing or converging is harder to assess than changes in the distribution of earnings. It is however an issue of importance for the analysis of the new order at the workplace level.

The relational contract of standard employment covered managerial and professional employees before it was extended downwards to some manual and lower-level white-collar staff. It was during the middle decades of the twentieth century, in the USA, that structured internal labour markets were broadened to cover lower-level employees (Edwards 1979). This extension of previously scarce benefits was partly a consequence of legislation by government in the area of employment relations, partly the result of trade union pressure, and partly because employers saw benefits to themselves from a more experienced, stable, and committed workforce (see also Baron and Kreps 1999: 167–88).

In Britain, the relational contracts and structured internal labour markets and careers of primary labour were found in their most developed forms among managerial and professional employees, particularly those employed in large organizations in the private and public sectors. Fully structured internal labour markets and internal career ladders were much less common among manual employees, because British companies chose to recruit from the external labour market to different job levels (e.g. to skilled jobs) and to provide less predictable career ladders. Indeed, the internal barriers between semi-skilled and skilled levels were often guarded by unions as much as by employers. However, many large organizations offered their clerical and manual employees considerable employment security, which often included the retention of staff during cyclical downturns in the economy and, when redundancy could not be avoided, by firing on the basis of 'last in, first out'. It was not unusual for manual employees to be promoted internally to supervisory or technical positions, and occasionally into management, although this was not a clearly structured and predictable process from the viewpoint of the individual employee (Blackburn and Mann 1979: 95–111). There was some further harmonization of terms and conditions between manual and non-manual employees in the 1980s. These tendencies led Russell (1991, 1998) to suggest that social class differences were in the long run being reduced, although she also noted previous occasions when benefits for manual employees had been eroded under the pressure of adverse economic conditions.

1.5.1. *Class Differences in Decline?*

Bolder claims about the eclipse of social class differences have been made by various macro-theorists of a new economic order, typically because these differences are seen as relatively slight in comparison to the massive global discontinuities that they believe are imminent (Gray 1998; Beck 2000: 18–24). However, there are also more specific claims about the declining role of social class differences, both in market economies generally and specifically in Britain.[20] One claim is that because of the increasing pressure of competition and the urgency of short-term results, it has become necessary for employers to reward managers and professionals less on the basis of seniority and service and more on the basis of current performance (Brown 1995; Savage 2000; see the critique in Goldthorpe and McKnight 2004). They thus become more like employees in other social classes, such as sales workers or production line operatives, for whom personal incentives are often important. It has also been argued, for instance by David Lewin (1994), that an important strand in recent HRM practice has been the attempt to identify and make explicit the previously implicit elements in all forms of relational employment contract.[21] Once these are explicit, then companies can offer individually tailored contracts, specify and monitor performance more effectively, and design better incentives. It is reasonable to assume that contingent pay and contingent work will involve more measurement. Thus, the formal codification of explicit obligations will undermine service contracts. The growth of a particular form of HRM systems in Britain, which has been referred to variously as 'reward management' or 'performance management', provides some empirical support for this interpretation (Smith 1992; Incomes Data Services 1997). These systems, which have been especially applied at managerial level (Gallie et al. 1998: 67–9), emphasize the setting of targets and objectives for individuals and their subsequent appraisal and reward on the basis of whether targets and objectives have been met.

The considerable limitation of these interpretations is that they do not directly address the special characteristics of the work situation of the managerial and professional classes, which are often referred to as the 'service class'. Without an analysis of these characteristics, it is difficult to judge whether the changes referred to are likely to make an important difference, still less whether they would result in something so fundamental as a convergence of social class positions. It is important at this point to consider the typology of employment contracts developed in the work of John Goldthorpe and colleagues (Goldthorpe 1982, 1995, 2000a; Erikson and Goldthorpe 1993; Goldthorpe and McKnight 2004). This analysis provides a deeper understanding of the sources of variation among conditions of employment, and has underpinned several major studies of social class mobility in Britain and Europe. Goldthorpe has made a number of revisions to his original formulation of employment relations, but the basic distinction remains that between *service, labour*, and *mixed* or intermediate employment contracts.

His social class scheme contains seven classes, which may be condensed into five for certain purposes (Goldthorpe and McKnight 2004). The service class contains professional, administrative, and managerial employees. This is subdivided into two separate service classes: the first includes the higher grades of these occupations; the second covers the lower grades of these occupations with the addition of higher-grade technicians. The intermediate social class is divided into a class of higher grade, routine non-manual employees, and a class that includes manual workers' supervisors and lower-grade technicians. The lowest social class, which corresponds to the conventional category of the 'working class', comprises three distinct classes: skilled manual workers; lower-grade, routine non-manual workers; and semi- and unskilled manual workers. The final social class includes small employers and self-employed workers.

In his formulation of these categories, Goldthorpe drew on David Lockwood's use of the Weberian concepts of market and work situations since these were, in his view, the two major components of social class position (Lockwood 1958).[22] Class positions 'are seen as deriving from social relations in economic life or, more specifically, from *employment relations*' (Goldthorpe and McKnight 2004: 1). The market character for those in service class relationships (particularly professional, administrative, and managerial employees) is qualitatively different to that of the wage worker. Exchanges between employer and service employees are more diffuse and have a longer-term orientation than those with waged-labour contracts. Here, Goldthorpe emphasizes the role 'played by rewards that are of an essentially *prospective* kind' (1982: 169), which include the expectation of salary increments, the promise of security both in employment and in retirement, and the availability of career opportunities. These are similar to the forms of deferred compensation that were considered in our earlier discussion of incentives. Wage earners, by contrast, typically have a labour contract, which is based on the exchange of a discrete quantity of effort for a discrete quantity of reward, usually on a short-term basis. In short, the defining element of professional, administrative, and managerial employment is one of 'service', while that of the wage-worker is a more market-like exchange (see also Goldthorpe 1987: 41; Erikson and Goldthorpe 1993: 41–2; Goldthorpe and McKnight 2004).

Goldthorpe (2000*a*; Goldthorpe and McKnight 2004) has revised his original model of employment contracts by incorporating ideas from transaction cost economics. He starts from the assumption that moral hazard and incomplete information are inherent to the employment relation. The two main sources of contractual hazards for the employer are, unsurprisingly, similar to those of Williamson (1981, 1985).

1. The difficulty of monitoring or controlling agents, because of the difficulty of observing and measuring the quantity and quality of outputs, and even of inputs.
2. The specificity of the human assets or capital possessed by agents that would be lost to the employer if they left this employment.

Goldthorpe shows that a two-dimensional typology of employment contracts or relationships derives from the two dimensions of contractual hazard. This typology is congruent with the distinction that he has long made between labour and service work. The dimensions reflect different types of work tasks and roles. Consequently, Goldthorpe argues, it is the nature of work that determines the contractual hazards faced by employers and influences the contractual solutions that they will choose.

The pure form of *labour* contract occurs where both the difficulty of monitoring performance and the specificity of human assets are low. It is particularly appropriate to the work performed by semi- and unskilled manual occupations, and is also found in a somewhat modified form among skilled manual and lower-grade non-manual occupations. Work is easily monitored. Monitoring may be achieved by output measures, which allow a direct link to be established between performance and pay, or by input measures such as hours worked, which allow variable pay that is based on time rates under direct supervision. If the work requires no skills or only general-purpose skills, then human asset specificity is not an issue for employers, who can hire adequate replacement labour on the external market.

A *service* contract is appropriate for the work performed by employees in a professional, administrative, or managerial capacity. Monitoring by the employer is very difficult, because information is distributed asymmetrically in the employee's favour. Thus, employees inevitably have an area of discretion and autonomy from supervision. Goldthorpe believes that monitoring service-type work via performance-related payment poses substantial risks to the employer. Because service jobs are typically multifaceted and it is not possible to devise payment systems that reward every facet, employees will concentrate on the work elements that are rewarded and not on those that are not. Thus, relating pay to performance risks creating perverse incentives. His view corresponds to those of a number of economists. Senior, higher-grade service employees in the upper service class typically perform multiple and disparate tasks and this is their value to the organization. Some of these may be specific and in principle capable of being measured for performance. But as Baron and Kreps (1999: 264) comment on jobs with multiple tasks, many tasks are

ambiguous, with measures of performance that are at best very noisy and at worst nonexistent. For multitask jobs that mix such disparate tasks, agency theory recommends very weak pay for performance and increased reliance on intrinsic motivation.

There is the very familiar risk, that rewarding specific outcomes which are measurable in the short term will have perverse consequences for the organization, if individual employees therefore pay less attention to the other important aspects of their jobs (Milgrom and Roberts 1992: 391–2, 423–46).

Human asset specificity is also high. Therefore, employers need to retain employees whose knowledge cannot easily be replaced via the external labour market. In these circumstances, the organization depends on the motivation and commitment of its employees to serve its interests: contractual obligations typically involve a diffuse and implicit exchange of service to the employer in return for rising career wages and long-term employment. Thus for Goldthorpe, structured internal labour markets appear to be definitive of the service contract of employment.

Mixed or intermediate contractual forms combine elements of both labour and service contracts. These occur either where work is difficult to monitor but human asset specificity is low, or where specificity is high but monitoring is easy. The first case covers routine non-manual occupations 'on the fringes of bureaucratic structures', for example, clerical and secretarial workers in large organizations, where, according to Goldthorpe (2000a: 222), contracts provide the fixed salaries and relaxed time-keeping typical of service work, but without the rising career wage of service contracts. The second covers the supervisors of manual workers, and lower-level technicians. Goldthorpe suggests that they are paid on a similar basis to manual workers with, for example, weekly pay and paid overtime and/or adjustments based on the monitoring of the hours worked. But their asset specificity is valued by their employers who are likely to offer income and employment security, and sometimes the prospect of promotion.

Finally, he questions whether the traditional service contract is in decline and business risk is being transferred on a large scale from employers to employees (Goldthorpe 2000*a*). He accepts that employers would naturally choose to erode service contracts and introduce labour contracts if they could do so, because contractual hazard is then easier to control. If the generality of service-class employees were to be employed on short-term contracts and paid on the basis of performance, this would suggest that service contracts were indeed under threat. However, in his view, there is little to suggest that the underlying logic of why employers in the past chose service contracts no longer holds. There may be short-term shifts in emphasis in response to external pressures. Nonetheless, if the logic has not changed or been transcended, then service contracts may be expected to survive.[23]

1.5.2. *Classes and Knowledge*

These debates can also be considered from the perspective of the development of a knowledge economy. Managers and professionals have always been 'knowledge workers', but some would argue that they are the groups now being most intensively 'informatized' and transformed by new knowledge, including knowledge about new ways of organizing work and services (Bresnahan 1999). This in fact adds further weight to the arguments put forward by Breen (1997), Goldthorpe and others, while helping to explain the increasing inequality of earnings that was discussed earlier. Those already at the top of the distribution of rewards remain the bearers of what is most valuable and most scarce, and so their relative value is increasing. At the same time, the organization must rely on their knowledge without itself knowing what it is, because the organization can never catch up with personal knowledge that is always being renewed and inevitably covers disparate multiple tasks. Therefore, it must continue to allow wide autonomy to its senior managers and professionals, and rely on long-term incentives and attachments to secure the benefits of their knowledge for itself. Thus, the knowledge economy adds to the power of internalized contracting systems and to the relative advantage of the higher occupational classes.

There are some contrary arguments. Cappelli (1999*a*, 1999*b*) claims that knowledge in the contemporary economy becomes quickly outdated and so there is less reason for employers to hold on to individuals, because the freshest knowledge can be purchased on the open job market. He also argues that individuals have incentives to achieve visible successes, which they can add to their CVs in preparation for their next job, and therefore they do not need the longer-term rewards that internalized career structures have offered in the past.[24] Furthermore, it may be that organizations in the knowledge economy gain the capacity to identify, specify, and measure the crucial aspects of performance as a corollary of the growth of informatization. Therefore, it would be sensible to base rewards increasingly on those elements of managerial and professional activity that relate to key short-term outcomes, that is the ones which are immediately valued by shareholders or governments. There are risks, and mistakes are likely, but organizations will, according to this view, gain by focusing the work of their most senior, higher-grade managers and professionals on what is most important. In short, since knowledge is not static, the structuring of work and reward is likely to grow. The result may be a decline in the autonomy of managers and professionals, and an increase in the importance of short-term over long-term rewards.

Such a possibility will become a reality only if the owners of organizations do learn how to systematize the knowledge of their most senior executives, measure their performance across multiple and disparate tasks, some of which have a long-term, strategic orientation that delivers results several years in the future, and can design effective HRM systems that do not depend on trust and reputation. There would be no inconsistency between such a development and continuing inequality of earnings, however, as long as senior managers and professionals continue to be the main holders of valued knowledge. Nor would such a development necessarily prove to be inconsistent with an overall internalized form of relational contracting. In this scenario, there might be a tendency for the lower grades of managers and professionals, who are members of the lower service class, to be moved from a pure service model of contracting towards a mixed contractual form.

Our view of these and the other issues discussed in this chapter is that they are not ultimately matters of logic. How the various tendencies work out in practice depends on choices made by employers and by employees, and on how these choices are modified in interaction with one another. If we eschew economic, technological, and social determinism, then we accept that prediction is hazardous. Theory suggests where we should look and what we should look for, but only close observation and analysis will tell us what is actually happening.

It is to be expected that employers should feel from time to time, and as circumstances allow, that it might be desirable to control their employees more closely, use the power of the market to provide stronger incentives for performance, shift risk away from themselves and onto their employees, and thus attempt to shape the terms of the employment relationship in their favour. Indeed it would be startling if they were not to do so, if they believed the outcomes would be unambiguously beneficial. We do not doubt that the changes mentioned above have happened somewhere and at some time, as has been reported in many case studies. However, we will show that it is misleading to use evidence from case studies alone in order to propose that there is a sustained and widespread change in any particular direction. Employers push in one direction and find that employees or their representatives resist. Employers provide incentives for particular performance goals and then find that others, which are perhaps just as important, are neglected. Employers try to escape from long-term commitments only to find that their best employees use their market power to go elsewhere, leaving behind those whom they would prefer not to keep. There is a normal waxing and waning of the power of any two sides to a bargain which depends partly on circumstances. What we seek to know is whether all the indications of change that we have identified amount to anything more than this.

1.6. The Structure of This Book

This chapter has considered the main theoretical debates concerning the development of a new economy or new capitalism. These lead to various inferences and questions about possible changes in British employees' experience of working life, and it is on this level—the level of the individual—that our research focuses. In the following chapters, we consider how employees have been faring at the turn of the new century, and set this in the context of observed changes over the preceding 10–15 years. We ask whether the experience of employment has in reality been a deteriorating one, and if so in what respects. Differences by class (and by gender in certain chapters) are examined in order to investigate tendencies towards sustained inequality or towards convergence. The aspects of employment that we consider include promotion and careers, job security or insecurity, standard and non-standard contracts, welfare benefits, unionization and individualized bargaining, controls and incentives, and working hours and work-intensifying practices. Among the outcomes that we consider are earnings, occupational benefits, work strain, family relationship strain, job satisfaction, and a new measure of job desirability that provides new insight into the nature of inequality at work.

Our analysis is intended to feed back into the theoretical debates with which we began. To this end, we ask whether the observed experiences of employees can be seen as the result of increasingly 'externalized' or 'marketized' forms of employment relationship, or of adaptations of existing 'internalized' employment relationships to external pressures.

The main sources of information used in the following chapters are national surveys of British employees carried out in 1992 and 2000–1, each of which systematically reviewed individuals' experiences in employment and conditions of work. The 2000–1 survey, known as Working in Britain in the Year 2000 (WiB 2000), was planned and designed by, amongst others, the present authors. The 1992 survey, known as Employment in Britain (EiB 1992), has previously been reported in Gallie et al. (1998). An aim of the WiB 2000 survey was to make comparisons with 1992 and for that purpose it replicated many of the questions contained in the earlier survey. The data and documentation of both surveys are accessible to the academic community through the UK Data Archive (www.data-archive.ac.uk). Most of the WiB 2000 survey was conducted during the latter half of 2000, and although the fieldwork continued into the early part of 2001, we shall henceforth refer to the research period as 2000 rather than 2000–1.

The two surveys provide cross-sectional national samples, obtained by a stratified random sample of private addresses with further random selection of one employed respondent per address. The achieved samples were 3,458 employees in 1992 (71% response rate) and 2,132 in 2000 (65% response rate), and the age range in both surveys was 20–60 years. Further details of the 1992 survey will be found in Gallie et al. (1998). Information in the 2000 survey was collected from respondents by means of a personal interview, using a structured questionnaire supplemented by a short self-completion form to cover more sensitive material.

The following chapters also make use, from time to time, of a number of other surveys. These include, on the side of employees, the Social Class in Modern Britain (SCMB) survey of 1984 (see Marshall et al. 1988); some of the British Social Attitudes (BSA) series, which take place annually; and also the Labour Force Surveys. On the side of employers, we make some use of the Workplace Employee Relations Surveys (WERS) 1998 and 2004 and its precursors (Workplace Industrial Relations Surveys: WIRS), and more extensive use of our own Change in Employer Practices Survey (CEPS 2002), which has been reported in White et al. (2004) and is also available in the UK Data Archive.

All these sources deploy national samples obtained by probability sampling methods. What we are discussing throughout the following chapters, therefore, is the situation for British employees as a whole at certain points in time. This viewpoint is different from studies of particular industries or occupations, or qualitative studies of purposively selected small samples, or case studies of particular workplaces or organizations. The perspective we adopt is appropriate for assessing the very broad and indeed global changes that have been suggested in the literature concerning the new economy and the transformation of work. These data permit us to draw inferences about what has actually been experienced, on average, by British employees, and to set these inferences against the hypotheses that can be derived from various theoretical positions. Our findings and conclusions will not necessarily hold for more local or specialized situations that can be accessed only through other kinds of research such as case studies.

Making comparisons of employee experience over a decade, using fairly large national samples and an extensive set of comparable questions, represents a considerable advance over what has until recently been possible. First steps in this direction were taken by Gallie et al. (1998) with the EiB 1992 survey, but data for earlier years were scanty. A more recent study using overtime comparisons, and deploying data from the same or similar sources, is that of Francis Green (2006). We hope that research such as these earlier studies and our own represents the start of a new tendency towards more systematic collection and analysis of employee data that is both large-scale and rich in content. It is certainly only a beginning.

Each of the following chapters contains its own further discussion of the conceptual and theoretical issues it addresses; these often extend some aspects of the present introductory discussion. Methods of analysis and forms of argument vary widely across chapters, and these too are explained as the chapters proceed. The remaining task for the present chapter is to explain briefly the content of the other chapters, while leaving each to make its own way in terms of theory and methods.

Chapter 2 begins by drawing on the well-known distinction between organization and market-oriented models of the employment before reviewing the literature on the 'internalization' of the employment relationship. We then outline the US and British literatures on the 'marketization' of the employment relationship in some detail as it constitutes much of the 'received wisdom' that we test in subsequent chapters. Following this, we examine the extent to which traditional career-type jobs have either been replaced or modified by more market-driven forms of employment. In particular, we examine evidence about the continuity of employment with a single employer, levels of 'non-standard' employment and employees' perceptions of the extent to which their jobs are still located within career tracks.

A wide range of contemporary sociological literature claims that social class is no longer a major source of social inequality. In Chapter 3, we focus on the work of two authors who have made such claims in relation to the distribution of employment conditions. However, the two authors differ with regard to the cause of this supposed change: one believes it is because the employment relationship is being subjected to a process of marketization (Sørensen 2000), while the other makes an argument that is consistent with the notion of a long-term trend towards the internalization of the employment relationship (Russell 1998).

However, the chapter begins by examining the empirical cogency of the recent Goldthorpe model of social class since we believe it has the potential to offer a compelling explanation for variations in the labour market experience of different groups. Indeed, the relationship between occupational classes, monitoring difficulty and human asset specificity is something that, to the best of our knowledge, has not so far been investigated. Then we illustrate how the relationship between class position, earnings, and fringe benefits has evolved between 1992 and 2000 in order to evaluate arguments about the declining significance of social class.

Chapter 4 covers the changing nature of employee voice in the context of long-term changes in labour market composition, partly because the subject is not only of interest in itself but also because it bears directly on claims of a radical restructuring of the employment relationship. Here, we examine whether recent changes in employee involvement represent the kind of 'return to contract' (Streeck 1987) that we might expect from a shift towards market-oriented employment practices. We also examine whether the absence of trade unions means that employees have lost the ability to influence decision-making within the workplace. Finally, in the context of a supposed shift from 'collectivism to individualism', we draw on research at the intersection of economics and psychology to examine the proposition that some sections of the labour force are less inclined, or even unable, to benefit from the kind of individualized employment relations polices associated with HRM.

Chapter 5 is the first of three that consider, from different points of view, the increasing work demands experienced by employees. This chapter asks whether employers rely on 'market discipline' to stimulate employees' effort. The prototypical model, derived from Marx, indicates that it is the market-induced fear of job loss that produces compliance with overwork. The chapter then analyses the effects of various forms of insecurity on employees' reported levels of work demands and work strain. Finally, it examines whether tendencies in British employers' human resource practices are consistent with the notion of increasingly marketized employment relations.

Chapter 6 considers acceptance of overwork as a quasi-rational effort–reward bargain that is manipulated by 'bureaucratic discipline', that is, the systematic use of controls and incentives by the employer. After charting increases in the methods of control and incentive, the chapter analyses the effects of selected types, first on earnings, and then on the work demands, work strain, and working time of employees. The chapter provides the first analysis of the extent and effects of computerized or ICT-based monitoring of individual work and performance. It also offers evidence about the gains in earnings of different class groups through appraisal systems and incentive payments.

Chapter 7 examines the interplay between work demands and family demands, and the experience of women and men is contrasted throughout. The chapter first examines the levels of dissatisfaction with hours, and the willingness of individuals to accept lower earnings as the price of reductions in hours. The analysis then considers how hours of work and involvement in a range of work-intensifying HRM practices affect family relationship strain, childcare satisfaction, and the sharing of housework. Comparisons between employees in single-earner and dual-earner couples are used to assess materialist interpretations of work–family spillover.

Chapter 8 takes up the issue of job quality. In one sense or another, all the chapters are concerned with the question of whether in recent years whatever changes have taken place in the workplace are, from the employee's perspective, changes for the worse. However, this chapter directly confronts the issue of measuring job quality in a generalized sense. It empirically identifies what it is that employees find desirable about their jobs and how their ratings of their jobs are affected by the type of contractual situation they find themselves in. It also investigates the way in which job quality is related to job satisfaction.

In Chapter 9, we provide an overview of the major findings and offer an explanation that seeks to bring the employment relationship back into contemporary analyses of economic restructuring. Too much of the current literature, in our view, tends to treat labour as another commodity and, consequently, fails to appreciate both the requirement for and variations within internalized employment relationships.

Notes

1. 'Liberal market economies' and 'coordinated market economies' are the terms used to describe two important varieties of modern capitalism by Hall and Soskice (2001). Britain, the USA, and Canada are also regarded as constituting a distinct type of economy by Castells (2000: 245).
2. Originally published in 1944.
3. Source: Historical series of trade and GDP, from National Statistics website; deflated by producer price index, authors' calculations.
4. World Bank forecasts released at the start of 2007 suggest that China will become the third largest manufacturer during that year.
5. The source for this estimate is the Change in Employer Practices Survey 2002: authors' own calculations from source data.
6. The G8 includes Canada, France, Germany, Italy, Japan, Russia, UK, and USA.
7. According to the statistical series of the socio-economic classification (NS-SEC) available on the National Statistics website, the proportion of managerial and professional classes (higher and lower levels) within total employment reached 40 per cent in autumn 2001, and rose to 42.9 per cent by winter 2005–6, the most recent available figure. Corresponding figures for combined semi-routine and routine classes were 26.4 and 24.3 per cent, respectively.
8. The nature of organizational restructuring in the UK during the early 1990s has been questioned. In a study of American, British, and continental European manufacturing companies located in Britain, which focused on the organization of product and process innovation, Hill, Martin, and Harris (2000) found a variety of responses to the new competitive environment. Delayering was normal, but vertical disintegration was not. Most companies remained relatively centralized, while some previously decentralized organizations had begun to centralize their research and development functions. Inter-functional integration was a critical issue for both centralized and decentralized organizations alike. The introduction of market principles into product innovation was rejected because of the risks of market failure. The authors suggest that the contemporary analysis of restructuring relies far too heavily on a particular interpretation of the history of organizational development in the USA, which ignores the range of forms found in the USA and elsewhere and the effects of path dependency.
9. Large Japanese companies which offered jobs for life and internal labour markets to core employees also traditionally hired others on less favourable, secondary terms (Clark 1979: 191–5). These included temporary staff, part-time staff, the employees of other companies seconded to the company (Castells 2000: 291–5). Women were more likely to find themselves in secondary labour markets. In effect, Japanese companies offered different sets of employment relationships to core and peripheral employees.

10. Harrison (1997: 258) claims that the proliferation of forms of work organization has now blurred 'the traditional distinctions between "core" and "periphery", "permanent" and "contingent", "inside" and "outside" employees, and "primary" and "secondary" labour markets'.
11. See also Beck (1992).
12. The growth of high-commitment HRM and its relationship with structured internal labour markets in the USA and Japan is discussed by Baron and Kreps (2000: 189–209).
13. Organizational psychologists have developed the concept of the 'psychological contract' (Rousseau 1995). As in the sociological view, this captures the sense that employees and employers have important expectations about the employment relationship and the rights and obligations entailed, most of which are implicit rather than formally defined. The main addition to the economic or sociological view of contract may be in pointing to the psychological consequences of honouring or violating the contract.
14. The term means literally power exercised by the holders of office, where office is assumed to reside within an organization.
15. See Goldthorpe (2000a) for a similar analysis.
16. In Chapter 6, it will be argued that ideas of control and incentive are complementary, rather than distinct. Here for the sake of simplicity we consider them separately.
17. The John Lewis Partnership is a classic British example of a major retail service organization with employee profit sharing as a fundamental principle, which combines superior financial performance with enlightened HRM.
18. Baron and Kreps (1999: 66) also refer to the role of 'goodwill and warm feelings or ethics' but do not discuss this further.
19. Similar arguments are developed by Cappelli (1999a).
20. The arguments of Sørensen (2000), who proposes a more general account of declining class differences, and of Russell (1991, 1998), who considers Britain specifically, are considered at greater length in Chapter 3.
21. But he notes that a different strand, which promotes non-financial participation, flexible teamwork, and 'strong' organizational cultures, may well point in the opposite direction.
22. 'Market situation' is defined by Lockwood (1958: 15) as 'the source and size of income, degree of job security, and opportunity for upward occupational mobility'. 'Work situation' refers to 'the set of social relationships in which the individual is involved at work by virtue of his position in the division of labour'.
23. Goldthorpe's scepticism as to whether there has been a fundamental shift in the service contract is echoed strongly in a recent debate in the USA. Jacoby (1999a, 1999b) argues that 'career jobs' may have changed on some dimensions, but in most respects there has been considerable stability over time and career jobs are not headed for extinction: managerial jobs that are full time,

long term, well remunerated in terms of pay fringe benefits are still normal. Cappelli (1999*a*, 1999*b*) agrees that there are still many 'good' jobs, but disagrees that these are 'career' jobs in the classic sense of the traditional internal labour market.

24. But not all the behaviour that organizations want to encourage and reward can be identified in terms of separable individual achievements, as noted above.

2

The marketization of the employment relationship?

2.1. Introduction

As the new millennium arrived, academics, management gurus, and journalists claimed that many of the characteristics that had come to define the employment relationship over the course of the twentieth century were being discarded. The spread of 'flexible' forms of employment (e.g. temporary and fixed-term contracts) seemed to suggest that the traditional full-time, open-ended employment contract was losing its status as the predominant means of engaging labour and possibly even becoming an arrangement enjoyed only by a privileged minority (Beck 1992; Hutton 1995; Scase 1999). Frequent media stories of job losses at major firms depicted a world of increased insecurity, a world where the idea of a 'job-for-life' was viewed with nostalgia, employment had been replaced by 'employability', and employers were reducing their workforces while simultaneously reporting profits (Bolger 1998; Buckingham 1998; Cassy and O'Hara 2000). Perhaps the most striking claim was that groups who were previously sheltered from market fluctuations, such as managers and technical specialists, had become the target of 'delayering' and 'outsourcing', a development that fuelled widespread fears about the demise of the organizational career (Kanter 1989; Brown and Scase 1994; Castells 1996).

How should we understand these developments? Is there an underlying trend that links these seemingly disparate claims? We propose to answer this question by returning to an old theme in the sociology of work: the commodification of labour under capitalism. The argument is that there is an inherent temptation within capitalism to treat labour as an impersonal commodity or 'factor of production', a tendency that reduces the relationship to an almost entirely economic form of exchange (Polanyi

1957; Fox 1974; Marx 1976). This idea has been taken up in recent years in a somewhat different guise, as a variety of authors insist that during the 1980s and 1990s employers shed many of the understandings about loyalty and mutual obligation that had grown up around the employment relationship. Instead, the newly received wisdom was that employers were increasingly seeking to marketize employment arrangements by using market forces to resolve any problems relating to the procurement, promotion, or payment of labour.

In examining whether there is a general movement towards market principles, it is, of course, necessary to clarify a starting point in order to understand what is supposedly being left behind. In Section 2.2, we do this by drawing on the well-known distinction between *organization*- and *market*-oriented employment systems (Dore 1973; Streeck 1987), before reviewing the influential US literature on the new market-mediated employment relationship (Cappelli 1999*a*, 2001; Cappelli et al. 1997; Harrison 1997; Sørensen 2000). We then provide a very brief review of the British literature to show how the idea of an increasingly market-driven employment relationship has been taken up in a different labour market context.

Following this, we assess a range of evidence relating to four areas of the employment relationship that are central to what we interpret as the marketization thesis. Although familiar claims of radical change have appeared in relation to each of these areas, we think it more useful to treat them as part of a wider phenomenon. The four areas are (a) temporary forms of employment, (b) job security, (c) career structures, and (d) remuneration. While the first three will be examined in this chapter, developments in the area of pay and appraisal will be analysed in detail in Chapter 6.

2.2. Organization- and Market-Oriented Employment Systems

In his classic study of comparative employment relations, *British Factory–Japanese Factory* (Dore 1973), Ronald Dore contrasted the Japanese 'organization-oriented system' with the British 'market-oriented system', and, in doing so, introduced an important distinction into the literatures on the sociology of work and industrial relations. According to Dore, each system consisted of a set of mutually reinforcing practices that were inscribed with a fundamentally different conception of the role of labour within the capitalist enterprise. For instance, the Japanese system,

Employer policy	Organization-oriented	Market-oriented
Labour market	Low turnover; permanent employees are differentiated from temporary workers and on-site subcontractors.	High labour turnover; hire and fire according to demand; 'numerical flexibility'.
Career	Organizational career Lower-level entry points Formal job ladders Firm-specific skills Promotion from within.	Inter-organizational ('Employability') Multiple entry points Limited ladders General skills External hiring - use of recruitment agencies.
Remuneration	Wages fixed by administrative principles; Use of appraisals; individual, group and organizational performance.	Wages fixed according to market signals, e.g. the 'going rate'.
Fringe benefits	'Single status' Harmonization of benefits.	Fringe benefits for 'core' staff 'Status divide' between blue- and white-collar.

Figure 2.1. Two models of the employment relationship.

Adapted from Streeck (1987), Dore (1990), and Gospel (1992)

which was found mostly in large firms, included lifetime employment, a seniority-plus-merit wage system, an organizationally-based career ladder, employer-based training and welfare schemes, enterprise trade unions, and a strong sense of corporate identity. The British market-oriented system, by contrast, was characterized by relatively high levels of staff turnover, market-based payment systems, self-propelled careers that involved moving between employers, state-supported training and welfare programmes, general industrial or craft unions, and a strong sense of identity with occupation or class (Dore 1973) (see also, Figure 2.1). In other words, the organization-oriented system relied heavily on internal policies and procedures for preparing, allocating, and paying employees for different jobs, while the British market-oriented system made much greater use of external market forces along with state provision.

Naturally, this summary raises the question of whether it makes sense to search for evidence of a general movement towards a market-mediated employment system in Britain, if this is the model that is already in place. What is frequently overlooked in Dore's book, however, is his then controversial argument that Britain was 'catching up' with the organization-based Japanese system. Dore's claim was controversial because the conventional wisdom among Western scholars was that

Japan was shedding its 'pre-modern' practices and becoming more like an Anglo-American market economy, as proponents of convergence theory had predicted. Somewhat provocatively, Dore argued that it was in fact Britain that was becoming more like Japan. To make the case, Dore pointed to the evidence of an increase in firm size (accompanied by a greater degree of bureaucratization), the growth of enterprise or plant-level bargaining structures, an increase in employment stability, and the integration of manual workers as 'full members' of the enterprise through participation and welfare programmes.

Dore restated his argument some fifteen years later, when he argued that changes in the nature of work and in market competition were such that the adoption of the organization-oriented employment system was a source of competitive advantage for firms, regardless of whether they were based in manufacturing or service industries (Dore 1989). To support the point, he presented evidence from Britain, Europe, and the USA in support of this so-called 'reverse convergence' thesis. For Britain, Dore drew heavily on Brown's empirical overview of developments in British industrial relations, which highlighted the increasingly enterprise-specific nature of training, the shift from multi-employer, industry-wide bargaining arrangements to single-employer arrangements, and the use of salary systems that were becoming increasingly insulated from external market influences (Brown 1986). A notable feature of the latter was the concern with providing a fair system of internal pay differentials, even at the expense of careful alignment of market rates. However, Dore stressed that progress towards the organization-oriented model was restricted to the 'core' workforce, and a sharper distinction was emerging between the 'core' of full-time, permanent employees and the part-time and temporary workers who made up the 'periphery'.

The possibility of a long-term trend towards the internalization of labour in Britain received further support in Howard Gospel's *Markets, Firms and the Management of Labour in Modern Britain* (Gospel 1992). Covering a significantly longer period than Dore, Gospel charts the growth of British industry and the evolution of the employment relationship from the middle of the nineteenth century until the 1980s. Like Dore, Gospel recognizes the historic influence of the market and the 'cash nexus' on employment relations in Britain. Both agree that British employers traditionally relied on market mechanisms for procuring labour, fixing its price, and disposing of it as demand subsided. Instead of developing formal organizational systems, employers relied on external market methods of coordination with the result being an employment relationship characterized by minimal commitment on the part of both employees and employers. As Gospel put it: 'the invisible hand of the market dominated labour management, and the visible handshake of closer and more lasting relations between employers and employees made only slow progress' (Gospel 1992: 10).

Nevertheless, Gospel's aim is to chart the slow and incomplete transition to internal strategies within British industry, especially as applied to manual labour. Internalization, according to Gospel, exists where employers make every effort to offer permanent employment; develop internal job ladders and use internal promotion whenever possible; fix wages according to internal administrative principles rather than market forces; and strive to extend the range of fringe benefits (Gospel 1992: 8–9). His account of this transition stresses the influence of product and labour market considerations on decisions about the management of labour, though, critically, market forces are mediated by differences in firm structure and the nature of managerial hierarchies. Historically, British employers have been reluctant to internalize the employment relationship because of the existence of fragmented product markets, the availability of a ready supply of manual labour, and the prevalence of small- and medium-sized firms.

During the 1930s, however, Gospel found some evidence of a general push towards internalization. The most significant development was the extension of industry-wide, multi-employer bargaining, which had the effect of taking wages out of competition. The trend was more evident during the post-war period, when the effects of labour shortages persuaded more and more employers that internalization was in their best interests and the state encouraged these efforts by introducing legislation that formalized the employment relationship (e.g. contracts of employment, dismissal, and redundancy). From the mid-1960s, employers started to adopt single-employer bargaining, which allowed for the introduction of more sophisticated personnel practices, especially in the area of wages and fringe benefits.

Nevertheless, Gospel acknowledges that Britain's 'late internalization' was still hindered by a dearth of qualified management, the tendency for larger organizations to be primarily holding companies with little central control, and a weak capacity for innovation. With the advent of the Thatcher government during the 1980s and the subsequent offensive against trade unions, the interest in non-standard forms and labour market 'flexibility' suggested that the shift towards internalization, however hesitant and uneven, had stalled. For Gospel, the late and somewhat

reluctant attempt to internalize has had profound economic consequences: it has failed to stem British economic decline and undermined
national competitiveness relative to the USA, Germany, and Japan.

2.3. Anglo-American Capitalism: From Organization to Market?

A number of US scholars have argued that, much of the substantial
restructuring activity undertaken by employers in the 1990s was driven
by a desire to make greater use of market forces in organizing the employment relationship (Abraham 1990; Cappelli 1995, 1999*a*, 2001; Cappelli
et al. 1997; Harrison 1997; Sørensen 2000). The most sophisticated and
detailed statement of this argument is contained in a major study by
Cappelli et al. (1997), which draws on a wide range of evidence to map
the spread of what they term 'market-mediated employment practices'.
Having outlined the *internal* (or organizational) model, which they claim
US employers had been developing since the late nineteenth century,
Cappelli and his co-authors insist that it is breaking down as employers
try to respond to more competitive product markets, an increased emphasis on shareholder value, the development of new management techniques (e.g. total quality management and benchmarking), and advances
in information technology. These responses have invariably included
attempts to reduce labour costs, especially those associated with sheltering
labour during periods of economic difficulty, and measures to promote
greater flexibility in the deployment of labour (see also, Streeck 1987).

Much of this study, and Cappelli's subsequent book, *The New Deal
at Work*, is given over to describing how these responses have led to
the demise of the traditional employment system and the emergence
of a more explicitly market-oriented set of arrangements. These include
the growth of 'arm's-length, market-mediated' forms of 'contingent' (or
temporary) labour; the rapid expansion of the temporary help industry;
and increasing instability in employment as indicated by a decline in job
tenure. Considerable emphasis is also placed on the decline of internal
labour markets, as an example of the contemporary 'deregulation of
the employment relationship' (Cappelli et al. 1997: 15). Although much
of this decline is attributed to the waves of organizational 'delayering'
that swept across US industry during the 1990s, Cappelli himself subsequently argued that the growth of executive search agencies represents
an important structural change in the labour market. The emergence of

the executive search (or 'headhunting') industry has had the effect of institutionalizing poaching between firms, with the result that employers have become increasingly unwilling to invest in long-term training and development programmes (Cappelli 2001: 237). Finally, Cappelli and colleagues point to the growing use of performance- and market-driven payment systems that seek to redistribute risk between employers and employees. Generally, such schemes are designed to increase the proportion of the overall wage bill that is determined by individual, group, or organizational performance. The result is that, firms are able to reduce the fixed costs of employment, while employees, on the other hand, face greater uncertainty over future earnings.[1]

Whatever the diversity of the market-mediated relationship, Cappelli and colleagues insist that contemporary employment restructuring shares an underlying logic that stands in contrast to that of the traditional system. Specifically, the new model makes individual employment relationships more sensitive to market forces. Product market pressures, for instance, are brought inside the organization by linking wages and job security to organizational performance. Pressures from the labour market are evident in the greater use of temporary and contract labour, increased hiring from outside for intermediate and senior positions, and the practice of developing careers across (rather than within) organizations. The result is that these changes push more of the risk of doing business onto employees at the same time that changes in work organization are demanding substantially more from them (Cappelli et al. 1997: 209).

For all the changes described in *Change at Work*, the authors are still somewhat hesitant about predicting the death of the traditional organization-centred employment system,and acknowledge that change in the reverse direction is also possible (Cappelli et al. 1997: 14). Indeed, Cappelli writes in his later work that the substitution of market solutions for internal, administrative rules does not spell the death of long-term employment (LTE). Here he draws an analogy with another social institution that was historically associated with lifetime commitment, namely marriage. Cappelli claims that 'the new employment relationship is like a lifetime of divorces and remarriages, a series of close relationships governed by the expectation going in that they need to be made to work and yet will inevitably not last' (Cappelli 1999a: 3).

Although the arguments presented by Cappelli and colleagues are consistent with much of the received wisdom about the contemporary world of work, they have been the subject of some searching criticism. One of the most stringent critiques comes from Sandford Jacoby, a leading

American business and labour management historian (Jacoby 1999a,b). Jacoby agrees with Cappelli that managers and executives have experienced substantial changes in career patterns and pay practices, and that aggregate job tenure rates have declined modestly since the late 1970s. However, he accuses Cappelli of being preoccupied with the experiences of managers and claims that this has distorted his overall view of the US labour market. For Jacoby, the most striking fact is that the majority of American workers continue to hold career-type jobs that provide fringe benefits, training, and the prospect of a future with their employment. Consequently, he insists that the current practices of US employers are not qualitatively different from those of the recent past (pre-1980s) because internal labour markets and long-term jobs have not died; they have merely adapted to a changing environment.

Instead of embracing a new market-mediated model, Jacoby claims that employers have long had a tendency to transfer risk onto employees at the bottom of the business cycle. In this respect, the recession of the early 1990s is no different than those of the 1970s or the 1930s, when employers also reduced their sense of obligation to their employees. For Jacoby 'the reallocation of risk—not the decline of career-type jobs—is the central imperative driving today's internal labour markets' (Jacoby 1999a: 135). Employees have been asked to bear more risk, notably in the form of contingent pay and reduced health insurance coverage. Employers are introducing more variability into their remuneration practices through group incentives, bonuses linked to organizational performance, profit-sharing, and stock options. Borrowing the language of economists, he accepts that more pay is 'at risk' but insists that this is frequently for employees who hold long-term jobs within traditional internal labour market structures.

Nevertheless, Jacoby insists that there are limits to this process of risk reallocation, and the most important limit is probably what he calls 'the organizational realities of managing a workforce' (Jacoby 1999a: 136). Employee loyalty and commitment still matter, especially with the growth of service-oriented and knowledge-intensive forms of work, where it is often difficult to supervise employees directly. Employee skills and tacit knowledge remain important and, though it may seem rather obvious, new employees will always require some training. This has, according to Jacoby, become all too evident to employers adopting new forms of work organization. Self-managing teams, for instance, work best when accompanied by stable, career-type jobs that promote the kind of interpersonal relations necessary for effective team work. Finally, high levels of employee turnover remain expensive for employers, but, against a background of new forms of work and fast-changing markets, they look distinctly irrational.

2.3.1. *Labour Market Flexibility and Job Insecurity in Britain*

Many of the contributions to the British debate about the restructuring of the employment relationship cover similar themes to those found in the US literature. For our purposes, the most important point is that the growing influence of the market features prominently in analyses of the changing world of work. Countless authors refer to the influence of the 1979 Conservative Government, with its programme of economic deregulation and flexible labour markets, the economic recession of the early 1990s and, more recently, the influence of global competition (e.g. MacInnes 1987; Hutton 1995; Gray 1998; Howell 2005). For instance, the social theorist Andrew Sayer, writing primarily about developments in the UK public sector during the Thatcher era, believes that there has been a shift from bureaucratic- to market-based forms of economic exchange, with a concomitant emphasis on 'contractualization' and the commodification of labour (Sayer 1997). Although the reasons for these changes differ between the public and private sectors, Sayer insists that the result is broadly similar across both sectors, as managers insist on the increased externalization of work and, concomitantly, the extension of the peripheral workforces, and the 'delayering' of organizations. The net result of these changes has been a decline in internal labour markets, with 'increased economic insecurity and often outright casualization of labour' (Sayer 1997: 55), while the professional norms and standards of performance that were once used to ensure quality in the public sector have been replaced by the bureaucratic measurement of work outcomes (see also, Heery and Salmon 2000*a*).

A somewhat similar set of ideas can be found in the work of Damian Grimshaw and Jill Rubery, who have perhaps done most to highlight the spread of 'market-led' employment solutions during the 1990s (Grimshaw and Rubery 1998; Grimshaw et al. 2001). Working from an institutional economic perspective, they claim that the British labour market has been *re-institutionalized* through a series of changes that undermine the traditional operation of internal labour markets, weaken the principles established through collective bargaining, and disregard the kind of understandings embodied in notions of 'custom and practice' (Grimshaw and Rubery 1998: 202–6). Reviewing a range of small-scale studies, they point, for example, to the impact of reforms on the public sector, where the use of compulsory competitive tendering has led to the contracting out of a wide range of services that are not considered to be part of the core business (e.g. maintenance and cleaning) and, subsequently, to the deterioration of employment conditions, or the loss of jobs. Another area they highlight is pay and payment systems, with significant developments in both the public and private sectors. In the public sector, for instance, the Conservative Government abolished national wage determination in favour of local bargaining (e.g. in the National Health Service). Employers in the private sector have also broken away from national and industrial agreements and this has left them free to put more emphasis on performance and less on seniority in making decisions about salary progression. Meanwhile, the composition of the labour market has changed following 'the well-known shift from full-time permanent employment contracts to the more "flexible" contractual forms of self-employment, part-time, and temporary work' (Grimshaw and Rubery 1998: 205).

Working with other colleagues, Grimshaw and Rubery also draw on case studies among a diverse range of organizations (e.g. from high street banks to privatized public utilities) to demonstrate the negative impact of downsizing on job security and career structures (Grimshaw et al. 2001; Beynon et al. 2002). While all of this is consistent with the general dismantling of labour market 'shelters', they acknowledge that it does not necessarily lead to a decline in job tenure. The reason is not so much that employers are cutting jobs but that employees are more likely to cling to their jobs during a recession, even jobs that are part of weak internal labour markets (e.g. few career opportunities) (Grimshaw and Rubery 1998: 205–6). In sum, 'internalizing the market' inevitably entails a drive to reduce labour costs, with the result being the break up of the structured employment conditions that provided many workers with steady improvements in pay, status, skills, and careers (Beynon et al. 2002: 260–1). Yet they acknowledge that, as much of this activity is driven by short-term gains, there is always a possibility that employers may wish to benefit from stable internal labour markets in the future. Indeed, some of their case studies indicate that while employers may be tempted by opportunities to reduce costs through externalization, the complications of dealing with subcontractors can lead them to reconsider. For instance, problems with the quality of work or, indeed, concerns about protecting the skill base over the longer term, may lead firms to keep activities in house (Beynon et al. 2002: 168–9; see, also, Rubery et al. 2002).

Despite their different orientations, each of these contributions alleges that the employment relationship is becoming increasingly market driven, though Grimshaw and Rubery acknowledge that there are limits on this process. Certainly, all agree that this re-commodification of labour has led to greater fragmentation and diversity and, ultimately, to a general deterioration in employment conditions. As such, the British literature resembles those describing the rise of market-mediated employment arrangements in the USA, though the contributions have been framed somewhat differently (see also, Appay 1998 on developments in France). What is also significant for our purposes is that in each case the form of employment (e.g. permanent or temporary), the degree of job security, the presence of career ladders, and the nature of payment systems are all central to the debate (see Figure 2.1).

That said, one of the major differences between the British and US debates is the attention given to trade unions in understanding the transformation of employment relations (Brown 1993; Purcell 1993; Millward et al. 2000). In contrast to the USA, British trade unions have had much higher levels of membership and a much greater role in collective bargaining at least until the 1980s (Western 1997). Since then, trade union membership has fallen, especially in the private sector where aggregate union membership halved from 56 per cent in 1980 to 29 per cent in 2000 (Brook 2002). Also, in 1980 seven out of every ten workers had their pay set through collective bargaining; by 1998 this had fallen to four out of every ten workers and appears to have stabilized around this figure (Kersley et al. 2006). In this context, it is easy to understand why several authors assume that British employers face relatively little organized opposition to their efforts to give the market a greater role in organizing the employment relationship (e.g. Breen 1997; Sayer 1997; Howell 2005).

2.4. Challenging Market Orthodoxy

Before we present some empirical evidence on the extent to which the employment relationship has been marketized, we would like to make a number of preliminary observations to clarify the task in hand. First, we must acknowledge that most employment relationships consist of a mixture of two elements, namely those derived from the *market*, which emphasize the *contractual* nature of the employment relationship, and those based on the idea of an *organization*, where labour enjoys membership of a particular organization and has a certain social and political status. Certainly, the extreme case of 'spot market' labour, where labour is hired on a daily basis according to the 'going rate' is relatively rare. Indeed, this idea is implicit in Cappelli's acknowledgement that market- and organization-oriented models represent the opposite ends of a continuum and not two fundamentally different or mutually exclusive phenomena (Cappelli 1995: 573).

Once we accept the idea of a continuum, however, the task of detecting a change, especially minor changes, becomes more difficult as the market and organization models blur into each other. This problem is compounded by doubts about whether the classic internal labour market was ever really that prevalent, a point that Cappelli acknowledges (2001: 237). It could be argued that such arrangements only ever covered a small proportion of the labour force and, even then, were dependent on a unique set of economic conditions. Yet labour economists Siebert and Addison produced some estimates for the 1980s which suggested that internal labour market arrangements were, in fact, quite common. According to their analysis, approximately 50 per cent of all British employees were covered by such arrangements compared with 40 per cent of those in the USA. A substantial part of the British proportion was, of course, due to the presence of a larger public sector (Siebert and Addison 1991: 77–9).

Fortunately for our purposes, the arguments advanced by Cappelli and colleagues in the USA, as well as those of Sayer and of Grimshaw and Rubery in the UK, all point to a sharp break with the past. More precisely, the logical implication of their arguments is that the long-term trend towards internalization has not merely been halted but actually reversed. Consequently, an important feature of our analysis concerns the nature of any changes, that is, whether they are based on a different logic to the policies that underpinned the organizational model.[2]

As Jacoby has argued, it is entirely possible that employers may seek to transfer more risk onto their employees without dismantling the fundamental features of the internal system. Accordingly, we shall occasionally use the concepts of risk and risk shifting to capture variations within and between both the organization- and market-oriented systems. We would also like to emphasize that the organization-oriented system seeks to share these risks between employers and employees, while more market-oriented systems may do so only for certain privileged white-collar groups.[3] Consequently, much of our analysis will compare the experiences of those in working-class jobs with those in service-class occupations.

Whatever the failings of the existing literature, it has, nonetheless, helped us identify those facets of the employment relationship that are central to this debate. In the remainder of this chapter, we will examine the evidence for change (if any) in a number of areas that are central to the debate about the changing nature of the employment relationship (Figure 2.1). These are temporary and fixed-term employment contracts, job security and job tenure, and, finally, careers and internal labour markets. Developments in pay are examined later in Chapter 6. Finally, we would like to stress that in selecting these areas, we focus on objective indicators of the policies and practices that make up the organization-oriented model, because these are central to debates about transformation in the employment relationship. More subjective elements of the employment relationship, such as satisfaction with working hours and perceptions of job quality, will be examined in Chapters 7 and 8, respectively.

2.4.1. *The Employment Relationship: Adaptation or Transformation?*

THE GROWTH OF MARKET-MEDIATED FORMS OF EMPLOYMENT?

As we indicated earlier, the apparent increase in non-standard employment is central to the market-mediated employment thesis. In a rare British review of risk and employment restructuring, Breen argues that employers are increasingly pursuing greater flexibility in employment by offering part-time, temporary, or casual employment contracts.[4] Such arrangements enable them to 'acquire an option' over employees, retaining them when market demand justifies doing so, and discarding them when it does not. In this way, Breen argues that employers have shifted risk onto employees, while the employees, for their part, have been unable to resist because of the fear of unemployment, the decline of trade unions, and the employers' willingness to take advantage of employment law (Breen 1997).[5]

Even if we restrict our indicators of market-mediation to various kinds of temporary employment, we are still assuming that these can be lumped together as arrangements governed by market forces. The organizational sociologist, James Baron, has criticized Cappelli's concept of 'arm's-length market-mediation', precisely because subcontracting and the use of temporary help agencies may all have the kind of relational contract associated with the traditional employment relationship. For instance, those employed by a subcontractor may simply be regular employees of another organization (e.g. a security firm). Similarly, those employed by 'temp' agencies may work in the context of a relatively long-term relationship between the agency and its client. Even some independent contractors may, for all intents and purposes, be regular employees of an organization that merely seeks to avoid paying tax and social security (Baron 2000).

Our view is that there is a more fundamental problem here with Cappelli's concept of market-mediated employment, which is that it conflates two levels of analysis, namely that directed at the level of the organization and that directed at the level of individual employees. At the organizational level, it would be entirely reasonable to argue that an organization makes use of market-mediated relationships when it uses subcontracting firms and temp agencies while also hiring workers on fixed-term and temporary contracts. However, at the individual level a security guard working for a subcontracted security firm may have a traditional employment relationship, even though Cappelli insists on treating it as an 'arm's-length market-mediated' employment relationship. We would argue that the analysis should be focused on the individual level because contemporary debates about the transformation of the employment relationship are mostly about the experiences of employees, either directly or indirectly. Otherwise, there is a real danger of confusing two different phenomena and, consequently, of exaggerating change.

CHALLENGING A WELL-KNOWN MYTH

In their account of employment restructuring in contemporary Britain, Grimshaw and Rubery (1998) argued that changes in the composition of the labour force were one reason why the traditional operation of internal labour markets was being undermined. Using evidence from Dex and McCulloch's analysis of labour force surveys (LFS) (Dex and McCulloch 1995), they compiled a table which seemed to demonstrate 'the well-known shift from full-time permanent employment contracts to the more "flexible" contractual forms of self-employment, part-time and temporary work' (Grimshaw and Rubery 1998: 205). Grimshaw and Rubery reported that the growth of self-employment, at the expense of regular employment, represented a transfer in the costs of economic adjustment

Table 2.1. 'Flexible' forms of employment, 1975–2004 (working age population 16–64)

	1975		1981		1986		1994		1999		2004	
	M	F	M	F	M	F	M	F	M	F	M	F
a. Full-time permanent	n.a.	n.a.	n.a.	n.a.	79.3	47.7	73.8	49.9	74.6	51.5	73.6	51.5
b. Part-time permanent	2.4	39.0	1.7	40.6	3.5	43.8	3.7	37.7	5.2	38.2	6.1	38.2
c. Self-employed with employees	5.1	1.7	7.2	2.9	5.6	2.1	5.3	2.1	4.7	1.5	4.3	1.7
d. Self-employed without employees	5.8	2.2	4.7	1.5	9.0	4.5	14.4	7.1	12.8	6.6	13.7	6.6
e. Full-time temporary	—	—	—	—	2.6	1.9	3.2	2.8	3.7	3.0	2.7	2.3
f. Part-time temporary	—	—	—	—	1.8	6.3	1.3	4.5	1.6	4.4	1.6	3.7
g. Government training scheme	—	—	0.3	0.4	—	—	1.6	1.1	0.7	0.4	0.5	0.4
b + d	8.2	41.2	6.4	42.1	12.5	48.3	18.1	44.8	17.9	44.8	19.9	44.7
All 'flexible' employees, b + d + e	—	—	—	—	15.1	50.2	21.3	47.6	21.6	47.8	22.6	47.1

Notes: For 1975 and 1981 the classification by permanent/temporary status does not exist. Weighted—including second jobs.

Source: Dex and McCulloch (1995, Tables 4.1 and 4.2); Grimshaw and Rubery (1998, Table 2) and Quarterly Labour Force Surveys (Spring) for 1994, 1999, and 2004.

while the expanding part-time category implied greater insecurity and instability.

As this table referred to the period from 1975 to 1994, we decided to update it in order to examine whether this trend has continued into the present century. Accordingly, we have brought the evidence up to 2004 while maintaining the categories used in Dex and McCulloch's original analysis (Table 2.1).[6] For comparative purposes, we also use Grimshaw and Rubery's measure of 'flexible' employment, even though we think it makes little sense to include 'part-time permanent' alongside 'self-employed' (without employees) and 'full-time temporary' workers (Gallie et al. 1998: 168–72).

Certainly, the proportion of full-time, permanent jobs held by males fell between 1986 and 1994 (by 6 points), as Grimshaw and Rubery reported in their account of the 'well-known shift' to flexible employment. It has, however, remained quite stable for the period between 1994 and 2004. Meanwhile, the proportion of such jobs held by women has increased, though somewhat modestly. Or, to put it another way, the proportion of all 'flexible' jobs has not changed dramatically since the mid-1990s.[7] Bringing these points together, we must reject the notion of an ever increasing trend or shift to non-standard forms of employment (e.g. Beck 1992; Gorz 1999). The 'well-known shift' that was evident in the earlier period may have been simply a response to the recession of the early 1990s and could yet be reversed by the sustained period of economic prosperity that has followed.

This general trend is also evident among the temporary and self-employed categories, two groups most associated with market-mediated forms of employment (Abraham 1990; Cappelli 2001). When we review the evidence in relation to the proportion of the labour force engaged on a temporary basis, we find that it remains fairly stable at around 5 per cent (not shown). The proportion engaged in temporary employment increased during recessionary periods in the mid-1980s and again in the early 1990s, only to fall back to 5–6 per cent on each occasion (combining 'full-time' and 'part-time temporary' in Table 2.1) (see also, Dex and McCulloch 1997: 96–7). Furthermore, the proportion in temporary jobs has been falling for the past few years and is now at much the same level as it was ten years ago, or indeed, twenty years ago. This trend also appears in the EiB (1992) and WiB (2000) surveys, although they only tell us what happened during the 1990s. For instance, the proportion working on temporary contracts, that is, of less than 12 months' duration, decreased (from 7.2% in 1992 to 5.5% in 2000), as did the proportion hired under fixed-term contracts, that is, of between 1 and 3 years (from 5.0% in 1992 to 2.8% in 2000). To put it another way, the proportion of employees in permanent employment actually increased during the 1990s, contrary to widespread claims of labour market fragmentation. Approximately, 92 per cent of all employees held permanent employment in 2000, according to the WiB (2000) survey, compared with 88 per cent in 1992 (EiB 1992 survey). In this respect, the standard employment relationship is substantially more resilient than some commentators would have us believe.

Similarly, there is no evidence to indicate that there has been a substantial increase in the proportion of the working population who would prefer to bear economic risk on their own. The proportion of men engaged in self-employment, especially those without employees, grew between 1986 and 1994 but has more or less remained the same since then (Table 2.1). Generally, much of the growth in self-employment was heavily concentrated in the 1980s, a period associated with the much celebrated, but ultimately short-lived, 'enterprise culture' of the early Thatcher government (Blanchflower and Oswald 1990; Robinson 1995). Although the rate of growth during that period marked Britain out from other comparable countries, it was, nonetheless, driven mostly by sector-specific, and indeed recession-prone, industries. The construction industry, for instance, accounted for approximately one-third of the growth during the 1980s and more than two-fifths of the decline between 1990 and 1993 (Robinson 1995: 169).

MARKET-MEDIATED FORMS OF EMPLOYMENT: COMPETING OR COMPLEMENTARY?

If we look beneath the headline figures, we find that the distribution of the so-called marked-oriented arrangements across the public and private sectors is rather uneven, so much so that it would be difficult to interpret it as part of a general movement from organization to market. Ironically, it is the insulated public sector rather than competitive private sector where the use of fixed-term contracts of twelve months or less is most prominent. According to Cully et al., almost three quarters of public sector workplaces had some employees on fixed-term contracts in 1998, compared with one-third of those in the private sector (Cully et al. 1999: 35). An earlier analysis of the WIRS (1990) evidence also revealed that the non-trading public sector contained a much greater proportion of 'high users' than the private sector (26% compared to 4%) (Casey et al. 1997: 46). This study also found that the proportion of employees on such contracts in either sector tended to be relatively small (median of 5% in 1990) (Casey et al. 1997: 45).[8]

This public–private division is significant because it highlights an obvious limitation in US accounts of market-driven employment arrangements, which are preoccupied with the private sector. Of course, those supporting the externalization thesis could counter by arguing that changes in the public sector represent prima facie evidence for their position. If so, they would then have to acknowledge the rather unique set of circumstances, such as public sector budget constraints, that have led to some forms of market-driven employment becoming more prominent in the public rather than the private sector. Moreover, they must then face the challenge of explaining how the unique experience of the public sector can provide a basis for expecting further, or perhaps even more radical, growth in the private sector.

Further support for our emphasis on the underlying continuity in the employment relationship can be found in the reasons that employers give for using various forms of non-standard employment. According to the WERS (1998) survey, the use of temporary agency workers and fixed-term contractors was not associated with any radical new flexibility strategy. Instead, the most commonly cited reasons for using office temps were short-term cover (59%) and efforts to bring the size of the labour force in line with demand (40%), with the latter also being the major reason for using fixed-term contracts. Cover for maternity leave was also important in deploying agency staff (22%) and fixed-term contractors (11%) (Cully et al. 1999: 37). More recently, the WERS (2004) survey found that fixed-term contracts were more commonly used to support an occupation that formed the core group of employees within a workplace (Kersley et al. 2006: 81).

What all of this suggests is that the use of non-standard labour has more to do with buttressing the position of those in full-time, continuing employment than offering an alternative to it. Above all, it does not support the argument that the introduction of these arrangements might be part of a general core-periphery strategy (Atkinson 1985) or a deliberate policy to discipline the workforce by bringing market forces inside the firm (see also, Hakim 1990; Casey et al. 1997).

2.5. Job Tenure and Job Security: No Long Term?

One of the defining features of the traditional organization-oriented employment system was the provision of secure jobs (Streeck 1987; Dore 1989). Whatever the prevalence of full-blown internal labour markets, the provision of a continuing, as opposed to a casual, employment relationship has long been recognized as one of the defining institutions of modern capitalism (Hodgson 1999: 164–7). For reasons that are still unclear, academics and journalists on both sides of the Atlantic interpreted job losses during the early part of the 1990s as evidence that the traditional LTE relationship was in decline. Although employers always made substantial cuts to their workforces during previous recessions, it somehow seemed as if the phenomenon was something new or special to an era of global competition. The most well-known manifestation was the preoccupation with rising employment insecurity and claims that job insecurity had become the norm for most of the working population (OECD 1997; Elliott and Atkinson 1998; Gray 1998; Heery and Salmon 2000*b*). Perhaps the most eye-catching claim of all was that insecurity had become as much of a problem for middle-class, white-collar employees as it had previously been for those in working-class jobs (Kanter 1989; Brown and Scase 1994; Heckscher 1995). For Cappelli et al., the fact that 'downsizing' programmes were disproportionately targeted at 'the top rungs of the corporate hierarchy' (Cappelli et al. 1997: 69) represented prima facie evidence of just how far the principle of market exposure was being extended up the organizational hierarchy (Cappelli 1999*a*: 118).

If this 'age of insecurity' (Elliott and Atkinson 1998) has indeed arrived, then we might expect to see a general decline in *job security*, especially in the form of job tenure and, consequently, increased instability in employment across the entire labour force.[9] If not, we might at least expect a decline in the proportion enjoying LTE, since this is one of the defining characteristics of the organization-oriented employment system.

In contrast to the start of the 1990s, we now have a fairly good idea of what has been happening to job tenure in Britain over the past quarter of century through the analysis of large-scale surveys. Using data from the Labour Force and General Household surveys, the labour economists Paul Gregg and Jonathan Wadsworth report that average job tenure remained relatively stable between 1975 and 1998 (Gregg and Wadsworth 1999: 109). For much of this period, changes in average tenure have been relatively small for most groups, somewhere in the region of 2–5 per cent (Gregg and Wadsworth 1999: 126). However, when the data is analysed by gender, age, and the presence of children, the evidence for change is somewhat more pronounced. Job tenure decreased slightly during the 1990s for three-quarters of the workforce, that is for men and women without dependent children (Gregg and Wadsworth 1996: 110–11; Gregg and Wadsworth 1999; Gregg et al. 2000: 54). At the same time, they also report that median job tenure actually rose for men by 10 per cent between 1975 and 1985 but then fell by 5 per cent in the period thereafter. Women, by contrast, experienced an increase in job tenure for the entire period, rising by 8 per cent in the period before 1985 and 17 per cent subsequently. Much of the increase for women is attributed by Gregg and Wadsworth to a dramatic rise in the proportion of women returning to work after childbirth. Consequently, average job tenure for men was around six years and ten months and four years and six months for women (Gregg and Wadsworth 1999: 116). The other notable development was the sharp decline in job tenure among older men. This finding is consistent with the general decline in labour market participation among older men (Disney 1999; Faggio and Nickell 2003). For men over 50 years of age, average tenure fell by 14 per cent after 1985 and stood at approximately 11 years by 1998 (Gregg and Wadsworth 1999: 122).[10]

Of course, those who insist that we have entered an 'age of insecurity' (Elliott and Atkinson 1998) might respond by arguing that the issue is not about average job tenure or employment stability (which could mean different employers), but rather the experience of those in long-term jobs with the same employer. The suggestion here is that such jobs are becoming so rare that they no longer provide a normative standard for aspiring labour market entrants. This idea was perhaps best captured in the memorable phrase 'no long term' by the American sociologist Richard Sennett when he argued that contemporary capitalism no longer treasures the kind of mutual commitment between employer, employee, and community that enabled individual workers to form stable social ties with their colleagues and neighbours (Sennett 1998: 22–7).

British research on long-term jobs is somewhat divided, without, however, pointing to dramatic change in either direction. According to Gregg and Wadsworth's analysis of the LFS, the share of jobs with tenure of ten or more years declined between 1985 and 1998 from 38 to 33 per cent.[11] If some modest decline is evident, the story gets somewhat more complicated when the evidence is broken down by gender and age. Once more the proportion of such jobs held by women with children increased by 4 percentage points, though that of men fell by 7 points and that of women without children by 4 points. Substantial change is also evident among men over 50 years of age, where the chances of being in a long-term job fell by around 9 per cent (Gregg and Wadsworth 1999: 125–6).

By contrast, the economic geographer, Kevin Doogan claims that 'there has been a significant and widespread increase in long-term employment in the UK' during the 1990s (Doogan 2001: 422). Doogan also uses evidence from the LFS, though his analysis is based on the EUROSTAT 'special extraction' used for comparisons with other European countries. For the period between 1992 and 1997, he finds that the proportion working ten or more years with the same employer (which he terms the 'rate of long-term employment') increased from 29 to 33 per cent, or approximately, 4 percentage points. Furthermore, this increase was evident among men (2 points) and, in particular, among women (7 points). Finally, Doogan reports that the proportion of managers, professionals, and skilled craft workers in long-term employment has increased.[12]

Given the discrepancy between Gregg and Wadsworth and Doogan, we have undertaken our own examination of the LFS, partly to examine the period under debate, and partly to extend the analysis to 2004. For comparative purposes, we use similar tables to Doogan to examine trends

Table 2.2. Long-term employment in the UK by gender, 1994–2004 (000s)

	1994	1999	2004
Total employment	24,816	26,265	27,388
Total LTE	7,797 (31.4%)	8,598 (32.7%)	8,348 (30.5%)
Male employment	13,534	14,206	14,670
Male LTE	4,967 (36.7%)	5,218 (36.7%)	4,870 (33.2%)
Female employment	11,282	12,059	12,718
Female LTE	2,830 (25.1%)	3,380 (28.0%)	3,478 (27.3%)

LTE—long-term employment

Source: Quarterly Labour Force Surveys (Spring).

in long-term employment (i.e. ten years or more) across three points in time: 1994, 1999, and 2004.

Our analysis of the LFS data shows that the overall proportion of employees in long-term employment has barely changed between 1994 and 2004 (Table 2.2). Again, differences by gender are somewhat more noticeable, with a decline of about 3 percentage points for men and an increase of 2 percentage points for women. In other words, our evidence supports the decades-old trends described by Gregg and Wadsworth: average and long-term job tenure have declined by a few points and, while male tenure is also falling, that of female workers continues to rise. Equally significant, our evidence reveals that the degree of change is nowhere near the somewhat hyperbolic claims of ever greater insecurity and instability that have been sold to the general public (Elliott and Atkinson 1998; Gray 1998; Sennett 1998).

As we indicated earlier, influential commentators in the USA and the UK have drawn attention to the apparently new phenomenon of middle-class employment insecurity, with the standard example being the large numbers of professional and managerial staff released by large blue-chip corporations undertaking 'delayering' exercises (Kanter 1989; Brown and Scase 1994; Heckscher 1995; Gray 1998). Yet, when we examine occupational class, as defined by the LFS, we are unable to find the kind of evidence that would convince us that there had been a fundamental redistribution in the risk of job loss. Instead, managers, professionals, technicians, and those in skilled trades tend to have higher rates of long-term employment than those in personal service or service and sales occupations (Table 2.3). Given all that has been written about the decline of managerial careers, the rise of inter-organizational job hopping, and the end of corporate loyalty (e.g. Elliott and Atkinson 1998; Gray 1998; Sennett 1998), we think it important to emphasize that the proportion of managers in long-term

Table 2.3. Occupational distribution of long-term employment, 1994–2004 (000s)

	1994			1999			2004		
	LTE	Total employment	%	LTE	Total employment	%	LTE	Total employment	%
Managers	1,654	3,914	42.3	1,797	4,159	43.3	1,647	3,995	41.1
Professionals	948	2,526	37.5	1,097	2,880	38.1	1,179	3,423	34.4
Technicians	737	2,367	31.1	895	2,694	33.3	1,216	3,782	32.2
Clerical workers	985	3,812	25.8	1,194	4,030	29.6	1,049	3,436	30.5
Service and sales	3,352	1,948	17.2	355	2,140	16.6	309	2,227	13.9
Personal service	614	2,502	24.6	707	2,906	24.3	476	2,136	22.3
Skilled trades	1,241	3,264	38.0	1,269	3,121	40.7	1,180	3,096	38.1
Machine operators	752	2,312	32.5	805	2,380	33.8	642	2,057	31.2
Other/elementary	516	2,134	24.2	477	1,981	24.1	651	3,173	20.5
Total	7,783	24,781	31.4	8,597	26,287	32.7	8,345	27,325	30.5

LTE—long-term employment.

Source: Quarterly LFS (Spring).

employment simply has not changed very much. Management, it seems, is relatively more stable than any other occupation.

Our confidence in these claims is supported by research on work history data by Gallie et al., which shows that the occupational class of a person's job is a critical factor in determining their vulnerability to unemployment. Over the period from 1950 to 1990, men from semi- and unskilled manual work have a much higher risk of becoming unemployed than those in professional or managerial occupations, as indeed have those in skilled manual jobs (Gallie et al. 1998: 134–5). A different set of analyses, this time by Burchell et al, also shows that white-collar employees enjoyed substantially greater levels of job security than blue-collar workers for the period between 1967 and 1985 (Burchell et al. 1999: 18).

Although the evidence from job tenure and work history data is very informative, we must acknowledge that they are primarily retrospective in nature. By definition, measures of job tenure must refer to the past. Fortunately, we have been able to compensate for this limitation by asking employees if they think that they will be laid off in the near future or if their employer has been cutting the workforce. When we compare the evidence from WiB (2000) with that from the earlier employment survey in 1992, we find little change. The proportion who thought that they would lose their job over the next twelve months because of the closure of their workplace is tiny and remains unchanged at approximately one in fifty (2% in 1992 and 1.5% in 2000). Similarly, small proportions thought that they would lose their job over the same period because of redundancy (3.4% in 1992 and 2.2% in 2000). Finally, only one in four respondents in 2000 said that the organizations they worked for had reduced their workforce in the previous two years compared with more than one in three respondents (40%) in 1992.

To conclude, the evidence on job tenure and long-term employment simply does not support grandiose claims about the demise of long-term jobs, the rise of market-driven employment practices, and the associated transfer of risk from employers to employees. Strictly speaking, some general decline in overall job tenure is evident, but the rate of decline is so slow that only those with a proclivity for gross exaggeration would insist on emphasizing increasing insecurity and the end of long-term jobs (see also, Auer and Cazes 2000). The idea that middle-class jobs are as insecure as those held by the working class is revealed to be little more than a scare story. Similarly, we have not uncovered any systematic evidence of a general redistribution of employment instability between working-class and middle-class occupations. Curiously, some of the more striking changes, particularly the increasing stability of women's employment and the sharp decline in tenure among men over 50 years of age, have been somewhat neglected.

Given the relatively stable picture that emerges from our research, the preoccupation with insecurity towards the end of the 1990s seems rather extraordinary (e.g. OECD 1997; Elliott and Atkinson 1998; Heery and Salmon 2000*b*). An analysis of this problem by Felstead et al. offers some possible answers (Felstead et al. 1998). Drawing on national data, Felstead et al. reported a significant redistribution of perceptions of insecurity between blue-collar and white-collar workers. During the 1980s, for instance, managers, professionals, and associate professionals felt quite secure, while those in low-paid occupations felt relatively insecure. By 1997, the situation was reversed. We suspect that this change accounts for the increase in the attention given to insecurity. In addition, Felstead et al. also found that perceptions of insecurity were closely related to unemployment rates within 'travel to work areas'. Remarkably, these perceptions persisted into the late 1990s, some years after unemployment began to fall. Felstead et al. suggest that once a person has experienced the pain of job loss, or lived in an area where unemployment is rife, then the memory of this possibility remains despite subsequent changes in the economic environment.

2.6. The End of Career-Type Jobs?

Of course, claims of rising insecurity were accompanied during the 1990s by the headline grabbing assertion that career-type jobs were disappearing as organizational job ladders were being pulled apart (Kanter 1991; Brown and Scase 1994; Heckscher 1995; Arthur and Rousseau 1996; Worrall et al. 2000; Grimshaw et al. 2001). According to this literature, much of which emanated from business schools, increasing insecurity and declining career structures (or internal labour markets) were part of a wider set of changes that included outsourcing, greater use of team-based forms of work, individual merit-based payment systems, and the replacement of secure but stale employment with a more dynamic model of 'employability'. Instead of being offered a secure, career-type job, employees, especially white-collar and managerial employees, were offered the chance to learn new skills, gain experience—typically at a 'blue-chip firm', and make a wide range of contacts, all of which supposedly enhanced their CVs and made them more appealing to other employers (e.g. Kanter

Table 2.4. Percentage of employees with current job as part of a formal career ladder by sector, 1984–2000

	1984			2000		
	Public	Private	Total	Public	Private	Total
Yes	57.7	36.4	44.4	60.0	45.3	49.8

Note: Based on those employed for more than 10 hours per week. N = 842 for 1984 and 1,817 for 2000.

Source: Class in Modern Britain (1984) and WiB (2000).

1989; Heckscher 1995; Grimshaw et al. 2001). The less than implicit message was that employers would no longer feel obliged to provide career opportunities and employees should treat themselves as commodities, as marketable human resources, to be traded across organizations for varying periods of time.

As we noted earlier, much of the empirical evidence for these developments was based on organizational case studies of unknown typicality. Admittedly, national evidence on career structures is all too rare, especially when compared with that on temporary employment or job security. Nevertheless, we are able to compare a small number of items from our WiB (2000) survey with earlier surveys conducted in 1992 and 1984.

Once again, our evidence challenges much of the received wisdom on what has been happening to career structures over the past twenty years. When we examine the evidence across these three different points in time, we find that the proportion of employees whose jobs belong to formal career ladders has, if anything, increased since 1984! More specifically, when the respondents were asked if their present job was a step in a recognized promotion or career ladder within their current organization, those saying 'yes' increased by 5 percentage points between 1984 and 2000 (Table 2.4). If an increase of 5 percentage points seems relatively small, especially when spread over a decade and a half, it is worth adding that approximately half of all British employees believed that they had a career-type job by the end of the period!

Given that these findings are at variance with much of the conventional wisdom on careers, we think it necessary to consider a range of further evidence on this topic. For instance, we used a more general question to ask if the respondents' type of work had a recognized career ladder, even if it meant changing employers. In other words, we extended the notion of a career to include occupational as well as organizational careers. Unsurprisingly, this shows that a slightly higher proportion believe that they have careers in this broader sense, though there has been relatively little growth over the period 1992–2000 (from 57% to 58%). If the level of growth seems rather small, the significant point here is that employees believe that their career ladders have not actually declined at a time when journalists, business school academics, and social commentators had been announcing the death of the traditional career.

Furthermore, when we examine the presence of job ladders by sector, we not only find evidence of more substantial growth, but also find that this is mostly in the private sector (9 percentage points increase compared to 2 points in the public sector). This is quite ironic, as many of the proclamations about the end of organization-based careers were based on case studies from the private sector, where increased competition, new technology, and management philosophies were believed to be driving organizations towards leaner and more competitive structures (e.g. Kanter 1989; Heckscher 1995; Grimshaw et al. 2001). Nevertheless, we must acknowledge that considerably higher proportions of those in the public sector reported that either their jobs or their 'sort of work' belonged to formal career ladders. This difference is also reflected in the employer survey (CEPS 2002), where three-quarters of the public sector organizations have well-defined career ladders, compared to three-fifths of the private sector. While this conforms to the popular idea that employment in the sheltered public sector is more likely to provide secure, career track-type jobs than the private sector, the employer survey also confirms our general argument that job ladders are as common as ever. Approximately two in three establishments state that they provide well-defined job ladders, with most of these (58%) being open to all grades of staff.

In addition to the provision of formal job ladders, another closely related feature of the organization-oriented model is a preference for internal candidates, particularly when filling positions above entry level. For labour economists, the logic of this policy is based, in part, on an information problem: employers know more about the qualities of existing employees, and getting detailed information on external candidates is often costly in terms of administrative effort. Cappelli, as we saw earlier, argues that the emergence of executive search agencies (or 'headhunters') undermines this policy by institutionalizing poaching and, consequently, reducing the incentive to continue with internal development (Cappelli 2001: 237).

If this development is as significant in Britain as Cappelli believes it is in the USA, then we might expect employers to place a fairly low value on promoting people from within. The corollary is that they should display an increasing inclination to use the external labour market to find suitable candidates. But once again, our evidence contradicts fashionable claims of radical change. According to the employer survey (CEPS 2002), seven in ten say that they recruit internally for professional and managerial positions where possible, while six in ten claim to do likewise for other posts (White et al. 2004: 56–7). Even for some of the more specialist managerial and technical positions, less than one-third of the enterprises use recruitment agencies for finding new staff. Of course, it is possible that this rather buoyant picture of career structures might be somewhat exaggerated by managers wishing to present their organizations in the best possible light. One way of dealing with this possibility is to see if the evidence from the employee surveys point in the same direction. When asked if there was any advantage in already working for their organization when a better job became available, the proportion saying that it was either 'essential' or a 'major advantage' increased by 6 points (from 53% to 59%) between 1984 and 2000. So, in terms of employee perceptions, the tendency to prefer internal candidates has increased. When it comes to 'getting a significant promotion', however, two in three (65%) employees believed that they were better off staying with their current employer in 1984. Although this fell to under one in two (46%) employees in 1992, it rose back towards the previous level by reaching three in five (60%) employees by 2000. While we might speculate about a possible link between the decline and the economic recession of the early 1990s, it is, nonetheless, quite evident that the majority of employees had restored their faith in internal promotion by the end of the decade.

This general argument receives further support from evidence in the employer survey on changes in the number of pay grades within establishments. If employees believe that their chances of making progress are best served by remaining with their present employer, then we might expect that grades would have expanded in recent years. This, it seems, is exactly what has happened. While there has been some contraction, the increase in the number of grades has been more than twice the decrease (White et al. 2004: 61–2). In other words, organizations appear to be *relayering* rather than delayering!

Of course, it was managerial careers that were supposedly most affected by policies that sought to reduce the middle ranks in an effort to produce 'flatter' firms. To address this issue, the employer survey asked if the proportion of managerial jobs had changed. Here it was found that the proportion increasing was almost double of that decreasing: management jobs were being reduced in one in eight establishments but increased in

Table 2.5. Percentage with job that is part of a formal career ladder by social class, 1984–2000

Higher managers and professionals		Lower managers and professionals		Intermediate workers		Lower supervisors and technical		Semi-routine		Routine	
1984	2000	1984	2000	1984	2000	1984	2000	1984	2000	1984	2000
78.0	74.8	66.5	65.5	40.8	46.1	52.0	46.4	25.2	36.0	17.9	21.5

Note: Based on those employed for more than 10 hours per week. N = 882 for 1984 and 1,917 for 2000.

Source: Class in Modern Britain (1984) and WiB (2000).

one in four. Further analysis of the data indicated that expansions in grades and in management jobs tended to be in workplaces that were experiencing growth (White et al. 2004: 62). The corollary, of course, is that the opposite tended to occur in establishments that had contracted during the previous three years.

Finally, we should mention that much of the literature on the demise of organizational careers gives the impression that it is a general development, a universal experience marking a profound shift within capitalist economies (Kanter 1989; Castells 1996; Gray 1998). For those familiar with the literature on social class, this represents an extraordinary claim because the idea of a career, especially one that involves regular increases in pay, status, and authority, has traditionally been associated with white-collar employment (e.g. Goldthorpe 1982). Even a relatively basic analysis of the incidence of formal career ladders by social class shows that it only begins to have a meaningful presence as one moves up into non-manual and, in particular, into lower managerial and professional employment (Table 2.5). To put it another way, the vast majority of those who hold managerial or professional positions (both higher and lower) have jobs that are part of an organizational career ladder, while the same is true only for a minority of those in semi- or routine working-class positions.

It follows, therefore, that the expansion of managerial and professional employment and the relative decline of blue-collar employment across much of the Western world during the post-war period (Crouch 1999: 134–7) has meant that career-type jobs have become more widespread. In other words, long-term changes in the composition of the labour force have produced more and more jobs where we might reasonably expect the incumbents to enjoy the old-fashioned idea of a career. It would appear that those proclaiming the demise of careers and career ladders are unaware of the significance of this change in our social structure.

Nevertheless, we should not ignore the relative increase in the perception of belonging to a formal career ladder that was evident among the semi- and routine categories during the 1990s. The 11-point increase within the semi-routine class, in particular, suggests that the traditional internal employment system is actually expanding at the bottom. Here, at least, is one piece of evidence to support Dore's controversial claim that the organization-oriented employment system is becoming more common in Britain, and, consequently, that Britain is 'catching up' with Japan (Dore 1989: 430–3).

2.7. Conclusion

Contrary to claims of increasing marketization (Cappelli et al. 1997; Sayer 1997; Appay 1998; Claydon 2004) as well as fashionable claims about the 'end of work' (Gorz 1999), the 'destandardization of labour' (Beck 1992), and the 'casualization of the labour market' (Hutton 1995; Gray 1998), we find little evidence to indicate that the traditional employment relationship has been transformed in the way such claims would suggest. Instead, we would argue that the standard employment relationship (i.e. full time and continuing) is still important, both quantitatively and normatively. Despite claims of a shift to non-standard work, the full-time, permanent job is still the principal means by which people engage in employment. Temporary employment may have become more common during the 1980s, but it is now no higher than in the late 1970s. It is, therefore, no surprise to learn from employer surveys that the use of temporary, agency, and contract staff has also remained relatively stable, or that these alternative forms of the employment relationship are used primarily to complement the existing workforce. More significantly, the proportion of employees in long-term employment remained relatively stable across the 1990s and into the early years of this century, while average job tenure has declined only slightly since the mid-1970s (Gregg and Wadsworth 1999). In sum, the major institutional fact of the contemporary labour market is that employers, by and large, employ the same workers in the same jobs this year as they did last year.

A similar story emerges in relation to careers. Once again, the conventional wisdom suggests that career ladders are in decline and, once again, we find that the general situation has remained fairly stable over the past decade and a half. Where there are signs of change, these are generally towards the expansion of organizational career ladders, notably within the private sector and among those lower down the socio-economic ladder. More significantly, however, it seems that the majority of British employers are following the organization-oriented model by providing career ladders of various kinds and supporting them with internal promotion policies.

This leads us to conclude that when it comes to *forms of employment*, much of the marketization, externalization, and transformation discourses appear to be unduly influenced by (downward) swings in the business cycle, such as that which occurred during the early 1990s. During that period, employers appeared to turn their backs on the implicit understandings that surround the traditional internal employment system (i.e. secure jobs and the prospect of a career). When the economy started to expand in the middle of the decade and unemployment declined, employers were in a position to restore these commitments, though the swing from employability back to employment has obviously not proved so newsworthy. Nonetheless, the very fact that the pendulum has swung back is testament to the power of what Jacoby calls 'the organizational realities of managing a workforce' (Jacoby 1999a: 135). Loyalty and commitment still matter, new employees have to be trained, and the provision of career-type jobs remains the best way of developing skills and teamwork. In other words, any tendency towards the commodification of labour has to be balanced with the need to secure employee consent while promoting the acquisition of new knowledge, skills, and routines.

However, just as our evidence does not support the marketization thesis, neither does it suggest that Britain is rapidly 'catching up' with the organization-oriented model associated with the Japanese economy (Dore 1973, 1989). Apart from the expansion of job ladders, most of the other indicators highlight the remarkable stability and durability of the employment relationship; the overall pattern is characterized more by continuity than radical change in either direction. We must, however, acknowledge that this claim relates to the *form* rather than the *content* of the employment relationship, and a more general assessment must await our examination of the evidence on fringe benefits and harmonization in Chapter 3, employee involvement in Chapter 4, and forms of payment in Chapter 6.

What is striking is the degree of variation across different sections of the labour force. Focusing on aggregate trends may help refute some of the prevailing myths about employment, but it also masks some important labour market trends. In relation to gender, for instance, Gregg and Wadsworth report that the average job tenure for men has fallen while that of women has increased substantially as more and more women return to work after giving birth. Similarly, the proportion of long-term jobs (i.e. tenure of ten years or more) held by men has declined while that held by women has increased. In both cases, the most conspicuous decline has been among men over the age of 50 years (Gregg and Wadsworth 1999).

The other major source of variation in employment relationships is social class. The majority of those in service-class positions (notably higher managers and professionals) claim to have jobs with recognized career ladders compared with less than half of those from the 'intermediate class' and one-quarter of those in the 'routine' category. Our analysis of the LFS also shows that managers, in particular, have the highest proportion in long-term jobs. Clearly, the impulse to internalize the employment relationship appears to be strongest among service-class occupations and much less prominent within intermediate and working-class positions. However, it is conceivable that British employers may have sought to extend white-collar conditions to blue-collar employees through the harmonization of fringe benefits and, perhaps, in the area of work organization. It is to these matters that we now turn.

Notes

1. While some authors have interpreted 'externalization' and 'market-mediated' employment as market-mediated *forms* of employment, such as temporary or part-time arrangements (Abraham 1990; Marsden 1999:236–7), Cappelli insists that his conception of the market-mediated employment relationship goes beyond the idea of 'core-periphery models'. More specifically, he argues that even when employment is offered on a long-term basis, the internalization of market principles in various human resource policies means that it is fundamentally different to its predecessor (Cappelli 2001: 207). We use the term *marketization* to capture Cappelli's broad interpretation of market-mediation.

2. A striking feature of the marketization literature is that claims of long-term change are frequently made on the basis of evidence that is inappropriate for the purpose. In our view, far too much of the literature is based on one-off organizational case studies rather than longitudinal labour market data. Consequently, much of the evidence for long-term change may stem from the kind of normal restructuring that occurs during a downturn in the business cycle.

3. One of the defining features of Dore's organization-oriented model is what he describes as the 'white-collarization of blue-collar employment'. His research indicated that white-collar employees are protected from the vagaries of the

    market in both Japan and Britain, while blue-collar workers are insulated only under the Japanese organizational model (Dore 1973: 264).

4. This is one facet of a more general exposition by Breen that has been outlined in Chapter 1.

5. We do not agree that all forms of non-standard employment can be interpreted as evidence of externalization. Part-time work, for instance, is frequently placed alongside temporary employment as a form of market-mediation (Abraham 1990), even though the two have little in common. The most obvious difference is that part-time employees have a much higher level of employment security (Gallie et al. 1998: 168–72).

6. We have chosen to replicate the tables used by Dex and McCulloch (1995) and later by Grimshaw and Rubery (1998) for comparative purposes. However, we must acknowledge two problems. First, we do not agree that part-time jobs should be treated as a 'flexible' form of employment. Second, neither Dex and McCulloch nor Grimshaw and Rubery explain how they account for 'second jobs'. This is important because the proportion of people with second jobs may vary over time. We have weighted the data to account for 'second jobs'.

7. Even if we were to include establishment evidence, our analysis of the CEPS (2002) indicates that some workplaces are increasing their use of non-standard employment (i.e. agency, freelance self-employed, outside contractors, and temporary employees), while others are cutting back. The net result is still only a modest shift towards external sources of labour (White et al. 2004: 21, 31–3). This is consistent with the WERS series, which finds that the proportion of workplaces containing employees on temporary or fixed-term contracts or from temporary help agencies remained unchanged between 1998 and 2004 (Kersley et al. 2006: 80–2).

8. Subcontracting is also more prevalent in the public sector according to the WERS evidence (Cully et al. 1999: 36).

9. Measures of job security tend to divide into objective indicators such as length of tenure, and subjective measures which capture feelings of insecurity. We concentrate on objective measures because the claims we are examining are primarily about changes in employment arrangements rather than attitudes or feelings.

10. Although we have followed Cappelli, Jacoby, and others in using job tenure as an indicator of continuity in employment, we must acknowledge that this approach is less than ideal. Inferences drawn from the kind of job tenure data contained in the LFS are problematic because they refer only to the incomplete spells of those currently in employment. For instance, job tenure, or observed incomplete spells of employment, may decrease during periods of economic growth as new workers are attracted into the labour market and others are encouraged to change jobs. By contrast, recessionary periods may lead to substantial job shedding and an increase in average job tenure for those

who remain in employment. What is required is data on all complete and incomplete spells in the labour market for cohorts of individuals. Regrettably, such data are not yet available.

11. They also report that the same trend is evident in the General Household Survey estimates for 1985–95.

12. Curiously, Doogan makes no attempt to reconcile his findings with the well-known work of Gregg and Wadsworth.

3
Inequality at work

3.1. Introduction

Many of those who insist that the employment relationship is increasingly being shaped by market forces believe that this will lead to changes in the prevailing pattern of social inequality. Cappelli et al., for instance, argue that the traditional divide between managers, supervisors, and routine blue-collar workers has been replaced by a new divide between executives and all other employees (Cappelli et al. 1997: 189–93). Several other researchers have pointed to a growing divide between standard and non-standard employees (e.g. Abraham 1990; Sayer 1997: 56–7; Appay 1998) while economists point to the emerging gap between highly skilled university graduates and the rest of the working population in an age of 'skill-biased technological change' (e.g. Katz and Autor 1999; Machin 1999).

Instead of exploring this myriad of new divides, we will concentrate on those associated with social class, partly because they are important in their own right and also because they feature in the work of researchers who may be placed within what we have loosely described as the marketization and internalization perspectives on the changing employment relationship. More specifically, we concentrate on two such claims, one from a Harvard sociologist, Aage Sørensen (Sørensen 2000), and the other from a British economic historian, Alice Russell (Russell 1991, 1998). Despite their different origins and orientations, both claim that traditional class-based forms of social inequality have either attenuated or taken on an entirely different form because of recent changes in employment practices. Here, however, the two authors differ because Sørensen's argument, as we shall see shortly, is essentially a variation on the idea that the employment relationship is being subjected to a process of marketization while Russell's history of the harmonization of employment conditions is consistent with the notion of a long-term trend towards the internalization of the employment relationship.[1]

Although we restrict our analysis to these two contributions, we should stress that claims about the declining significance, or even the death, of social class have become quite influential over the past fifteen years or so (Clark and Lipset 1991; Beck 1992; Pakulski and Waters 1996). But where others emphasize the influence of developments outside the world of work, such as the growth of the welfare state, the emergence of consumption classes, and the politics of identity, Sørensen and Russell base their claims on changes in the employment relationship.

Before we examine these competing claims, we will undertake some important preliminary analyses that are designed to test the concept of social class that informs this study. Here we investigate whether Goldthorpe's conception of social class (Goldthorpe 2000a), which we outlined in Chapter 1 (Section 1.5.1), has any correspondence with the kind of variations in work organization that he proposes. To that end, we were able to include a series of measures in the WiB 2000 survey that were designed to capture the underlying concepts of asset specificity and ease of monitoring. Although this exercise is essentially one of construct validation, it has, potentially, much wider implications. If we can demonstrate that there is a different logic to the employment relationship for different social classes, then we have a good basis for understanding why variations exist in the distribution of job rewards across the class spectrum.

3.2. Employment Relations and Social Class

We begin our discussion of class analysis with a simple observation: in modern societies the employment relationship is taken for granted. We rarely ask why enduring relationships of exchange between employers and employees exist, let alone why the content of this relationship varies in the way it does. That it is not 'natural' or inevitable is clear—in the nineteenth century, many British workers worked on their own account or in some trades hired themselves out by the day or the hour (Stedman Jones 1971). In these circumstances, the 'contract' that existed between parties was often just a verbal agreement to supply a service or to carry out a specific task for a given sum of money. In both cases, the time horizon of the 'contract' was limited and, even if repeated, it was potentially subject to renegotiation of the terms on each occasion of re-engagement.

It is easy to see why an employer might find spot markets attractive. They make it easy for employers to assure themselves that they pay no more than they need to in order to get the job done. Yet, it is also easy to see that spot markets will not work well as a way of hiring labour for some tasks. University teaching, for instance, could be arranged by having a line-up outside the university entrance at the beginning of every term with potential teachers competing on price for teaching courses. Of course, no higher education system in the world works like this. In many, there are tenure systems which guarantee jobs until retirement or even for life. One of the reasons is that a spot market for university teaching would create a perverse incentive for teachers to misinform their students. In a spot market, well-taught students will enter the line-up and compete against their professors. It would be like expecting turkeys to vote for Christmas to expect professors to do a good job of educating the competitors who may take the food from their children's mouths!

Clearly, some jobs can be organized more easily through a spot market than others. They work best when what has to be done is well defined, performance can easily be monitored, and the skills that are needed to perform the job are widely available. A good example of this sort of job is stevedoring where, before containerization, labour was hired by the day or for however long it took to unload a particular ship.[2]

Some jobs, like university teaching, are difficult to organize through spot markets. The skills are not widely available, the objectives are diffuse, or take a long time to achieve, and it is difficult to monitor performance without destroying things—for example, the inculcation of a love of knowledge among students—that the work is supposed to produce. Many other jobs, often organized in bureaucratic hierarchies, share, to a greater or lesser extent, these characteristics. They tend to be organized according to the principles of a service contract (see Chapter 1, Section 1.5.1).[3]

This way of thinking about employment relations helps to make sense of the concept of social class in an age when the vast majority of those who work sell nothing but their labour and are the employees of organizations. In this situation, the Marxist distinction between proletariat and bourgeoisie does not help us to understand heterogeneity in the employment relationship and cannot explain why the working conditions of some employees are clearly more favourable than those of others. Of course, none of this has stopped sociologists from building their intuitive notions into conventional distinctions between different grades of employee—for example, the blue-collar/white-collar distinction. Indeed there has been a minor industry attempting to set out where exactly this dividing line lies and what the criteria of demarcation should be (see Lockwood 1958 for an early empirical example). However, once we accept the idea that jobs may be differentiated in terms of how difficult it is to monitor performance and how much human asset specificity they entail (see Chapter 1, Section 1.5.1), we have a scheme for predicting the way in which the content of the employment relationships will vary along these dimensions. It is this variation in the content of the employment contract that is captured in the groupings of occupations embodied in sociological class schema, such as the one proposed by Goldthorpe (Erikson and Goldthorpe 1993: 35–47; Goldthorpe 2000a: 206–29).

It is one thing to propose a scheme for understanding the way in which different social classes may be differentiated, but it is quite another to show empirically that they are in fact so differentiated. As far as we know there are no direct tests of this version of Goldthorpe's theory of social class.[4] In the next section, we carry out a simple validity test.

3.3. Social Class, Monitoring Difficulty, and Human Asset Specificity

The test is straightforward: we select indicators of monitoring difficulty and human asset specificity, use them to define a two-dimensional space, and plot the positions of social classes within this space. We then ask whether the configuration of occupations corresponds to that predicted by Goldthorpe's theory? What the theory predicts is illustrated in Figure 3.1, which is taken from Goldthorpe (2000a: 223). The service classes (I and II) are in the North Eastern quadrant, indicating that monitoring difficulty and human asset specificity is high. In the South Western quadrant are the skilled (VI) and unskilled (VII) working classes along with unskilled service sector workers (IIIb) and farm labourers (VIIb). Job performance in these classes is relatively easy to monitor and asset specificity is low. The more interesting cases are those sitting off the main service/labour contract diagonal, the so-called mixed cases. Supervisors of manual labour and lower level technicians (V) are likely to have quite a lot of organization-specific know-how that cannot be easily bought from the external labour market and may even be quite difficult to replace internally. At the same time, the results of the work performed are straightforward to monitor. The opposite is more typical of the work of routine non-manual workers (IIIa). Here the skills are easily bought from the external market—hence the existence of temping agencies—but

---

Box 3.1. MONITORING DIFFICULTY ITEMS

HMUCH How easy or hard would you say it is for your supervisor or manager to know how much work a person in a job like yours does in a week?

QUAL How easy or hard would you say it is for your supervisor or manager to know the quality of the work that is done by a person in a job like yours?

SEEN Do you carry out your work in a place where you can be seen all the time by a supervisor or manager?

GLANCE Most of the time can your supervisor or manager tell at a glance how your work is progressing?

TCON Whether a machine or assembly line determines effort or a computerized log/record is kept and used to check performance?

POT Whether the respondent is paid for any overtime they work?

APPRAI Someone formally appraises job performance on a regular basis and it affects earnings or prospects.

TARG Whether targets are set by management/supervisor and they affect pay/promotion and are checked on a long cycle?

HHOUR Are working hours decided by the employer or by the employee?

HCON Are your starting and/or finishing times checked by a supervisor/manager or by a time clock or by a signing on (or similar) system?

BREAK Can you take a break from work for 10 min without having to ask permission?

ERRAND If you need to go on a private errand can you leave your workplace for about half an hour without informing a manager or supervisor?

---

outputs may be more difficult to monitor—at least in the short term. The mixed cases are crucial to the validation of the theory. If all classes lie on the main service/labour diagonal, then monitoring difficulty and asset specificity contain much the same information about the relative position of the classes and the two dimensions can be reduced to one. However, if class V and IIIa occupations are found to lie on the minor diagonal in the way predicted, this should count as evidence for the utility of the theory.

In what follows we use data collected by the WiB 2000 survey. The items used to index monitoring difficulty and human asset specificity are listed in Box 3.1 and 3.2, respectively. The relevance of some of the items is obvious and needs no further explanation. We comment briefly below only on items that require a little more justification.

It is difficult to think of a job in which performance is completely impossible to monitor. Even jobs which primarily involve the delivery of intangibles, for instance the spiritual salvation promised by the Church of England clergy, involve some tasks where either inputs or outputs can

---

Box 3.2. HUMAN ASSET SPECIFICITY ITEMS

RESDUR Standardized residual from regression of duration of current employment episode on age.

OUTOP If you were to lose your job . . . when you did get another job, do you expect you would get at least as much pay as you do now, or would you have to take a job with lower pay?

PROM Generally speaking, when it comes to getting a significant promotion, do you think someone like yourself is better off staying with the same employer or moving around between employers?

BARG After starting their current job has the respondent ever asked their employer for a wage increase and got it?

DOJOB How true is it that your supervisor or manager could do your job if you were away?

OWNWAY In order to perform your job well how important are ways of working that you have developed on your own?

---

be evaluated, for instance the length of the sermon or the quality of the seed cake at the annual church bazaar. Performance monitoring is not an 'all or nothing' thing; there is a continuum of difficulty and different points on this continuum tend to call forth different institutional mechanisms ranging from hourly direct observation by a person through longer-term target setting on to sophisticated annual appraisal schemes. What we have tried to do is select indicators of different positions on this continuum.

Modern methods of work control do not require direct observation by a person. Computerized technology can keep track of work flow and performance (see Chapter 6). The variable TCON (standing for technical control) combines information on whether effort is controlled by the pace of a machine or an assembly line and/or a computerized log is kept of performance. Overtime payment (POT) implies that discrete units of work effort can be identified and rewarded when performed outside of the standard hours of work—for example, extra hours to meet a delivery date, or deal with temporarily increased volumes of activity, or cope with unexpected circumstances such as the repair of a broken plant or equipment. In these circumstances, it is usually clear what exactly has been done in the overtime hours. This is likely to be less clear when the overtime hours are unpaid. Appraisal (APPRAI) implies observable performance criteria against which the individual's actual behaviour can be evaluated, as does the existence of targets set by managers or supervisors

(TARG). In the latter case, however, we identify specifically the kind of targets the achievement of which can be monitored only over a relatively long cycle (at least quarterly), implying that it is difficult, or meaningless, to monitor results in real time. HHOUR and HCON indicate employer control over working hours—which we take to be a way of monitoring work effort and indirectly measuring output by assuming that there is a relationship, albeit a less than straightforward one, between inputs and outputs. In the same spirit, BREAK and ERRAND are treated as indicators of the ease of input monitoring.

Human asset specificity is somewhat more difficult to measure with survey instruments than is monitoring difficulty, so our indicators are, *faute de mieux,* more indirect. The longer employees stay with an organization, the higher the probability that they acquire job-relevant knowledge that is specific to that organization and personal to them. A long-serving ICT specialist will know, for example, the quirks of her network—which undocumented patches and workarounds have been implemented to keep the system going. In a cross-sectional survey, such as WiB 2000, employee age and length of service are by design correlated, but we can fix this by working with the residual of job tenure after it has been regressed on employee age (RESDUR). DOJOB and OWNWAY also tap the extent to which the employee has performance-enhancing knowledge, gained through learning by doing and not known to others. An important indicator of human asset specificity is the fact that employees are paid more in their current job than they would be in an otherwise comparable job in the external market (OUTOP). One reason for this is that asset specificity creates an economic rent and employees and employers are able to bargain over its division. BARG identifies those employees who have been able to mobilize their bargaining power to achieve a salary increase that their employer would presumably not agree to if they could easily replace the employee by an external hire.

What we are aiming for is an empirically generated map of the relative position of occupations that is isomorphic with the scheme illustrated in Figure 3.1. To generate this, we work with twelve occupational groups defined by the Office for National Statistics (ONS) in their national statistics socio-economic classification (NS-SEC).[5] The twelve aggregated categories we use are described in Table 3.1 along with examples of the sort of occupations included in each group. We need scores for each NS-SEC category on the two dimensions which we obtain from two regressions in which membership of an NS-SEC category is predicted by the monitoring difficulty and asset specificity indicators, respectively.

Table 3.1. NS-SEC groups and indicative occupational titles

Short label	ONS NS-SEC category title	Five most common occupations in a category	% of all employees; $n = 2,132$
HM	L2 Higher managerial occupations	Marketing and sales manager; production and works maintenance manager; computer systems and data processing manager; treasurer and company financial manager; local government officer	5
HP1	L3.1 Higher professional occupations—'traditional' employees	University teacher; medical doctor; solicitor/barrister; software engineer; chemist	6
HP2	L3.2 Higher professional occupations—'new' employees	Computer analyst/programmer; management/business consultant; underwriter, claims assessor, broker, investment analyst (managers/supervisors); taxation expert; management accountant	2
LP1	L4.1 Lower professional and higher technical occupations—'traditional' employees	Nurse; secondary school teacher; primary/middle school teacher; welfare, community, and youth worker; underwriter, claims assessor, broker, investment analyst (employees)	13
LP2	L4.2 Lower professional and higher technical occupations—'new' employees	Technical and wholesale sales representative; other sales representative; professional athlete sportsman; importer/exporter	1
LM	L5 Lower managerial occupations	Other managers and administrators; other financial institution and office managers; manager in service industries; manager in building and contracting; marketing and sales managers	7
HS	L6 Higher supervisory occupations	Account and wages clerk, bookkeeper, other financial clerk (supervisor); clerk (supervisor); production and works maintenance manager (supervisor); counter clerk and cashier (supervisor); other secretaries, personal assistants, typists, etc. (supervisor)	4
INT	L7 Intermediate occupations	Clerk; account and wages clerk, bookkeeper, other financial clerk; other secretaries, personal assistants, typists, etc.; filing, computer, and other record clerks; civil service administrative officers and assistants	17
LS	L10 Lower supervisory occupations	Sales assistant (supervisor); bar staff (supervisor); other plant and machine operatives (supervisor); metal working, production, and maintenance fitters (supervisor); other childcare and related occupations (supervisor)	9
LT	L11 Lower technical occupations	Metal working, production, and maintenance fitters; electricians, electrical maintenance fitters; motor mechanic, auto engineer; gardener, groundsman/woman; other crafts and related occupations	5
SR	L12 Semi-routine occupations	Sales assistants; care assistants and attendants; counterhands, catering assistants; receptionists; educational assistants	18
R	L13 Routine occupations	Cleaner, domestic; drivers of road goods vehicles; storekeepers and warehousemen/women; other childcare and related occupations; packers, canners, bottlers, fillers	14

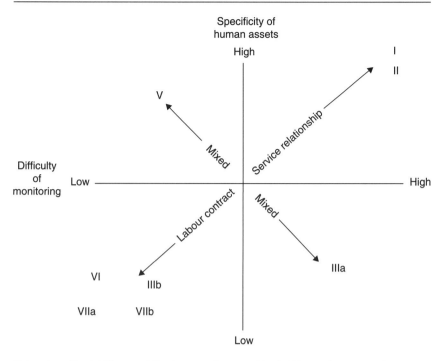

Taken from 'Social Class and Employment Contracts' in Goldthorpe (2000*a*; 223)

Figure 3.1. Predicted positions of Goldthorpe social classes in the monitoring difficulty/human asset specificity space

A by-product of the technique we use is scale scores that indicate the 'distance' between the occupational categories.[6]

The result of this exercise is displayed in Figure 3.2, which is an empirical version of Figure 3.1. The outcome is quite encouraging for advocates of the Goldthorpe class theory. In general, the occupational groups lie on a North East to South West line, indicating that monitoring difficulty and human asset specificity are positively correlated. This means, for example, that employees whose work is not easy to monitor are likely to have high levels of firm-specific knowledge. However, there is also local North West by South East separation, most noticeably between lower technical/lower supervisory employees and intermediate occupations. The former are relatively high on the asset specificity dimension but low on the monitoring difficulty dimension while this ordering is reversed for the latter. These are precisely the groups that are

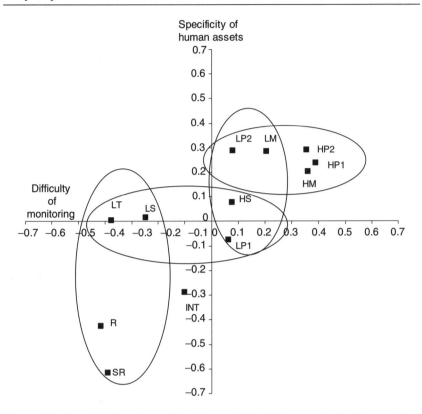

Figure 3.2. Empirically estimated positions of NS-SEC categories in the monitoring difficulty/human asset specificity space

termed 'mixed' with regard to the labour/service contract distinction and this pattern is as predicted in Figure 3.1.[7]

What is not predicted by the theory, but emerges empirically, is the step-like structure of the relationship between the occupational groups. Starting in the South Western quadrant we have the routine, semi-routine, lower technical, and lower supervisory occupations, which have similar monitoring difficulty values but vary in terms of asset specificity. The LT and LS occupations belong to a second group along with the higher supervisors and lower professionals 1 which are similar in their level of asset specificity but vary along the difficulty monitoring dimensions. In turn, the HS and the LP1 belong to a third group with the lower professionals 2 and the lower managers; they are similar in monitoring difficulty but differ in asset specificity. Finally, the LP2 and LM belong to a fourth group that includes the higher professionals 1 and 2 and the higher managers. This group is similar in terms of asset specificity but varies along the monitoring difficulty dimension. The only occupational groups that do not fit easily into this scheme are the intermediate occupations, clerks, secretaries, and other lower level clerical and administrative positions, exactly the group whose ambiguous position in the class structure prompted Lockwood (1958) to explore the nature of the distinction between white-collar and blue-collar work.

In short, the model of the class structure displayed in Figure 3.2 is somewhat like a green stick: it bends at particular breakpoints but is still continuous. Occupational groups are differentiated first according to one principal and then according to another. Groups similar in terms of monitoring difficulty are differentiated by their degree of human asset specificity, and those with the same level of human asset specificity are differentiated in terms of monitoring difficulty. Some occupations appear to belong to one group in terms of one criteria and a second according to the other. There is nothing 'contradictory' about this; it is a natural outcome of employers finding it rational to offer different contractual conditions to groups who differ along one or more 'problem' dimensions.

Before moving on, we have one more major remark to make. There is a literature that claims to discern within Goldthorpe's service class distinct professional and managerial class fractions (see Butler and Savage 1995; Guveli 2006; Guveli and De Graaf 2007; Guveli, Need and De Graaf 2007). That managers and professionals differ in all sorts of ways is scarcely to be denied. From the point of view of those interested in the theory of social class, the point is not whether they differ, but whether they differ for the right reasons. Goldthorpe's claim is essentially that different classes are treated differently by employers (have different contractual statuses) because the occupations that comprise them differ with respect to monitoring difficulty and human asset specificity. Variation along these dimensions defines what class (in Goldthorpe's conceptualization) is and any evaluation of the empirical adequacy of the conceptualization has to be made in terms of these dimensions. Figure 3.2 makes it obvious that in terms of the relevant criteria no clear-cut managerial grouping exists distinct from a clear-cut professional grouping: managerial and professional occupations are intermixed. Higher professionals are very similar to higher managers on both dimensions and the LP1 group is about as far away from the LP2 group on the asset specificity dimension as it is from the lower managerial group and much closer to the higher supervisors.[8]

All we have done so far in this chapter is show that some conventional occupational groupings, which we call social classes, differ with respect to the difficulty they pose for a principal (employer) who wishes to extract work from an agent (employee). What we turn to now is how the fruits of employment—wages and fringe benefits—are distributed between the social classes. In particular, we focus on whether there has been a significant change during the 1990s in interclass differences in these distributions. We start by presenting the reasons why some commentators appear to believe that changes have either occurred or are likely to occur in the near future.

3.4. Social Class, Wages, and Fringe Benefits

Differences in pay and fringe benefits, notably between manual and non-manual workers, were once considered to be symptomatic of the class-ridden nature of British industry. During the late 1960s, a series of pioneering studies highlighted major differences in working conditions between blue-collar and white-collar employees, with those in blue-collar occupations being less likely to enjoy a range of 'status privileges', such as employer-based pension plans and sick pay schemes. Further evidence of their 'second-class' status was indicated by having to 'clock-on' to record attendance, suffering wage deductions in the event of being late for work, and having to take time off without pay in the event of family illness (Craig 1969; Wedderburn and Craig 1974; Townsend 1979). But perhaps the most striking indicator of class differences in the everyday lives of British workers was the provision of separate workplace entrances, canteens (or dining rooms), and toilets (Craig 1969), differences that constituted a form of 'industrial apartheid' for one commentator (Bugler 1965). The persistence and prevalence of this 'status divide' in employment conditions was eventually recognized as a major industrial relations problem during the 1970s, when trade unions, the Donovan Commission on Industrial Relations, and, subsequently, the Labour Government called for the removal of 'invidious distinctions' not based 'on the requirements of the job' (Donovan 1968: para 42; Crouch 1977: 99).

By the end of the twentieth century, however, a number of authors claimed that such class-based forms of workplace inequality had either attenuated or, else, been replaced by more individualized forms of inequality. As indicated earlier, we concentrate on the claims advanced by two such authors, Sørensen and Russell, because they represent different sides of the marketization–internalization debate. While both accept that vestiges of these structures might remain, they insist that these no longer serve as the primary source of inequality in employment conditions. Instead, Sørensen claims that social inequality has been experiencing a process of individualization so that individual factors, such as human capital, are now the major source of differentiation in job rewards (Sørensen 2000). By contrast, Russell draws on a large range of literature from industrial relations and HRM to claim that employment conditions have been harmonized across the class divide and the major division is now that between men and women, or between standard and non-standard workers (Russell 1998).

3.4.1. *Rent, Employment Relationships, and Inequality*

To understand Sørensen's specific claims about the changing nature of inequality, we need to provide a brief outline of his general argument (Sørensen 2000). Sørensen seeks to overcome weaknesses in Marxist and Weberian treatments of social class by conceptualizing social class as a form of personal wealth, that is, the assets an individual controls. His basic idea is that individuals will typically seek to maximize their wealth by seeking to get the best possible return from their assets, which might include inherited economic capital, along with personal investments in human, social, and cultural capital. With regard to the wealth obtained from employment relationships, Sørensen distinguishes between 'normal' market returns and rents, where the return is greater than that which would be achieved under conditions of perfect competition (Sørensen 1996). In other words, '[r]ents are payments to assets that exceed the competitive price or the price sufficient to cover costs and therefore exceeding what is sufficient to bring about the employment of the asset' (Sørensen 2000: 1536).

Employment relations can create rents in a number of ways once they deviate from the kind of 'spot-market' exchanges that characterize Sørensen's counterfactual of perfect competition. Although they are relatively rare, spot markets constitute 'open employment relationships', where an individual is completely dependent on his or her human capital, ability, and talent (Sørensen 2001: 297). By contrast, under 'closed employment relationships' employees are insulated from market forces and consequently enjoy rent, as their income exceeds that which might be obtained in a competitive market. This means, for example, that permanent, or open-ended, employment contracts may create a rent when both the employer and the employee benefit from continuing the relationship. The employer benefits when the employee learns firm-specific skills and knowledge, and the employee appreciates that these skills are less saleable elsewhere (Sørensen 2001: 306–7). Similarly, internal labour markets, which typically seek to develop and retain firm-specific knowledge, serve to increase rent. Even though such promotion ladders may provide less than the market wage at entry level, when they are open to outsiders, they typically provide an overall surplus over a lifetime, and become increasingly closed or insulated in the process (Sørensen 2000: 1546).

Having set out this elaborate conceptual map, Sørensen proceeds to argue that it is in the interest of employers 'to produce a labour market conforming to the assumptions of neoclassical economics' (Sørensen 2000: 1554) and this, indeed, is what he believes has been happening in recent years. Here he identifies a number of developments, such as the increase in earnings inequality, the subcontracting (or 'outsourcing') of work, and the downsizing of organizations. Although they may appear to be rather different phenomenon, Sørensen insists that each represents a deliberate attempt by employers to eliminate rents from the labour market.

For Sørensen, the inevitable result of these developments is a 'structure-less society', one in which 'rents will disappear from structural locations in the labour market' (Sørensen 2000: 1555). Inequality will certainly persist but it will no longer be based on class position as determined by 'closed employment relations'. Rather, the resulting spot market will reward individual endowments in the form of human capital, effort, or natural talent. To put it another way, employment relationships become less important in determining inequality than the labour market capacity of individual workers. In this context, inequality will become much more highly differentiated and fragmented. To support this claim, Sørensen refers to evidence on increasing inequalities in earnings in the USA, which show that structural locations have become less important in explaining variations in earnings than do individual attributes such as human capital (Sørensen 2000: 1552).

Sørensen's argument is significant for our purposes because it suggests that class structure is becoming less important in explaining labour market inequality. While others, such as Beck (1992), have also argued that there is a new individualization of inequality in capitalist societies, Sørensen's account is more useful because it clearly identifies the source of this change in the rent-removing practices of employers. The latter is particularly significant because many of these same practices have already received considerable attention in Britain. In relation to earnings, for instance, Britain is regarded as being second only to the USA in terms of earnings inequality with a dramatic increase during the 1990s (Machin 1999; Nielsen and Alderson 2001). More significantly, much of the widening of income inequality is attributed to increasing returns to education and skill, and, contrary to conventional wisdom, this trend is not confined to a small band at the very top of the income hierarchy (Machin 1999). There is also evidence to indicate that the subcontracting of work has increased, notably in the privatized public utilities and in the public sector following various forms of government deregulation (O'Connell Davidson 1993; Morgan et al. 2000). Indeed, the best available evidence from employers indicates that some 90 per cent of all workplaces engage in some kind of outsourcing (Cully et al. 1999). But perhaps the most highly publicized development during the 1990s was the attack on the 'corporate fat' with many 'blue chip' British-based firms reducing the middle ranks of their organizations through 'delayering exercises'. One direct consequence of this practice was the erosion of internal labour markets in large organizations (Brown and Scase 1994; McGovern et al. 1998; Grimshaw et al. 2001). In short, these parallel labour market developments, which may well be the product of an underlying 'Anglo-Saxon capitalism', indicate that there are good grounds for examining Sørensen's claims in the British context.

3.4.2. Harmonization and the Death of the 'Status Divide'

Russell's accounts of the changing nature of workplace inequality differ from Sørensen's in several respects, yet they share an underlying message (Russell 1991, 1998). She too argues that class-based forms of inequality have more or less disappeared and while inequalities remain, these can no longer be captured by the concept of social class.

Her basic thesis is that the twentieth century was marked by a long-term trend towards the harmonization of employment conditions in Britain, notably between blue- and white-collar workers. Early developments in occupational welfare at the end of the nineteenth century developed into full-blown waves of harmonization during the second half of the twentieth century. Although Russell claims that much of this activity was spearheaded by a select group of British manufacturers in the 1960s and 1970s, the process was accelerated during the 1980s by the increased demand for flexible labour, the arrival of multinational firms from the

USA and Japan, and by the then Conservative Government's policies of labour market deregulation.

Many of the reasons that Russell gives for the convergence in employment conditions are essentially the same as those given for the internalization of the employment relationship (Cappelli et al. 1997: 16–22). For instance, employers introduced integrated pay and grading structures with harmonized benefits as a means of promoting greater flexibility following the introduction of robotics and computer-controlled equipment. There were also returns to scale in that employers increasingly accepted that it was administratively inefficient to maintain two separate sets of employment conditions. Furthermore, this process was boosted by the Conservative Government's support for a general movement from centralized multi-employer pay bargaining to enterprise-level bargaining as it enabled employers to internalize decisions about pay and conditions.

Although some British firms had introduced single status policies before the arrival of US and Japanese firms, Russell's argument suggests that it was the economic performance of the Japanese firms and, in particular, their reputations for high productivity and 'good industrial relations' that demonstrated the benefits of the organization-oriented model of employment (Russell 1998: 98–107). Here Russell draws upon Oliver and Wilkinson's influential 'Japanization of British industry' thesis, which proclaimed that a large proportion of British-owned firms were adapting substantial elements of Japanese production and employment practices, with the introduction of 'staff' benefits being one of the most common changes (Oliver and Wilkinson 1992: 179).[9]

While others have written about the demise of the 'status divide' (Evans 1980; Arthurs 1985; Price 1989), Russell is the only one to address the implications for social inequality generally and class-based inequality in particular. Her conclusion is that there has been a fundamental transformation in the class structure of modern Britain as the 'timeworn workplace divide which had buttressed class consciousness' has more or less disappeared (Russell, 1998: 168). The death of the status divide marks the demise of 'the class structure and the class identities of the mid-twentieth century' (Russell 1998: 189). Yet, Russell acknowledges that inequalities remain, though the most significant workplace divide is now between those in full-time, permanent employment and those in temporary, part-time, or self-employed jobs (Russell 1998: 186). Nonetheless, she concludes by describing her study as another contribution to the growing literature on 'the death of social class' (Clark and Lipset 1991; Pakulski and Waters 1996).

Although Sørensen and Russell believe that the effects of social class are being attenuated, it is fairly obvious that there are substantial differences between them as to how this process is taking place. Sørensen's account, for instance, points to a deterioration in employment conditions as employers seek to move towards a basic spot-market exchange of wages for labour. Russell, by contrast, believes that social class is becoming irrelevant because of a general improvement in the conditions of blue-collar workers.

Underlying both, however, is a failure to recognize that it may be neither possible nor desirable for employers to provide the same employment relationship to employees engaged in different kinds of work. More specifically, variations in asset specificity and ease of monitoring (such as those described earlier in this chapter) may lead to different kinds of employment relationships and these in turn can give rise to persisting inequalities of a class-based kind. The significance of this for Sørensen's argument is that it is not always in the employers' interest to move towards a spot-market type relationship because of the problems of work monitoring and asset specificity. For example, the employment of managers on such a basis is quite likely to be counterproductive as the basic spot-market exchange would not enable the employer to develop and retain the kinds of firm-specific knowledge that characterize a large part of managerial work. As Goldthorpe himself argued in response to Sørensen:

From the standpoint of organizational effectiveness, it is in fact the basic labour contract that I would see as being the form of regulation of employment with the most limited range of application: that is, to types of work where little more than labour in its elementary sense is involved. (Goldthorpe 2000*b*: 1579)

3.5. Measuring Inequality in Employment Conditions

In reviewing the evidence on workplace inequality in Britain, we were struck by Peter Townsend's remark that

[A]ttempts to investigate how far conditions of work in one industry are characteristic of conditions in another, and to develop common standards of comparison, especially in relation to trends over time, have scarcely been made at all, or only fragmentarily. (Townsend 1979: 432)

Certainly, much of the early research on differences in employment conditions was biased towards large, manufacturing enterprises (e.g. Craig 1969; Robinson 1972; Wedderburn and Craig 1974). Townsend's work represented a significant advance in that it was the first to draw on a nationally representative survey and used indicators that were not specific to manufacturing (Townsend 1979: 432–75). His results were also significant because he found that 'deprivation at work' was broadly related to occupational class, and while there was indeed a divide between manual and non-manual workers, there were also further divisions within non-manual employment, notably between those in routine non-manual grades (mostly women) and those in professional and managerial grades (almost entirely male) (Townsend 1979: 443).[10]

Although Townsend's research was conducted in the late 1960s, there were no further improvements in nationally representative evidence on employment conditions until the advent of the WIRS/WERS surveys of British workplaces in the 1980s. Even so, the evidence raises the question of whether widespread assumptions of harmonization are little more than a myth. Using a summary measure of single status that included provision of an employer pension scheme, company car or car allowance, private health insurance, four weeks of holidays (or more), and sick pay beyond statutory entitlement, Cully et al. (1999: 73–4) found substantial differences in the distribution of fringe benefits during the 1990s. After defining 'single status' workplaces as those that existed wherever there was no differential between managerial and non-managerial employees in the availability of these benefits, they found that only two-fifths (41%) of all workplaces met this criterion. Furthermore, such workplaces were more likely to have a recognized trade union, though the presence of a union made little difference among private sector workplaces.

Despite the value of the WERS-based studies in pointing to the persistence of inequality (see also Millward 1994: 104–13), the analyses failed to build on Townsend's focus on divisions among white-collar and blue-collar occupations in addition to the traditional manual or non-manual divide. The contribution of Millward (1994), for instance, is confined to establishments employing only manual and non-manual employees. Similarly, the analysis undertaken by Cully et al. (1999) is restricted to differences between managerial and non-managerial employees. Indeed, much of this literature, including Russell's detailed historical studies (Russell 1991, 1998), displays a marked tendency to slip from the status divide into a two-class model of society, a practice that flies in the face of the Goldthorpe class schema and, indeed, most of the sociological literature, whether Weberian or neo-Marxist.

In the remainder of this chapter, we examine both Sørensen's individualization thesis and Russell's harmonization thesis by drawing on the more sophisticated categorization of social class used in both the EiB 1992 and WiB 2000 surveys.[11] Although much of the neglected literature on the status divide was preoccupied with the distribution of fringe benefits, we also consider class differences in hourly earnings because it is central to Sørensen's claim that inequality is increasingly based on individual attributes, such as human capital, rather than social structure. Finally, we appreciate that for those familiar with the literature on social stratification in modern Britain, it will not come as a surprise to learn that social class remains an important source of inequality. Consequently, we shall, instead, concentrate on the question of whether social class has become less important as a source of inequality over time.

3.6. Social Class, Earnings, and Benefits

Table 3.2 shows how estimated pay levels vary over social classes, how average pay within classes has changed over the 1990s, and how pay variation within classes has evolved. It also contains information about the proportions within each class that fall below two conventional 'poverty wages' levels—the legal minimum wage prevailing in 2000 (there was no minimum wage in 1992) and the earnings level corresponding to 60 per cent of median earnings in the relevant year.[12]

The best single number indicator of wage levels to focus on is median hourly earnings and the stand-out finding is the big difference in the fortunes of those at the top and bottom of the class structure.[13] During the 1990s, the average inflation-adjusted hourly earnings of higher managers increased by about a quarter, while median earnings for routine and semi-routine employees appear, if anything, to have declined slightly. Lower technical employees and the lower managerial grades also seem to have done rather well, with increases of 15 and 10 per cent, respectively. Wage increases for all other groups have been modest and the predominantly public sector lower professionals have apparently taken a pay cut in real terms. While we should be careful not to read too much into some of these numbers—they are only estimates—the increase in salary levels for higher managers is quite stunning and we should bear in mind that these are not in the main just 'fat cat' CEOs. In fact, the NS-SEC category of higher managers reaches quite far down the executive hierarchy. The 'fat cats' have been quite generous in the distribution of the cream among their own tribe.

Table 3.2. Hourly earnings, level, and dispersion by social class grouping (NS-SEC) 1992 and 2000

	% in NS-SEC	Mean £	% Change in mean	Median £	% Change in median	10th Percentile	90th Percentile	Inter-quartile range	Standard deviation	% Below 2000 minimum wage levels	% Below 60% of median
Higher managers											
1992	4	9.88		10.85		5.76	18.82	7.21	1.82	6	6
2000	5	14.61	48	13.41	24	6.99	27.35	10.56	1.73	0	0
Higher professionals											
1992	6	11.20		11.42		6.78	17.84	5.65	1.59	1	1
2000	8	13.22	18	12.07	5	6.99	23.35	7.69	1.74	1	3
Lower professionals											
1992	16	9.50		9.99		5.54	16.33	5.13	1.65	3	5
2000	14	9.82	3	9.74	−3	6.07	15.39	4.96	1.53	1	2
Lower managers											
1992	7	8.17		8.12		4.57	16.66	6.05	1.76	5	9
2000	8	9.82	20	9.03	11	4.95	20.24	6.89	1.75	2	6
Higher supervisors											
1992	3	7.85		8.36		4.44	13.18	5.90	1.67	4	7
2000	4	8.72	11	8.59	3	5.24	14.84	5.24	1.20	1	4
Intermediate											
1992	17	6.55		6.80		4.21	11.51	3.46	1.58	7	11
2000	16	7.06	8	7.02	3	4.50	12.20	3.52	1.54	5	10
Lower supervisors											
1992	6	6.21		6.35		3.71	11.50	3.94	1.56	10	22
2000	8	6.42	3	6.54	3	3.89	10.80	4.10	1.56	6	19

Lower technical											
1992	6	7.08		7.26	15	4.24	11.60	3.81	1.19	3	9
2000	5	7.95	12	8.01		4.80	13.18	4.73	1.50	1	5
Semi-routine											
1992	19	5.24		5.38	−5	3.33	8.91	2.92	1.53	14	30
2000	18	5.28	1	5.09		3.50	9.23	2.52	1.58	12	37
Routine											
1992	16	5.31		5.30	−3	3.33	9.07	2.97	1.63	12	27
2000	14	5.39	2	5.16		3.60	8.33	2.80	1.58	10	35
All											
1992	100	7.03		7.02	5	3.81	13.81	4.98	1.72	8	15
2000	100	7.56	8	7.37		4.00	15.14	5.43	1.76	5	16

1992 EiB $n = 3{,}480$; 2000 WiB $n = 2{,}132$. Employees only. Data are post-stratified and weighted with weights derived from the Quarterly Labour Force Survey for the relevant year. Missing data are filled in by multiple imputation, $m = 5$, see Appendix 2. All amounts at 2000 prices.

What Table 3.2 also makes clear is that occupational earnings uncertainty has roughly mirrored growth in earnings levels. Among the higher managers and professionals, the lower managers, and the lower technical employees the spread of earnings has increased, whereas among the other occupational groups it has either remained stable or actually declined slightly. In essence, the members of occupations that have on average done well during the 1990s have become more heterogeneous or internally stratified in wage terms. Most have done well, but some have done very well.

The last two columns of Table 3.2 illustrate just how poorly the worst off have done in relative terms. The introduction of the national minimum wage appears to have been effective in reducing the proportion receiving the very lowest pay levels. However, if we focus on relative pay—60 per cent of median earnings—we see that the proportion of routine and semi-routine workers falling below this level has unequivocally increased. In 2000, just over a third of employees in routine occupations and almost 40 per cent of employees in semi-routine occupations had hourly earnings below this threshold. The story is rather nicely summed up in two numbers: in 1992, NS-SEC explained 21 per cent of the variance in hourly earnings; in 2000, the comparable figure is 33 per cent. Over the 1990s, social class became a *better* not a worse predictor of earnings. This fact does not sit well with Sørensen's prediction of a movement towards what might be described as a structureless 'neoclassical soup' (Goldthorpe 2000*b*: 1581).

A sceptic might reasonably ask what our data show when we condition on other relevant variables. If we re-estimate the wage prediction

Table 3.3. Fringe benefits available to employees, 1992 and 2000

	1992	2000
Occupational pension scheme	65%	63%
Sick pay beyond the statutory entitlement	61%	64%
Subsidized/free meals	33%	25%
Sports facilities	26%	NA
Company car/van	25%	20%
Private health insurance	23%	21%
Help with travel costs	20%	16%
Finance/loans for house purchase	16%	12%
Profit sharing/share options	16%	15%
Mean number of days of paid sick leave without certification	4	4
Mean number of days of paid holiday	19	22

Source: 1992 EiB and 2000 WiB.

equations and control for age, gender, ethnic group (1992 only), educational qualifications, hours, duration of service with the current employer, industrial sector, organization size, private sector, and trade union presence, we find the same pattern of (highly significant) class differences though the magnitude of the effect is attenuated. We can get a concise summary of the changing magnitude of the class effects by comparing the standard deviation of the 1992 and 2000 conditional class slope parameters. In 1992, their standard deviation was 0.045; in 2000, it was 0.149.[14] Again we are forced to conclude that even when we control for human capital indicators, social class distinctions have become more, not less, marked.

We now turn to fringe benefits and other aspects of working conditions. Table 3.3 lists nine fringe benefits and two additional indicators of conditions of service that have traditionally distinguished the white-collar and blue-collar workforce—the number of days of self-certified sick leave permitted by the employer and the number of days of paid holiday the

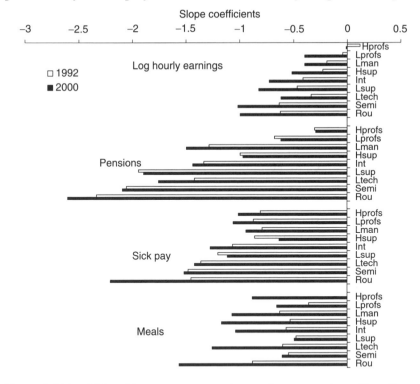

Figure 3.3(a). OLS and logit parameter estimates from regression of benefits on social class, 1992 and 2000.

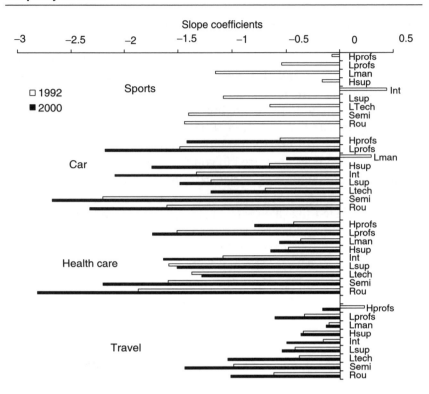

Figure 3.3(b). Logit parameter estimates of benefits on social class, 1992 and 2000.

employee is entitled to. Respondents were asked in 1992 and 2000 to say whether they were entitled to any of the benefits regardless of whether they actually made use of them. Between the two dates, there have been some minor changes in the proportions entitled to some of the benefits, but by and large the picture has remained quite stable. Our interest is not in the overall level of entitlement but in differences between social class groups in entitlement levels.

Figures 3.3a through 3.3c allow us to see how class differences have changed over time. The length of each bar in the figures represents the magnitude of a coefficient from a regression—a logistic regression for binary responses such as benefit entitlement and an ordinary least squares (OLS) regression for continuous responses. Bars are plotted for all social classes except the higher managerial employees who are assigned a value of zero. Thus, the availability of benefits to each class group must be interpreted as a comparison with the level prevailing among

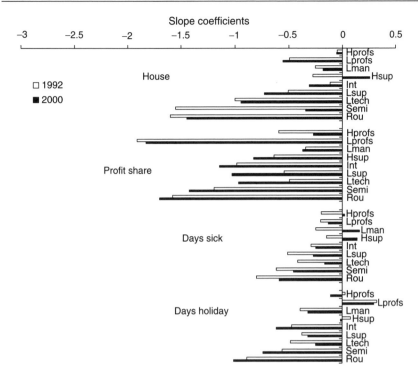

Figure 3.3(c). Logit parameter estimates from regression of benefits on social class, 1992 and 2000.

the higher managers. As the bars get longer in a negative direction, the distance between the benefit level in a particular class and the level in the higher managerial group gets greater. For purposes of comparison, we also include in Figure 3.3a information about class differences in earnings.

Naturally, we are not surprised that there is a strong class gradient in all of the figures. Our concern is whether that gradient has shrunk, grown, or remained constant during the 1990s. The results are very easy to summarize: in all domains except one, class differences have either remained stable or have actually increased. The exception is days of self-certified sickness absence, and the movement towards equalization of contractual conditions here is due primarily to changes in employment law. The overall pattern is quite contrary to what we would expect from Russell's account. Rather than an inexorable movement towards classless, single status industrial citizenship most change is again actually in the direction of *more* not less stratification.[15]

3.7. Conclusions

We would like to conclude this chapter by providing a brief summary of the main results before turning to the question of how we might explain the persistence of social class differentials in job rewards. We began by showing that conventional Goldthorpe class categories can be mapped into a simple two-dimensional space defined by axes that index the severity of two problems that bedevil all organizations: the ease of collecting information about how well an employee is performing and the extent to which the employee has knowledge and skills that are not easily replaced by external hire. Of course, there are no jobs where it is completely impossible to judge performance and nobody, given sufficient time, is irreplaceable. These things are a matter of degree. Where occupations end up in this space is dictated primarily by the nature of the tasks that define the job. Locations within this space create contractual design problems that require different solutions. The solutions are the typical service, mixed, and labour forms of contract. Again, this is just a typology and in practice there will be considerable variation around the themes. Nevertheless, the institutional details of the contractual solutions are in a sense the fabric of the class structure.

In the second half of the chapter, we examined a set of claims about the rigidity of the class structure. For different reasons, both Sørensen and Russell claim reason to believe that social class no longer has the same power to structure the institutional details of workplace inequalities that it once had. By looking at two sets of institutional details—wages and fringe benefits—we were able to show that there is almost no evidence to support this claim and that on the contrary there is evidence that over the 1990s social class differences became wider rather than narrower. It would seem that the death of class has been greatly exaggerated.

How then do we explain the unequal distribution of pay and benefits across the class spectrum? Here we believe Goldthorpe's recent re-conceptualization of the origins of *employee* classes, which draws heavily on the work of institutional economists, provides the most parsimonious solution. As we indicated in Chapter 1 (Section 1.5.1), the employment relationship is founded on an incomplete, implicit contract in which employers face the basic problem of turning labour power into labour. This problem is complicated by variations in the organization of work, especially where it is either not possible or economically counterproductive to monitor the efforts of employees in detail. Accordingly, employers will, over time, use a mixture of incentives and forms of supervision that are most appropriate given the requirements of the job. It follows that higher managers, for example, receive a higher level of pay and a wider range of fringe benefits because their work is difficult to monitor and they clearly have considerable firm-specific skills that are valued highly by their employers. By contrast, most of the jobs in the routine working class category do not require skills that are difficult to find in the external labour market and, furthermore, are such that employee performance is easily judged. Generally, the level and type of rewards that an employee receives are those that are most likely to maximize their performance given the nature of their work and the value of their skills. This, then, is the compelling logic of economic efficiency that lies behind Goldthorpe's conception of social classes.

There is, however, a complication in that the distribution of certain kinds of fringe benefits cannot be explained by such economic functionality. Instead, we have to return to the idea that the provision of these benefits serves no other purpose than to indicate the elevated social status of the beneficiary. The 'company car' is, perhaps, the most well-known contemporary example. Providing company cars to higher managers is unlikely to make them more efficient than their secretaries, particularly when neither of them needs a car to do their jobs. Yet they are significantly more likely to have this benefit when compared with almost any other class group (Figure 3.3b).[16] In sum, we would contend that employment conditions of this kind simply reflect the prestige, or status, of employees in the same way that having separate bathroom and dining facilities marked the social distance between white-collar and 'cloth cap' for much of the twentieth century. If so, then it would appear that the ancient tradition of 'status privileges' remains alive and well in twenty-first-century Britain.

Notes

1. We would like to add that Sørensen's and Russell's work was also chosen because they represent popular contemporary ideas within the literature on social stratification and HRM. Sørensen presents a plausible version of the argument that social inequality has become increasingly individualized while Russell is intent on showing that blue-collar employment conditions have basically converged on those of their white-collar colleagues.

2. As anyone who has watched the Elia Kazan movie *On the Waterfront* will know, there was often much more 'organization' of the hiring process than is implied

by a pure spot market (see Bell 1960 for a classic account of the 'organization' of labour on the New York waterfront).

3. As the name suggests, these types of arrangements typically have their origins in state bureaucracies, ecclesiastical hierarchies, or the military. For example, Marco Polo in *The Travels* reports the following about Kubilai Khan's military organization:

   . . . We shall now relate how he dealt with those barons who acquitted themselves well in battle . . . he promoted those who were commanders of 100 men to the command of 1000, and commanders of 1000 to the command of 10000; and he gave them lavish gifts of silver plate and tablets of authority, each according to his rank . . . all who have these tablets also have warrants setting forth in writing all the powers vested in them by their office. (Marco Polo, *The Travels*, 1958, Penguin Classics p. 91)

4. See Evans (1992) and Evans and Mills (1998, 2000) for tests of the validity of Goldthorpe's earlier conceptualizations of social class.

5. We use the NS-SEC categories rather than Goldthorpe classes because they are more firmly based on Goldthorpe's class theory than are his own categories (see Rose and Pevalin, 2003), and thus in a Popperian spirit we test the strongest available version of his theory.

6. The model used here is the so-called Stereotyped Ordered Regression (SOR) model (Anderson 1984; DiPrete 1990; Hendrickx 1999). The model can be expressed as

$$\log\left(\frac{P(Y=q)}{P(Y=r)}\right) = a_q - a_r + (\varphi_q - \varphi_r)(\beta_1 X_1 + \beta_2 X_2 + \ldots + \beta_k X_k)$$

   In words: the log odds of an observation being in any one category (q) of the NS-SEC classification rather than in an arbitrarily defined reference category (r) is a function of the difference between two constants (denoted by the Greek letter a) plus a weighted linear combination of a set of predictor variables (in this case either the indicators from Box 3.1 or those from Box 3.2) *multiplied by* the difference between two further constants (denoted by the Greek letter φ. It is these φ parameters that give us the distances between the NS-SEC categories. The model is estimated by maximum likelihood using public domain STATA code written by Hendickx. We fit two models, one for the monitoring difficulty indicators and another for the asset specificity items. In both cases, the model fits somewhat less well than a multinomial logistic regression but is always preferred by the Bayes' information criterion (BIC) statistic. In Figure 3.2, we have rescaled the arbitrary range of the φ parameters so that they are identical for both of the plotted dimensions.

7. The intermediate NS-SEC group corresponds to Goldthorpe's class IIIa while the lower supervisory NS-SEC group forms a part of class V. The NS-SEC

lower technical occupations are a mixture of parts of Goldthorpe's class V and class VI.

8. There are a couple of caveats we should add to our story. First, it would be dishonest if we did not point out that there is, of course, uncertainty about the class coordinates in Figure 3.2. The precise coordinates plotted are simply the 'best' estimates under the model we have assumed; others are also plausible. Second, it is possible to argue about the name that should be attached to each dimension. We believe on face validity grounds that the items we have chosen really do index monitoring difficulty and asset specificity; however, others may disagree. It seems implausible, given the item content, that a very different label could be given to the monitoring difficulty dimension. Given the difficulty of finding good indicators for asset specificity there is more room for interpretation here. Looking at the overall configuration of the vertical dimension of Figure 3.2, the most plausible alternative interpretation is in terms of skill level (for an argument that skill requirements is indeed the critical dimension underlying the Goldthorpe class schema; see Tåhlin 2007). Telling against this however is the inversion in the order of the routine and semi-routine groups and the second and first lower professional groups. The LP1 occupations typically require the acquisition of a higher level of formal qualifications than do the LP2 occupations, which typically involve a lot of learning by doing and organization-specific knowledge.

9. Curiously, Russell neglects to mention other management rubrics that emerged during the same period and also recommended the adoption of single status policies. Both the 'new industrial relations' and 'HRM' approaches to employee relations emphasized the need for employers to remove differences in the treatment of salaried and waged workers (Millward, 1994; Storey 1992; Wood 1996).

10. Townsend's contribution was completely ignored in Russell's history of the rise and fall of inequality at work. This is unfortunate because much of the empirical evidence that she uses to defend her account is of doubtful or, at best, of an unknown value. Like many of the later contributions on the status divide (e.g. Price, 1989; Price and Price 1994), she tends to draw on case studies (e.g. Toshiba) and surveys (IRRR 1989, 1993) that report only the successful introduction of harmonization policies. Consequently, there is a real danger that the evidence is representative only of a self-selecting group of 'progressive' or 'best practice' companies and not British industry in general.

11. Since we follow Townsend in examining the distribution of employment conditions across the general working population, we are unable to comment on the distribution of 'status privileges' within particular workplaces. Even so, if there has been a general movement towards harmonized conditions then we might expect to see this in our data.

12. In the tables and figures that follow we have reduced the twelve NS-SEC categories we have so far worked with to ten by combining the two higher professional groups and the two lower professional groups.

13. Mean hourly earnings, which are provided for comparison, are heavily influenced by extreme values in the tails of the distribution and there are reasons to believe that errors of measurement tend to accumulate in the tails of wage distributions (see Skinner et al. 2002).

14. The ratio of the standard deviation of the unconditional effects in the later period to that in the earlier is also approximately 3 (0.451/0.151).

15. It seems implausible to believe that we would find anything but a very similar result if we are able to analyse the monetary value of the benefits rather than simply their presence or absence.

16. A similar argument can be made in relation to the number of days of paid holidays (Figure 3.3c) as well as a range of other benefits, including access to flexible working hours and the ability to take a short break without requiring official permission (not shown).

4

Representation, participation, and individualism

4.1. Introduction

Like most social relationships, long-term employment relationships depend, among other things, on the willingness of both employer and employee to listen, consider, and respond to the concerns of the other party. This was a relatively straightforward task in the small firms of early capitalism, where regular contact between workers and owners created a relationship that often went beyond mutual economic benefit. However, the task became much more complicated with the arrival of modern industrial capitalism where the growth of large organizations, the separation of ownership from control, and the emergence of elaborate managerial hierarchies generated a much more impersonal set of relations between employers and employees. This in turn led many employees to join trade unions, notably during the interwar years (Fox 1985), as close personal ties were replaced by a much more instrumental set of exchanges centred on the 'cash nexus'. In subsequent decades, trade unions became the primary means by which employees articulated their concerns and negotiated over wages and benefits.

However, the dramatic decline in trade unionism since 1979 has generated a major debate about what, if anything, has replaced trade unions as the voice of those who sell their labour to make a living (Towers 1997; Millward et al. 2000: 83–137; Howell 2005: 164–73). The emergence of new management rubrics during the 1980s and 1990s provided one alternative in the form of employee involvement. Indeed, managerially-oriented proponents of these practices argued that they were much more appropriate for the highly educated and achievement-oriented employees of the late twentieth century (Lawler 1986; Wickens

1987). Unsurprisingly, some commentators have sought to summarize these developments as a shift from *indirect* or *representative voice* to *direct voice* or, more grandly, as a general shift from *collectivism* to *individualism* (e.g. Storey and Bacon 1993; Brown et al. 1998; Gospel and Wood 2003).

In this chapter, we examine the evidence on employee representation, participation, and individualism to address aspects of the transformation literature introduced in Chapter 2. More specifically, we assess whether recent developments in representation and participation correspond with the neo-Taylorist authoritarianism associated with the emergence of a more marketized employment relationship (Sayer 1997). We also consider the alternative possibility that interprets the increased use of employee involvement practices as part of a long-term tendency towards the internalization of the employment relationship (Streeck 1987). In addition, we also examine the changing nature of employee voice in the context of long-term changes in labour market composition, partly because the subject is of interest in itself, but also because it bears directly on claims of a radical change in the employment relationship. Here we focus on three broadly related questions. The first asks whether the expansion of white-collar employment and the rise of female employment are associated with a decline in union membership. More specifically, we investigate whether women and white-collar workers have a lower propensity to join trade unions than men and those in working class jobs. Second, we examine whether the absence of trade unions means that employees have lost the ability to influence decision-making (e.g. Millward et al. 2000: 83–117). Much of the literature assumes, either implicitly or explicitly, that trade union representation constitutes a highly effective form of employee participation and, consequently, that the decline in union membership since the peak years of the late 1970s represents a decline in employee influence. Instead of assuming that employees in non-union settings have little or no *voice* we propose to compare employee responses from unionized and non-unionized to see if there is indeed a difference in perceptions of influence.

The final area that we investigate relates to the supposed new world of individualism in employment relations. In contrast to much of the existing research, which focuses on the ways in which employers advance individualized employment relations policies, there is an extraordinary lack of research on individualism among employees (see Deery and Walsh 1999 for a rare example). We address this gap in the literature through a simple, but highly revealing, study of individual bargaining behaviour. Here we draw on research at the intersection of economics and psychology to explore the possibility that some sections of the labour force are less inclined, or even unable, to benefit from HRM policies that promote greater individualism with respect to pay and conditions.

4.2. Market, Contract, and Participation

The historical evolution and future direction of the employment relationship cannot be adequately understood without reference to the organization of work, and the representation and participation of employees. As Marx pointed out some time ago, one of the ways in which the employment contract differs from other kinds of commercial contracts is that the employer hires only *labour power* (or the employees' capacity to work) rather than actual *labour* (or the product of their work). The problem is resolved mostly, if not entirely, by giving the employer the right to organize work and to direct, evaluate, and discipline employees. As it happens, the employment contract is usually defined as a contract where the employee agrees, within limits, and in return for a certain level of remuneration, to place themselves under the authority of an employer (see, for example, the discussion in Hodgson 1999: 164–9). Consequently, relations of authority and the organization of work are tremendously important for understanding how the employees' capacity to work is turned into work. But how do these areas relate to contemporary debates about transformation in the employment relationship?

Writing against the turbulent background of the 1980s the German sociologist Wolfgang Streeck provided an incisive, ground-clearing formulation of this problem when he set out the two basic strategies that employers may take during a period of economic crisis (Streeck 1987). Under the first strategy, which he termed a *return to contract* (the market solution), employers seek to treat labours as a disposable commodity that can be hired and fired as demand dictated. One of the hallmarks of this strategy is 'numerical flexibility'—the use of temporary and other kinds of non-standard employment to overcome the labour market rigidities associated with the spread of employment protection legislation and social security payments.

What is significant for our purposes is Streeck's argument that when the contractual elements of the employment relationship are predominant then workers are not expected to do more than that which is contractually stipulated (Streeck 1987: 287). Typically, the work is organized in such a way that employers are not dependent on the extra-contractual

	Return to Contract	*Extension of Status*
Labour market orientation	External	Internal
Employment status of workers	'Temporary'	'Permanent'
Numerical flexibility	'Hire and fire' Substandard contracts	Flexible working time, overtime, short-time working
Functional flexibility	'Hire and fire' Managerial discretion	Broad job descriptions Self-regulated job rotation
Work organization	Taylorist	Team working, 'Quality Circles'
Qualifications sought	Narrow, specific Functional	Broad, unspecific professionalized' Extra-functional
Wage determination	Industrial engineering Payment by activity	Payment by ability Bonus pay, Share ownership
Management style	Unilateral use of managerial prerogative	Consultation, Participation, Co-determination

Figure 4.1. Two ways of achieving organizational flexibility

Source: Streeck 1987: 294.

(or 'extra-functional') contributions of employees. Instead, managers rely heavily on a combination of monetary incentives and detailed job descriptions to ensure appropriate levels of productivity (Figure 4.1). Also, as workers are not expected to exceed that which is formally specified under such 'Taylorist' arrangements, it follows that they cannot expect to participate in, or be consulted about, managerial decisions. Indeed, one of the defining characteristics of the 'return to contract' is the insistence upon, and acceptance of, the restoration of managerial authority over matters that may previously have been open to discussion. In such situations, 'management's right to manage' is justified on the grounds that the economic needs of the organization are of paramount importance. The alternative approach, which Streeck calls the *extension of status*, is consistent with the organization-oriented policies that Dore found among large Japanese firms (Dore 1973) (see Chapter 2). Like other non-Marxist scholars, Streeck accepts that the long-term evolution of the employment relationship includes 'the decontractualization of relations between workers and employers' (Streeck 1987: 293), a process that has seen gradual imposition of a range of status rights onto what was previously almost entirely a contractual matter. Here Streeck provides the example of legislation that seeks to provide employment protection (e.g. against unfair dismissal). If the status of employees has become more formalized under such arrangements, their obligations to their employer are notable for being relatively open-ended and marked by a sense of obligation.

Accordingly, when employers seek to introduce policies that represent an extension of status, these typically require 'an extra-functional element of voluntary cooperation which is difficult to mobilize through hierarchical authority' (Streeck 1987: 294). Rather than seeking to extend the hierarchical element of the organization, employers instigate a series of decentralized responses. Work, for instance, may be organized around teams, 'quality circles' may be introduced, and the organization may develop an extensive programme of training and employee development. Streeck argues that this strategy will entail a greater degree of functional flexibility, with general training, job rotation, and a willingness to work overtime, or even outside normal hours if required. At the same time, the workers' sense of obligation to the firm and, indeed, their status as members of the organizational community will be recognized through policies that seek to enhance their 'voice'. Generally, the aim is to improve cooperation and reduce hierarchical forms of interaction in the context of a relationship that both parties treat as being long term.

Admittedly, Streeck was writing during a period when many of the major western economies were going through a recession and neoliberal policies were in the ascendancy in Britain and the USA. In this context, a possible 'return to contract' seemed to be in keeping with a *zeitgeist* that was shaped by the rise of the 'New Right', the collapse of the USSR, and the apparent 'triumph of capitalism' as an economic system. By the late 1990s, however, macroeconomic conditions had improved, employment had expanded, and employers and government departments seemed to have become much more interested in employee involvement (see, for example, Marchington et al. 1992). Although some case studies drew pessimistic conclusions about the prospects for employee involvement (Danford 1998; Hales 2000), large-scale survey evidence from Gallie and his colleagues identified a number of changes that were likely to have positive long-term implications for non-union forms of employee participation. The most significant of these was a sustained trend towards upskilling, which, along with the adoption of new technologies, meant that employers had more reason to delegate decisions to employees in complex environments (Gallie et al. 1998).

4.3. Trade Unions and the Changing Composition of the Labour Force

In his analysis of the strategic choices facing employers, Streeck noted that few were more important than the decision to include or exclude trade unions from workplace governance. What Streeck did not anticipate was that trade union organization and influence would continue to fade, even during a lengthy period of economic prosperity, and that this was only partly because of strategic choices taken by employers and trade unions. Within the British context, the programme of anti-union legislation introduced by Margaret Thatcher's Conservative governments is frequently presented as a major reason for the decline in trade unionism during the final decades of the twentieth century. Although this legislation created a more hostile environment for trade unions, industrial relations scholars generally reject the idea that the collapse in membership can be attributed to a single causal factor. Instead, they emphasize a combination of factors that include the changing composition of the workforce, the shift from manufacturing to service industries, the birth of new (non-union) organizations, in addition to legislation and the policies of employers and unions themselves (see, for instance, Gospel and Wood 2003; Waddington 2003; Fernie and Metcalf 2005).

Even so, much of the British debate about trade union decline has concentrated on organizational characteristics, such as the sector, size, and age of establishments, probably because the arrival of the WIRS/WERS data has coincided with the emergence of a generation of labour economists skilled in quantitative techniques (e.g. Disney et al. 1994; Machin 2000; Millward et al. 2000). By contrast, the influence of long-term social change, as expressed through the changing occupational structure or the growth of female employment, is of interest only to a few sociologists (e.g. Gallie et al. 1996a). This is unfortunate because the growth of white-collar employment, the increased labour market participation of women, and the spread of non-standard employment arrangements have all been associated with lower levels of unionization across Europe (Ebbinghaus and Visser 1999).

4.3.1. *Have Trade Unions Become a Middle-Class Phenomenon?*

Within the sociological literature, the long-term expansion of white-collar employment combined with the dramatic decline in manual employment, notably since the 1980s, is often cited as one of the major reasons for the decline of the labour movement. Classic studies from the 1950s by C. Wright Mills and David Lockwood suggested that white-collar workers were reluctant to join trade unions because their work is quite individualized in nature; they enjoy relatively high levels of job security; and they identify closely with the interests of their employer (Mills 1951; Lockwood 1958). Within a couple of decades, however, industrial relations researchers were struggling to explain the remarkable growth in white-collar trade unionism during the 1960s and 1970s, a development that clearly challenged the received wisdom on the lack of interest in trade unionism among white-collar workers (Bain 1970; Lockwood 1989: 253–9). The economic restructuring of the 1980s accelerated the increasingly white-collar nature of British trade unionism, as large numbers of jobs were lost in manufacturing—a traditional union stronghold—while union density remained fairly stable in the mostly white-collar public sector (Morgan et al. 2000; Waddington 2003).

Unfortunately, assessments of the changing composition of union membership by social class have been undermined by the use of rudimentary occupational categories that focus mostly on differences between manual and non-manual workers. The danger with such measures is that they conceal important differences within the ever expanding non-manual category, while the very distinction between manual and non-manual is itself of little relevance to an increasingly post-industrial labour force. Gallie has sought to overcome these limitations by using the Goldthorpe class schema to examine changes in union membership across the 1980s (Gallie 1996; Gallie et al. 1998: 100–6). Comparing evidence from 1986 with 1992, he and his colleagues found that union membership had become more prevalent among professional and managerial employees (47%) than either skilled manual (42%) or semi- and non-skilled manual employees. They contend that this was mostly because of a small decline in membership (1%) among the professional and managerial ranks compared to greater decline among non-skilled manual workers (5%) and, in particular, among skilled manual workers (11%) (Gallie et al. 1998: 102–3).

Although it contains some limitations, we recognize that Gallie and colleagues broke new ground by providing the first national snapshot of changes in union membership by social class over time. Taken at face value, their results raise the intriguing possibility that the expanding middle classes may have become the last bastion of trade unionism (see also Gallie et al. 1996b: 24). This would be rather ironic in historical terms as trade unions were once the preserve of manual workers employed in relatively insecure jobs on low wages rather than white-collar employees in secure career-type jobs. In any case, we propose to revisit this question later in the chapter by using a more finely grained set of social class distinctions that will enable us to compare membership propensities across the class spectrum.

105

4.3.2. *Have Women Become More Trade Union Oriented?*

Historically, the accepted view in the industrial relations literature was that women were substantially less likely than men to become union members (Bain and Elsheikh 1979; Bain and Price 1983; Bain and Elias 1985). Certainly, unionization was considerably lower among women for much of the post-war period and a ten percentage point difference was evident as recently as 1991 (Brook 2002). Since then, however, there has been a sharp fall in membership among men while among women that has risen to the point where it is broadly similar to men (Grainger 2006). This development is all the more remarkable because women are heavily concentrated among part-time workers (Hakim 2004: 59–73), a category that trade unions have traditionally found difficult to recruit. Indeed, the reluctance of part-timers to join trade unions is a long-established and consistent finding within the literature on trade union membership (Sinclair 1995; Gallie et al. 1998; Walters 2002: 104–5).

Even so, there is some evidence to show that where women work full-time their membership levels are broadly similar to men (Gallie 1996: 158; Gallie et al. 1998: 103). This suggests that the problem lies in the nature of employment rather than with women per se. Further support for this idea comes in the WiB 2000 survey where we find that approximately one in three full-time workers is a union member, with little difference between men (35%) and women (34%). However, it would be rather naive in statistical terms to conclude that women have finally become as union friendly as men while considering only one other fact (nature of employment).

4.4. Marketization, Employee Involvement, and Individualism

Returning to the general theme of transformation in the employment relationship, we might expect employers to have greater freedom to dictate patterns of communication, consultation, and work organization as trade union influence declines. Freed from the shackles of trade unions, it seems plausible that employers may have instigated a strategy in which the marketization of the employment relationship is accompanied by a 'return to contract' in the areas of work organization and managerial style. If so, we would certainly not expect to see employee involvement policies becoming more prevalent and we might even see evidence of a decline if the thesis is to be taken seriously.

4.4.1. *Who Has More Say?*

Taking this theme further, we propose to examine employee perceptions of their influence over decisions relating to their jobs because it is here that employers' policies of encouraging employee involvement are supposedly targeted. Following the spirit of the marketization thesis, we might expect that any such policies are unlikely to be perceived as having a tangible influence over the way employees go about their work. In other words, their influence is purely at the symbolic level. In this context, we might expect that the presence of a trade union will be associated with the perception of having an input into the decision-making process. The alternative view, following the logic of internalization, would be not only increased direct participation but also that involvement policies would be associated in employees' minds with having a real impact on decision-making.

In setting out these propositions, we acknowledge that policies of direct voice are unlikely to provide employees with an influence over wages and conditions in the same way that trade unions do under direct, or representative, forms of voice. At this point, we think it is useful to distinguish between decisions affecting work organization, such as task assignment, and those affecting industrial relations, such as pay. Our analysis focuses explicitly on decisions affecting work organization, as this is an area where we might reasonably expect employees to have an influence regardless of whether their workplace contains a trade union.

4.4.2. *Individualism for All?*

To date, much of the employment relations literature on the supposed shift from collectivism to individualism has concentrated on employer policies (e.g. Storey and Bacon 1993; Kessler and Purcell 1995; Roche 2001). Within this literature individualism is interpreted as individualized HRM practices, such as open door policies, performance appraisals, and merit-based payment systems. Policies of this kind are supposedly based on the philosophy that employees are unique individuals whose skills, knowledge, and contributions must be formally identified, recognized, and rewarded. This contrasts with the traditional pattern of industrial relations where employees were treated as indistinguishable members of a collectively organized and managed labour force (see, for instance, Guest 1989; Storey and Bacon 1993). Generally, the spread of individualized HR policies is interpreted as evidence of a 'secular drift' towards individualism and the rupturing of collectivist forms of industrial relations (Storey and Bacon 1993; Bacon and Storey 1995).

We propose to contribute to this debate from a different, though no less important, direction by asking a rather simple question: what kinds of employees pursue individual bargaining? This approach is, arguably, more consistent with the traditional conception of individualism as a 'moderate selfishness' that disposed individuals to be concerned only with themselves and their family (de Tocqueville 1835/1966). A similar conception can be found in Alan Fox's magisterial history of the British system of industrial relations, where he introduced the notion of *atomistic individualism* to capture a form of Tory philosophy in the late nineteenth and twentieth centuries. Fox defined atomistic individualism as a process by which individuals not only pursue their self interest, having first defined those interests for themselves, but also act independently of others. This contrasts with *instrumental collectivism* where individuals, while still pursuing their self-interest, find it expedient to act in concert with others (Fox 1985: 191–2).

As sociologists, we have an expectation that such atomistic individualism, to the extent that it exists, will be influenced by a range of personal, social, and organizational factors. To illustrate this point, our analysis will focus on a question that relates to what is termed the *gender gap* in pay. Explanations of women's inability to achieve comparable earnings to men point to a range of structural and personal characteristics. Neoclassical economists, for example, emphasize differences in human capital between men and women, while feminist scholars emphasize the constraints imposed by an unequal division of labour in the household and a lack of affordable childcare (Padavic and Reskin 2002: 39–55). Another possible factor, which comes from recent research at the interface of economics and psychology, suggests that women may be more reluctant than men to put themselves forward for pay rises.

In a book entitled *Women Don't Ask*, two American scholars, Linda Babcock and Sara Laschever, cite a wide range of evidence from social experiments, surveys, and in-depth interviews, to show that women are less likely to speak up for themselves in a range of situations requiring direct negotiation. Needless to say, the result is that women incur substantial economic costs throughout their working lives. One of Babcock's own surveys, for instance, reveals that the starting salaries for college graduates are noticeably higher for men precisely because they are eight times more likely to ask for more money (Babcock and Laschever 2003: 2). Another found that women's starting salaries for their first jobs after completing an MBA were 6 per cent lower on average than men's even after adjusting for the industry they entered, the city where they worked, the functional area of employment, and their pre-MBA salaries. What was perhaps even more remarkable was that the yearly bonuses, which they negotiated on a personal basis, were 19 per cent smaller than those for men (Babcock and Laschever 2003: 59–60).

So why are women afraid to negotiate? Babcock and Laschever provide a range of answers to this question, with the most prominent being a lower sense of entitlement combined with a greater uncertainty about the value of their work. Particular emphasis is placed on the role of social expectations. Many women are so grateful to be offered a job that they accept whatever salary is offered. Those that do negotiate tend to be more pessimistic about the amount of money that is available. Consequently, Babcock and Laschever (2003: 42) conclude that women enter the work-force expecting to be paid less than men and so they are not disappointed when those expectations are met.

Nonetheless, we think it would be simplistic to conclude that gender alone would explain variations in the ability to ask for a raise. Like many other empirical regularities, we suspect that a range of variables, along with the inevitable random variation, will be correlated with a willingness to speak up for oneself. Aside from personal characteristics, which are usually fairly predictable, there may be other influences relating to the nature of the occupation, the organization, and the general working environment. For instance, members of the service class, such as higher managers and professionals, may be disposed to seeking pay rises because it is considered normal practice for people who move from one highly paid job to another. Also, following from the literature on collectivism and individualism, we might expect those who are not in trade unions to be more likely to pursue individual negotiation. The corollary is that trade union members do not ask for pay rises because they pay union officials to do this for them. In addition, they may also feel that negotiating on an individual basis might undermine the collective solidarity that is the essence of trade unionism.

4.5. The Changing Nature of Employee Representation

We begin our analysis with a descriptive account of changes in member-ship by social class since the mid-1980s before undertaking a more sophis-ticated analysis that allows us to assess the effects of selected structural

Table 4.1. Trade union membership by social class, 1984–2000

	1984	1992	2000
Higher manager & professional	45.9	36.6	25.4
Lower manager & professional	50.0	46.0	43.1
Intermediate workers	41.5	40.3	29.7
Lower supervisor & technical	57.5	46.0	31.4
Semi-routine	50.6	36.8	27.1
Routine	51.6	45.1	28.8

Note: Employees working more than ten hours per week only.
Sources: SCMB 1984; EiB 1992; and WiB 2000.

and personal characteristics on union membership (see also Gallie et al. 1998: 100–6). In addition to social class, we examine the influence of gender, employment status, and ownership (public or private), partly because they consistently appear as significant determinants in previous research and partly because they have been the subject of substantial compositional changes over the past decade and a half.[1] We recognize that there are limits to the kind of causal inferences that can be made from the statistical modelling of cross-sectional data, particularly in estimating changes over time, but we believe that it can help separate out the effects of different structural and personal characteristics on the propensity to unionize.[2]

Over the period 1984–2000, we find that trade union membership remains much more prevalent among professional and managerial employees, though we must emphasize that this is among the *lower* managerial and professional class (Table 4.1). More specifically, union membership for lower managers and professionals remains close to half of those employees over this period (43%) while it has fallen to somewhere between one third and one quarter for higher managers and professionals (25%), intermediate workers (30%), lower supervisors and technicians (31%), semi-routine (27%) and routine (29%) workers. To put it another way, union membership has contracted least among lower managers and professionals (seven percentage points between 1984 and 2000). The other slight exception is intermediate workers where the proportion fell by one in ten (twelve percentage points).

Why does union membership appear to have held up so much better among lower managerial and professional occupations? In an earlier analysis of this issue, Gallie and colleagues claimed that professional and managerial employees as a whole were more likely to work in environments that were conducive to unionization, notably in large

Table 4.2. Effects of personal and workplace characteristics on union membership

Independent variable	β	Significance
Gender		
[Ref. cat. Male]		
Female	−0.480	**
Employment contract		
[Standard (full-time & permanent)]		
Full-time temporary	−0.757	**
Part-time permanent	−0.829	**
Part-time temporary	−1.100	*
Social class		
[Higher manager & professional]		
Lower manager & professional	1.530	**
Intermediate	0.872	**
Lower supervisor & technical	1.576	**
Semi-routine	1.445	**
Routine	1.510	**

Note: Logistic regression; multiplicative effects on odds; n =1,939; * significant at 0.05; ** significant at 0.01; ns = not significant. Control variables were age, establishment size, gender-based workplace segregation, and public/private sector.

Source: WiB.

organizations, and in the public sector (Gallie et al. 1998: 100–6). In Table 4.2, we examine the relationship between trade union membership, gender, and social class while controlling for some of these other influences (i.e. establishment size, public/private sector). Starting with gender, our analysis indicates that women are still less likely to become union members, even after controlling for employment in part-time and temporary jobs. Specifically, the odds for women are 0.619 times lower than those for men, which is a non-trivial difference. This confirms our earlier suspicion that the comparable rates of unionization among women and men in full-time employment might not hold once other factors are taken into consideration. Women, it seems, are still less likely to join trade unions.

At the same time, part-time and temporary workers (especially part-time temporary workers) are also noticeably less likely to be union members. Again, this finding is consistent with earlier research (Gallie et al. 1998: 104) and confirms the widely held view that non-standard workers present a substantial organizing problem for the union movement.

Turning to social class we find that relative to higher managers and professionals, all the other classes have higher propensities to union membership, once other factors are controlled, and that they are broadly similar to one another except for the intermediate class whose propensity lies in between. If lower managerial and professional employees are no more likely to belong to trade unions than routine working class employees, this still represents a substantial change from the situation in the 1950s when the classic literature found that white-collar workers were, by comparison, much less inclined to take up union membership than their blue-collar counterparts.

So how do we explain the finding that union membership has held up much better among lower professionals and managers? Here our analysis concurs with the earlier work of Gallie and colleagues which shows that professional and managerial employees are more likely to be union members because they work in large workplaces and or in the public sector (Gallie et al. 1998: 103). Yet it is also evident that higher managers and professionals, who share similar work environments, are the least likely to belong to trade unions, other things being equal. Perhaps they view union membership as being incompatible with their status and or with the exercise of managerial authority. Or perhaps they believe that they can do much better by negotiating for themselves. If so, then they must also constitute that section of the labour force for whom claims about substantive individualization and individualistic orientations are most appropriate.

4.6. Communication, Participation, and Internalization

Turning from indirect to direct forms of voice, we now consider the survey evidence on employee communication and consultation policies in the context of claims of transformation in the employment relationship. We know already from organizational case studies and from employer surveys that there was some interest in such policies during the 1990s (Cully et al. 1999; Geary 2003). But has this been maintained into the current century?

When we compare the results from WiB 2000 with those of the earlier EiB 1992, we find a small increase of around four to five percentage points in the availability of information-oriented meetings (from 71 to 75%) and also in meetings that allowed for discussion (from 64 to 69%) (see Table 4.3). If changes in the order of four to five percentage points seem rather small, it should be noted that they come over a relatively short period and that, furthermore, both are in the same direction. Perhaps the most significant point is that the majority of the workforce was covered by such policies by the year 2000: three quarters of all employees were able

Table 4.3. Information and consultation by union presence, 1992–2000

	Reporting (%)					
	1992			2000		
	All	Unionized	Non-union	All	Unionized	Non-union
Briefing meetings	70.5	80.3	57.5	74.6	85.1	64.9
Discussion meetings	63.5	70.1	54.5	68.8	76.4	62.9

Sources: EiB 1992 and WiB 2000.

to attend information briefings and more than two thirds participated in discussion meetings. The WERS 2004 provides a helpful elaboration on the prevalence of discussion type meetings as it asked managers how much time was allowed during briefing meetings for employee questions or comments. The results reveal that some time was allowed in nearly every workplace and roughly two thirds (64%) claimed to devote at least one quarter of the time available to discussion (Kersley et al. 2005: 17).

Furthermore, the employee surveys show unionized workplaces having a greater proportion of these practices than non-unionized settings throughout the period. In our 2000 survey, for example, we find that just over three quarters (76%) of respondents from unionized establishments report discussion meetings compared with under two thirds (63%) of those from unorganized settings. Nevertheless, it would be wrong to infer that the dominant emerging category across the British economy is of trade union representation and direct employee voice policies coexisting together. The simple reason is that the proportion of workplaces containing trade unions has contracted sharply as a proportion of all British workplaces. In 1980, two of three establishments recognized trade unions; by 1998, this had fallen to two of five (Millward et al. 2000: 96). The corollary is, of course, that the proportion of non-union establishments has grown and with that, workplaces where only direct voice policies exist. In fact, the most recent WERS evidence reveals that while the use of team briefings or workforce meetings has increased since 1998, this has occurred mostly in the private sector where union membership is at its lowest (Kersley et al. 2005: 17).

Turning to work organization, we used our employer survey (CEPS 2002) to ask if the organization contained 'groups or teams which organize their own work without a supervisor' and if 'the amount of formally designated team working' had changed over the previous three years. Our analysis found that four in ten establishments contained self-managing teams, nearly three in ten had increased their use of formally designated teams, and that hardly any said that they were reducing this form of work organization. Although the more well-known WERS series, which refers to 'some core employees in formally designated teams', finds little change between 1998 and 2004, their definition of teams suggests that almost three in four (72%) establishments use this form of work organization (Kersley et al. 2005: 10).[3]

Another work-unit-based form of participation, namely quality circles, continues to have a healthy presence, with the employee surveys reporting an increase of almost ten points between 1992 and 2000 (21 to 30%). (We should acknowledge that the wording of the 2000 survey is open to a more generous interpretation of what constitutes a quality circle.) Our companion employer survey from 2002 indicates that nearly four in ten workplaces (39%) have quality circles, with a further one in five (22%) planning to introduce or extend the practice during the next twelve months. Stephen Hill noted that quality circles were created as one component of a total system of quality management in Japanese companies, and that US and British organizations had adopted these in the 1980s without understanding the whole (Hill 1991; Hill and Wilkinson 1995). So this continuing interest in quality circles may be fuelled by the adoption of a more encompassing set of quality management practices (which is why we have moved away from a narrow focus on quality circles per se).

In sum, the evidence we have reviewed so far does not support the idea that British employers are adopting the kind of neo-Taylorism associated with the market-oriented model of employment. Instead of a 'return to contract', we find a gradual trend towards increased employee consultation and involvement with greater use of formal communication, consultation, and team-working practices. Admittedly, our surveys do not include the comprehensive range of work organization and human resource policies specified by various forms of high performance, or high commitment, management literatures (Wood and de Menezes 1998; Appelbaum et al. 2000). For instance, one possible omission relates to the selection and training of team members. That said, Streeck's account of the organization-centred *extension of status* strategy emphasizes policies that promote functional flexibility through general training and job rotation. As it happens, we were able to include a small number of items in both the 2000 employee survey and the 2002 employer survey to assess the prevalence of functional flexibility.

Given that British trade unionism was associated with restrictive work practices for much of the twentieth century, we thought it would be

Table 4.4. Cross-training and flexibility by unionization

| | Employees (%) | | |
	All	Union	Non-union
Trained to perform different tasks if necessary	67.9	73.0	62.3
Sometimes perform different tasks to help cope with pressure	65.7	68.5	62.7
Sometimes perform different tasks if someone sick	55.8	57.8	53.6

Source: WiB 2000.

informative to cross-tabulate our indicators of functional flexibility by the presence of a trade union in the respondent's workplace (Table 4.4). The results are striking: two thirds of employees in the 2000 survey are 'trained to perform different tasks if necessary' (68%) and 'sometimes perform different tasks to help cope with pressure' (66%) while half of all respondents 'sometimes perform different tasks if someone is sick' (56%).

Unionized work settings are also more disposed to providing cross-training and to have employees who will take on other tasks when colleagues are sick or under pressure. The difference reaches close to eight percentage points in the case of cross-training (73% vs. 62%). A three-way cross-tabulation by workplace size (not shown) fails to explain away the variation as the percentage of respondents reporting cross-training is greater in unionized workplaces regardless of whether they are large (500+ employees) or very small (1–10). Further analysis would be required before we can be certain that the higher scores in unionized settings are not the product of some other variables. Doing so, however, only confirms that it is no longer easy to associate trade unions with restrictive work practices.

Analysis of the companion employer survey from 2002 has revealed that the adoption of greater functional flexibility is one of the most significant areas of change in contemporary work organization (White et al. 2004: 41–3). Nearly half of all workplaces say that employees are taking on an increasing variety of tasks while three in ten establishments have been making greater use of job rotation schemes. This analysis also finds that different forms of flexibility, particularly cross-training and functional, or task flexibility, tend to appear together (33%). Although we are unable to trace change over time, we can, however, turn to the WERS series for help on this point. The 2004 WERS finds that two thirds (66%) of workplaces had trained at least some employees to be functionally flexible and that this proportion had barely changed since 1998 (69%) (Kersley et al. 2005: 11). Or, to put it another way, a relatively high level of functional flexibility would appear to have been in place for some time.

Those familiar with research on HRM practices will not be surprised to learn that these practices are associated with workplace size and that respondents from larger workplaces are more likely to be covered by such policies (results not shown). This is probably because large organizations are more likely to have well-resourced HRM functions and people management practices (Gallie et al. 1998: 95–100; Millward et al. 2000: 53–6; 213–4).

Overall, the results are easily summarized: they consistently point away from the rigid Taylorist forms of work organization associated with the marketization thesis. Instead, there is a general movement towards greater employee involvement and this holds across both unionized and non-union workplaces.

4.6.1. *Who Gets to Have a Say?*

The diffusion of various forms of employee involvement leads us to ask a rather obvious, if much neglected, question: What do employees perceive their level of influence to be? Fortunately, we included some questions in the WiB 2000 survey (see Box 4.1) that enable us to make comparisons not only with the 1992 survey but also with BSA surveys dating back to the mid-1980s (Hedges 1994).[4]

Box 4.1. MEASURES OF PARTICIPATION IN DECISION-MAKING

Influence on Change

Q: Suppose there was going to be some decision made at your place of work that changed the way you do your job. Do you think that you personally would have any say in the decision about the change or not?
A: 1. Yes; 2. No.

How Much Influence?

Q: How much say or chance to influence the decision do you think you would have?
A: 1. A great deal; 2. Quite a lot; 3. Just a little.

Satisfaction With Influence

Q: Do you think that you should have more say in the decisions that affect your work, or are you satisfied with the way things are?
A: 1. Should have more say; 2. Satisfied with the way things are.
Sources: BSA 1985, 1989; EiB 1992; and WiB 2000.

Table 4.5. Employees' say in decisions affecting their work, 1985–2000

	Employees' saying (%)			
	1985	1989	1992	2000
Have a say	62	50	56	65
Should have more say	36	44	48	43
Satisfied with the way things are	63	54	52	57

Note: See Box 4.1 for details of measures.

Sources: BSA 1985, 1989 adapted from Hedges (1994: 48); EiB 1992; and WiB 2000.

The results in Table 4.5 are surprising in that they do not show the kind of straight-line trend that might be expected to follow an authoritarian 'return to contract' or the diffusion of waves of employee involvement across the 1980s and 1990s. Instead, we find that just under two thirds of employees (62%) believed that they would have a say in such changes in 1985; the proportion then fell to half in 1987 and in 1992 (as reported in Gallie et al. 1998: 90) before rising again to just under two thirds (65%) by 2000.[5] Meanwhile, those who wanted a greater say increased between 1985 (36%) and 1992 (44%) before falling back in 2000 (43%). Similarly, satisfaction with the level of participation followed the same pattern falling between 1985 and 1992 before rising again in 2000 (see also Kaur 2004). So, whatever the reason for the decline in the early 1990s, perceptions of influence and satisfaction with the degree of perceived influence are certainly not falling in a manner that would be suggestive of increasingly authoritarian workplaces.

At the same time, we accept that a substantial share of the working population have an unmet need for participation (see also Gospel and Willman 2005: 135–40). What kinds of employees hold these views? Do they work in low-level routine occupations where they have to do as they are told? Or, alternatively, do their workplaces lack modern employee involvement policies? To answer these questions, we included these and other variables in analyses that examine the influence of employment characteristics on whether employees have 'any say' as well as if they think they should have 'more say' (Table 4.6). The results are worth examining in detail.

First, our analysis confirms that those in working class occupations, specifically semi-routine and routine employees believe that they have little, or no, influence on changes affecting their jobs when compared to higher professional and managerial employees. The finding that 'intermediate' employees also feel that they have little say is quite striking

Table 4.6. Effects of employment characteristics on whether employee 'has any say' about changes in his/her job (Model 1); and on whether employees 'should have more say' in decisions that affect their work (Model 2)

Independent variable	Model 1		Model 2	
	'Has any say'		'Should have more say'	
	β	Significance	β	Significance
Meetings where you can express views				
[Yes]				
No	−0.770	**	0.437	**
Quality circles				
[Yes]				
No	−0.669	**	0.308	**
Suggestion scheme				
[Yes]				
No	−0.116	ns	−0.062	ns
Union presence				
[Yes]				
No	0.587	**	−0.559	**
Social class				
[Professional/managerial]				
Lower manager & professional	−0.182	ns	0.337	*
Intermediate	−0.602	**	0.058	ns
Lower supervisor & technical	−0.427	**	0.442	*
Semi-routine	−0.690	**	0.392	*
Routine	−0.638	**	0.290	ns

Note: Logistic regression; multiplicative effects on odds; Model 1: $n = 1,672$, Model 2: $n = 1,795$; * significant at 0.05; ** significant at 0.01; ns = not significant. Control variables were employment contract, establishment size, and public/private sector.

Source: WiB 2000.

because the traditional wisdom was that this category had considerable autonomy, with several requiring sub-degree level qualifications for entry (see, for example, Lockwood 1989). Yet they are not among those who would like to have more influence, in contrast to those in the semi-routine and lower supervisor and technical categories. The latter groups lack influence and desire more. Surprisingly, those in routine occupations are less likely to insist on having a say, even though they also feel excluded.

Once again, these results confirm that the nature of the employment relationship varies across social class groupings with those in working class and intermediate blue-collar occupations reporting little influence over what happens to their jobs. While the results for those in the semi-routine and routine working class might be expected, it is clear that there is also a substantial demand for greater involvement further along the social class spectrum. We believe that these findings have implications for the literature on employee involvement, and indeed for other research on managerial practices, because these generally focus on organizations rather than occupations. Providing briefing meetings or suggestion schemes does not alter the nature of the work that people do within the lower levels of organizations nor does it change the way in which they experience decision-making. We would, therefore, argue that occupations and occupational classes remain important, if unduly neglected, units of analysis in the study of HRM, work organization, and employment relations (see also McGovern 1998).

We also think it is significant that employees in non-union settings are less likely to report a participation/representation gap than their unionized counterparts. That is, they believe that they have the ability to influence decisions and do not want any more. How might we explain these results? There are at least two plausible explanations. The first is that trade unions may curtail the opportunities for employees to speak as individuals. Changes to work organization, for instance, may be passed through a process of formal, collective agreement that leaves little room for individual views. Such an argument would, however, be unable to account for the coexistence of non-union and unionized forms of voice (Table 4.3), as well as the relatively high levels of cross-training and flexibility reported in unionized settings (Table 4.4). The second argument suggests that trade unions emerge as a response to overly hierarchical forms of authority that cause widespread employee dissatisfaction. In other words, the problem lies with the workplace regime rather than trade unions per se. Explanations of this kind have used in an attempt to explain why job satisfaction is consistently lower among unionized workers than non-unionized workers (e.g. Gordon and Denisi 1995; Bender and Sloane 1998). But without additional evidence on managerial style and workplace practices, we are unable to reach a stronger conclusion.

Finally, compared to employees who can take part in meetings that allow for discussion, those in workplaces without such a policy are significantly less likely to have a say while also being more likely to insist that they should have more. Similarly, employees who do not participate in quality circles are more inclined to state that they have no ability to influence decisions and that they would prefer to have more. These findings are quite important in substantive terms because they show that policies of an organization-centred kind can have more than symbolic value for employees, at least in matters of work organization.

4.6.2. *Who Pursues Personal Negotiation?*

Earlier, we noted that despite extensive reference to the individualization of employment relations, there is a surprising lack of evidence on the willingness of employees to engage in individual negotiation over their terms and conditions (i.e. individualism). This is all the more remarkable because we might anticipate a rise in individual bargaining, given the contraction in collective bargaining since the 1980s. Unfortunately, the 1992 survey did not include any questions on this topic so we are not in a position to comment directly on change over time. Instead, we address this issue by examining the propensity to pursue individual negotiations with the explicit aim of testing for gender differences following the Babcock and Laschever thesis that we outlined earlier (Babcock and Laschever 2003).

In the WiB 2000 survey, we first asked the respondents if they had been able to negotiate personally with their employer over pay when they first joined. We then asked if they had ever subsequently asked for a pay rise or a change in working hours. In both cases, we also asked if their requests had been successful. Basic tabulations reveal some gender differences at the descriptive level. While the WiB 2000 survey indicates that nearly three in ten employees were able to negotiate personally over pay on entering the job (29%), the proportion rose to one in three (33%) in the case of men and fell to under one in four (23%) for women. Similarly, of those who ever subsequently asked for a pay rise (31%), more than one third (38%) were male and one quarter (24%) were female. The gender differences were, however, reversed when it came to asking for a change in working hours. Of the one in five (21%) who have ever asked for such a change, there were nearly three times as many women (31%) as men (12%). So, these descriptive statistics might tempt us to conclude that there are clear gender differences in whether, and what, employees are prepared to negotiate on a personal basis.

Yet it is also possible that these differences do not support the claim that women are more reticent: they may simply ask for different things because they face different constraints and opportunities. For instance, there may be few women employed in senior professional and managerial positions where individual negotiation may be a common practice. Indeed, when we compare employees from different social classes we do find variations in the propensity to pursue a personal pay rise. Specifically, two in five higher managers and professionals (41%) have asked for an increase compared with one in five (20%) from the semi-routine occupational class.

Table 4.7. Factors relating to individual pay negotiations

Independent variable	Model 1		Model 2	
	Negotiated pay on entry		Negotiated pay subsequently	
	β	Significance	β	Significance
Gender [Male]				
Female	−0.339	**	−0.168	ns
Union member [Yes]				
No	0.805	**	0.343	**
Social class [Professional/managerial]				
Lower manager & professional	−0.352	ns	−0.345	ns
Intermediate	−0.781	**	−0.932	**
Lower supervisor & technical	−1.054	**	−0.258	ns
Semi-routine	−1.442	**	−1.141	**
Routine	−1.169	**	−0.680	**

Notes: Logistic regression; multiplicative effects on odds; Model 1: $n = 1,942$, Model 2: $n = 1,941$; * significant at 0.05; ** significant at 0.01; ns = not significant. Control variables were education, employment contract, establishment size, and public/private sector.

Source: WiB 2000.

Can we be confident that a gender difference will still exist once we take these other factors into consideration? To answer this question, we will concentrate on pay as this is central to Babcock and Laschever's thesis, as well as to our analysis of individualism in employment relations (see Chapter 6 for further analysis of working hours). A simple tabulation of the data reveals that more than two thirds (69%) of those who ever asked for an increase in pay were successful. As further analysis revealed no statistically significant differences between men and women, or between social classes, as to who receives an increase (after asking for one), the key question is whether employees are prepared to ask at all.[6]

In Table 4.7, we present logistic regression analyses of the propensity to negotiate pay on entry to the current job (Model 1) and subsequently (Model 2). Compared to men, the odds of women asking for more pay on joining decrease by a factor of 0.712, which is a substantial difference. However, the effect disappears when it comes to looking for pay after taking up the position (Model 2). Consequently, it would be difficult to support an essentialist argument that women are always less likely to ask for a raise by virtue of their biology or early socialization. Instead, whatever reluctance they may have initially subsequently declines as they become more comfortable in their new role. This means that we cannot simply blame women for their inability to ask for more pay generally. Instead, we would prefer to see more research on why gender matters in some negotiation situations and not others (see also Bowles et al. 2005). Why, for instance, does gender matter in the propensity to negotiate on entering a job but not subsequently? Clearly, these are striking results that ought to be taken up in future research on the gender gap in pay.

Turning to social class, we find that those in routine, semi-routine, and lower supervisory and technical classes are significantly less likely to seek more pay at entry than those in the higher managers and professional category (Model 1). This finding fits the popular image of 'high fliers', or even would be 'free agents' who can negotiate their own deals. It may also reflect the nature of their labour, which may be relatively scarce because of their skills and knowledge and difficult to monitor because of high levels of discretion and responsibility (see Chapter 3). What is perhaps even more striking is that the odds for them subsequently seeking a pay rise are also much greater than other groups (Model 2). In this respect, their employment relationship is unusual in that they clearly believe that it is open to renegotiation and, significantly, such renegotiation is to their advantage.

Unsurprisingly, those who are represented by trade unions are indeed less likely to ask individually for more pay, both on entering and in the time thereafter (Models 1 and 2). Common sense might suggest that these are trivial findings because employees are bound to ask for pay rises where there are no trade unions. Rather, the significance of these results is that they point towards an increase in individual bargaining as collective bargaining continues to decline and non-union workplaces become more prevalent. Of course, this assumes that the union effect on inhibiting individual deals also applied in earlier periods. As trade unions were much stronger in the past, we have no reason to think that this would not be so.

4.7. Conclusion

Our aim in this chapter has been to provide a fresh perspective on employee participation and representation, primarily by analysing them in relation to debates about the transformation of the employment relationship and against a background of long-term changes in the composition of the labour force. We now wish to conclude by commenting on the three areas that were the focus of our analyses: internalization, employee participation, and social inequality.

In relation to the first of these themes, those familiar with the evidence from the WIRS/WERS series will not be surprised that our analyses of employee and employer surveys show that direct participation is increasing while indirect participation through trade union representation continues to decline. Formal communication, consultation, and team-working practices have all become more widespread while various forms of functional flexibility and cross-training are now quite common within British industry. Moreover, these developments cannot be dismissed as being merely symbolic. Here we attach considerable significance to our modelling of perceptions of participation which indicated that the presence of briefing and discussion meetings along with quality circle type arrangements are all positively associated with the belief that employees actually have a say. Certainly, these results are consistent with the idea of a progressive swing from union voice to union and direct voice and, finally, towards direct voice alone (Millward et al. 2000: 121–2). But given our interest in the overall nature of the employment relationship we prefer to interpret them as part of a long-term tendency towards internalization or, as Streeck puts it, an extension of status (Streeck 1987). The general aim of this strategy, as Streeck explained, is to enhance the employees' sense of membership in an organizational community where management trust them with extra responsibilities, where they feel obliged to engage in extra-functional activity, and where they believe their voice matters.

Turning to the subject of employee representation and voice, our analyses show that some of the compositional changes in the labour force, such as the increased participation of women, and the use of non-standard job arrangements undermine trade union representation. Women, in particular, are still less inclined to join trade unions, even when controlling for the influence of employment in non-standard arrangements. Even so, this does not rule out the possibility that the increased participation of women in full-time employment may eventually reach a tipping point where little or no significant difference exists in the male–female propensity to unionize.

At the same time, our assessment of union membership by social class supports Gallie's argument that the growth of non-manual employment need not undermine trade union organization (Gallie 1996). Union membership levels certainly held up better among lower managers and professionals than any other class category across the 1990s. That said we would not go so far as to agree that this class has become 'a more solid bastion of trade unionism than the manual working class' (Gallie 1996: 150).

This is because our modelling of trade union membership shows that the propensity to join trade unions remains as high among the routine working class and among lower supervisors and technical workers.

If, by some miracle, union membership rates were to increase our examination of the factors associated with employees having a say over decisions affecting their jobs does not indicate that employees will have more voice. Instead, our results provide a direct challenge to those who see trade unions as the best way to satisfy a general demand for greater employee participation (e.g. Towers 1997; Howell 2005). To put it crudely, becoming a union member may mean that employees have less rather than more influence over decisions affecting their work. What employees may gain in terms of bargaining power, they may lose in terms of direct participation. In defence of trade unions, we did note the possibility that this perception may result from an underlying problem that led employees to join trade unions in the first instance. Either way, this is a question that deserves further research.

In relation to inequality, we believe that the interaction between internalization and individualization will contribute to greater inequality in earnings in two respects. First, those in service class employment are more likely to benefit materially from what Brown and colleagues call 'substantive individualization', that is, increasing differentiation in employees' pay and non-pay terms and conditions (Brown et al. 1998: i). Of course, it could be argued that this may always have been the case because higher managers and professionals were never constrained by union membership. In response, we would point towards the greater use of individualized bonuses and incentive payments, which allow for much more variation in earnings than seniority or job measurement-based schemes. In our view, individualized payment schemes give legitimacy to substantial individual inequalities in earnings (see also Chapter 6). We would, as a consequence, argue that the greater propensity of higher managers and professionals to ask for pay rises has to be considered as a contributory factor to the increasing inequality in earnings witnessed over the past few decades (Machin 1999; Nielsen and Alderson 2001).

The second area with the potential for greater inequality is that of gender. The reluctance of women to ask for more pay when taking up a new job inevitably means that a significant proportion will start on lower pay than their male colleagues. A further problem for women is that research by psychologists indicates that performance appraisals invariably include subjective assessments and these tend to result in lower ratings for women (Nivea and Gutek 1980; Dipboye 1985; Martell 1991). Even where performance appraisal ratings do not differ, men are still more likely to benefit from the subsequent translation of appraisal ratings into salary adjustments (Drazin and Auster 1987). Finally, the outcome of such salary adjustment processes generally lack transparency, particularly in the private sector (Neathey et al. 2003: 35–6). As it is considered gauche to ask others about their salaries, that is, if it is not forbidden by company policy, employees have no way of knowing whether they earn more or less than comparable colleagues.[7] Consequently, female employees rarely have sufficient grounds to challenge inequities in pay, assuming they even suspect that a problem exists.

Taken together, these findings suggest that categorical inequality, such as that between men and women or between different social classes, will be reinforced when employers direct their HRM policies towards employees as individuals rather than seeking to treat them as part of a collective group with standardized pay and conditions. We would, therefore, wish to emphasize that the long-term extension of the internally oriented employment system need not reduce social inequality; it may simply perpetuate it in a more opaque fashion.

Notes

1. We are able to improve on the earlier analysis by Gallie and colleagues in three important respects. First, we cover a longer period of time—sixteen years (1984–2000) compared to six (1986–92). Second, each of the surveys that we use is based on a nationally representative sample while the 1986 data that Gallie and colleagues use is based on surveys of six urban areas and cannot, therefore, be treated as being truly representative of the national situation. Finally, we use a six-item version of the Erikson–Goldthorpe class schema to capture possible differences between the higher and lower professional and managerial classes that may be hidden within the five-item version used by Gallie et al. (1998: 32).
2. Our confidence in these surveys was reinforced by finding that their estimates of union membership for the period are broadly similar to those based on other, better-known sources (e.g. Millward et al. 2000). For instance, we find that union membership fell from around half of all employees (49.7%) in 1984 to less than one in three (32%) by 2000.
3. We suspect that our more modest figure results from the use of a narrower definition of self-managing teams. If we compare this with Harley's analysis of the 1998 WERS data, which found that fewer than 7 per cent of British workplaces contained self-managing teams, our 2002 data points to a reasonable amount of growth in this area (Harley 2001).

4. Like the WiB 2000 survey, the BSA survey is designed to yield a nationally representative sample of adults aged 18 and over. The sampling frame is also based on the Postcode Address File compiled by the post office and the data are also weighted to allow for the fact that not all of the units covered in the sample have the same probability of being selected.

5. The BSA surveys from 1987 and 1991 also report that the proportion having a say was around half of all employees (51 and 54%, respectively).

6. Using the same controls as in Table 4.7, we conducted (binary) logistic regression analysis of whether the respondent received an increase having ever asked for one. The only relevant variable to reach statistical significance showed that those in non-union settings were more likely to get an increase. This is to be expected given that they have a much greater propensity to ask for a pay rise (Model 1 Table 4.7).

7. Under employment legislation introduced in April, 2003, women can submit a questionnaire to their manager to find out whether they are being treated less favourably. Refusing to complete the questionnaire can count against an employer at an Employment Tribunal, but employers are under no obligation to do so.

5

Overwork and market discipline

5.1. Introduction

In the competitive market economies that typify Britain and most of the post-industrialized world, the achievement of high levels of performance has become a central concern of employers. To achieve the organization's performance goals, employees are required to accept growing work demands, whether in terms of long and variable hours, sustained physical, mental, and emotional effort, or an increasing pace of work. By the late 1990s, the assumption that most employed people are overworked had spread through British society and its media.

There is an extensive vocabulary of overwork. The term itself appears in the title of a best-selling book by Judith Schor (1991), who particularly examined long working hours in the USA. Another widely used concept is work intensity or intensification, referring to the amount of work required in each unit of time (Nichols 1991; Green 2001, 2006; see also various chapters in Burchell, Ladipo, and Wilkinson 2002). Those who wish to focus on the psychological experience of overwork often employ the concept of work strain or work stress. This is by now the subject of an immense literature, and of extensive empirical studies (e.g. a remarkable longitudinal study of civil servants: Marmot et al. 1991; Marmot 2004; or the Bristol Stress and Health at Work Study: Smith 2001). Starting with Arlie Hochschild (1983), sociologists have drawn attention to emotional labour as a burden of much contemporary work, especially in services that involve continual interaction with customers and clients (see Korczynski 2002 for review).

Terms such as overwork, work intensification, or work strain are of course value-laden and suggest that there are alternative states of affairs where work would be (or should be) at a normal, more relaxed, and less stressful level. By using such terms, one engages in a contestation around practice. There is no way of avoiding this engagement, even if one wished to. *Effort*, perhaps the nearest one can get to a neutral concept, is nonetheless subject to an endless negotiation process between employers and employees (Behrend 1957; Baldamus 1961), and to discuss and analyse it, in any of its various forms, is to become involved in that process. One can acknowledge that, at the level of subjective experience, effort can be enhancing, for example, when the individual engages in an effort as an expression of personal commitment or a means of self-discovery. At other times however effort is degrading or diminishing, where, for example, it results from an external imposition that is felt as exploitative, or leaves the individual 'used up' or 'burnt out', hence unable to enjoy a full life of choice. Whatever the subjective experience of effort, however, this does not affect its contested position in the employment relationship. It is around this position that the current chapter, and the following two, revolve.

There is little reason to doubt that the effort demanded of British employees has in fact been rising. The survey evidence is consistent with the sources already cited in pointing that way. In 1992, 31 per cent of employees strongly agreed that their jobs required them to work 'very hard', but in 2000 this had risen to 40 per cent.[1] In 2000, moreover, 56 per cent of employees said they were working harder than two years previously, while only 12 per cent said they were working less hard. A well-validated questionnaire measure of work strain (Warr 1990), used in both the 1992 and 2000 surveys, also shows a mean increase of 4 per cent over the period, which is statistically significant. The largest increases in work strain were observed for higher managers and professionals (up 9%). Although these percentage increases may seem small, they should be viewed against the evidence (see Gallie et al. 1998: 219–31) that work pressures and work strain were already at a high level by 1992.

One of the contemporary circumstances believed to be associated with increasing work demands of various types is the reorganization of work into more flexible forms (see Chapter 1). Multi-skilling and multitasking, combined with 'delayering' to reduce management and supervisory support and increase self-management for the remaining employees, make employees responsible for filling their own time with a variety of tasks, a process graphically described by Maria Hudson (2002). Flexibility is also the underlying rationale of work systems such as 'just-in-time' that have spread from their manufacturing origin into the supply chains of retailers, hospitals, and many other organizations: they have the effect of accelerating the flow of work. Another conspicuous development is the growth of systematic HRM practices that are geared to high commitment or high performance (Huselid and Becker 1996; Wood 1996; Huselid, Jackson, and Schuler 1997; Ichniowski, Shaw, and Prennushi 1997; Appelbaum et al. 2000; Ramsey, Scholarios, and Harley 2000). Innovation in workplace practices, whether to pursue flexibility or develop higher personal performance, is itself part of a wider pattern of increasing organizational and technical change that has become very prevalent (Bresnahan 1999; White et al. 2004). The process of change in turn imposes pressures on employees, and especially on the managers who drive it and are driven by it (Worrall and Cooper 2001). The technology of control also comes into the picture. A large literature has grown up on the pressures of working in call centres, under the control of computerized monitoring systems (e.g. Bain and Taylor 2000; Yeuk-Mui 2001; Bain et al. 2002; Deery, Iverson and Walsh 2002; Taylor and Bain 2005); more will be said about computerized monitoring in Chapter 6.

In a recent major study that provides further analysis and reflection on many of these developments, and has an international perspective, Francis Green (2006) concludes that the increasing demands or pressures of work are mainly associated with change in work organization, flexibility, and the repercussions of information technology on ways of working. He concludes, of the intensification of work, that 'its detrimental impact on well-being is unambiguous' (Green 2006: 174).

So existing knowledge about the workplace circumstances connected with overwork is extensive. Yet, while changes in work organization or in work techniques indicate how overwork develops, they do not explain why these changes are chosen and agreed by the social actors involved. If the impact of these changes, in terms of work demands on employees (including managers), is unambiguously negative, *how or why do employees go along with them?*

This question opens another window onto the relative importance of market mechanisms and of mechanisms internal to the organization. For many commentators (as outlined in Chapter 1), work intensification is of one piece with market uncertainty, job insecurity, and the transfer of risk from employer to employees. Fear of job loss compels individuals to accept a ratcheting up of work demands, and employers can rely on insecure market conditions to simplify their task in extracting more from the workforce. In opposition to this view, however, one can place an interpretation based on the growth of internal systems of control and incentive that organizations can apply to achieve higher performance.

According to this contrary view, organizations wishing to shape employee behaviour rely not on the external market, which they cannot control, but on their own know-how in configuring checks and rewards to produce reliable results: what Amitai Etzioni called 'remunerative power' (Etzioni 1975). The debate, then, is between market discipline and bureaucratic discipline: between the discipline produced by threatening external conditions, and the discipline produced by internal command and control.

This chapter considers the first set of ideas, linking overwork to external, market discipline, while the next chapter deals with the explanation in terms of internal, bureaucratic discipline. Section 5.2 begins with a discussion of ideas behind the market discipline thesis about overwork. The conceptual issues are less simple than might appear at first sight, with a crucial requirement that job insecurity or fear of job loss must generalize beyond a short-term crisis into longer-term behaviour. Following this conceptual discussion, the third, fourth, and fifth sections of the chapter assess how the market discipline thesis stands up to evidence. Initially, the focus is upon the relationships between various insecure circumstances and employees' levels of effort. Then the workplace policies of employers are considered, specifically those intended to produce high levels of commitment and effort. Finally, class differences are examined, cross-cutting the chief questions of the chapter.

5.2. Markets, Fear, and Overwork

The popular idea is that people work harder when they are afraid of losing their jobs. This idea, however, fails to explain why in Britain employees have gone on working harder during an exceptionally long period of economic prosperity. Jobs have been getting more plentiful, not scarcer, so employees should have been losing their fear and slacking off. A simple idea of effort responding to fear can only explain short-term increases in effort. The trick is to explain how effort can continue to rise even when the initial shock that made people afraid for their jobs has passed by. To put this more formally, how can temporary changes in market conditions result in a longer-term change in workplace effort, and even in a progressive rise leading to overwork, despite reversion of market conditions? To provide a satisfactory answer to this question requires a more elaborate model of how effort is determined between employers and employees. It is instructive to return to the early critiques of overwork that began to appear in the nineteenth century in Britain. That surely was a period when fear was abroad in the workforce, and it was certainly a period of extraordinarily long working hours. These conditions evoked what was probably the first coherent attempt at constructing a market model of overwork.

5.2.1. *Starting with Marx*

The role of market mechanisms, of the commodification of labour, and of fear in producing overwork was famously suggested in Karl Marx's writings.[2] He was by no means the first, of course, to comment on the extremely long hours that characterized British industry in the first half of the nineteenth century. He was however the first to provide an explanation that coherently addressed the behaviour of both employers and workers.[3]

Importantly, Marx did *not* simply present employers as exploiters and workers as exploited. He interpreted employers' desire for long work hours in terms of remaining profitable against a background of rapid technical change. Workers were required to work long hours because machinery had to work long hours, to produce a return on investment before becoming obsolete. The employer who, in the conditions (and, one should add, the state of knowledge) of the early nineteenth century, did not enforce long hours of work risked being driven out of business by not being able to replace machinery as frequently as competitors. Thus, employers' behaviour, while responding to the profit motive, was also a function of structural conditions in the product market.

Workers meanwhile were unable to resist the imposition of long hours because of conditions in the labour market. Rapidly increasing population and the flight from country to town produced abundant labour for industry, further increased, as Marx emphasized, by the introduction of great numbers of women and children into factories and mines. The labour surplus was a 'reserve army' permitting employers to transfer the pressures of the product market onto workers. Furthermore, restrictive laws prevented workers from combining against employers or from otherwise exercising what little power they might have.[4] Workers' main choices, in effect, were between accepting what were universally long hours, and destitution.

This account reveals the essentials for a market-based model of overwork. Note, first, that there are two kinds of market involved: the product market and the labour market. Employers seek to obtain more labour from employees at all times, but the form in which they do so depends on the structural conditions in the product market: at that time, long hours were desired by employers because they wanted to work their machinery before it could become obsolete. (Whereas nowadays, perhaps, employers seek flexibility from their employees to cope with uncertain and rapidly changing demand.) Whether employers can get what they desire also depends, however, on structural conditions in the labour market. The labour surplus that Marx perceived was only part of the reason why employers could impose long hours. They could also do so because no alternative hours were on offer (long hours were the norm) and because employees lacked the organization or the regulatory support to oppose employers' will.

Marx does not explicitly state how long hours could be *persistent* even in times and places with a shortage of labour, but he could readily have done so with the elements that he identified. Once the initial competitive conditions had provided the impetus to establish long hours as the norm, there would be a considerable social and economic inertia to prevent employers from deviating: social, because they would be 'rocking the boat' for all employers at other times and places, and economic, because they themselves would continue to fear the long-term costs of shortening hours. On the employees' side, meanwhile, the structural conditions constraining their opposition to employers' policy would also be little affected by temporary labour market improvements; indeed, the legal and judicial framework in place at that period existed to prevent workers from exploiting conditions that would otherwise favour them.

Yet the observations that Marx made did not always fit his model. He noted, for instance, that employers were only partly successful in implementing long hours. There was a widespread problem of workers' absence on Mondays and, not infrequently, on Tuesdays as well, and employers struggled with this problem, then as now. If power in the labour market had been as one-sided as Marx stated, surely employers would simply have dismissed absent workers and filled their places with others who complied. The fact that workers were often able to cut their actual hours by absence suggests that they were not totally dominated by fear of job loss; they already had some informal bargaining power. Further, Marx describes at some length what happened when, subsequently, government imposed regulation on working hours and brought the era of very long hours to a close. Employers then discovered, much to their surprise, that they could achieve even higher levels of output per worker, with these shorter hours, than they had achieved in the previous regime. This again suggests that the market discipline previously imposed on workers was not in its final outcomes very effective.[5]

5.2.2. *Contemporary Models of Market Discipline*

For a model of market discipline to reach the standard set by Marx, it must account for both employer and employee behaviour in terms of market developments and structures, and must also provide a mechanism that carries short-term change into long-term effects. This section considers some market models for the contemporary employment relationship that meet these criteria. Before turning to these models, though, it may be useful to re-emphasize the extensive and varied nature of current competitive pressure, which renders the 'market discipline' thesis more plausible and more general. Chapter 1 outlined the evidence for increasing competition and its sources in the world economy, and it is not necessary to reiterate it. We would however stress two points from the earlier discussion: first, that financial markets are as important for market discipline as product markets and labour markets; and that the pressures of change have affected the public sector as well as the private sector.

In the tighter financial regimes that apply to managements in both the private and the public sectors, it is hardly surprising if they press for greater effort on the part of employees. Indeed, many employees, whether in the private or the public sector, see a direct link between these background pressures on management and the work intensification that they themselves face (Burchell 2002). What, though, is the nature of this supposed link between competitive pressures and work intensification and overwork? Do employers in practice rely on competitive market conditions to discipline employees into higher levels of effort? How might this be achieved?

5.2.3. *Job Insecurity*

Perhaps Marx's fear-based model of overwork can be applied directly to the present labour market. Job insecurity has been a focus of much research and commentary in Britain, and has been extensively discussed in two important collections of papers (Heery and Salmon 2000*b*; Burchell, Ladipo and Wilkinson 2002). The connection between job insecurity and work intensification is more suggested than formally stated in these sources, but the elements for a model (with Marx in mind) are present.

The argument initially relies on the recurrence of high unemployment during the 1980s and early 1990s, and the widespread feelings of anxiety that resulted. The evidence for high levels of job insecurity in the early 1990s, a period when high unemployment was rapidly unleashed, is indeed rather strong (Gallie et al. 1998). It was at this time—about a decade behind similar developments in the USA—that leading British employers began publicly to disown their reputations for offering long-term employment. Yet since the mid-90s, Britain has experienced continuous economic growth, falling unemployment, rising employment, reduction in temporary working, and the restoration of internal labour markets (see Chapter 2). One might agree that employees were in no position to resist work intensification in the early 1990s, but why should they continue to comply a decade later? One possibility is that the periods of mass unemployment changed something longer-term: they generated new institutions, or norms, that have continued to create anxiety or fear even after mass unemployment has ended.

Such a change, plausibly, is in the use of redundancy as a *normal* method of adjusting workforce numbers even in good economic conditions (Turnbull and Wass 2000). This normalization of redundancy took place in the period of massive restructuring in the 1980s, was consolidated in the recession of the early 1990s, and then appears to have carried over into the more prosperous period from the mid-1990s onwards. The failure of efforts to mount a collective resistance to mass redundancies in the 1980s and the progressive contraction of unions thereafter help to explain why there was little opposition to redundancies in the 1990s. Data from WERS 1998 reveal that job cuts took place, during the single year 1997–8, in workplaces employing 37 per cent of private-sector employees. The corresponding proportion for public-sector employees was 29 per cent.[6] So even at a time when the economy was buoyant, redundancies were widespread. Indeed, redundancies have come to form a larger share of total labour turnover during periods when the economy is doing well and unemployment is low (Turnbull and Wass 2000). Employees must surely be aware of this, not only because they hear of redundancies at their own workplace but because large-scale redundancies and the closure of sites are given prominence in the British media.

At any one time in a prosperous economy, naturally the proportion of employees personally facing redundancy is small (see Chapter 2). Even so, when redundancy is a normal part of employer policy, employees may well be fearful that they could be out of a job at *some* time. Although in good economic conditions a new job will generally be found before long, employees may still have much to lose in terms of pay, benefits, and pensions as they move to a different employer. The motivation then is to reduce the risk by staying off the employer's shortlist of least-desired employees. In the 2000 survey, four in ten employees thought that if they lost their job they would probably be unable to get another with as good pay as their present one. Moreover, three in four of all employees said that they would be glad to trade off some pay for a job with a greater degree of security. One obvious way of reducing the probability of job loss is to mark oneself out as a hard-working and compliant employee.

Job insecurity has also been a feature of the US labour market since the 1980s, where downsizing came early (Harrison and Bluestone 1988) and has perhaps led to more profound changes in the employment relationship (Cappelli 1999a, 1999b). Some aspects of Cappelli's account have already been discussed in Chapter 2 of this book, but there are other aspects that relate to effort or overwork. He is particularly intrigued by the consequences of employers' reneging on the previous psychological contract of job security and career progression, and their general abandonment of fair treatment as a principle of conduct towards employees. These changes might have been expected to *reduce* levels of effort or performance, as employees became disillusioned and cynical, but what was observed instead was sustained and improving performance (Cappelli 1999a: 128–36). The question that interests him, accordingly, is how these adverse consequences were avoided: what substituted for the commitment and trust that large employers, in particular, previously assumed as the basis for motivation?

Fear of job loss, or what Cappelli calls the 'frightened worker model' (Cappelli 1999a: 130–2), is an important part of the explanation he offers. Employees are fearful of showing their resentment towards management policies when their jobs may be on the line, and so employers are able to make demands without meeting resistance. In addition, Cappelli suggests, the resentment of employees towards exploitative treatment may actually be less intense when similar adverse developments are seen taking place throughout industry. Employers' reputation in the job market suffers less following downsizing and job cuts when such policies are being widely followed by others (see discussion in Chapter 1, especially Section 1.4.4).

The British literature on job insecurity and redundancy norms and Cappelli's frightened worker model under repetitive downsizing go a considerable way towards providing a plausible account of how effort can be raised by exposure to market competition. What is needed to complete the explanation, however, is a determination on the employer's side to change employment policies and employment relationships in such a way as to harness the motivation of insecurity. When employers adopt such an approach, one can talk of marketization of the employment relationship and of a 'market discipline' model.[7] This again leads to the question 'why?'. Why would employers give up established ways of managing the employment relationship to adopt market discipline as their preferred approach? The general answer to the foregoing question would be because market discipline is more profitable or more cost-effective. This might be very difficult to demonstrate since other approaches, such as HRM, can also deploy efficiency arguments. Another reason might be that repeated exposure to market fluctuations reduces the employer's reputation and the credibility of long-term promises so that fear of job loss becomes the only effective means of extracting more effort (see, again, the discussion in Chapter 1). There is, however, another idea that is worth noting.

5.2.4. *Market Individualism*

In the account provided by Cappelli (1999*a*), an attempt is made to cut through efficiency debates and suggest a simple answer. As markets become more volatile, a process sets in that compels employers towards marketized employment relations. First, they are obliged to drop their offers of internal career tracks, because of turbulent market conditions, and instead focus on recruiting the skills they need for the short term at the price set by the job market. Then, in reaction, employees cease to see themselves as dependent on the company and begin to see their future as depending on themselves. In short, they begin to construct their own careers in the wider job market rather than internally to their current employer. (This also accords with principles of 'employability' that were popular among employers in the 1990s: see Waterman, Waterman and Collard 1994.) Moreover, many people get to like this new market regime, once the initial shock is over: it offers them a kind of freedom that the old corporate career stifled. Their motivation becomes an individualistic one: they work to learn skills that will stand them in good stead, and to accumulate achievements that will grace their CVs. Employers then find that, even if they wished to reduce their reliance on the external job market, the changing attitudes of employees prevent them from doing so.[8]

The concept of market individualism has a special feature. It seems to apply especially well to people with a high level of skill, talent, or qualification: in short, to people who are well able to move around in the job market. Insecure employment conditions have revealed what they can do, unaided. Market individualism in this way complements the job insecurity version of market discipline.

5.3. Employees' Overwork and Job Insecurity

The ideas of market discipline are plausible as a source of overwork, but need to be tested against experience and evidence. The investigation begins on the side of employees (employers are considered later). From Marx through to Cappelli and the recent British literature on job security, there is an assumption that fear of job loss leads to increased effort. This section directly examines the assumption. If overwork is accepted or self-imposed by employees because of insecurity and fear, then the more they are exposed to insecure conditions, the greater their level of overwork will be.

Employees' effort is analysed for the year 2000 when the British economy was buoyant. To investigate the role of job insecurity, measures reflecting circumstances in the workplace have been preferred to attitudinal questions such as 'satisfaction with security'. This is largely because the attitudinal types of question may be influenced by personality differences that cannot be taken account of in the analysis. However, the three measures of insecure employment conditions, which are described in Box 5.1, are all negatively associated with individuals' satisfaction with job security, and this suggests that they are experienced by employees as threatening to themselves.

Of the three measures used, the most important conceptually is the employee's report of whether the workplace has contracted during the previous three years. Where a workplace has had this experience, there will often be a continuing anxiety about further job cuts (popularly referred to as 'survivor syndrome'). Despite the favourable economic conditions of the late 1990s, still one quarter of employees in the 2000 survey (27%) reported contraction taking place, so this remains a widespread circumstance. A potential limitation of this measure is that it excludes cases where jobs have been cut in some sections of the workforce, while there has been compensating recruitment in other sections, leading to overall stable or even expanding employment. However, previous experience with a variety of such measures leads us to believe that minor adjustment or reshaping of the workforce generally has little effect on employees' outlook. It is overall reduction of the workforce that has the crucial effect: for example, it has a clear negative influence on employee commitment (Gallie et al. 1998: 240–2).

The second indicator of insecurity in the analysis is the employee's judgement that she will lose her job during the following year as a result of redundancy or closure of the workplace. Very small proportions expected

---

Box 5.1. INDICATORS OF INSECURE EMPLOYMENT CONDITIONS

Three variables are constructed to represent insecure employment conditions.

  a. Workforce contraction: 'In the past three years has the number of people where you work in your current job got larger, got smaller, or stayed the same?' (If respondent has worked for less than three years in current job, accept answer for shorter period in current job.) The responses are coded as dummy variables.

  b. Quick dismissal: 'From this card, how long do you think it would be before a person in your organization, doing your sort of job, would eventually be dismissed if they persistently arrived late at work?' Responses shown on the card are within a week, within a month, within six months, within one year, more than a year, or never. Quick dismissal is defined as 'within a week' or 'within a month'.

  c. Expected closure or redundancy: This question was presented in the self-completion questionnaire because of its personal nature. 'How likely or unlikely is it that you will leave your present employer over the next twelve months?' Responses: very likely, quite likely, not very likely, or not at all likely. Those responding 'very likely' or 'quite likely' are asked to indicate one or more reasons from a list of nine, the first two of which are 'Firm will close down' and 'I will be declared redundant'. Selecting either or both of these responses codes the respondent to a dummy variable.

Note: To assess construct validity, associations with 'satisfaction with job security' were obtained, by cross-tabulating each item with the seven-point satisfaction measure. All were negatively associated, as follows: workforce contraction, $p < .001$, dissatisfied responses 17% vs 6% for those in workplaces with expanding or static employment; quick dismissal, $p = 0.02$, dissatisfied responses 13% vs 9% for those perceiving slower dismissal as the norm; expected closure or redundancy, $p < .001$, dissatisfied responses 66% vs 7% for those not expecting to leave for these reasons or not at all.

---

that this would happen to them (just 3% of the 2000 sample), yet where this does occur it appears to provoke extreme dissatisfaction with job security (see Box 5.1).

Apart from redundancy and downsizing, it is also relevant to consider the individual's exposure to dismissal on personal grounds because the employer is quick to fire employees. The question probing this asked how long it would take for employees at the workplace to be given the sack if they were persistently late for work. Six per cent said that this would happen within a week, and a further 23 per cent said it would take more than a week but less than a month. These two replies are taken together as indicating readiness to dismiss.[9]

Box 5.2. MEASURES OF EFFORT

Effort has been treated in economics as a unidimensional concept (a cost). This facilitates the development of formalized models. However, there is no single accepted measure of effort or of its cost. Additionally, if one is attentive to how people speak and think about work, one is aware that effort is experienced as (at least) two-sided. It can express pride or weariness. Rather than attempting to construct a comprehensive measure of effort, we confine ourselves to two facets that reflect this contrasting experience. These are intended to represent the 'brighter' (positively toned) and 'darker' (negatively toned) sides of the concept.

High work demands is based on a single question that asks how far the employee agrees with the statement, 'My job requires that I work very hard'. The answer 'strongly agree' is taken as the indicator of high work demands. Semantically, this statement expresses a relation between oneself and one's job, and because of the word 'requires' and the repeated 'My . . . I', this relationship is normative and possessive. By strongly agreeing with this statement, the individual claims to be a 'good worker' and committed to the job. Consistent with this interpretation, this indicator is positively and significantly associated with 'satisfaction with the work itself'.

Work strain is a scale derived from four questions (below) about feelings at the end of a workday and after coming home, and taps into ideas of tension and exhaustion brought on by work. The questions were devised by Warr (1990) and have excellent reliability. The wording of the questions is shown below. Answers are scored from one to six and are summed into an overall score. The work strain scale reports negative experience arising from effort. High scores suggest situations that are pushing individuals beyond what is reasonable. The scale is uncorrelated with 'satisfaction with the work itself', but it is negatively and significantly associated with 'overall job satisfaction'.

'Thinking of the past few weeks, how much of the time has your job made you feel each of the following?'

A. After I leave my work I keep worrying about job problems.
B. I find it difficult to unwind at the end of a workday.
C. I feel used up at the end of a workday.
D. My job makes me feel quite exhausted by the end of a workday.

(Responses: Never, occasionally, some of the time, much of the time, most of the time, or all of the time.)

Along with these three indicators of insecure circumstances, the analysis uses two outcome measures related to work effort or overwork. The two outcome measures, which will be used throughout the next chapter as well as in this one, are described in some detail in Box 5.2. The reason for using two measures, rather than relying on a single measure, reflects a point made in the introduction to this chapter: the concept of effort

Table 5.1. Insecure conditions and work effort in 2000

Insecurity indicators	Measure of effort used as dependent variable	
	Work demands[a]	Work strain[b]
Workplace contracted over past three years[c]	7.8* ($t = 2.35$)	9.2** ($t = 4.0$)
Workplace expanded over past three years[c]	6.9* ($t = 2.37$)	6.0** ($t = 2.74$)
Would be dismissed within one month if persistently late for work	1.1 ($t = 0.33$)	−0.00 ($t = 0.02$)
Expect to lose job because of redundancy or site closure within one year	−7.2 ($t = 1.11$)	10.1[†] ($t = 1.75$)
N	2,101	2,016

Notes: Significance symbols: [†] significant at the 10% level; * significant at the 5% level; ** significant at the 1% level. The models have controls for gender, age, highest qualification, social class, temporary contract, size band, public sector, unionized workplace, and region.

[a] Binary variable: logistic regression model. Estimates in this column are for marginal effects on probability (percentage points), evaluated at the means.

[b] Natural logarithm of quasi-continuous scale: OLS regression model. Estimates in this column represent the percentage change in work strain.

[c] Compared with no change in employment over the past three years.

Source: WiB 2000.

has both positive and negative connotations, and a balanced treatment should consider both. The measure labelled 'work demands' lies somewhat on the positive side, while the measure labelled 'work strain' has negative connotations.

In each analysis, all three measures of insecure conditions were included so that the estimated effect of each is net of the effects of the others. The analyses also controlled for a wide range of workplace, individual, and job characteristics. The chief results, shown in Table 5.1, encompass the following main points.

- Those who had witnessed their workplaces contracting in the previous three years on average had higher levels of effort, on both the 'work demands' and 'work strain' measures, than employees in workplaces with static employment. The probability of experiencing high work demands was 8 percentage points greater than in workplaces experiencing no change, and the average level of work strain was higher by 9 per cent.

- However, employees in workplaces that had grown in the past three years also had higher levels of effort, on both measures, relative to those in workplaces with static employment. Broadly speaking, high work demands and high work strain were as much a feature of employees' experience in growing as in contracting workplaces.

- Employees' sense of work demands was unaffected by expectations of redundancy or site closure over the coming year. Work strain was however somewhat higher among these employees, by an estimated 10 per cent, although this effect was on the borderline of statistical significance because of the small number in the group.[10] This adds some further evidence of increased effort in conditions where job insecurity was at an acute level.[11]

- Employees' sense of high work demands and of work strain were unaffected by the severity of their employers' readiness to dismiss.

Overall, the results provide reasonably good evidence that employees exert high levels of effort in insecure conditions. This applies both when personal job loss appears imminent, so that anxiety about insecurity is likely to be acute, and still more clearly in the medium-term aftermath of wider workforce reductions. The latter is particularly crucial for the market discipline thesis since employers can only rely on insecure conditions to provide a motivational 'stick' if the effect on effort is persistent.

This main finding must however be qualified in an important way. The levels of effort among employees in contracting workplaces are high relative to workplaces with static employment, but *not* relative to workplaces that have been growing. Presumably, conditions of growth provide other motivations to effort, such as greater chances of promotion and greater customer demands. Over the 1990s, moreover, expansion overtook contraction. Reviewing the three years up to 1992, nearly twice as much contraction as expansion was reported by employees (38% of employees against 21%). In the three years to 2000, the picture was reversed: 27 per cent of employees reported contraction against 37 per cent expansion. This underlines the need for employers to have employment policies that are adaptable to different circumstances. How employers actually developed their employment practices over the period is the focus of the next main section. Before that, however, the notion of 'market individualism' deserves some further examination.

5.3.1. *Market Individualism and Effort*

Market individualism is an idea that has been little explored previously and we can do little more than make a start on it. The first task is to find some measure that will indicate, at least roughly, how widespread market individualism may be. The idea of market individualism is that employees move opportunistically around the job market and do not see their careers in terms of a single employer. The following question, present in the 2000 survey, gets part of the way towards this notion: 'There are many career opportunities I expect to explore after I leave my present employer'. Overall, just under four in ten (39%) of the 2000 survey either agreed or strongly agreed with this expression of individualistic or opportunistic career attitude.

Were employees in workplaces that had contracted in recent years more likely to have this attitude, by comparison with employees in static or growing workplaces? In analysing this, the same set of controls was used as for the analysis reported in Table 5.1.[12] The result provided some evidence in support of Cappelli's concept: individualistic or opportunistic career attitude was indeed fostered by the experience of workplace contraction, both compared with those in static workplaces and those in growing workplaces.[13] Alongside experience of insecurity, other influences that significantly raised this type of career attitude were of a plausible type: being male, being young, having degree- or sub-degree-level qualifications, being on a temporary contract, and living in the London and South-East region.

The second stage of analysis was to compute the simple associations of individualistic or opportunistic career attitude with the two measures of effort. This was done for the sample as a whole, and also separately for employees in the higher managerial and professional class, and in the lower managerial and professional class. The results from these analyses provided no evidence that such a career attitude was related to effort, whether measured in terms of positively toned work demands or in terms of negatively toned work strain. In view of the lack of association at this simple level, no further analysis of a multivariate type was attempted.[14]

The experience of insecure conditions at work appears to stimulate a certain aspect of individualism or opportunism, and this is something that employers would need to take account of in framing their employment policies. But individualistic or opportunistic career attitude is, as far as one can see, of no consequence for overwork. Of course, market individualism is doubtless many-sided, so an analysis of just one attitudinal measure cannot claim to be conclusive.

5.4. Employer Policies and Market-Based Overwork

The analysis so far has shown that employees working in 'downsized' workplaces are likely to work harder, compared with those in a stable workforce. They are also more likely to become individualistic in the job market, although this seems to have nothing to do with effort. On the assumption that employers are aware of these influences, how would they shape their policies and practices to motivate employees? One reasonable response, surely, would be to dismantle those costly internal policies and practices that are intended to develop performance, and to control work effort. Why retain complex systems of incentive payment, with all the costs of recording and updating that are involved (let alone the incentive pay itself), if the firm could rely on fear of redundancy to keep employees running hard? The firm could also save costs by dismantling pay progression systems, with time-consuming appraisals and pay reviews each year, not to mention built-in employee expectations of continual wage and salary raises. Then too it could cut down on internal training provision, especially as much of the value of the training provided would tend to pass to other employers when employees left, as they are more likely to do when they are individualistic. Instead, the employer could minimize labour costs by taking on experienced employees at the going market rate, offering pay increases only when external conditions make it harder to recruit and retain, and firing employees as soon as demand falls or different skills are needed.

Such changes as these would result in a much smaller personnel or HRM function. Indeed, as Cappelli notes (1999*a*: 68), one consequence of the rise of market-based practice in the USA was some very public calls for HR departments to be disbanded. Indeed, the ideas at the root of HRM are at the opposite pole to the ideas of marketized or commodified employment practice (see Chapter 1). The involvement and development of employees in a cooperative enterprise requires a long-term perspective that is inconsistent with reliance on market opportunism. Accordingly, if employers are tending to opt more for the latter, one should see the diffusion of HRM practices coming to a halt and even going into reverse. This provides a simple though indirect test of the marketization thesis: one can look at whether HRM practices are diminishing, static, or increasing over time. If they are growing, that makes it less likely that a market-based approach is also gaining ground.

From the survey data (both 1992 and 2000/1), a set of thirteen practices has been assembled to represent the notion of HPWS. This notion was developed in an influential study of US manufacturing industries by Eileen Appelbaum et al. (2000), and has many common elements with other attempts to define 'best practice' in the development of HRM. HPWS is a version (or perhaps a subset) of HRM that, as its name implies,

143

Table 5.2. Development of 'HPWS' practices, 1992–2000

	Employees covered (%)	
	1992	2000
Problem-solving group	21	30*
Group working	46	58*
Group control	36	34
Group incentives	5	17*
Merit pay	38	37
Profit sharing	16	15
Individual incentive	15	22*
Workplace incentive	21	25*
Appraisal for pay	19	20
Appraisal for promotion	32	32
Appraisal for training	33	44*
Briefing groups	70	74*
Two-way meetings	63	69*
Average number of practices per employee	4.17	4.78

Note: * Indicates that the difference in proportions between the surveys is statistically significant at the 5% level or above.

Sources: 1992—EiB (N = 3,458); 2000—WiB (N = 2,132).

is particularly focused on orientating employees towards higher levels of performance.[15] It is therefore particularly relevant to an investigation of effort and overwork. The HPWS concept, as defined by Appelbaum and colleagues, consists of a combination of teamworking, incentives, personal development, and communications.[16] These practices involve considerable managerial and administrative resources to put in place and maintain.

Table 5.2 shows how the percentages of employees involved in each of these practices changed across the decade. The picture given by this table is certainly not of employers cutting back. Rather, it is of unspectacular but steady growth in the use of the practices, with the following points as highlights.

- Over the decade, the average number of practices that employees took part in increased by about 16 per cent (see bottom row of Table 5.2).

- Five of the thirteen practices remained static (none declined to a significant extent), but eight became more prevalent to a statistically significant degree.

- The proportion of employees saying that they took part in an appraisal system that helped to plan their training and development increased from 33 to 44 per cent. This was one of the largest shifts in practice detected between the two time-points. Increasing internal development of employees is in sharp conflict with the idea of purchasing needed skills in an *ad hoc* manner on the job market.

- There were substantial increases in teamworking (up from 46 to 58% of employees), in the use of problem-solving groups—sometimes called quality circles (up from 21 to 30%), and in the application of group or team incentives (up from 5 to 17%). These are all indications of a move towards more cooperative group-based forms of working that are generally considered central to HPWS.

A limitation of the picture provided by Table 5.2 is that it deals with the practices in a piecemeal way, whereas the widely accepted idea of HPWS, or more generally of 'strategic' HRM, is that practices must be *combined* in order to achieve effects on motivation and performance. To get some purchase on this idea, one can collect the practices into subsets or 'bundles'. Following the ideas of Appelbaum et al. (2000), four bundles can be defined: teamworking (the first three items of the table), incentives (the next five items), development (the three items concerning the uses of appraisal systems), and communications (the last two items). An employee participating in *more than one* teamworking practice is designated a 'strategic' participant in teamworking, and similarly for each bundle of practices.[17]

There were significant increases in 'strategic' participation in all four domains. Strategic participation in teamworking was up from 30 to 38 per cent of employees, in incentives up from 25 to 31 per cent, in communications up from 59 to 65 per cent, and in development up from 29 to 32 per cent.[18] One can also count, for each employee, the number of bundles of practices on which she is a strategic participant. If three out of four are taken as the pass mark for being a strategic participant in HPWS as a whole, there has been a significant increase in strategic HPWS involvement (from 19 to 26%) over the period 1992–2000.[19] Another way of expressing this is to say that over the period, the proportion of employees taking part in a systematic and performance-focused form of HRM rose from just under one in five to just over one in four.

This set of findings suggests that British employers have on balance not been moving towards a more marketized set of employment practices, but rather in the opposite direction, towards a more intensive investment in raising the performance of existing employees. This conclusion has not been reached by focusing on types of employer practice that are unusual or esoteric. Most employees take part in some of these practices, and the average number per employee now approaches five. This ensures that the test is appropriate for an overall assessment of the direction of change in employment practices in British workplaces. The evidence just presented also complements the picture already developed in Chapter 2 relating to promotion prospects and flexible forms of employment. Both types of evidence show internalized employment policies advancing rather than retreating.

There is however still one other possibility to consider. Perhaps there is a degree of segmentation in employment practice with employers that pursue downsizing relying on the motivational stick of insecurity, while employers with more stable or expansive conditions are moving more towards HPWS. If that were the case, then the diffusion of HPWS would not hinder a parallel move by other employers towards reliance on market discipline. Such an interpretation would have been arguable in 1992, when indeed (as shown in Table 5.3) employees in contracting workplaces had relatively low exposure to intensive HPWS compared with employees in less insecure conditions. By 2000, however, as the table also shows, employees in both contracting and expanding workplaces were considerably more likely to be involved in intensive HPWS than were static workplaces. In terms of HPWS exposure, employees in expanding and contracting workplaces had not become more segmented but more similar.[20]

Of course, the nature of the contracting, static, and expanding groups certainly changed over this period. Workplaces were presumably contracting in 1992 for the most part because they were hit by the recession, whereas in 2000 this can no longer be assumed: by then many would be thriving organizations engaged in an active downsizing strategy. Apparently, by 2000 employers were quite capable of combining downsizing policy with intensive HPWS. The estimated proportion of all British employees who were in workplaces, where there was contraction

Table 5.3. Intensive HPWS practices and change in workforce size, 1992 and 2000

	Each cell participating in intensive HPWS (%)	
	1992	2000
Workplace contracted over past three years	14	29
Workplace expanded over past three years	20	35
Workplace stayed same size over past three years	24	20

Sources: 1992—EiB; 2000—WiB.

without intensive HPWS, fell from nearly a third in 1992 (32%) to under a fifth (18%) in 2000. There is substantial evidence, then, that by the turn of the millennium HPWS, probably indicative of HRM more generally, was advancing, even in workplaces that had practiced downsizing.[21] To explain why, one must consider the attractiveness of HPWS to employers.

5.4.1. HPWS and Effort

In focusing on HPWS practices in the context of overwork, the assumption is that at least part of employers' interest is to extract more effort from employees. But is there in reality a positive relationship between HPWS and effort? This is a serious question since many critics of HRM and HPWS have expressed doubt about the efficacy of the practices.

Because of the multifaceted nature of HPWS practices, there are many ways in which their relationship with effort could be analysed: for present purposes, there is much to be said for simplicity. HPWS was therefore represented by a single binary variable already introduced in the foregoing section: it takes the value 1 when an employee participates at the 'strategic' level (more than one practice) in at least three of the four domains of HPWS. The variable distinguishes between the one-in-four employees participating in an intensive or strategic level of HPWS, and the remainder. This variable is then added to the analysis for which the main results were earlier presented in Table 5.1. The chief results of the new analysis are shown in Table 5.4.

Table 5.4. Workplace contraction, intensive HPWS practices, and work effort

	Measure of effort used as dependent variable	
	Work demands[a]	Work strain[b]
Workplace contracted over past three years[c]	7.8* (t = 2.30)	9.1** (t = 3.98)
Workplace expanded over past three years[c]	6.4* (t = 2.20)	5.8* (t = 2.58)
Intensive HPWS	7.9** (t = 2.74)	3.8† (t = 1.74)
N	2,101	2,016

Notes Significance symbols: † significant at the 10% level; * significant at the 5% level; ** significant at the 1% level. Explanatory variables included in model but not shown: quick dismissal; expect redundancy/closure. Controls as for Table 5.1.

[a] Binary variable: logistic regression model. Estimates in this column are for marginal effects on probability (percentage points), evaluated at the means.

[b] Natural logarithm of quasi-continuous scale: OLS regression model. Estimates in this column represent the percentage change in work strain.

[c] Compared with no change in employment over the past three years.

Source: WiB 2000.

The analysis provides reasonable evidence that HPWS practices, when provided in a systematic form, do tend to raise levels of employee effort. For those in the intensive HPWS condition, the probability of experiencing a high level of work demands is raised by 7 percentage points, and work strain also increases by 4 per cent. Both of these effects are statistically significant, albeit the latter at the 10 per cent significance level. Note that the analysis is *not* comparing employees involved in strategic HPWS with employees having no involvement in HPWS. Rather, employees under intensive or strategic HPWS are being compared with all other employees, many of whom are working under partially developed HPWS or HRM policies. The test is, therefore, quite a severe one.[22]

A further point of some practical importance, which emerges when Table 5.4 is compared with Table 5.1, is that the estimated effects on effort of workplace contraction and of workplace growth hardly change when the HPWS variable is added to the analysis.[23] Insecure employment conditions, and HPWS, are additive in generating higher levels of employee effort,[24] and the supposition that HPWS, or more generally HRM practices, are only effective when accompanied by secure employment (see, for instance, Kochan and Osterman 1994) is not supported. This suggests one reason why employers may pursue HPWS or more generally HRM practices (which can be seen as stepping-stones to HPWS). Potentially, HPWS extract additional effort both in conditions of workforce contraction and workforce expansion. The versatility of HPWS is an important advantage when market conditions are uncertain.

5.5. Are There Class Differences?

The analysis so far has given an average picture that encompasses all types of employee. It is worth considering whether there are differences lurking beneath the average: perhaps the marketization and commodification of employment is concentrated within certain groups of employees, while internalized practices continue to advance elsewhere. Here, a focus on class appears relevant. In discussing the commodification of employment, Richard Breen (1997) has argued that differences between classes will be deepened, with those in the salariat (managerial and professional employees) largely protected from corrosive market forces while conditions worsen for other classes (see also Chapter 1).

An analysis of participation in HPWS by social class is shown in Table 5.5. The measure used here is the percentage change in the average

Table 5.5. Change in HPWS practices, by class

	Change in average number of practices, 2000 vs 1992 (%)				
	Team practices	Incentive practices	Development practices	Communication practices	All HPWS
Higher managers and professionals	+42	+41	+7	0	+20
Lower managers and professionals	+29	+37	+20	+9	+22
Intermediate	+14	+10	+19	+13	+14
Supervisory and technician	+28	+6	−9	+8	+10
Semi-routine	+6	+21	+39	+18	+18
Routine	−1	−24	−17	−4	−10

Note: Team practices are the sum of the first four items in Table 5.2; incentive practices, the next five items; development practices, the next three items; communication practices, the last two items.

Sources: 1992—EiB (N = 3,458); 2000—WiB (N = 2,132).

number of practices that employees took part in, under the four domains of HPWS practice; this is also summed into an overall measure of inclusion in HPWS practices. A simple finding jumps out from this table. Between 1992 and 2000, all classes but one took part in greater numbers of HPWS practices: the exception being employees in 'routine' jobs (broadly, the least skilled in the class system). For employees in the routine class, there was an actual decrease in inclusion in all types of HPWS practices over the period, with an overall 10 per cent fall.

For managers and professionals, teamworking and incentives are the two HPWS domains with the most rapid growth. Employers are clearly *not* simply relying on, or resigning themselves to, competition in the job market to obtain the managers and professional staff that they need, or to maintain their levels of effort. Instead, they are developing these most intensive kinds of internalized employment policies. Already by 1992, experience of HPWS was highest within these groups, yet over the period to 2000 employers invested still more in extending HPWS among them.

However, the progressive diffusion of HPWS is by no means confined to the managerial and professional classes. It is present among the 'intermediate' administrative class, and *still more so* among employees in the semi-routine class, where many of the jobs formerly thought of as skilled manual are located. Indeed, the semi-routine class has experienced substantial growth in all four domains of HPWS (though starting from a base that was far below that of managerial and professional employees). In terms of HPWS *levels*, one might reasonably speak of a class gradient, with the highest levels of inclusion at the top. But in terms of *rates of change*, there is no clear gradient, rather a general advance across classes, with just the one conspicuous exception for routine occupations.

As routine-class employees are being treated so differently from other classes, it is of interest to see how this affects their levels of effort. Despite quite small numbers in the routine class for 2000,[25] a satisfactory analysis proved possible with the same variables as for the whole sample; this included the variable for participation in intensive HPWS, as well as those relating to the experience of insecure conditions. The main features of this analysis (no table shown) were as follows:

- None of the employment conditions affecting job security was significantly related to a high level of work demands.

- Work strain was on average 19 per cent higher for routine-class employees in workplaces that had experienced contraction relative to those in workplaces with static employment,[26] and 17 per cent higher than those in growing workplaces.

- Unlike for the whole sample, growth of the workplace did not link to higher effort for routine-class employees.

- Again unlike for the whole sample, participation in intensive HPWS did not link to higher effort for routine-class employees.

- Work strain was on average 27 per cent higher for routine-class employees who expected to lose their jobs in the next year because of site closure or redundancy. This estimate however refers to a very small group of employees.[27]

What matters in this set of findings is not the numbers, but the overall pattern of results. Employees in routine-level occupations are strongly affected by insecurity, and this is reasonable enough, given their relative lack of transferable skills and their exposure to job loss and unemployment. Equally important from the employer's viewpoint, perhaps, is the apparent inefficacy of intensive HPWS practices (in terms of effort) within the routine class.

The analysis focusing on the routine class provides the best evidence for the existence of the market discipline or 'frightened worker' model. For members of this group, levels of work effort are highly sensitive to insecure employment conditions, and they are involved in HPWS to a small and decreasing extent. These findings, taken in combination, are suggestive of an increased reliance among employers on market-based, hire-and-fire practices for routine-level employees specifically. Even for this group, though, employers may not be relying entirely on the external market to extract effort. That judgement will have to wait to the end of the next chapter, after looking at other kinds of internalized practices aimed at increasing effort.

5.6. Conclusion: Limits to Market Discipline

Overwork is a widespread condition among employed people in Britain, and is also present in other post-industrial countries. It is reasonable to infer that overwork grew up as part of intensifying competitive pressure, and associated public-sector reforms, that characterized these economies by the 1980s. These conditions gave rise to widespread insecurity, and a weakening of employees' capacity to resist employers' demands for more intensive working or longer work hours. What is harder to explain is why overwork has continued through the mid- and late 1990s and into the 2000s, a period when the British economy experienced extraordinarily sustained growth, with rising prosperity and confidence. It is not obvious why employees would continue to comply with overwork demands under these conditions.

This chapter has considered 'market discipline' as a general explanation of persisting overwork. One version of this explanation is that employers have perpetuated job insecurity by normalizing downsizing and redundancy, even in buoyant conditions. Employees have then continued to comply with overwork demands as a way of insuring themselves against the threat of job loss. On the employer side, it would then become possible to withdraw progressively from costly internalized employment systems, and to rely more simply on market pressures to maintain effort at a high level.

These ideas have a considerable degree of plausibility and are worth testing. Two main types of test have been constructed. The first asked whether those experiencing insecure employment conditions work harder. The second probed whether employers were increasingly relying on the external job market to produce the pressure: as this is hard to assess directly, an indirect method was used, looking at the diffusion of intensive human resource practices. These HPWS represent the opposite pole to marketized or commodified employment relations, since they require an intensive investment by the employer in staff development and involvement, which only makes sense within a long-term employment relationship.

Two main conclusions emerge from these analyses:

- First, insecure employment conditions in Britain have indeed been associated with high effort not only in the short term but also into the medium term. Effort is higher both when job loss appears imminent and within a three-year period following workforce reductions. Moreover, these findings refer to the buoyant economic conditions around 2000, whereas the previous recession ended in 1993.

- Second, employers have steadily increased their systematic use of performance-focused HRM practices.

Additional findings suggest some reasons why employers were adopting these resource-intensive, internalized practices rather than more simply relying on market discipline. The intensive practices were linked to high levels of effort among participating employees, and this was the case whether or not employees were exposed to workforce contraction. The practices therefore seem versatile across conditions of growth or contraction. Employers indeed were adopting the practices at about an equal rate under both conditions.

This set of findings is incompatible with claims of a general growth in employers' reliance on external market discipline. There remains, however, the possibility of more limited claims relating to particular classes of employee, and the best case for such a claim concerns employees in routine occupations. Employees in this class reported specially large increases in work strain when they experienced insecure conditions. Furthermore, employers appeared to be progressively excluding them from HPWS, in sharp contrast to all other classes.

Even in a buoyant economy, conditions of competitive pressure and periodic recourse to downsizing have been persisting. These conditions partly explain why employees raise their effort levels, contributing to overwork. But this has not been leading towards a fully marketized or commodified employment relationship, except perhaps in the case of the routine class, because employers place limits on the process through their preference for supposedly performance-enhancing internalized systems. The next chapter will focus on those features of internalized systems that are most likely to contribute to overwork.

Notes

1. The sources are, as usual, the EiB survey for 1992 and the WiB survey for 2000. In both years, 90% of employees either strongly agreed or agreed that their jobs required them to work very hard. The increase in 2000 among those

strongly agreeing was balanced by a reduction among those merely agreeing. An analysis with numerous individual and workplace controls still estimated that the proportion strongly agreeing was higher by 9 percentage points in 2000.

2. In Book 1 of *Capital*, originally published in 1867. See also *Wages, Price and Profit*, 1865.

3. This chiefly draws on Part Four, Chapter XIII of *Capital*. In discussing this period, the term 'workers' is used rather than (as elsewhere) 'employees' because labour was often purchased in units of a day or a half-day, so the notion of an employee in the modern sense would be anachronistic.

4. For a recent historical account of the legal and judicial restraints on labour, see Deakin and Wilkinson (2005).

5. Understanding of the counterproductive effects of long hours was not achieved until the Great War when a different kind of fear again led to very long hours schedules, with poor results in terms of output (Vernon 1977).

6. Source: own calculations from WERS 1998 data. The measure refers to reductions in any section of the workforce. Workplaces with less than ten employees are absent from the data.

7. Our use of this phrase is related to, but different from, the concept of market discipline developed by Bowles and Gintis (1993). These authors use the term to refer to employers who set wages above the market-clearing (full employment) level, conceptualizing this additional pay as an 'enforcement rent' that makes it easier for the employer to gain employee compliance. The Bowles and Gintis concept does not depend on job insecurity as such (or it defines job insecurity in terms of potential loss of job rents). Our notion of market discipline (following Cappelli) is more general in applying even where individuals receive only the going market wage. This is because individuals have 'relationship-specific assets' (Baron and Kreps 1999: 65–6; see discussion in Chapter 1) that they are likely to lose with their jobs and are partly non-financial.

8. While the fear-based mechanism is derived by Cappelli explicitly from Marx, this market individualism evidently has much in common with recent formulations by European sociologists concerning the individualization of the life-course (e.g. Beck 1992).

9. Variant analyses used the full set of seven categories, ranging from one week to 'never'; these variants provided no additional information.

10. The number of employees who expected to lose their jobs through redundancy or site closure, within the analysis sample of 2016, was 71.

11. It might be supposed that employees who believe they will lose their jobs will lose existing motivation to work hard. However, if as often happens the contraction of the workforce is spread over a period, employees may work to maintain their jobs as long as possible; or employees may be required to take on additional tasks in a transitional period while a site is being run down.

12. An ordered logit model was used, with $N = 2006$.

13. The marginal probability of 'agreeing' with the attitude statement was 7 percentage points higher, and of 'strongly agreeing' 2 percentage points higher, for the employees in contracting workplaces relative to both those in static and those in growing workplaces; these differences were all significant at the 1% significance level. These marginal effects were computed holding other variables at their mean values.

14. Any such attempt would in any case have been questionable because the estimates would potentially be biased by the unobserved effects of personality on individualistic career attitude as well as on effort.

15. See Wood (1999), Edwards and Wright (2001), and Godard (2001) for critical discussions of the links between HRM and performance.

16. At a detailed level, this set of practices differs from those in Appelbaum et al. (2000), reflecting differences in management methods between the UK and the USA.

17. For similar approaches to defining strategic or intensive HRM or HPWS, and discussion of the underlying rationale, see Godard (2001), Forth and Millward (2004), and White et al. (2004).

18. The increase in development was significant at the 10% level ($p = 0.08$); the increases in communications, incentives, and teamworking were significant at the 1% level.

19. This difference was significant at the 1% level.

20. Comparisons when the marginal distributions are changing are most reliably made in terms of relative odds-ratios. In 1992, the relative odds of an employee in an expanding workplace participating in intensive HPWS was 1.52 times greater than that of an employee in a contracting workplace. By 2000, this relative odds-ratio had fallen to 1.32.

21. White et al. (2004: 140–2), using information from employers, show that HRM strategy is as likely to be found in workplaces practicing downsizing as in workplaces with no downsizing.

22. The analysis was also performed with the variable being participation in at least one component of strategic HPWS, rather than participation in at least three. This analysis, which compares these employees with all others not participating in any kind of systematic HPWS, produced virtually the same result as that reported here, except that the effect of HPWS on work strain was significant at the 5% level.

23. There was also little change in the estimated effects on effort for the other measures of insecure conditions; as they are less important, they have been omitted from Table 5.4 in the interests of simplicity.

24. In further variant analyses, the interaction term between workplace change in employment and the HPWS variable was added to the specification. The interaction between the variables was not significant.

25. $N = 294$ for the analysis of work demands and $N = 279$ for the analysis of work strain.
26. The t-statistic was 2.85, significant at the 1% level.
27. The t-statistic was 2.21, significant at the 5% level; the number of routine-class employees in the sample expecting to lose their jobs because of site closure or redundancy was 14.

6

Bureaucratic discipline and overwork

6.1. Introduction

Why do employees accept work demands that adversely affect the quality of their lives? Chapter 5 considered one possible answer: people work harder because they are afraid of losing their jobs while employers have adapted to uncertain conditions by turning towards short-term employment policies. The evidence suggested that employees did tend towards overwork when faced with insecure employment conditions, but there was little indication that employers were relying more on the external job market. Instead, there was a progressive diffusion of intensive HRM practices to foster higher levels of employee involvement and performance. While insecure conditions at the workplace were associated with employees' reports of higher effort, the same also occurred when systemic HRM practices were present. Moreover, the HRM practices were versatile: they extracted higher effort from employees both when workplaces were contracting and when they were expanding. This may partly explain why employer policy was increasingly moving in that direction rather than relying on external market discipline.

The present chapter turns to a second type of explanation of employees' compliance with the demands of overwork. This interpretation highlights the use of *internal systems of control and incentive* to achieve higher performance. According to this view, organizations wishing to shape employee behaviour rely not on the external market, which they cannot control, but on their own know-how in configuring checks and rewards. This is what Etzioni (1975) called 'remunerative power', and he saw it as the only means by which complex organizations with a 'commercial' type of aim could get employees to work in a coordinated fashion so as to produce dependable results. The embedding of this type of power into a systematic framework of impartial rules was part of Max Weber's concept of modern bureaucracy, and so the label used for it in this chapter is 'bureaucratic discipline'.

Section 6.2 considers the theoretical underpinnings of bureaucratic discipline. Two different theoretical strands, one concerned with controls and the other with incentives, indicate various ways in which employers can in principle extract more effort from employees while employees in return obtain financial (and sometimes non-financial) benefits. The two theoretical positions are considered in turn: it is argued, however, that controls and incentives are interdependent and that the two theories are complementary. Yet there is a key difference in perspective between the main theories, which concerns the role and nature of bargaining or contestation.

After this conceptual introduction, three sections of evidence follow:

- The first section of evidence describes how employers were developing control and incentive practices across the 1990s, with apparent implications for overwork. In part, this section is a more detailed account of some of the developments already sketched in Chapter 5. Additionally, the remarkable growth of ICT-based monitoring systems is highlighted.

- The second section examines whether employees gain in earnings when they take part in control and incentive systems. Although this is not directly concerned with overwork, it is crucial to the overall argument to test whether these systems produce compensation for effort in order to obtain employees' compliance.

- The third and final section of evidence looks directly at whether incentive and control systems, including ICT-based monitoring, affect employees' experience of work effort.

Differences between classes are examined throughout the empirical sections. The central issue is whether control and incentive systems are being developed in ways that lead to class convergence, or whether they further separate the managerial and professional classes from others. The final section of the chapter, after summarizing the findings, discusses implications of this new evidence about the salariat, and considers the emerging space of contestation around overwork.

6.2. The Bureaucratic Project: Control, Incentives, and Effort

6.2.1. *Starting with Weber*

Coupling 'bureaucracy' with 'work intensification', 'effort', or 'performance', may seem paradoxical or provocative. This is because in everyday English, the epithet 'bureaucratic' suggests a sclerotic, rule-bound, unenterprizing organization, probably a branch of government that demands little of its employees. In contrast, Weber[1] developed the idea of bureaucracy as an organization with a developed, hierarchical administrative function that reflected on and improved productive efficiency and operated under objective rules and procedures to select and advance the most qualified and capable individuals to higher office. Weber argued that this form of organization was the most efficient for the conduct of large-scale activity (including government, armed forces, and churches, as well as economic production), and indeed the only feasible method for integrating this kind of activity.

How, potentially, does the nature of modern bureaucratic organization offer an explanation of overwork? Although Weber did not expressly formulate this question, he emphasized that the underlying rationale of bureaucracy lay in its construction of authority, discipline, and control. Importantly, discipline and control applies throughout the organization, including those at very senior levels. Coupled with this is his identification of 'free selection' for all positions as essential for efficiency. Only in a free labour market with competition based on competence can innovation proceed.[2] So bureaucracy is not a closed system that can operate independently of the market, rather it is a system that obtains advantages from competitive markets but then exploits them through internalized systems. Especially, bureaucratic organizations provide careers with promotion based on achievement. These features, it can be inferred, give rise to a competitive striving among the bureaucratic organization's management to obtain increases in performance, whether through improved technical solutions or through greater effort on the part of subordinates in response to 'imperative coordination' from above.

6.2.2. *Control and Incentive: A False Contrast*

While Weber's theory of bureaucracy helps to explain the emergence of modern performance-orientated managements, it still leaves open the question of why employees comply with the demands of a bureaucratic system, other than because they are powerless to resist. One answer, present in the literatures of economics, management, and sociology (and most Weberian in flavour), emphasizes the crucial importance of control (or monitoring, the term more usual in economics) to ensure not only that employees work in accordance with their duties and the organization's aims but also to provide information and analyse and improve performance. Another, prominent in the economics and management literatures and to a lesser extent within sociology, stresses the central role of incentives in signalling to employees what is important for them to do, and in providing the motivation to increase effort in that direction.

What should be stressed at the outset, however, is that these two types of explanation are in practice inseparable.[3] They are two ways of looking at and talking about the same aspects of employer–employee relations. Incentive pay, for instance, cannot affect behaviour unless it is linked to behavioural criteria and to a method of monitoring and assessing that behaviour (Behrend 1957). Even at the simplest level, piecework payments can only be made if the pieces are counted. At the other extreme, appraisal systems in professional organizations often involve huge inputs of the time of highly paid staff in setting objectives and criteria, gathering and assessing information about individual performance, and conducting discussions (see Baron and Kreps 1999, Chapter 10). A general issue for the use of incentive pay is the costs of the monitoring that is needed in support, for the value of any incentive system to an employer is the added production it stimulates *minus* the monitoring cost. In practice, also, methods of control such as appraisal systems are interwoven with a variety of practices that give employees an interest in taking part: these include annual pay rise evaluations, career ladders, training budgets, the chance to influence targets and objectives, or even just the opportunity to talk about personal and work issues with senior colleagues. All these things have a value and a cost. In this broad sense, we postulate that in the long run (or in equilibrium) the behavioural differences made by controls are compensated: there are incentives for controls, as well as controls for incentives. Why else would employees accept controls unless they too benefited?[4]

6.2.3. A World of Control?

In his book *Contested Terrain* (1979), the radical economist Richard Edwards maintained that internal control was employers' means of solving their basic problem, which is continually to extract more actual effort from the labour contract (Edwards 1979: 12). Furthermore, Edwards used historical evidence and contemporary case studies to argue that controls are continually being expanded and created by employers, partly in their fundamental search for more effort and partly to divert conflict. If this theory of expanding controls remains valid now, it predicts the rising overwork that is currently observed, since intensified competition will give rise to increased development of effort-extracting controls by employers.

The development that Edwards perceived between the late nineteenth century and the modern period was from simple and personal forms of control, notably direct supervision, towards systematic, structured, and encompassing forms of control. He used the phrase 'bureaucratic control' to describe how employers, typically the large business corporations, had extended their power over performance to their supervisory, administrative, and professional cadres. As these groups of employees expanded greatly, it became imperative for employers to achieve control over them so as to focus their behaviour on corporate aims. The solution, bureaucratic control, was to create systems of individual progression including career ladders, grade structures, and personal evaluations or appraisals, with a range of rewards, benefits, and privileges conditional on service. These systems of progression offered inducements to conformity with the company's demands. Employers later applied bureaucratic control to production work as well. While Edwards stressed the role of bureaucratic control in avoiding conflict and weakening unions, it is easy to see it developing a stronger performance-related role as performance targets and objectives, especially those of a quantitative type, become more widespread.

Alongside bureaucratic control, technical control is particularly relevant to the issue of overwork in recent years. This is control structured by machine systems, and Edwards illustrates it mainly through the well-known story of the development of flowline manufacture and assembly.[5] However, in another prescient passage (Edwards 1979: 122–5), he points to the introduction of minicomputers, numerical control, and microelectronic devices, and indicates that these too are a development of technical control. Without much stretching, the recent development of ICT-based monitoring systems, that extend far beyond manufacturing in such areas as call centres and retail checkouts, can be fitted into the concept of technical control. Arguably, then, it is technical control, just as much as bureaucratic control, that provides the new developments. The advent of ICT-based monitoring also resonates within incentive theory, as it promises a profound reduction in monitoring costs, the importance of which has already been noted. The picture then is of a world that is filling up with controls.

6.2.4. *A World of Incentive?*

Incentives have not been a prominent topic in sociology within recent years, but have been a focus of great interest in economics. To provide a theoretical framework for discussion, building on the foundations of Chapter 1 (Sections 1.4–1.5), one can turn to the 'personnel economics' of Edward Lazear (1995, 1998). The central issue considered in personnel economics is how employers can make *incentivizing bargains* with their employees so as to extract effort and direct it to the organization's aims. Personnel economics assumes that work has 'disutility' for the individual, who will prefer 'shirking' (paid leisure) to working if all else is equal. Coupled with the assumption of a fully competitive labour market, in which employees can move freely between jobs, this produces an important conclusion: effort has to be bought. According to personnel economics, the world of employment is full of incentives. It has to be, or work would not happen.

Lazear's distinctive contribution has been to reveal that incentives lurk in many familiar personnel practices. Promotion systems, for instance, and the pay differentials between job levels are shown to be important sources of long-run incentive even for those not immediately in the running. Again, salary structures and pensions that downplay reward in early career, but over-reward long service, are shown to be efficient incentives especially when monitoring costs are high (Lazear 1981). This is because employees themselves produce additional effort to ensure that they stay around to collect their long-term rewards. Similarly, Edwards (1979: 151–2) flags rewards for seniority, coupled with below-productivity pay in early career, as a powerful element of bureaucratic control, and offers case study evidence of how this operates in practice. Additionally, the incentive efficacy of either promotion or deferred compensation can be magnified when connected to appraisals and other systematic processes of targeting and monitoring performance.

If the world of work is already full of incentives, how can it become more incentivized, yielding still more effort? Broadly speaking, by moving from weaker to stronger forms of incentives, since stronger incentives produce more effort, other things being equal. For instance, incentives based on measuring output generally produce more effort than those based on input (Lazear 1995: 19–23). But output incentives require a higher degree of measurement and so monitoring costs go up. In practice, it is often more profitable for the firm to use simple incentives, such as straight pay with the potential for increases, rather than payment-by-results requiring the support of complex measurement systems. If monitoring costs go up, incentives tend to shift to weaker types while if monitoring costs go down, the predicted shift is towards a larger proportion of employees becoming covered by stronger types of incentive.

Changes in monitoring costs lead to important predictions about the sources of overwork. Although flexibility in skills, in work tasks, and in work organization has been claimed to increase work intensity (Green 2006), clearly these developments make coordination and monitoring more costly and so tend in themselves to reduce the use of strong incentives. One way of overcoming this constraint is by offering incentives based on the total achievement of groups of individuals whose work is partially interchangeable. Although Lazear is sceptical about group incentives because of the formidable 'freerider' problem that they face (Lazear 1995: 47–8), he does not take account of the low-cost monitoring that the firm can acquire when members of a team 'supervise' one another (called 'concertive control' by Barker 1993; see also Baron and Kreps 1999: 262–3). The growth of group or team incentives is therefore to be expected so long as flexible work organization continues to expand.

Another route to lower-cost monitoring is through the use, already mentioned, of ICT monitoring systems. With the growth of computers connected into communication networks, monitoring can be increasingly automated, and applied at very low cost to the growing proportion of jobs that are 'online'. As Lazear notes (1995: 21), once an organization has collected information on performance, 'it always pays to use the information [for incentive purposes] in some way'.[6] Since information is generated as a virtually free by-product of computer-networked activities, it is to be expected that here too controls and incentives for employees will expand, with obvious implications for overwork.

6.2.5. *Control, Incentive, and Contestation*

Economic incentive theory and the radical theory of control evidently have much in common. They share the assumption, introduced by Marx, that effort is determined in the work situation and not in the labour contract. Although one side emphasizes incentives in extracting effort and the other side emphasizes controls, they both cross-refer: for instance, bureaucratic control depends on deferred compensation while all incentives depend on some system of monitoring. Most fundamentally, perhaps, they agree that the effort involved in market work has to be compensated.

There is nonetheless an important difference in emphasis or perspective. Incentive theory assumes that the financial arrangements between employer and employee fully compensate the disutility of effort, and the individual provides just so much effort as is paid for.[7] This is the best bargain that the two sides can make and there is no reason to depart from it, at least until circumstances change. In the radical theory of control, however, it is assumed that the interests of employees remain in conflict with those of employers, even when they fully comply with employers' demands under inducements. There is always an implicit resistance to the employer's solution. Somewhat similarly, Wilhelm Baldamus (1961) advanced the theory of the 'effort–reward bargain',[8] emphasizing that current arrangements are generally unsatisfactory to management as well as to employees because of the compromise involved. Management seeks to 'manipulate' the bargain, to gain an employer advantage, but they are continually opposed by workers, who try to pull the bargain in the opposite direction.[9] Bargaining, or contestation, is inherent to systems of incentive and control, and bargains generally leave unfinished business. Unlike in incentive theory, it is possible for effort and compensation to be out of step, as one side or the other gains the ascendancy.

6.3. The Changing Shape of Controls and Incentives

Theories of control and incentives offer possible explanations for the observed increase in overwork in contemporary Britain. This will depend, in the first place, on whether employers have actually been putting their faith in systems of control and incentive. It will also depend on how widely such systems are being applied, and perhaps also in what specific forms. An issue that is becoming increasingly important with the continued growth of the managerial and professional classes is whether principles of control and incentive can readily be applied to this group. Because managers and professionals perform such variable work, difficult to define let alone to monitor and incentivize, it has usually been assumed by sociologists that they have to be on the outside of control-incentive systems, working on a basis of discretion and trust, and rewarded only by salary and promotion (see the discussions in Chapters 1 and 3). If this is the case, then control-incentive systems might be in retreat rather than in expansion mode.

To address these initial questions, this section reviews what has been happening to the main components of control and incentives over recent years. In Chapter 5 (see Table 5.2), some evidence was already presented that suggests growth in certain types of incentive that are part of 'HPWS'. Here the evidence is considered over a more extensive range of control and incentive practices. If there has been a contraction in the overall use of control and incentives, or even if there has been no increase in their use, this would tell against the idea that they lie behind employees' acceptance of overwork. If on the other hand there has been an expansion, this is prima facie evidence that employers are modifying their internal policies to seek and support more effort.

6.3.1. *Appraisal Systems*

Appraisal systems have been at the centre of the 'reward management' or 'performance management' systems that became widespread in Britain in the 1980s (Incomes Data Services 1992; Smith 1992). Reward management and performance management, in their turn, formed the foundation of British HRM practice. Implemented in a great variety of ways, appraisal systems are essentially formalized procedures for making qualitative judgements or decisions about personnel. They can be used to communicate and agree objectives and targets, to obtain suggestions, to provide judgements of performance, to decide and plan training, to influence promotion, and to determine or adjust what pay increase an individual will get. From a control viewpoint, they ensure that employees know their managers' assessments of themselves and know also that these assessments make a difference. In principle, they also provide a means by which employees can individually transmit some influence upwards.

The basic question asked about participation in appraisals in the 1992 survey was, 'Does someone formally assess your job performance on a regular basis?' and this was followed by several questions that asked how appraisals were used. In the 2000 survey, by which time the term appraisal had come into general use, a slightly modified question was posed: 'Does someone formally assess or appraise your job performance on a regular basis?' In both surveys, the question emphasized formality, regularity, and a focus on performance. It did not however define appraisal in terms of the process or method used, since these are known to vary greatly in type and sophistication.

Already in 1992 the proportion of employees receiving formal performance appraisals had reached 53 per cent, an appreciable increase on 1986 (Gallie et al. 1998: 68). By 2000, this had increased further to 57 per cent. The proportions of employees who saw appraisals as directly influencing pay increases (one in five of all employees) remained approximately the same in 1992 and 2000. However, there are several indirect ways in which appraisal can influence pay and advancement, and it is these as much as direct use for determining pay increases that give it an incentive character. One in three employees saw appraisal as influencing promotion decisions, a figure that was unchanged across the 1990s. Meanwhile, there was a marked increase in the use of appraisals to plan training and development, from 33 to 44 per cent of all employees, presumably reflecting a growing human resource development orientation in Britain. Through improved access to training, employees could indirectly expect to improve their earnings or promotion prospects. Also, nearly four in ten employees reported in 2000 (the question not being asked in 1992) that appraisals were used to set or revise their targets or objectives. Overall, then, the tendency was towards a greater density of appraisal, in the sense that appraisals were being used to do several things at the same time, all of which would impact on the individual's prospects and provide reasons for the individual to increase her or his work effort.

6.3.2. Appraisals and Class

The overall figures for growth in appraisals conceal wide variations between classes, which are shown in Table 6.1. Appraisals were originally an instrument of white-collar control and there continued to be marked differences by class according to the 1992 survey, but with a notable diffusion into manual occupations. Between 1992 and 2000, there was

Table 6.1. Participation in performance appraisals by class, 1992 and 2000

	1992 (%)	2000 (%)
Higher professional/managerial	71.6	76.8
Lower professional/managerial	54.7	68.3
Intermediate administrative etc.	57.2	64.7
Lower supervisory/technical	47.3	46.9
Semi-routine	42.5	49.5
Routine	41.9	32.6
N	3,458	2,132

Sources: 1992—EiB; 2000—WiB.

a further intensification of appraisals in the administrative, technical, managerial, and professional classes, and especially among associate professionals and managers where the proportion of appraisees rose from 55 to 68 per cent; the increase for higher-level managers and professionals was from 72 to 77 per cent. Across the semi-routine and routine occupational classes, however, there was an overall halt to the development, with the proportion of appraisees static at 42 per cent. This masked a sharp divergence between semi-routine and routine occupations, the former increasing their proportion (by seven percentage points) while the latter's fell (by nine percentage points). This is part of a wider tendency to exclude employees in the routine class from intensive HRM practices, as discussed in Chapter 5.

6.3.3. *Performance Incentive Pay*

Performance incentive pay refers to any variable pay that depends on a measurement of performance; it is distinct, therefore, from more general incentives such as promotion or seniority pay. To assess the use of 'individual incentives', for instance, the two surveys asked about receipt of 'any incentive payment, bonus, or commission based on your own performance'. Similar questions asked about payments based on team or group performance, and about payments based on the results achieved by the organization or the workplace. Additional questions asked specifically about pay rises being given to 'those workers who work hard and perform well' and about the existence of a 'profit-sharing scheme, employee share scheme, or share option scheme'. Together these cover most, though probably not all, varieties of 'performance incentive pay' commonly recognized. Table 6.2 shows what proportions of employees received the various kinds of incentive pay in each year.

The surveys reveal increases over the 1990s in the receipt of performance incentive payment based on individual, group, and workplace (or organizational) performance. The sharpest increase was in the use of group incentive pay, from a low base of one in twenty workers in 1992 up to one in six in 2000. This fits predictions, made earlier in the chapter, based on the growth of team-based work organization to achieve flexibility, coupled with the low cost of peer supervision. Although the use of workplace or organizational incentives increased, they grew less than individual or group incentives; also, profit-sharing or share schemes remained static. These latter findings are of incidental interest, as they cast doubt on the idea, noted in several previous chapters, that employers have

Table 6.2. Employee receipt of incentive pay, 1992 and 2000

Percentage of employees receiving	1992 (%)	2000 (%)	Significance of difference between years
Pay increase based on performance	38	37	
Individual incentive/bonus	15	22	**
Group incentive/bonus	5	17	**
Workplace incentive/bonus	21	25	*
Profit sharing or share scheme	16	15	
Any 1+ of above	53	54	
Any 2+ of above	25	31	**
Any 3+ of above	12	18	**
N	3,458	2,132	

Note: * significant at the 5% significance level; ** significant at the 1% significance level.
Sources: 1992—EiB; 2000—WiB.

been pushing business risk on employees. If that were the case, business-related incentives should be growing strongly.

Despite the increases in particular kinds of performance incentives, overall the same proportion of employees in both 1992 and 2000—a little less than one-half of the total—received *none* of the incentive pay elements. The increases in performance incentives took the form of multi-incentives, where the same employee's pay depends on more than one kind of performance (Table 6.2, lower panel). For instance, the proportion receiving three or more of the performance incentives rose from 12 to 18 per cent. The contrast in practice between non-incentive regimes and performance incentive regimes was therefore deepening.

6.3.4. Incentives and Class

The growth of multi-incentives has a marked class dimension. Whereas the growth of incentives across all employees was modest, in the upper reaches it was remarkably rapid. The proportion of higher professionals and managers getting three or more types of incentive pay more than doubled between 1992 and 2000 (from 17 to 37%), and it nearly doubled for the associate professional-managerial group (from 14 to 25%). For the routine-level occupations, on the other hand, the proportion actually fell (from 10 to 6%), and for the semi-routine (more skilled) it rose only slightly (from 7 to 10%).[10] These class differences were less marked if only one or two types of incentive are considered, but the routine-level occupations experienced a decline in incentive pay receipt whatever the criterion. Conversely, by 2000 it was the higher professionals

Table 6.3. Receipt of group incentive pay by class, 1992 and 2000

	1992 (cell %)	2000 (cell %)
Higher professional/managerial	5.1	27.5
Lower professional/managerial	5.0	21.2
Intermediate administrative etc.	3.5	13.2
Lower supervisory/technical	7.6	18.1
Semi-routine	4.6	14.2
Routine	9.0	8.7

Sources: 1992—EiB; 2000—WiB.

and managers who emerged as the most incentivized. Three in four of them received some form of incentive pay, and for 39 per cent this was an individual incentive payment (rising from only 17% in 1992). There was also a doubling of individual incentives for lower professionals and managers (from 14 to 28%). In the intermediate administrative, supervisory, and technician group, there was a slight increase in participation in individual incentives (from 16 to 19%). In the semi-routine and routine group, participation overall in individual incentives remained static at 15 per cent, although there was an upward shift for employees in the semi-routine class and a downward shift for employees in the routine class.

In view of the rapid rise of group- or team-based incentive pay, which reflects the growth of team-based work organization, it is also interesting to see how this was disposed across the classes. All classes except routine occupations were involved in the increase, but once again the greatest increase was for the highest occupations, where the use of group incentives increased more than fivefold. The findings are shown in Table 6.3.

6.3.5. *The Value of Promotion*

As the earlier discussion of incentive theory made clear, many aspects of traditional personnel practice, besides what are commonly known as incentive schemes, have an incentive interpretation. Indeed, promotions and deferred compensation are the most widely available of incentives, in the broader sense. Already in Chapter 2, it was shown that career and promotion opportunities remained widespread and if anything had been growing, not contracting, in Britain during recent years. A further perspective can now be added.

Employees in the 2000 survey were asked specifically for their views about the 'financial rewards for getting promoted' over the past five years.

The most common opinion, held by about one-half of employees, was that they had not changed, but those believing that the rewards had increased outnumbered those thinking they had decreased by more than two to one.[11] On balance, then, the perceived financial incentive of promotion had strengthened. Moreover, this applied fairly evenly across classes, although the associate managerial and professional class had a particularly positive view of the issue. The perception of employees, including those in the non-managerial and non-professional class positions, appears well-informed, since in Chapter 3 it was shown that the differences in material rewards between the classes was in fact growing, so that promotion was becoming more valuable. The enhanced prizes in the promotion 'tournament' provide another possible reason for employees' overwork.

6.3.6. *The Advent of ICT-Based Monitoring*

The general picture so far is of steady extension of incentive and control. Yet this on its own would constitute a gross understatement of the current position. For largely new methods of performance monitoring entered the scene during the 1990s: those based on continuous recording through ICT. This arises for employees connected to electronic point-of-sales (EPOS) systems at retail checkouts, for call centre operators on computer-controlled switchboards, for clerical staff updating online computer databases, and (potentially at least) for all kinds of staff, including professionals and managers, who use networked computing services including e-mails, intranets, and the Internet. ICT-based monitoring is also used to track the progress of goods (most of which now have electronically readable identifying codes) in a diversity of manufacturing, warehousing, and transport applications. In all these cases, computers are capable of recording and timing units of activity at an extremely detailed level, such as the item, the telephone call, or the keystroke. Once the activity of individuals or the progress of materials and goods has been connected to a computer system, it can be used to record events or progress to any degree of detail desired by management, and performance analysis of various kinds can then be generated. ICT monitoring can also be applied to detect infractions of rules, such as telephone calls to unauthorized numbers, or forbidden use of the Internet.

Precisely to quantify the growth of this kind of monitoring is impossible because the early stages of the development remain vague and unrecorded. No questions relating to the topic were contained in the

---

Box 6.1. QUESTIONS ABOUT ICT-BASED MONITORING

These questions were asked in the 2000 survey (WiB) within a module covering uses of ICT in the employee's job.

'Does a computerized system keep a log or record of work you are doing?' (Yes, No, Do not know)

If answer is 'Yes': 'Is the information recorded on that system actually used to check how you are performing in your work?' (Yes, No, Do not know)

These questions define three levels of ICT-based monitoring: no monitoring, recording only, and individual performance checking.

1992 survey, nor so far as we are aware were any other national data collected at around that time. It seems reasonable to suppose, however, that ICT-based monitoring was at a low level in 1992, although certainly present on some manufacturing assembly lines. The 2000 survey appears to be the first to collect national data on some of the main developments, and this was developed further in the employer CEPS 2002. Even so, the available information is broad-brush (see Box 6.1) and a detailed study of the various types of ICT-based monitoring remains to be done.

Yet the available information is remarkable enough.

- By 2000, one-half of all employees (52%) reported that a computerized system kept a log or record of work they were doing.[12]
- Nearly one quarter of all employees (23%) stated that the information recorded was actually used to check their performance in their work.

In case employees' responses might be thought to include an element of misinformation or of paranoia, one can also look at evidence from the employer CEPS 2002. In that, managers were asked whether 'a computer system or automatic data recording system keeps a continuous record of the work being done by any employees', and to estimate what proportion of employees was included. One-half of employers said that they were operating such a system, with about 30 per cent of all employees covered (White et al. 2004: 90). The two surveys therefore lead to a roughly similar picture, and it is certainly one of an extensive new form of monitoring being put in place. At one in five workplaces, management claims to have all employees covered by an ICT-based monitoring system. The 2002 employer survey also shows that ICT-based monitoring was most often encountered in larger workplaces (except in the public sector) and in growing workplaces; these are further indications that the use of this technology is likely to continue spreading (White et al. 2004: 86–93).

ICT-based monitoring is new and little investigated so far apart from call centres, which are unlikely to be typical. The strength or the intensity of monitoring, and the behavioural control based on it, probably vary greatly, even after excluding the many cases where records are not being converted into performance checks. However, further details from the 2002 employer survey indicate that in most workplaces, reports generated by the recording system are seen by management, in one-third of cases feedback is provided to employees, and the majority of managers consider that use of the information in training will be an important application. The major purpose of the systems is reported to be the monitoring of progress, while one in five employers uses the information directly for individual performance evaluation (White et al. 2004: 91–99). Overall, it seems that ICT-based monitoring is a development with serious substance.

6.3.7. *ICT Monitoring and Class*

Currently, the proportion of employees actually having their performance checked through ICT-based monitoring is rather even across the classes: 22 per cent for managerial and professional (including associate level), 27 per cent for supervisory and technician, and 21 per cent for semi-routine and routine. This contrasts with the picture for appraisal, where the class gradient is steep. But perhaps what is surprising is that the proportions in the classes other than semi-routine and routine are reported to be so high. ICT-based monitoring can be seen as an extension of technical control (Edwards 1979), which developed primarily for manual employees. However, employers have a tendency to extend each type of control across boundaries (Edwards 1979), and here they have the versatility of ICT to make that possible. That said, the type of ICT monitoring may be very different across classes because of the different kinds of work they perform.

ICT-based monitoring of employees' work has considerable implications for incentives, including but not confined to performance incentive pay. Because monitoring is less costly, incentives can be extended and (in principle) employers can afford to pay more for performance. There is some case study evidence that call centre employees see improved chances of rapid promotion because the best performers stand out (Belt 2002). Whether the new technology of control actually generates any increases in earnings, is one of the issues for the next section.

6.4. Paying for Effort

Section 6.3 has shown how controls, incentives, and methods of monitoring expanded and grew denser in Britain over the course of a decade, providing the potential for employers to extract additional effort with employees' compliance. One can reasonably infer, from this picture, that employers have been intending to exact more effort from employees. But whether this will actually happen depends on whether employees comply as well as on the efficacy of the systems put in place by employers.

Theories of control and incentive within bureaucracies provide a plausible explanation of why employees might accept increasing demands for effort and so shift towards overwork. Employers have the power to extract effort by paying for it, and it is control that expresses power and links effort and reward. Ultimately, what needs to be shown is whether controls and incentives have actually had the result of increasing effort. But it is also important, as a step towards understanding overwork, to gauge the magnitude of the financial returns to employees who take part in systems of incentive and control, for that supposedly provides the mechanism by which overwork becomes accepted.

6.4.1. *Appraisals, Individual Incentives, and Earnings*

The focus, then, is on assessing how much employees gain when they take part in various kinds of control system or incentive practice. As it is not technically feasible to analyse every kind of control and incentive together, the method will be illustrative rather than comprehensive.[13] One prong of the analysis examines the consequences of personal performance appraisal, the most widely used method of control, and one that potentially links employees to many kinds of rewards. The other main prong of the analysis is performance incentive pay. This is divided into two groups: regimes that include individual incentives, with or without the addition of group and/or workplace incentives, and group and/or workplace incentive regimes that make no use of individual incentives. The essential difference in the incentive regimes to be analysed, then, is whether individual incentives are present, or not. This focus on individual incentives is because they have usually been regarded as the strongest, and of course have played a large part in the history of workplace control (Friedmann 1954; Lupton 1972; Hirschhorn 1984). Employees participating in either individual or 'other' incentive regimes are compared with those having no participation in performance incentive pay.

The nature of the pay outcome in this analysis could easily be misunderstood, and so needs some emphasis. The analysis is *not* designed to show the size of the salary increase that follows an appraisal, nor the proportion of earnings coming from performance incentives.

Box 6.2. ANALYZING THE INFLUENCES ON EARNINGS AND EFFORT

Figure 6.1 and Tables 6.4–6.8 present findings from the analyses in a selective way. They estimate the effects of certain aspects of incentives and control that play an important role in the theoretical exposition of the chapter. In producing these estimates, the analyses also take account of external influences that are likely to influence the incentive or control variables, and the outcome measures (earnings or effort).

For the analyses of earnings, the control variables were as follows: gender, age, age-squared, socio-economic class, highest qualification, use of IT in job, hours, hours-squared, temporary contract, previous part-time contract, size of workplace, industry, union presence, and region. The dependent variable in the analyses was the natural logarithm of gross weekly earnings. A measure of earnings was used, rather than the more customary hourly wage measure, because hours worked are both a determinant of pay and a component of effort. The inclusion of hours among the control variables makes the estimates roughly comparable with those from models of wages. The estimation method is OLS regression. The estimated effects for (say) appraisal represent the percentage by which earnings are changed for an individual participating in appraisals, compared with not participating. The class-specific models of earnings included the same control variables, except class.

The analyses of work demands, work strain, and hours had the same control variables as in the analyses of earnings with the exception of hours and region. For work strain, the dependent variable was the natural logarithm of the work strain index, which was treated as quasi-continuous. The estimation method was OLS regression, and the estimated effects for (say) appraisal represent the percentage by which work strain is changed for an individual participating in appraisals, compared with not participating. For hours, the dependent variable was the hours actually worked (including paid or unpaid overtime) in the most recent pay-period, converted where necessary to a weekly figure. The estimation method was again OLS regression, and the estimated effects are changes in hours worked.

For the analyses of work demands the dependent variable was binary (see also Box 5.2 in Chapter 5), and the estimation method was logistic regression analysis. Unlike OLS regression, in logistic regression the estimated effects vary across individuals with different values on the other control variables. The percentages shown in the relevant tables are marginal effects on probabilities, calculated at the mean values of the control variables. For example, the estimated marginal effect for appraisal represents the change in probability of experiencing 'high' work demands for the 'average' individual when participating in appraisals, compared with that 'average' individual when not participating.

The class-specific models of effort included the same control variables, except class and industry.

Such measures, although of interest in their own right, would say nothing about the net gain for employees: employers might use such incentives in tandem with a below-market or an above-market level of basic pay.[14] Instead, we estimate the size of the gain in total earnings when the employee takes part in appraisal systems and/or individual performance incentives by comparison with not taking part (see Box 6.2 for further details of the analysis method).

The results, depicted in Figure 6.1, show that both appraisals and individual incentive regimes can make a tangible and far-from-trivial difference to total pay. Furthermore, 'other' incentive regimes (based on group or workplace performance) contributed substantially to overall earnings. So all the forms of control or incentive included in the analysis produced gains for employees.[15]

There is, however, an important difference between the results over time. Appraisal and performance incentive pay both contributed significantly to earnings in 1992.[16] If an individual participated in *both*, she or he could expect on average increased earnings of about 15 per cent. The results for 2000 were strikingly different from 1992 in one respect. The average gain from participating in appraisal systems fell sharply to a little under 2 per cent of earnings, a figure that was not statistically distinct from zero. This change did *not* apply to performance incentives. Individual performance incentive regimes remained steady, and although

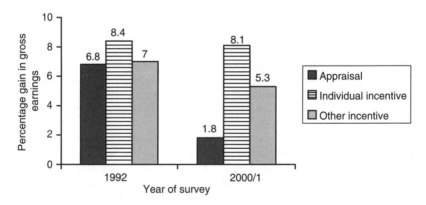

Figure 6.1. Estimated gains in earnings from appraisals and incentives.

Note: See text for explanation of 'Individual incentive' and 'Other incentive', which are mutually exclusive. The estimates are derived from analyses described in Box 6.2. The estimated effects are statistically significant at least at the 5 per cent level, except for Appraisal in 2000, which is not significant at the 10 per cent level.

Sources: 1992—EiB; 2000—WiB.

other (group/workplace) incentive regimes appeared to fall a little in their effect, statistically speaking there was no reliable difference between the two years.

Why did the rewards to participants in appraisal systems fall at a time when business profitability was rising very strongly?[17] A possible interpretation is that during the 1990s British employers began to feel that appraisals had become too costly. Nationally, the amount of additional earnings resulting from appraisals in 1992 was greater than from individual incentive pay because a larger proportion of employees took part in them, especially in the higher-paid managerial and professional classes. (According to these estimates, additional earnings from appraisals amounted nationally to about £16bn in 1992.) In addition, while performance incentive pay is a variable addition calculated periodically (it can disappear when performance declines), the result of appraisal is usually an addition that is consolidated into the basic wage or salary. One might also surmise that appraisals were under continuous and increasing pressure as individuals developed bargaining tactics with their own managers and as more elaborate superstructures, such as appeals procedures, also developed. The difficulty of operating an effective and stable appraisal system is discussed at length by Baron and Kreps (1999: Chapter 10).

6.4.2. Class Contrasts in Incentive Pay?

If employers were deliberately reining back the cost of appraisals, it then becomes much easier to see why multilayered incentive pay was being developed during the 1990s, and why this incentive development was particularly being aimed at the higher occupational groups that have participated to the greatest extent in appraisal systems. This broaches the issue of class differences in the returns from appraisals and from incentive pay. Because of sample size limitations in the surveys, it was impractical to mount a separate analysis for each class, but a useful picture can be obtained by grouping the classes in three: higher and lower managers and professionals form the first, intermediate administrative along with technical and lower supervisory form the second, and the semi-routine and routine classes form the third. These groups are sometimes referred to as (respectively) the higher, intermediate, and lower occupational classes. The key results for the three groupings can be seen in Table 6.4.

All these class groupings followed the overall pattern in terms of how appraisals affected earnings. In 1992, they all gained to about the same

Table 6.4. Class analysis of appraisals, individual incentive pay, and earnings, 1992 and 2000

	Estimated effects on gross weekly earnings	
	1992	2000
Professional/managerial		
Appraisal	6.8%*	4.3%
Individual incentive pay	10.4%**	9.1%*
Other incentive pay	10.2%**	10.0%+
N	848	621
Administrative and technical/supervisory		
Appraisal	5.8%*	4.3%
Individual incentive pay	2.8%	4.9%
Other incentive pay	4.4%	−2.2%
N	766	598
Semi-routine and routine		
Appraisal	5.5%*	−2.4%
Individual incentive pay	11.8%**	17.0%**
Other incentive pay	11.3%*	9.2%+
N	897	580

Significance: + 10% level; * 5% level; ** 1% level (other estimates are not significant at the 10% level). See Box 6.2 for details of analyses and control variables.

Notes: 'Individual incentive pay' and 'other incentive pay' are mutually exclusive, and are compared with 'no incentive pay' (see text).

Sources: 1992—EiB; 2000—WiB.

extent from appraisal, and by 2000 these gains had largely disappeared for all alike. Where the class groups differed was in the effects of incentive regimes:

- The group in semi-routine and routine occupations did gain substantially from incentives.

- The intermediate group did not gain appreciably from incentives in either year.

- More surprisingly, the group in managerial and professional occupations gained from incentive pay to a similar extent, broadly speaking, as did the semi-routine and routine occupations.

What interpretation of employer policy can be read into these findings? For managers and professionals, at least, the policy thrust seems clear. While the financial value of appraisals was run down, the value of all kinds of performance-related incentives held steady even while many more managers and professionals became entitled to them. On balance, the incentivization of managers and professionals was clearly being extended. For semi-routine and routine-level employees, the financial value of performance-related incentives was also maintained, and in the case of individual incentive regimes increased somewhat, but against this there was no expansion in entitlement. The declining role of appraisals as an incentive also has to be considered: these covered more than twice the proportion of employees in these classes as participated in individual incentives. The net effect is a roughly static situation, with increased returns from individual incentive regimes offset by falling returns from appraisals. Finally, for employees at intermediate levels—administrative, clerical, supervisory, and technicians—earnings gains from appraisal were run down, as with other groups, and across both years there was little financial value in their performance incentives. The necessary conclusion is that incentivization has fallen for this group. Overall, then, it was only with managers and professionals that a clear overall increase in financial reward tied to control and incentives could be discerned.

However, one potentially important change has so far been left out of the account. That is the introduction of ICT-based monitoring, which is likely to be especially salient for the intermediate group of employees that contains many computer-using clerical or call centre staff.

6.4.3. ICT-Based Monitoring and Earnings

As shown earlier in the chapter, ICT-based monitoring was entering the scene rapidly at the end of the 1990s, with potential gains for employers in terms of lower system costs and greater efficiency. However, it appears that any such gain was not shared with employees. In an alternative analysis for the 2000 survey, incorporating measures of ICT-based monitoring (see Box 6.1), the estimates of its effects were always statistically non-significant. Accordingly, the efficacy of ICT-based monitoring in generating more effort might be doubted: surely employees would not increase their effort for no reward? But if time lags in bargaining are brought into the picture, a different interpretation is possible. As a very new addition to employers' methods of exerting control over performance, it is possible that employees had not yet begun to press for compensating rewards. This might provide a further explanation of why employers were able to rein back the rewards dealt out by their appraisal systems: they could see other less costly ways of proceeding. However, to support this intuition one must be able to show independently that ICT-based monitoring systems are in truth extracting effort.

6.5. Controls, Incentives, and Overwork

The previous section has established that employees who submit to certain widely used control and incentive practices usually gain financially. This provides them with a reason for increasing their work effort. The final stage in the analysis is to examine whether these same control and incentive practices actually do extract more effort from participants, so contributing to the growth of overwork, and whether systemic differences in financial gain correspond to systemic differences in effort.

The analysis uses the same two measures of effort, or work intensity, that were described in Chapter 5 (in Box 5.1). As before, the measures are referred to as *work demands* and *work strain*, and each is used as the dependent variable in separate analyses. (Recall that work demands represents the more positively toned or bright side of effort while work strain represents its negatively toned or dark side.) In addition, however, a third measure of effort is introduced: the actual hours worked by the employee. There are two main reasons for considering it here.[18] First of all, long hours are widely perceived as a special problem in Britain, and are commonly viewed as part of an overwork syndrome. Second, for jobs where the level of work intensity is hard to measure or assess, such as many professional jobs, hours worked may well be used as a proxy for effort, both by the employer in judging the individual's performance, and by the employee in signalling her contribution to the employer. It might however be supposed that the effect of working hours is transmitted through the measure of work strain, and so a separate analysis of hours is superfluous. In fact, the correlation between hours and work strain in 2000 was 0.22, so that they have only 5 per cent common variance or 'overlap'. By including hours among the outcomes to be analysed, a fuller picture of effort should be obtained.

Otherwise, the analyses are constructed in much the same way as for earnings. They estimate how much difference it makes to work demands, to work strain, or to weekly hours worked, if an employee takes part in an appraisal system or in an individual performance incentive regime. Additionally, with the data for 2000 we also look at the effect when ICT-based monitoring is brought into the reckoning. The set of results concerning work demands is summarized in Table 6.5. The parallel analysis for work strain is in Table 6.6 and for hours worked in Table 6.7.

The effects on work demands were fairly complex and need careful unpacking.

Table 6.5. Controls, incentives, and 'work demands', 1992 and 2000

	Estimated effects on work demands (% probability of high demands)	
	1992	2000
Appraisal	5.2%*	5.3%*
Individual incentive	8.2%**	4.7%
Other incentive	2.8%	3.0%
ICT recording only		1.1%
ICT performance checks		0.3%
N	3,123	2,101

Significance: * 5% level; ** 1% level (other estimates are not significant at the 10% level). See Box 6.2 for details of analyses and control variables.

Sources: 1992—EiB; 2000—WiB.

Table 6.6. Controls, incentives, and 'work strain', 1992 and 2000

	Estimated effects on work strain	
	1992	2000
Appraisal	5.6%**	2.6%
Individual incentive	2.3%	1.6%
Other incentive	2.7%	2.0%
ICT recording only		3.3%†
ICT performance checks		7.5%**
N	3,016	2,016

Significance: † 10% level; * 5% level; ** 1% level (other estimates are not significant at the 10% level). See Box 6.2 for details of analyses and control variables.

Sources: 1992—EiB; 2000—WiB.

Table 6.7. Controls, incentives, and hours worked, 1992 and 2000

	Estimated effects (additional hours/week)	
	1992	2000
Appraisal	0.57	0.05
Individual incentive	2.72**	2.23**
Other incentive	1.26*	0.39
ICT recording only		1.47*
ICT performance checks		1.60*
N	2,884	1,947

Significance: * 5% level; ** 1% level (other estimates are not significant at the 10% level). See Box 6.2 for details of analyses and control variables.

Sources: 1992—EiB; 2000—WiB.

- Both appraisals and individual performance incentive regimes raised individuals' work demands.
- 'Other' incentives—those that lacked an individual performance element—*did not* raise work demands to a significant degree. ICT-based control also made no difference to work demands, when it was included in the analysis for 2000.
- Looking across years, one finds that the effect of appraisal was about the same in both years, which is somewhat surprising in view of the falling financial value of appraisals that was revealed in the previous section. The effect of individual incentive regimes was conversely larger in 1992 than in 2000, despite financial gain from individual incentives in both years. The effect was statistically significant only at the earlier time, although the difference between years was itself also not significant.[19]

The picture for work strain was different, and again quite complex.

- Appraisals start off in 1992 with rather a strong effect on work strain, but this declines in 2000, in line with the falling earnings premium for those in appraisal systems.
- Performance incentives—whether individual or 'other'—*did not* have a well-defined effect on work strain in either year.
- The major new influence on work strain in 2000 is the advent of ICT-based monitoring. Even when the employee feels it is only used for recording purposes, not for checking her own performance, there are signs of work strain increasing.[20] The increase in work strain becomes marked when ICT control is used to check individual performance. *An addition of nearly 8 per cent to work strain* is then estimated.

Finally, the picture for hours worked was again different.

- Appraisal systems had no effect on hours worked.
- Individual incentive regimes were associated with longer hours in both years—between two and three hours per week, on average.
- 'Other' incentive regimes had a smaller but significant effect on longer hours in 1992, but this disappeared in 2000.
- Working under an ICT-monitoring system increased hours by about 1.5 hours in 2000. It made little difference whether the system was seen as merely for recording purposes or as a direct check on individual performance.

Overall, appraisals were associated persistently with work demands, but with work strain only in 1992. Incentive regimes that included an individual component were also associated with work demands, and also with long hours; these effects were reasonably persistent across years. 'Other' incentive regimes affected only hours worked in 1992, and nothing at all in 2000. ICT monitoring, entering the scene in 2000, had a strong effect on work strain and a moderate effect on longer hours.

Controls and incentives generally increased effort, in at least some respect, although incentive regimes that lacked an individual component were of marginal relevance for effort. (Employers may have other purposes in mind with these, such as fostering cooperation.) But the effects of controls and incentives did not always closely correspond to their effects on earnings. Most conspicuously, ICT monitoring increased both work strain and hours worked even though it made no contribution to earnings. Before coming to overall conclusions, however, it is useful to look at some results when class-groups are viewed separately.

6.5.1. *Class Differences in the Effects of ICT-Based Monitoring on Work Strain*

To make the presentation manageable, classes are condensed into three groups as before, and only the results for 2000 are shown (Table 6.8). Also in the interests of simplicity, the results for 'other' incentive regimes (those without an individual component) are omitted from the table: there were no significant and positive findings for this either in 1992 or in 2000. The initial purpose of this analysis is to see how the overall results for 2000 are built up from the class-specific results.[21]

Starting with appraisal, one can see from Table 6.8 that the effect on work demands (significant across the whole sample) was fairly evenly spread across the class-groups. Although the effect was not significant in any of these sub-samples, one can attribute this to reduced sample size and conclude that for all classes alike, appraisals probably have the effect of increasing work demands.

In the case of individual incentive regimes, there is one particularly simple finding visible in Table 6.8. These are associated with significantly longer hours for every class-group, and the size of the effect is rather similar, around 2.5–3.0 hours per week.

The table also casts further light on the impact of ICT-based monitoring on work strain and on weekly hours worked. For employees in semi-routine and routine occupations, ICT-based monitoring increased

Table 6.8. Class, controls, incentives, and effort, 2000

	Work demands Probability (%)	Work strain %	Hours
Professional/managerial			
Appraisal	4.5	0.0	1.35
Individual incentive	−3.9	−0.0	2.47*
ICT recording only	−7.1	−0.2	0.41
ICT performance checks	−4.3	0.3	0.93
N	754	724	700
Intermediate/supervisory/technician			
Appraisal	5.5	0.1	−0.37
Individual incentive	7.7	6.5	2.52**
ICT recording only	4.6	4.4	0.53
ICT performance checks	2.3	10.2**	0.75
N	685	660	647
Semi-routine/routine			
Appraisal	4.1	4.2	−1.5†
Individual incentive	4.2	−0.1	2.89*
ICT recording only	5.5	8.5*	3.75**
ICT performance checks	2.4	8.1	2.36*
N	662	632	600

Significance (see text for interpretation): †10% level; * 5% level; ** 1% level (other estimates are not significant at the 10% level). See Box 6.2 for details of analyses and control variables.

Sources: 1992—EiB; 2000—WiB.

work strain by around 8 per cent: it made no difference whether the employee thought of this merely as a recording system or as a means of checking her own performance.[22] For employees in the intermediate-level administrative, technical, and lower supervisory occupations, there was no clear effect if ICT-based monitoring was only a recording system, but there was a marked effect on work strain, of 10 per cent, if it was used for personal performance checking.[23] For employees in the professional and managerial occupations, ICT-based monitoring had no effect on work strain. Finally, the effects of ICT-based monitoring on weekly hours were mainly concentrated among the lower class-group consisting of semi-routine and routine occupations. Although the effects were in the same direction for the higher and intermediate class-groups, they were considerably smaller and statistically non-significant.

By comparing the results shown in Table 6.8 with corresponding results for 1992 (for which the table is not shown), one conspicuous change over the period can also be expressed in class-specific terms:

the reduced effect of appraisals on work strain was concentrated in the higher and intermediate class-groups. In 1992, participating in appraisals raised work strain for managers and professionals by 5.8 per cent and for intermediate administrative, supervisory, and technician occupations by 5.5 per cent: these effects were significant,[24] and had disappeared by 2000.

Overall, both appraisals and individual incentive regimes had effects on effort that were rather similar across class-groups, but the effects of ICT-based monitoring were concentrated on employees below the professional/managerial level. A reasonable supposition about this difference is that the monitoring is being applied to quite different kinds of task. For employees in managerial and professional jobs, ICT-based monitoring possibly applies only to minor aspects of their work, such as monitoring e-mail usage. For employees at lower levels, ICT-based monitoring can be applied to much of the daily work: examples are flowline assembly operators, call centre operators, database clerks, or retail checkout staff. In cases like these, naturally, the pressure exerted by this kind of monitoring technology, and by the control systems that they serve, is much greater.

6.5.2. *An Overview of Pay and Overwork*

One can now look across the whole set of results concerning controls and incentive regimes, taking account of their effects on financial value as well as on work demands and work strain. The most general point to make is that all the incentives and controls have some effects on employees' finances and/or on one or more of the three facets of effort. But these effects can change over time, and sometimes there is a marked misalignment between an incentive/control element's effect on effort and its corresponding effect on earnings. The complications increase because the three aspects of effort that have been considered in the analysis (work demands, work strain, and hours) respond somewhat differently to controls and incentives of different types.

Change over time, misalignment, and varying relationships to the types of effort are all exhibited in the case of appraisal systems and their effects. Taking part in appraisals initially yielded substantial gains in earnings for employees, but later these financial gains fell away. Corresponding to this fall in financial value, the link between appraisal and work strain was initially strong but then weakened. On the other hand, appraisals went on influencing employees' feeling of working under high work demands, even when its reward-value declined. As discussed earlier in the chapter, appraisal systems may offer employees a variety of non-financial gains, such as increased opportunities for communication and involvement, and it is possible that these gains were sufficient to motivate positively toned work effort.

The clearest case of a disjunction between reward and effort was that of ICT-based monitoring. It produced much the greatest effects on work strain in 2000, and was also associated with longer work hours, but at that time it was producing no financial gains for the employees it affected. This disjunction might in part come about because the monitoring technology had been introduced very recently; there might be a time lag in adjusting reward to the additional effort extracted through control systems using the technology. Another relevant factor may be the overlap of ICT monitoring with personal use of ICT in the employee's job. Being an ICT user did raise earnings in 2000, after controlling for numerous personal, job, and workplace characteristics; this has of course been found in numerous other studies, though the genuineness of the effect remains a controversial issue. If employees who use ICT *feel* that they are better-paid than the average, they may thereby *feel* that they are being compensated for the increased pressures resulting from ICT monitoring, and this will reduce bargaining pressure. Statistically speaking, this feeling on the part of employees, if it exists, is erroneous. Many of the employees under ICT monitoring are not themselves active users of ICT in their jobs, and vice versa: the effects of ICT use in the job, and of ICT monitoring are entirely distinct.

Overall, these results seem consistent with an interactionist, bargaining view of the effort–reward relationship. Disjunctions between effort and reward occur because bargains do not completely meet the goals of one, other, or both parties. This view would be further strengthened if evidence could be produced of actions being taken in response to misalignments between effort and reward, especially in the case of ICT-based monitoring. One relevant finding is that, in 2000, employees under ICT-based performance checking appeared to be a little more likely to be planning to leave their jobs. This finding is statistically weak,[25] but it does accord with observations of high staff turnover at some of the call centres that have been notorious users of ICT monitoring technology. Exit is just one of the ways that employees can exert counter-pressures on control systems that they experience as unfair. Others will be considered in the concluding discussion that follows.

6.6. Conclusions

This chapter, like the previous one, started out from perceptions of rising overwork that have been widely voiced by commentators. In a competitive economy and society, it is easy to see that more work by employees is attractive to employers. The question that is less clear, and that accordingly has been taken as the focus in this chapter and the previous one, is *why* employees allow it to take place: why they agree to it or comply with it. This question is crucial unless one submits to some form of determinism, whether economic, social, or technological.

The interpretation of employee compliance, taken as the focus of this chapter, is that employers have extracted more work effort by the systematic use of incentive-and-control systems, with additional effort financially compensated. This line of enquiry also provided a further opportunity to look at differences between classes, resuming the theme from earlier chapters about differentiation or harmonization of class outcomes.

The evidence points towards considerable increases in incentives and controls for British employees over the 1990s. There was a moderate overall increase in appraisal systems, in various forms of performance incentive provision, and in rewards for promotion as seen by employees. Additionally, there was a marked tendency for each kind of control or incentive to be linked with others, forming an increasingly dense control-incentive web, especially for the managerial and professional classes. The most remarkable development, however, concerned new methods of monitoring based on the use of ICT. These emerged rapidly from obscure beginnings to cover one-half of employees by 2000 and to contribute directly to control over performance in the case of one in four employees.

Further analysis showed that it made a difference to total earnings and/or to various measures of effort, when employees participated in appraisal systems, in performance incentive regimes, or in control systems using ICT monitoring. These effects could be substantial (of the order of 10–15% above expected market pay; of the order of 5–10% above average levels of work strain; of the order of 2–3 hours added to the work-week). However, the effects varied in magnitude and significance across years and across class groupings, and there were some striking disjunctions between the effects on effort and the effects on reward. Most notably, ICT-based monitoring was found to increase work strain (except for managers and professionals), but not to be compensated by any upward shift in total pay. It appeared to be wholly negative in its implications for employees, while apparently providing employers with a free lunch.

Overall, then, the idea of bureaucratic discipline contributes substantially to explaining why overwork has been accepted by employees (and thereby further undermines the case for the market discipline thesis). Additional earnings provide employees with the motive to increase effort, and employers have developed methods of monitoring and control to ensure that effort is increased. But this simple conclusion gives a picture of the relationships that is much too stable, and much too conservative. What appear, overall, as moderate rates of change in the systems themselves become massive shifts for particular classes, notably managers and professionals. Furthermore, the large changes over time in the impacts of particular elements of incentive and control, such as appraisals, and the observed disjunctions between effort and reward, notably in the case of ICT monitoring, suggest processes that involve considerable contestation, strain, and distortion. These aspects require further discussion to conclude the present chapter and to connect with the following one.

6.6.1. *Class and Overwork*

Control and incentive systems have in recent years been re-focused to a remarkable extent on managers and professionals, the group sometimes referred to as the salariat. On the face of it, this suggests that the aim of many employers has been to put more pressure on the salariat to perform according to some criteria, against which they will be judged and rewarded. Against this interpretation, there is the argument that the work of the salariat is too complex and too diffuse to be monitored, manipulated, and subjected to short-term incentives. Those who take this view suggest that where incentives are applied to this group, it is either tokenism with no real impact or an opportunistic way of creaming off profits for the personal gain of those in authority. Either way, there is no major implication for behaviour.

This chapter's class-specific analysis shows that managers and professionals make substantial financial gains from participation in incentive regimes of various kinds. Moreover, the analysis reveals two ways in which the effort of managers and professionals is affected by participating in certain kinds of systemic controls and incentives. One is that managers and professionals share, with other classes, a sense of increased work demands when they take part in appraisal systems. The other is that managers and professionals who receive individual performance incentive pay (with or without other types of incentive) on average work longer hours. As the proportion of managers and professionals that took part in individual performance incentives was increasing rapidly over the decade, this latter effect was of major practical importance. Accordingly, one has to resist the suggestion that the incentivizing of the salariat lacks substance: it has real implications for their effort as well as for their earnings.

This conclusion, however, does not mean that all issues concerning the salariat, incentives, and effort have been satisfactorily resolved. In particular, the analysis has yielded no explanation about work strain in the salariat in 2000. Managers and professionals recorded the highest level of work strain in that year, and the greatest increase relative to 1992, but appraisal systems, incentive regimes, and ICT-based monitoring did nothing to account for this. Doubtless there are other ways in which competitive pressures affect the strain experienced by managers and professionals, perhaps including the individualized bargaining discussed in Chapter 4, and the competition for increasingly attractive promotions suggested by findings in Chapters 2 and 3 as well as earlier in the present chapter. But these are speculations that we cannot test and must leave as an issue for future research.

It must also be stressed that the progressive incentivization of the salariat does not offer simple support for ideas of class convergence. It is true that managers and professionals are affected by appraisal systems and by individual incentive regimes in ways that are somewhat similar to the experience of other classes. In one crucial respect, however, the recent experience of managers and professionals has been distinctive. Their effort has been little affected by the introduction of ICT-based monitoring, yet for those in the intermediate and lower class-groups this technology has been the source of large increases in work strain. Indeed, a reasonable interpretation of the evidence as a whole is that for the salariat the main development is taking place through individual performance incentives while for other classes the main development is through ICT monitoring. This suggests divergence rather than convergence.

6.6.2. *Contracting, Contestation, and Overwork*

Disjunctions between effort and reward, and changes over time in the relationships involving effort and reward, are indications of an effort–reward bargaining process that is incomplete and subject to distortion. Most starkly, ICT-based monitoring of individuals' work in Britain generates a substantial increase in work strain, very much as would be expected on the basis of the call centre literature, yet generates no additional compensation. This disjunction between the effort experienced and the reward received fits better with the radical view of the employment relationship, and especially its emphasis on manipulation and contestation rather than fully rational contracting. Employers manipulate the arrangements in their own favour, when they can, and employees contest the arrangements to do the opposite. This permits effort and reward to be out of balance, over some periods.

According to this interpretation, the advantage that employers currently get from their application of ICT-based monitoring is temporary, presumably the result of the technology's novelty. Employees who work under ICT monitoring perhaps find it difficult to make effort–reward comparisons with other situations, and do not yet know how or on what grounds to contest the technology. Eventually, however, employees' contestation is likely to develop. This will partly occur through informal means such as difficulty in recruiting, or quit rates, but also through industrial action and through campaigns of opposition. In July 2003, for example, an extraordinary wildcat strike took place at London's Heathrow Airport in opposition to an electronic time recording system that the management of British Airways was attempting to impose, and there have subsequently been several local actions by Royal Mail staff against electronic monitoring systems. It is through actions such as these, and their outcomes, that employees learn how ICT monitoring can be contained or what compensation can be extracted for accepting it.[26] Another strand of contestation is the increasing association of workplace ICT monitoring with wider issues of social surveillance. For example, early in 2007 large-scale opposition emerged to the British government's ideas about 'road pricing', partly on the grounds that this would involve electronic monitoring of vehicle movements; yet many drivers of commercial vehicles already operate under corporate monitoring of this type. As surveillance for business reasons becomes connected with infringement of civil liberties, employers may have to pay a heavier price for using it.

These are merely examples of the continually varied processes of negotiation that are involved in shaping effort–reward bargains. Employers seek to gain power over effort through internalized systems of control and incentive, but their ability to achieve this is limited by the power of employees, individually and collectively, and by the permeability of the organization's boundaries to external signals and to the norms and preferences of society. Chapter 7 argues, indeed, that contestation is entering a new phase as overwork interacts more insistently with family values.

Notes

1. The present discussion largely draws on Weber (ed. Parsons) 1947: 129–40.
2. This emphasis on innovation is especially clear in Weber (ed. Roth and Wittich) 1968: 128–30.
3. With the proviso that *to the extent that they affect behaviour*. There are trivial controls for which no incentives are needed and trivial incentives for which no controls are needed.
4. For further insight into how employees can use controls for their own benefit, see Edwards and Wajcman (2005).
5. A more complete account is provided by Hirschhorn (1984), who also stresses the role of standards and measurement developed in Taylorized work systems.
6. As a pertinent example, the statutory requirement in England for schools to report pupil attendance and lateness statistics has been followed by the production of individual certificates of good attendance and punctuality for children as young as five.
7. This is also roughly the view of Etzioni (1975) and Lane (1991), who approach the issue from a largely non-economic viewpoint.
8. An 'effort bargain' was earlier proposed by Behrend (1957), who argued that effort bargaining was a means of adjusting workplace pay to market conditions. One might also mention that Friedmann (1954), best known as the originator of the 'deskilling' thesis, characterized the work intensification produced by Scientific Management as a problem of industrial relations.
9. Informal workshop bargaining or contestation was vividly described in a number of the industrial sociology classics of the 1950s and 1960s (e.g. Roy 1952; Lupton 1963).
10. The relative odds of a higher professional/manager getting three or more incentives, as opposed to a routine worker's, increased by a factor of 1.9 between 1992 and 2000.
11. In total, 28 per cent perceived increased rewards from promotion, 12 per cent decreased rewards, 48 per cent no change, and 13 per cent could not give an opinion.
12. In most cases, this would mean only some of their work or particular aspects of their work. Even in call centres, where ICT-control is thought to be most complete, staff have suggested that the technology only analyzes about one-half of the skills they apply to the job (Yeuk-Mui 2001).
13. The obstacle to estimating the effects of all kinds of incentives in a single analysis is that they tend to occur together and so are highly correlated.
14. Suppose that the employer pays 80 per cent of the basic market wage and a 25 per cent average bonus. Then total earnings gain for the average employee is zero. If on the other hand the employer pays 110 per cent of the market wage and a 10 per cent average bonus, then total earnings gain for the average employee is 21 per cent.

15. The 1992 estimates for the earnings effects of performance incentive pay are broadly similar to those of Booth and Frank (1999), who used data from the British Household Panel Survey 1991 to estimate an effect of 'performance-related pay' of around 9 per cent.

16. Because 'individual' and 'other' incentive regimes are mutually exclusive by definition, any one individual can benefit from only one of them. But a person benefiting from either can also benefit from appraisal-based earnings increases, if available.

17. In the late 1990s, British companies were for a time the most profitable, on average, of any country, and were still in fifth position in 2000 (source: National Statistics website).

18. It was less appropriate to consider hours in Chapter 5 because conditions of workplace contraction or expansion could affect the hours required by the employer, independent of any influence on the effort of the employee.

19. As the difference in the effect of individual incentive between 1992 and 2000 is itself not statistically significant, one cannot exclude the possibility that the difference is random.

20. Statistically, the effect is at the borderline of the 10 per cent significance level ($t = 1.65$).

21. The results of the overall analyses and the class-specific analyses are not strictly comparable, since it was necessary for technical reasons to omit industry dummies from the analysis specification for the latter.

22. The 'ICT recording only' effect was significant at the 5 per cent level ($t = 2.28$) while the 'ICT performance checking' effect was not significant at the 10 per cent level ($t = 1.60$). The joint effects were significant at the 10 per cent level.

23. The effect was significant at the 5 per cent level ($t = 2.54$).

24. The effect for the higher class-group was significant at the 5 per cent level ($t = 2.50$) and for the intermediate class-group at the 10 per cent level ($t = 1.75$).

25. In a model of individual leaving intentions over the following year, ICT-based performance checking increased the relative odds of intending to leave by a factor of 1.36 (the marginal probability of intending to leave rose by four percentage points), with a t-statistic of 1.75 (significant at the 10% significance level).

26. For extensive historical examples of industrial action in relation to technology and control systems, see Friedmann (1954).

7

The family challenge

Chapters 5 and 6 described rising work demands and work strain among British employees and explained why employees accepted overwork partly as the result of insecure employment conditions, and partly as the interlocking effects of organizations' work incentive and control systems, which provide reward for effort and extract effort for reward. However, Chapter 6 also argued (in the spirit of Baldamus 1961 and Edwards 1979) that effort–reward bargains are provisional and continually open to contestation. Among the ways in which employers' imposition of long hours, or control over effort, can be challenged is by invoking political, social, and moral values, so that contestation not infrequently arises from shifts in ideological climate. Such a potentially challenging development is now in view. It involves opening the effort bargain to the interests of a new set of outsiders: the employee's family. Previously excluded from the very idea of an employment contract or an employment relationship, their voice is at last beginning to be heard.

During the late 1990s and early years of the new century, the family was often the focus of a moral panic in Britain. The concerns expressed were many-sided, including such diverse topics as the replacement of marriage by cohabitation, the high rate of divorce and partnership breakdown, and the incapacity of parents to control rebellious and antisocial children. While many interpreted such developments as signs of terminal decline in the institution of the family, others maintained that it remained strong and suffered only because so much more was demanded of it. Among the evidence supporting the latter view are results from questions asked in the WiB (2000) survey, where respondents rated their families far more important to them than work, leisure, friends, religion, or politics.[1] At the same time, the pressures facing families seem undeniable.

One of those pressures, by common consent, comes from the increasing demands of paid work on family time. The two-earner family, rather than the 'male breadwinner' model, has become standard: three in four employed men in couples also have an employed partner.[2] Most women now return to paid work within a year of the birth of their first child, although a generation ago the proportion was only one in four (Daniel 1980; McRae 1991; Callender et al. 1997; Hudson, Lissenburgh, and Sahin-Dikmen 2004; see also Smeaton 2006). Women have made remarkable gains in entry to professional and managerial jobs,[3] despite continued sex discrimination, and increasing proportions are following a career, which typically involves increased pressures and difficulties when combined with family work (Crompton, Brockmann, and Wiggins 2003). The time pressures on couples, however, do not all come from changes on the woman's side. Britain has evolved into an economy dependent on long working hours, somewhat on the lines of the USA, with one in four men in 2000 working in excess of the supposed upper limit (under the EU's Working Time Directive) of 48 hours a week.[4] The failure of relationships through pressures of job and career has become a clichéd theme in TV drama.

According to media accounts (which presumably reflect public perceptions), the adverse consequences of expanded paid-work time, such as exhaustion and stress, fall primarily on 'working mums', and then secondarily on wider family relations. There is reason in this assumption, for women (collectively speaking) have continued to do most of the housework and the childcare alongside their paid employment. Time-budget research shows that the time women spend on housework has not fallen as quickly as their paid time has grown, and moreover both men and women on average now spend *more* time on childcare than used to be the case (see Gershuny 2000 for details). It has also been pointed out (Brannen and Moss 1991) that in most couples it is the woman who plans and organizes the shopping, the meals, and the childcare, a cognitive task that becomes more complex and potentially more fraught as she does more paid work. Indeed, the importance of the home planning function has been underlined in recent innovative research from the USA (Lee 2005). Some conclude that the varied demands on employed women with children are impossible to reconcile, and there have been repeated suggestions that the State should offer stay-at-home, child-rearing women some financial compensation to encourage more to follow their example. During 2006, this became part of the policy platform of the opposition Conservative Party in Britain.

Much criticism for these work-related difficulties of families has been directed at employers. It is not hard to find evidence in support of such criticisms: for example, the adoption of policies to assist working parents has recently languished at the bottom of managers' priorities for change (White et al. 2004: 113–15), and WERS (2004) reveals that nearly two in three managers still believe that it is up to the individual, rather than the employer, to sort out these difficulties (Kersley et al. 2006: 271). Yet many of the ideas to develop a response have in fact come from the employers' side. The notion of 'work–family balance', promoted in the British financial sector in the early 1990s, was intended as corrective thinking to the assumption that career-seeking women (and men) must give themselves wholly to the organization. The terminology was soon modified to 'work–life balance' so as to include single people who also felt they needed something more beyond paid work. The practical agenda however remained largely focused on the family, with 'family-friendly practices', another piece of managerial terminology, as the central thrust. Such practices have included, in different workplaces, everything from enhanced maternity and paternity leave provisions to career break schemes and contracts geared to the school-term. Through ideas and practical steps such as these, employers have at least accepted the legitimacy of family concerns within the employment relationship. This has been further underlined through work–life balance campaigns promoted by employers' organizations and by that largest of employers, the government.[5]

Even so, employers do not seem fully to have grasped the logical consequences of what they are doing. The family is the chief remaining locus of moral feeling in a secularized society, giving its concerns immense authority. The implication of admitting these concerns into the employment relationship is that they will act as a binding constraint on what the employer can demand and what the employee will agree to. In apparent disregard of all this, however, employers have been pressing on with the 'HRM agenda', including to construct 'HPWS', as discussed in Chapter 5. Through concerted use of HRM/HPWS practices, many British employers seek to enhance employees' commitment to the organization and, ultimately, the performance of the organization itself.[6] But can commitment to the organization and its goals increase without impinging on employees' commitment to their own family relationships? Can a drive for greater personal performance in the job be consistent with encouraging employees to devote adequate time and emotional energy to the family?

It is not just employers who face a challenge from the family. Individual women and men are confronted continually with decisions about how to reconcile their family relations with their desire to earn more money and the demands of their jobs and careers. Assuming that employers are now more open to a kind of bargaining about work–family balance, how do employees exploit that possibility, and what priority do they give to family over paid work? Assuming, as most do, that work–family conflicts are concentrated in two-earner families, what are members of such couples doing about it? For example, do they individually work shorter hours, and do they use their combined earning power to 'buy off' home problems via nannies, home helps, and the like? Can couples avoid the pressures by maintaining the alternative, traditional, one-earner structure, as conservative commentators imply?

These are specific points that this chapter examines. More generally, this chapter considers similar basic questions as those treated in Chapters 5 and 6, here transposed to the family context. Why do employees accept work pressures that have adverse consequences for their family relations, and what forms do these adverse consequences take? Following the introduction, the argument is developed through four sections that interlace theory with evidence:

- An initial section considers how employees, especially those with marital partners, contest overwork in the views they express. These findings not only illustrate the embeddedness of long hours in British employment but also reveal a growing dissatisfaction with actual hours that may reflect the growth of social opposition.

- The second section begins with a review of the influential 'time-squeeze' theory of overwork and the family, and argues that this needs to be extended to take account both of employers' internal policy development and of the non-materialist values within family relationships. The section then examines how employers' practices impinge on family relationship strain (FRS) and dissatisfaction with childcare. The underlying debate is whether current 'best practice' in managing the workforce results in 'mutual gains' for employers and employees, or whether on the contrary it inexorably conflicts with employees' family values.

- The next section reverts to an employee perspective and considers differences in family outcomes between one-earner and two-earner couples. The sometimes counter-intuitive findings of this section indicate the incompleteness of the dominant time-squeeze formulation of work–family conflict and lead on to a review of alternative formulations incorporating identities and commitments.

- The fourth section goes further inside the family by considering influences on the sharing of household work between partners, an important issue for gender equality. The section also continues the analysis of employers' policies: does employer pressure affect intra-family negotiation, and if so with what consequences?

The analyses of this chapter naturally include family characteristics as well as workplace characteristics. It is important to recognize that family characteristics are distinctive, in that they are constructed through personal and family choices. Being in a couple relationship; having children or not; and both partners being in paid work, or only one, all these are the result of choices that (most of the time) involve two people. Ideally, the background influences on these choices would be explicitly taken account of in our analyses, but here (as in most research on family and work) they are largely unknown. Accordingly, when one uses family characteristics to account for outcomes, one needs to be most careful in interpreting the results; but it is rarely the case that only one interpretation is possible. Where a finding appears counter-intuitive, we are at pains to test it through alternative analyses which embody different interpretations. Compared with previous chapters, therefore, this chapter contains a relatively high proportion of discursive, and sometimes speculative, interpretation. Nonetheless, we believe that the main findings are sufficiently robust to have serious implications for issues about work demands on families.

7.1. Voicing Hours Preferences and Complaints

The presumption that one meets continually in media discussions, and in much of the academic literature, is of an unmet need for shorter hours, so as to leave more time for family.[7] Such a preference on the part of employees would immediately secure them the moral high ground, and the assumption that this is indeed their position is convenient for those who would like to make a case for working time reform (including, indeed, the present writers).

It turns out, however, that this is not the nature of things, at least in Britain. What people want, in terms of hours, seems distressingly like what they have already. As Table 7.1 shows, about two-thirds of employees in 2000 wanted no change in their hours and earnings—they appeared to have more-or-less found their preferred combination. Furthermore, of

Table 7.1. Employees' preferred hours in 2000, by sex and family structure

Would prefer	Women (%)		Men (%)	
	Single	Couple	Single	Couple
Longer hours and earn more	29	15	38	23
Same hours and earn same	63	71	55	65
Fewer hours and earn less	5	10	5	9
Do not know	3	4	2	3
N	440	671	315	706

Source: WiB (2000).

the remaining minority who would have liked a change in hours and earnings, those seeking more hours and more pay greatly outnumbered those wanting fewer hours and prepared to give up some earnings in return. Admittedly individuals with partners were less likely to desire long hours, and more likely to desire short hours, than those without partners. Yet even so, only around one in ten individuals in a couple was prepared to trade pay for shorter hours, whereas one in seven women in couples, and nearly one in four men in couples, would prefer longer hours and more pay. These proportions change rather little if one focuses on those individuals whose partners are also in paid work: even here there is a remarkable appetite for still more paid hours of work.

One likely reason for the lack of demand for shorter hours is because many people have already succeeded in changing their own hours within their job, on an individual basis. Women frequently acted in this way, with nearly one in three[8] making a request for an hours change subsequent to joining their current employer, and 90 per cent of requests being granted. Men less often asked for a change—only one in eight did so with his current employer—and less often got what they asked for; but still two-thirds of requests succeeded. We do not know whether employees more often asked for longer or shorter hours, but in the case of women there is circumstantial evidence suggesting it was often the latter. Among those with a dependent child, about four in ten had asked their current employer for a change in hours, and if they had a child under three, the proportion rose to 55 per cent. It is plausible that many of these requests were for shorter hours after returning from childbirth. The fact that so few people expressed a desire for shorter hours with less pay could therefore indicate that most of those who wanted a change towards shorter hours already asked for it and got it. The main point, in any case, is clear: the supposed rigidity of employers over hours has been exaggerated, even though doubtless there remain some who are completely inflexible.

Another way of calibrating people's response to their paid-work time is by seeing if they are more likely to seek another job when they are *not* getting their preferred hours. About one in four of those wanting longer hours and one in five of those wanting shorter hours were intending to change employers, whereas among those preferring to keep their present hours only one in seven was intending to move.[9] The result shows that having undesired and inflexible hours certainty did make people unsettled. Still, only 2 per cent of the sample both wanted shorter hours *and* were intending to change jobs.[10]

The interim story therefore seems to be simple: few employees are seeking the shorter hours that their families might appreciate, and if they do want a change, they have a fair chance of getting one if only they ask. Yet, as will be found time and again in this chapter, dig a little more and simplicity is soon dispelled.

7.1.1. *Expressing Discontent*

If most people have the working hours they want or prefer, does that mean that they are 'satisfied' with their hours? Only on a naïve view of what is happening when individuals express their satisfaction or dissatisfaction in words. Although there is by no means a consensus among specialists in this major field of research, one of the main and long-standing interpretations is that these verbal expressions are made relative to some *expectation* that is lurking in the background (Locke 1976). Because expectations differ between social groups (for instance, those with higher-level qualifications have higher expectations of interesting work and progressive careers than those with only elementary qualifications), even cross-sectional comparisons of satisfaction require the most careful interpretation (see also the further discussion and analysis in Chapter 8). Moreover, it seems likely that expectations rise over time, as people become better informed and more demanding in their outlook. Declining satisfaction may of course reflect declining conditions of employment at constant expectations. But it may also reflect constant or even improving conditions of employment against rising expectations. Unfortunately, it is far easier to obtain measures of satisfaction than it is to obtain measures of expectations (though for an attempt at the latter see Section 8.9 of Chapter 8).

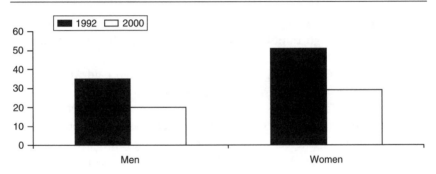

Figure 7.1. Per cent 'completely satisfied' or 'very satisfied' with their hours, 1992 and 2000.

Sources: EiB (1992) and WiB (2000).

Bearing these complications in mind, Figure 7.1, focusing on the positive end of the satisfaction scale, shows how satisfaction with hours of work changed between 1992 and 2000. The absolute figures for 2000 might not appear special, but comparison with the earlier year reveals that there was a large downward shift over the period. Employees were becoming less satisfied, with the main change being from large proportions saying they were completely satisfied or very satisfied at the earlier time, to large proportions at a relatively lukewarm or indifferent level of satisfaction at the later time. This shift was somewhat greater for women than men, as Figure 7.1 indicates. Marital status, the employment or non-employment of the partner, and the presence or absence of children, all made little or no further difference to satisfaction with hours.

There is a seeming paradox in these findings when combined with those that came earlier in the section. Although most employees were saying that they were working at their preferred hours (conditional on earnings), their satisfaction with hours was shifting hugely in the negative direction.[11] To see this in perspective, however, it is important to realize that expressed satisfaction had declined for *most* aspects of people's jobs. There was a *general* increase in discontent, or in its expression, over the period.[12] So interpreting the declining satisfaction with hours involves interpreting the overall trend. It is implausible, first of all, to attribute the increased dissatisfaction to a general decline in employment conditions. The earlier survey, EiB (1992), was carried out at a time of severe economic depression, whereas the second half of the 1990s and the early 2000s witnessed prolonged economic stability and steady growth in employment and earnings. Further, as documented in Chapter 2, employers over the period turned away from temporary employment practices and reaffirmed their in-house development and career policies. This is not to say that *no* aspects of employment conditions contributed to declining satisfaction. But to account for such a widespread decline, one surely needs to bring rising *general* expectations into the account.

There are indeed indications that the end of the twentieth century was a period when British society was applying more severe criticism to many aspects of current experience, such as politics, public services, and professions. This comes about in part because of higher levels of education, and the breakdown of dominant ideologies of religion, politics, and social status. People stop being deferential and are no longer afraid to criticize and make demands. These developments are not, in principle, new, but part of a tendency that goes back at least to the Enlightenment of the eighteenth century.[13] What is new, however, is an enormous increase in the efficacy of the media in disseminating information that provides the basis for criticism, and in amplifying the expression of criticism. The ability of media criticism to bring about changes in the policies of many institutions—government, public services, and business—has become apparent.[14] These developments in combination encourage individuals to reflect critically on their working lives and identify themselves with critiques for change. Satisfaction with working time is likely to be influenced as part of the general tendency towards greater criticism of employers.

It seems likely, though, that there is also a *separate* element involved in growing dissatisfaction with hours. Even at a time of growing expressed discontent, the *largest* downward shifts in satisfaction took place in relation to hours of work and to another aspect of work with a connected meaning: 'the amount of work'. As noted earlier, more people were working for very long hours in 2000 than in 1992, and as Chapter 6 showed, employers have been increasing the range of methods to control work and to extract work effort. In the better economic conditions at the turn of the decade, people may well have expected work to get easier but found it got harder.

7.1.2. *Pragmatism and Aspiration*

Now that we have carefully interpreted dissatisfaction with paid-work hours, we can revisit the apparently contrasting results from the question about hours preferences, and ask once again, 'How can employees who are apparently working their preferred hours be dissatisfied with those hours?'

A reconciliation comes by seeing the two types of question as pitched in different levels, or frames. The question about hours included the repercussions between hours and earnings, and so pinned individuals down to the pragmatic level. In accepting a job with pay and hours attached, an individual in a sense accepts that that is the best compromise to be had (otherwise she would take the better alternative). This, the economist's 'revealed preference', depends on the individual seeing the world from which the job offer emerges as more-or-less fixed, or anyway beyond her capacity to alter. Most people eventually settle for long periods in one job and so proclaim that the world of 'fact' offers them nothing more. In Wittgenstein's dismissive dictum,[15] *This is how things are.*

In expressing their satisfaction or dissatisfaction, individuals may stay within the framework of pragmatic expectations or they may move to a critical perspective in which expectations are aspirational or normative. Such a shift of perspective is allowable within the general idea that satisfaction is relative to expectations, a concept encompassing varied senses. If individuals remain within the pragmatic framework (constrained expectations), then there would tend to be agreement between expression of preferences, and expression of satisfaction. If, however, expressions of satisfaction move to a higher aspirational level, they can diverge from pragmatically constrained preferences. In other words, the employee's dissatisfaction then relates to the framework in which the pay-hours contract is fixed, not just to the pay-hours contract itself. It becomes a criticism of the system that has limited the range of available contracts in a way that falls short of the individual's aspirational values. The constraints on one's practical life cease to be the constraints on one's evaluations.[16]

To illustrate this, consider Figure 7.2 that displays the average dissatisfaction with hours in 2000 for women and men who answered the question about preferred hours in different ways. Also shown is the average level of dissatisfaction with hours, for all women and men, in 1992. In 2000, those who said they would like either longer or shorter hours than at present (with corresponding changes in earnings) were considerably more dissatisfied than those who preferred to stick with their current hours. This variation indicates relative dissatisfaction with contract at the pragmatic level: these employees feel they have a bad deal, and probably could get a better one: as mentioned earlier, above-average proportions of these are planning to leave their current employer. But this is only one half of the story, for even the employees who want to stick with their current hours are considerably more dissatisfied than the average of all employees in 1992.[17] This is indicative of an increasing gap between what

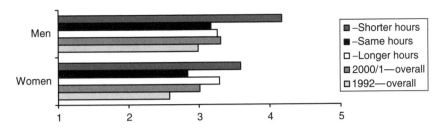

Figure 7.2. Average dissatisfaction with hours (7 point scale), by hours preferences, for men and women.

Sources: EiB (1992) (last bar only) and WiB (2000) (top four bars).
Note: A longer bar indicates greater dissatisfaction.

is available and what is aspired to. Even the people who feel that they are not going to find a better deal in practice are becoming less accepting of the social order which produces these kinds of hours constraints.

7.2. Market Power and the Family

We are provisionally interpreting the combined results on hours preferences and dissatisfaction with hours as showing that employees have constrained choices of hours that diverge from their social aspirations. Yet the data also show that individuals are rather successful in changing their hours, when they ask. What then is the nature of the constraint that they experience? The clearest answer to this question is that of Juliet Schor in her book *The Overworked American* (Schor 1991), which Chapter 5 also briefly referred to. Employees, argues Schor, are constrained in the hours they work by unequal market power.

It is first necessary to explain why employers want long hours, then how they can impose them.[18] Schor sees employers as needing to extract increasing returns from labour in the face of competitive pressure. This, as previous chapters have made plain, is a widely shared and variously confirmed interpretation of recent market capitalism; the intensification of competition in the third quarter of the twentieth century is little contested. What made longer hours attractive to US employers, in Schor's account, was an increased opportunity for obtaining *unpaid* hours. This was associated with the growing proportion of white-collar employees in the occupational structure, for these occupations have little tradition of premium overtime payments. It was also partly associated with an increase in the bargaining power of employers relative to that of labour during the economic depression of the 1970s and 1980s. These details, however, are not of great concern to the issues of this chapter, especially as labour market conditions have changed considerably since the period of which Schor speaks. The *general* point to be extracted from her argument so far is simple: upward pressure on hours arises in part because employers use their bargaining power to pursue them.

What makes Schor's analysis more interesting is her treatment of the supply side. She accepts that widespread increases in hours could not have occurred without employees being takers of the hours on offer (as of course the data discussed earlier in this chapter have indicated for the case of Britain). Part of Schor's story is that families themselves chose long hours and demanding jobs to fulfil material ambitions. At the same time, these choices have been strongly influenced by a consumer society that has developed powerful forms of advertising and credit. Increases in paid-work hours permit increased consumption, but consumption also locks people into working extended hours, because they need to service their personal debt. So the choices made by employees or families are heavily constrained by consumer market frameworks. Bluestone and Rose (1997) add to this argument by emphasizing the falling wages of US families in the least-skilled, lowest-paid sections of the job market, who have needed to work more hours merely to maintain their standard of living. In Britain, earnings inequality has also risen (see Chapters 3, 4, and 6), and there is the additional role of the housing market, where the presumed long-term advantage of ownership under rising property values has led many families into burdensome mortgage commitments. While the details vary by country, the underlying argument is similar. Capitalism works on both sides of the market, consumption and labour. Employers do not directly create the financial commitments of their employees, but they are aware of them and able to gain leverage from them.

7.2.1. *Widening the Interpretation of Work–Family Conflict*

Schor's book provides a powerful explanation of how individuals can choose the paid-work hours they have, yet experience conflict between those hours and their family life. But while this account has a compelling simplicity, it achieves this through a somewhat narrow view both of family outcomes and of employer policies. On the family side, the problem is seen as a shortage of hours, or 'time squeeze' (Schor 1991: 17), and this shortage of hours is presumed to be the complement of the family's paid hours. Sociological issues about how family *relations* are affected by changes in hours are either ignored, or perhaps assumed to correspond directly with the shortage of hours: less time = poorer family outcomes.[19] Similarly, by focusing exclusively on market constraints, Schor gives little recognition to the changing values and aspirations involved in women's participation in the labour market and their careers. Again, the monolithic representation of market power gives few clues about differences in employers' policies and practices. This is of course consistent with the emphasis on shortage of family hours as the fundamental issue: in that perspective, nothing about employers' policies matters except the hours extracted from their employees. Yet that is to ignore the extensive and varied development of work intensification practices, some of which were considered in Chapters 5 and 6. What affects individuals' family relations is not just paid-work hours but the totality of work demands made by the employer.

Schor's identification of family problems with the time squeeze has influenced much of the research that has taken place more recently. One consequence has been an almost exclusive concentration on two-earner families. One-earner families have largely disappeared from this literature (see review by Perry-Jenkins et al. 2000), yet little has been done to explicate on a theoretical or conceptual basis why adverse effects should especially fall on dual-earner couples. Rather, this has been left as a self-evident or 'common sense' implication of increasing work-time for family units and especially those with children. For example, Batt and Valcour (2003: 189), noting that 'dual-earner families now constitute the typical American family', go on to infer that: 'As a result, the difficulty of managing work and family demands has increased for many working adults'. Similarly, Schneider and Waite (2005) begin an essay entitled *Why study working families?* with a description of a woman juggling responsibilities to job, husband, and children, and imagine that she 'reflects on the pace and demands of her life and how it differs from that of her mother' (Schneider and Waite 2005: 3).

For sociologists, however, the concept of 'demands' that is used in these (and many other) papers cannot be correctly specified in terms of a physical quantity such as time. Demands are socially imposed and socially accepted: they have an obvious normative significance. If one wishes to speak of demands on families, or on individuals in a family context, one must pay attention to the socially defined roles and identities through which demands are socially constructed. Again, the crucial outcomes, from a sociological viewpoint, cannot be expressed in terms of quantities of time. They have to be expressed in terms of the qualities of relationships. These will be influenced not only by material constraints such as availability of time (important though these are likely to be) but also by the meanings and values that are attached by each family member to the roles that others and themselves play.

The basic time-squeeze model therefore has to be developed in two ways, one relating to a more extensive treatment of employers' work demands, and the other relating to a deeper examination of the role of family structures and relationships. These two types of development provide the agenda for the remainder of this chapter.

7.3. Employers' Practices and Family Relations

The 1992 and 2000 employee surveys make it possible to examine employers' work demands in an extended way and see how they impinge on family relations.[20] Following Schor's lead, we take the actual hours of work (including unpaid hours in the job) as primarily determined by the market via the employer. The employee does make choices, but only within a system of constraints that is largely controlled by the employer or by the market system in which the employer is embedded. This then is a primary measure of the employer's policy through which work is demanded.[21]

For employers, however, it would be futile to control the hours of work without controlling work intensity per hour worked. To investigate work intensification, a measure is constructed consisting of practices that are widely regarded as essential elements of HRM. However, they are not intended to cover all kinds of HRM practice. The focus is on the kinds of practices that are widely regarded, among management theorists and among managers themselves, as generating higher commitment and performance. Furthermore, from within this set of high-commitment or high-performance practices, the selection is confined to those where previous research shows them to have the potential of raising work pressures (see White et al. 2003). The resulting set is very similar to the set of 'high-performance work practices' considered in Chapter 5, even though the two sets were constructed according to partly different criteria. The present set excludes the items on communications that were present in Chapter 5 but includes additional items relating to appraisals and to team-working.

The entire set of HRM practices is summarized in a single score, representing how many practices the individual employee encounters in

---

Box 7.1 A SUMMATIVE MEASURE OF WORK-INTENSIFYING HRM PRACTICES

The use of a summative measure is chiefly justified on conceptual grounds. The management and industrial relations literature on HRM practice, and especially on HRM that is orientated to high performance, maintains that the effectiveness of these practices depends on combined use of practices, often referred to as 'bundles', rather than the use of particular practices in isolation. Reflecting this prescription, summative measures are widely used in research on HRM (e.g. Delaney 1996; Delery and Doty 1996; Huselid and Becker 1996; Huselid, Jackson, and Schuler 1997; Ichniowski, Shaw, and Prennushi 1997; Godard 2001). Since most employers have *not* achieved comprehensive use of the practices, the summative measures can be interpreted as indices of progress towards full adoption.

There is no general agreement on the aspects of practice that should be included in measures of HRM. Items used in the present summative score focus mainly on what have been called 'on-line' practices, meaning practices that directly affect an individual's job or work, while omitting 'off-line' practices, such as communication meetings (see Godard 2001); however, the final item below, 'problem-solving group', can also be partly interpreted as an off-line practice. The items refer to (a) appraisal systems: any participation in appraisal, appraisal influencing pay, appraisal influencing promotions, appraisal influencing training and development, and appraisal influencing hard work; (b) incentives: individual-based, team-based, organization-based, profit-sharing or share scheme, and merit-based pay increases; (c) team organization: group working, group influencing hard work, and problem-solving group. The items can be recombined in several ways to relate to other concepts in the literature on 'HPWS', for example, some appraisal items relate to 'skill' and others to 'incentive' dimensions used by Appelbaum et al. (2000).

Statistical support for the use of a summative score is provided by the Kuder-Richardson measure of scale reliability (analogous to the Cronbach Alpha measure), which returns a value of 0.72 for the set of fourteen binary items in 1992 and 0.76 in 2000.

---

the course of her own job. What is of interest is *not* the effect of each particular practice on family relations: we know from previous research (White et al. 2003) that there are numerous specific effects, and that these are complicated. Here we abstract from these specific effects and seek the *average effect per HRM practice*—asking, in effect, what happens to family relations as employees face increases in the number of these practices in the workplace. Box 7.1 provides further details of the measure and justification of its use.

The idea that HRM practices can adversely affect family relations is a particularly challenging one for those who see HRM evolving towards a 'best practice' model that meets the performance goals of organizations precisely by nurturing the self-realizing aspirations of individuals. For example, Appelbaum et al. (2000) in their influential study of US manufacturing showed that companies not only achieved their performance aims better when they implemented 'HPWS'[22] but also had more satisfied, trusting, and committed employees in doing so. Findings of this kind have led some commentators to label best-practice HRM as 'win–win' systems since both employers and employees supposedly come out better off. Some writers on the 'new service economy' have extended this to a 'win–win–win' model in which customers as well as employers and employees are the beneficiaries of best-practice HRM, adapted to include customer service values (see Korczynski 2002 for review).

The analysis also takes account of recently developed management practices, already noted in this chapter's introduction, which are intended to be helpful to work–life balance. It has been shown, in both the USA and Britain,[23] that workplaces with many HRM practices tend to have more family-friendly practices. One approach is to offer employees more choice or flexibility over working time so that they can get a better fit with family demands. Another approach is to make provision specifically for those who have (young) children, for instance through career breaks or workplace crèches. These are the two kinds of practices that occupy centre stage in current policy discussions of work–family balance. By including these within the analysis, one can assess potentially positive as well as negative influences on family relations. If HRM practices are usually teamed with family-friendly practices, the net impact of the developments on family relations could be positive even if the HRM practices on their own have adverse effects.

In the analyses, each family-friendly or balance-friendly practice is included as a separate variable, with no attempt to collect them into a single measure as in the case of HRM practices. There is little indication in management discourse to suggest that employers have a strategic or integrative policy in connection with this domain, and a detailed analysis, using employer data from WERS (1998), suggested that practices of these types were adopted by British employers in a somewhat diverse and fragmentary manner (Wood, de Menezes, and Lasaosa 2003).

A final point about how the analysis represents work demands is that it does *not* include ICT-based monitoring, which was one of the salient influences on effort uncovered in Chapter 6. Variant analyses indicated that this feature of employer practice did not significantly influence family pressures, and it was therefore omitted in the interests of simplifying an already complex set of results.

Box 7.2 MEASURING FAMILY RELATIONSHIP STRAIN

The measure is based on three questions, asked in 2000 as follows:

'How often would you say the following statements are true of yourself:

"After work I have too little time to carry out my family responsibilities as I would like."

"My job allows me to give the time I like to my partner or family."

"My partner/family get a bit fed up with the pressure of my job."'

In 1992, the second item was worded in a negative sense ('does not allow'). This difference in wording does not affect the sense of the scale, and in the analysis the two surveys are always treated separately. A 5-point response scale was used, with responses 'almost always', 'often', 'sometimes', 'rarely', and 'never'.

The first and second items refer to time shortage, but also to normative interpretations ('responsibilities', 'I would like', 'I like') of the individual's family role. The third item refers more directly to the respondent's perception of partner's or family's frustration with her or his job pressures.

The reliability (Cronbach alpha) was 0.85 in 1992 and 0.75 in 2000. The items are combined into a single measure by means of their principal components factor score. The factor accounts for two-thirds of the variation of the three items. Positive values indicate more FRS. Use of the factor score, rather than a summative measure, here improves the approximation to a continuous distribution.

7.3.1. *Measuring Pressures on the Family* [24]

To assess overwork as a family experience, one needs ways of representing pressures on the family. The chief measure performing this role in the analysis is called 'FRS'.[25] It is constructed in an analogous way to the work-strain measure used in Chapter 6. Box 7.2 provides the details of the questions. The main limitation of the measure is that it does not appear to express *acute* family relationship problems. One might prefer to know whether partners were throwing the crockery at each other or contemplating divorce. Stronger questions of that type, however, cannot be included in a survey that chiefly concerns experiences of employment. Yet even to answer the available questions at the unfavourable end of the response scale may point to a considerable degree of strain in relationships.[26] The scale correlates well with the work-strain index and the measure of workload dissatisfaction,[27] an indication that a high score places the individual in a problem-zone. Table 7.2 shows the proportions that gave indications of FRS in 2000. Men experienced somewhat more frequent FRS because of their work than did women, but the differences were not large.

Table 7.2. Responses to the family relationship strain items, by gender, 2000

	Women (%)			Men (%)		
	Almost always	Often	Sometimes	Almost always	Often	Sometimes
Too little time for responsibilities	8	17	36	8	21	37
Partner/family get fed up	3	9	23	5	13	30
	Never	Rarely	Sometimes	Never	Rarely	Sometimes
Give time I like to partner/ family	4	11	25	5	14	30

Note: See Box 7.1 for full wording of items and responses.
Source: WiB (2000).

The measure of FRS is applicable to nearly all employees (not just those with partners or children).[28] For a second measure of pressure on the family, the individual's degree of dissatisfaction with childcare arrangements, the focus is confined to employees with children below the age of 12. Childcare includes all types of care while the parent is away at the workplace; it includes, for instance, care by a partner or relative as well as paid childcare, but because of the way the question is worded, excludes the individual's own role in providing childcare. A 7-point satisfaction scale, ranging from 'completely satisfied' to 'completely dissatisfied', was used, but few people gave explicitly 'dissatisfied' answers. Despite this limitation, and despite the restriction of the question to people with children under 12 years of age, which considerably reduces sample size, the analysis of satisfaction with childcare produced statistically significant results. This reflects the emotional involvement that parents have in childcare arrangements: any fall below complete satisfaction is likely to be a matter of intense concern. The childcare satisfaction scale acts as a sensitive detector of family pressures.

7.3.2. Workplace Influences on Family Pressures

The initial aim of the analysis is to assess how the hours worked by the employee, and the extent of the HRM practices in which she or he is involved, affect the two measures of family pressure. (Further details of the analysis are shown in Box 7.3.) To start with, how did workplace practices impact on FRS? The main results can be summarized briefly:

- The longer the hours that people worked, the greater the FRS they experienced. The effect was similar in both 1992 and 2000, and women and men were about equally affected.[29]

Box 7.3 ANALYSING PRESSURES ON FAMILY RELATIONS

In this chapter, results from a set of analyses are presented in a selective way, with qualitative conclusions in the text and some statistical details in footnotes. The focus is on those aspects of employers' practices that are hypothesized to either increase or reduce pressures on family relations. In producing these estimates, the analyses also take account of external influences that are likely to influence both workplace practices and the family outcome measures. Two forms of statistical model are used. When FRS is the dependent variable, the model is OLS regression, as the outcome is measured on a quasi-continuous scale. When dissatisfaction with childcare, or male share in household work, is the dependent variable, the ordered logit model is applied.

Details of the main explanatory variables (workforce practices) are as follows. Actual hours are weekly and range from 1 to 100; scores on the summative measure of HRM practices range from 0 to 14 practices; categorical or dummy variables represent flexible working hours and personal control over hours worked, which are compared with having fixed hours with no choice. In addition, the analyses provide comparison between single employees, those in one-earner couples, and those in two-earner couples.

All models are estimated separately for women and men, within survey year.

Control variables included in the analyses of FRS and of male shares in household work are age, age-squared, hours in second job, job tenure, tenure-squared, class, the age (banded) of the youngest child (with no child the reference category), change in workplace size, and dummy variables for union, fair supervisor, own employment commitment, and financial orientation. For the model of dissatisfaction with childcare, where the sample size is small and the sample composition more homogeneous, a reduced set of controls is used, consisting of class, age of youngest child, and fair treatment by supervisor.

Sample size for the 1992 analyses (using the EiB survey) is reduced because some of the questions relevant to these analyses were asked only of a randomly selected one half of the full sample.

- Additional HRM practices increased FRS.[30]

- The adverse effect of HRM practices increased markedly for women between 1992 and 2000. The average effect on men was weaker than women and did not change appreciably between 1992 and 2000.

- In 2000 (not 1992), flexible time practices produced some helpful effects in reducing family strain.

- The important flexible practices were different for women and men. Women benefited when they had a system of flexible working time, and men when they had complete control over what hours they worked. The benefit for men was slight, but represented a large improvement on 1992, when time discretion for men was associated with higher, not lower, family strain.[31]

What of satisfaction or dissatisfaction with childcare? The overall picture is again quite straightforward. Recall that this analysis was applicable only to those with a child under 12 years of age so that the sample size is much reduced.[32] There was one main finding here:

- Additional HRM practices increased dissatisfaction with childcare for both women and men in 2000.[33] They had previously made no difference in 1992, so the pressure from HRM appears to have increased for both women and men over the decade.

Beyond this, working parents' satisfaction with childcare appeared to be little affected by their employment conditions. Working hours, which were so important for FRS, were here unimportant, possibly because, as suggested earlier in this chapter, the employer is often willing to adjust hours to personal circumstances. The situation is quite different with HRM practices. Individuals have a hard time to opt out of the pressures these generate.

Flexible hours and family-friendly provisions also made little difference to childcare satisfaction or dissatisfaction, although one might have expected, or hoped, that they would improve matters here. In 2000, none of the flexible hours control practices made a difference either way to childcare satisfaction. Previously, in 1992, having flexible hours actually had an adverse rather than a helpful effect on childcare satisfaction for men, and made no difference either way for women.[34] In the main analysis, childcare assistance from the employer made no difference either way to childcare satisfaction.[35] This, however, might be because such assistance is offered to, or taken up by, only a small proportion of employees in any one year.[36] Alternative analyses were therefore run to look at the effects of enhanced maternity pay and at career break schemes, which apply to a larger proportion of parents.[37] Once again, though, these made no difference to levels of childcare satisfaction or dissatisfaction.

Over the two analyses, the findings provide a prima facie case that both working hours and HRM practices adversely affect the family, though in partly different ways. Additionally, the effect of working time flexibility is not as consistently favourable as is often assumed, although it does have some positive results. However, to arrive at a more complete interpretation, each of the analyses needs to be examined in more depth.

7.3.3. *Interpreting the Effects on Family Relationship Strain*

The effect of weekly working time is the natural point to start a more probing interpretation. It connects with the time-squeeze literature and will provide a helpful key for quantifying other results. In the analysis of FRS, the effect of hours was represented as *linear*. On this assumption, the results show that for every additional hour at work, FRS increases by a fixed amount. The same increase in strain results when someone changes hours from (say) twenty-five to twenty-six as from (say) fifty-five to fifty-six. Moreover, the increase in strain is five times greater when hours change from twenty-five to thirty as when they change from twenty-five to twenty-six. This assumption considerably simplifies the practical interpretation of the whole set of results, but is it reasonable?

From the viewpoint of popular discussion on work–life balance, the assumption may well seem rather strange. The usual focus of criticism is 'long hours', whether for either partner or for the couple in combination. This might suggest that paid work only creates a problem when it goes on for more than an average, or normal, amount of hours. In that case, FRS would not rise at all while paid-work hours were at a low or below-average level; strain would only start to climb when some threshold of high work hours was reached. More generally, the relationship might be curvilinear rather than a straight line, partly because people with rather different values, or tastes, may be found in different sections of the hours distribution, and the work–family trade-off may vary accordingly.

Figure 7.3 displays what kind of relationship exists in the data, which in this case are pooled across both surveys, to give a more reliable picture, but split first by sex and then by marital or partnership status. The method that underlies the charts, locally smoothed regression, allows the fitted line to follow the data, whatever its shape; the charts are truncated at 70 hours per week, since above that level the observations are sparse and the fitted line wanders wildly. The charts do in fact show that FRS rises steadily across the whole range from 1 to 70 paid hours, for both sexes and for both single people and those in couples. There is the suggestion of a slight kink at about 55 hours per week, above which point FRS rises a little *less* steeply. For men and for single people, there is also some indication that the slope of the curve increases once it gets close to about 35 hours and is less steep below that point.[38] Nonetheless, it is also clear that a straight line gives a good approximation to the empirical curve for each of these groups.

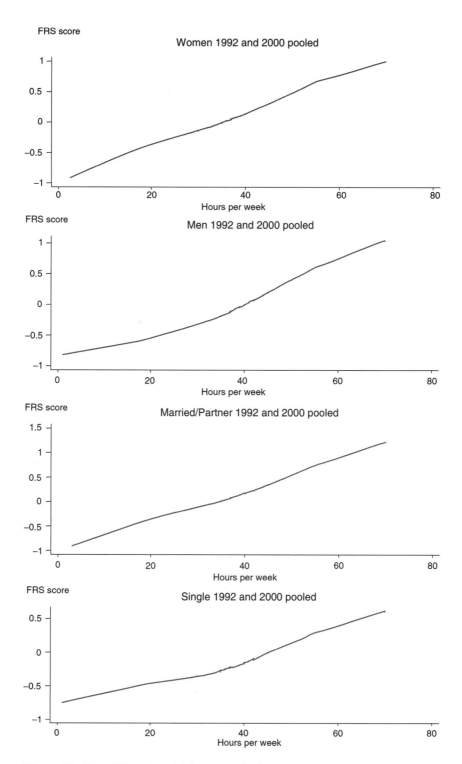

Figure 7.3. How FRS varies with hours worked.

This point has been laboured partly because it has considerable practical consequences. If the relationship between hours and FRS is approximately linear, one can claim that every hour's work makes a difference to family relations. But equally, one has to accept that what constitutes a 'balance' between paid work and the family is entirely a matter of social negotiation. There is *no* level of hours below which the problem of FRS is conclusively 'solved'.

Apart from this crucial policy point, the linear relationship makes it much easier to interpret the other influences on FRS. The FRS is not measured on a familiar scale like kilos or litres, but everyone knows what an hour is and most people probably have a feel, from their own experience, of what it means to have to stay at work for an extra hour. Given the linear relationship, one can make use of these understandings to quantify the effect of other influences on FRS in relative terms, compared with the effect of working hours (see notes 31–3 for the underlying numbers and Chapter 8 Section 8.5 for a similar use of this strategy).

In the case of men, an additional HRM practice had an effect on relationship strain that was similar to, but slightly lower than, an extra hour's weekly work. After converting this to an annual perspective, an additional HRM practice was like an extra 44 hours' annual work in 1992 or an extra 35 hours' annual work in 2000, from the viewpoint of FRS. In the case of women, the relative effect of HRM practices was greater. An extra HRM practice 'cost' women employees the same as 1.4 extra weekly hours, or about 70 hours annually, in 1992, and this rose steeply to an equivalence with 2.4 weekly hours, or somewhat more than 120 annual hours, in 2000.

This quantification helps to bring home two qualitative points. First, adding these kinds of HRM practices to a workplace's repertoire on average has implications for FRS that are of the same broad order of magnitude as adding to working hours. There is little justification in paying attention to the one while ignoring the other. Second, for women the relative effect of these HRM practices is greater than for men and growing over time. Indeed, by 2000 the effect of HRM practices on family relationships— measured relative to the hours standard—was about 3.5 times as great for women as for men.

Using the same measurement method, one can also assess the value of flexibility over choice of hours. Flexibility did become more valuable between the early 1990s and the start of the next decade. Perhaps employers were operating these methods differently by 2000 (flexibility associated with working from home?), or perhaps employees were learning to use them more effectively for their own benefit. For women, only a system of flexible hours was useful, and in terms of reduced FRS, it equated to a reduction of working time of about 8 hours per week or 400 hours per annum. For men, only autonomy over their own hours was useful, and it equated again to about 8 hours per week. So the potential of flexibility in hours for work–family balance has not been exaggerated. The trouble is that only a minority of employees has it. In 2000, the proportion of women employees with flexible working hours was still below 1 in 4 (23%), while the proportion of men with autonomy over hours was only 1 in 7 and most of these were managers or professionals. This can be contrasted with the wide application of HRM practices, particularly appraisals and group-based work organization, both of which are applied to more than one half of all employees. Indeed, the number of these HRM practices affecting employees, on average, was about four in 2000. Averaging across all female and male employees in 2000, HRM practices equated to about 300 hours-worth of FRS per annum, while flexible hours practices equated to a reduction of roughly 75 hours-worth of the same.

7.3.4. *Interpreting the Effects on Dissatisfaction with Childcare*

Turning to parents' degree of dissatisfaction with childcare arrangements, unfortunately one cannot use linear modelling assumptions to quantify the effects (see Box 7.3). To achieve a useful interpretation, one can instead focus on how the probability of being 'completely satisfied' is shifted by the presence of an additional HRM practice for a person with otherwise average characteristics.[39] The answer is that, in 2000, it was shifted down by 2.5 percentage points in the case of women, and by 1.8 percentage points in the case of men.

This may appear a surprisingly small difference for a statistically significant effect. Remember however that the majority of parents are at the 'completely satisfied' end of the scale, indicating how important it is to parents to get childcare right: any shift towards lower satisfaction is a correspondingly serious matter. Additionally, the number of these HRM practices varied considerably across workplaces in 2000, with the median employee experiencing four such practices while one-quarter of employees faced seven or more. Multiplying the effects by three therefore gives a reasonable indication of the implications for childcare satisfaction of working at a workplace that is highly orientated towards HRM, relative to one that is middling. When HRM practices come in large 'bundles'—as management experts exhort employers that they should—this means that parents will not only experience considerable work pressure on themselves but will also consequently struggle to achieve fully satisfactory childcare.

Some further interpretation is called for concerning flexible hours or autonomous control over hours. Their failure to increase satisfaction with childcare seems extremely surprising since one would suppose that such flexibility is important for parents in smoothing over the cracks in their childcare cover. One possibility is that where flexible hours are on offer, parents relying on this tend to push themselves harder, so losing some of the potential advantage from the viewpoint of easing childcare stresses on themselves. Moreover, the most likely situation is that one parent has flexible arrangements, while the other does not. Indeed, if the availability of flexible hours to one partner is independent of their availability to the other, only one in twenty couples will enjoy a situation where *both* have flexibility. It is not hard to see that the main load of coping with childcare emergencies will then fall on the flexi-mum or flexi-dad, making her or him less happy with the overall arrangements.

An important general point, putting the findings about childcare satisfaction alongside those for FRS, is that the influences of the workplace are not necessarily the same across different family outcomes. Indeed, only the HRM practices affect both FRS and childcare satisfaction, and they do so in an adverse way.

7.4. Critiquing the Time Squeeze

If one wishes, ultimately, to reform policies and improve work–family balance, then one has to understand how different kinds of families are differently affected by the problems at work. As discussed earlier, the time-squeeze literature points towards two-earner couples as particularly affected, and this is certainly the assumption of current public debate in Britain, where the Conservative Party, and conservative commentators, are pressing for policy changes that will reduce the financial pressure for both parents to work. Is it true, however, that two-earner couples experience more family pressure from their work situation?

The evidence of our 2000 survey, conducted at a time when paid hours and work pressures were increasing, says 'no'. If the time squeeze determines FRS in a straightforward way,[40] then those in two-earner families would on an average have higher strain than those who are sole earners

Table 7.3. Adverse family relationship strain, for women and men in one-earner and two-earner couples, 2000

	Women (%)_		Men (%)	
	One-earner	Two-earner	One-earner	Two-earner
Too little time for responsibilities—almost always or often	28	25	36	30
N	95	548	255	418
Partner/family get fed up—almost always or often	16	12	29	17
N	96	549	254	417
Give time I like to partner/family—never or rarely	15	15	30	18
N	97	551	255	418

Note: Percentages for other responses not shown; see Box 7.1 for full wording of items.
Source: WiB (2000).

in a couple. Table 7.3 compares sole earners with those in two-earner couples, showing the proportions who gave stressed responses to each of the questions in the FRS measure in 2000. It shows, for both women and men, that sole earners consistently had *higher* proportions of stressed respondents.

True, the differences are sometimes small (especially among women), and the simple percentages shown in Table 7.3 do not take account of the many other possible influences that were controlled in the main analysis, which may bias comparisons between two-earner and one-earner couples. In the full analysis, when the separate questions are combined into an overall measure, numerous controls are applied. With the full controls, those in two-earner couples should (according to the time-squeeze hypothesis) have higher FRS.[41] However, the opposite again holds true even when the full multivariate analysis is carried out. The main finding therefore is simple:

- In 2000, people had *lower* levels of FRS if they were members of two-earner couples than if they were the sole earner in a couple.

The differences in 2000 were both statistically significant and large.[42] *Being the earner in a one-earner couple, by comparison with being in a two-earner couple, was like working an extra 10 hours a week in terms of its adverse impact on FRS.*

Results are more in accord with preconceptions when one turns to satisfaction with childcare. Here, men who are sole earners are more satisfied than men in two-earner couples. However, to interpret this in terms of the time squeeze would be implausible and forced. Unsurprisingly, childcare is nearly always performed by their partners while these sole-earner men are at work: that men on the whole prefer this probably reflects persistent gender role attitudes. Women on the other hand appear to be moving away from these attitudes: in 1992, they too were somewhat more dissatisfied about childcare if both they and their partners were in paid work, but by 2000 their dissatisfaction with childcare arrangements was no longer affected by whether they were sole earners or in two-earner couples. Clearly, this set of gender differences cannot be explained in terms of family time: gendered differences in attitudes and values towards childcare can more plausibly be invoked. Although this is speculative, one might suppose that in 1992 the adverse job market played a dominant part in whether partners of employed women were non-employed, and these men would be childcarers through constraint. By 2000, there could be more men who preferred a household role and were childcarers through choice. Even so, women in one-earner couples became relatively less likely to see this as better than other kinds of childcare arrangement.

The evidence points to a stark conclusion: the prevailing preconceptions about how family characteristics affect pressures on the family are too simplistic. If sole earners experience more FRS than those in two-earner couples, a family time squeeze cannot be the basic problem because one-earner couples unequivocally expend less time on paid work than two-earner couples. This has important implications, not only for research on work and the family but also for the public policy debates about work–family balance, with their focus on two-earner couples and 'working mothers'.

7.4.1. *Can the Time Squeeze Be Salvaged?*

The issues, however, are not yet entirely resolved. There are two objections that might be raised in defence of the time squeeze, objections about aspects of the couple's situation that have been ignored in the analysis. Each of these aspects, if shown to be important, also has an interpretation for policy. First, we consider issues to do with money and then issues to do with variation in partner's hours of work.

One-earner couples suffer from a lack of income in comparison with two-earner couples. Perhaps it is a lack of money that creates family tension, while the relative affluence of two-earner couples buys off that strain. Childcare services, house-cleaning services, and home and garden maintenance services can all be purchased on the market. Income can also be used to buy products that cut the time needed for household work, for instance labour-saving equipment, or convenience foods. More income tends to give children more space for play, more toys, games, and creative materials, more stimulating activities and travel, and many other advantages. Child development studies have frequently shown income to be a potent factor for cognitive attainment. Perhaps two-earner couples do experience greater family strain than one-earner couples *at a given income level*?

Perhaps, on the other hand, the time squeeze does not work across all two-earner couples, but still applies where *both* partners work long hours. In other words, so long as one of the partners (usually the woman) works relatively short hours, a very common situation in Britain (for discussion see Crompton 1999), the couple can manage everything without much strain. But when both partners are heavily committed in terms of paid hours, the situation becomes difficult. Conversely, one could however argue that when women and men have similar hours, they will have still better family relations because then they are closer to equal shares. A US study that provides some evidence along these lines is that of Milkie and Peltola (1999). In that study, men whose partners worked longer hours reported greater personal success in achieving balance between job and home.

To address these points, further variant analyses were carried out. The 2000 survey did not ask for details of the partner's earnings. However, it did collect their job titles and the hours they usually worked. From this, it was possible to make a reasonable division of partners, in the two-earner couples, into those that were probably in the upper half of the earnings distribution (by sex) and those in the lower half. Additionally, there are of course full details of the respondent's own earnings.[43] When this additional information was added to the analysis, what happened?

- The higher relationship strain of those in two-earner couples was unaffected.
- Respondents with higher earnings also had higher FRS—even after taking account of their partner's working (or not), their own job level, their own working hours, and a host of other factors.

- This was the case for both men and women, but the adverse effect of their own higher earnings on FRS was much larger for women than men.[44]

- Respondents whose partners had above-average earnings also tended to have higher FRS. This difference however fell short of being statistically significant.

To quantify the own-earnings effect, for women an extra £100 per week adversely affected the FRS about the same as working an extra 6 hours a week; for men, the effect was roughly one-third of this. These results imply that the difference in FRS between one-earner and two-earner couples would be *still greater* if it were not for the *adverse* effect of the higher income that the two-earner group has.

The framework of Chapter 6 conveniently interprets these results. Effort and reward are linked by employer-incentive and -control policies and employer–employee negotiation. The extra effort and accountability that individuals have to commit to, in order to increase their earnings, means more pressure on family relations. There is no reason to doubt that extra earnings do offer the benefits for families that were mentioned earlier, such as the ability to buy-in household services and to spend more on children's development. But from the viewpoint of the FRS, it is not these benefits that matter but the additional pressures of earning more.[45]

The idea that the time squeeze might be concentrated in two-earner families where both partners work long hours was approached in a similar way to the analysis of earnings. The two-earner couples were divided into those where the partner's hours were below the median (for that sex of partner) and those where the partner's hours were above the median. The FRS was then compared between these two-earner groups and one-earner couples. It was then found that:

- Two-earner couples had lower FRS than one-earner couples, whether their partners worked above-average or below-average hours for their sex.

The differences within the two-earner couples were not statistically significant. Even when the partner works relatively long hours, respondents from two-earner couples experienced less FRS than did respondents from one-earner couples.

Overall, these additional analyses certainly added some useful points to the understanding of FRS. However, they do not undermine the important finding that *the employed member of one-earner couples experiences more relationship strain than members of two-earner couples.*

7.4.2. Rethinking Work–Family Conflict

Seen against the prevailing discourse about the time squeeze for two-earner couples, the finding that two-earner couples cope relatively better than one-earner couples may seem strange. However, from a sociological or social-psychological viewpoint, it is rather the belief that material variables (such as time or money) map directly into personal relationships that is a *non sequitur*. The survey data collected in the present research do not permit us to test other, more qualitative explanations of the difference in FRS between families with different characteristics, and we prefer not to bet on interpretations that would be entirely speculative. Yet there is no lack of relevant lines of explanation in the literature on families, and it may be useful to offer some signposts to this literature before moving on to the final topic of this chapter.

One of the most far-reaching explanations is in terms of individuals' personal *identification* with, or *commitment* to, work and family domains. According to Bielby and Bielby (1989), people become committed to work and family roles simply as a result of their continuing involvement with work and family activities and responsibilities. At the same time, however, commitment involves a process of identification with the assumed role. A crucial and still controversial issue, discussed by these authors, is whether identification with one role involves a trade-off against other roles, or whether people have the capacity to engage with multiple roles involving complex identification. There have been voices arguing for the potentially enriching nature of multiple roles (see especially Barnett 1999). However, much of the research on multiple roles is confined to an individual perspective. Especially in the context of the family, the allocation of roles and the interaction between partners' roles should be central (Marks and MacDermid 1996). One possibility is that when the members of a couple share the breadwinning role, they have more sympathy with each other's role-strains, whereas in one-earner couples difficulties may arise because the commitment or identification of each member is different from the other's.

Any discussion of social identities or roles also has to include norms. Returning to Bielby and Bielby (1989), one finds a strong emphasis on social norms as influences on the identities and roles by gender. They claimed, for example, that women are expected to take on multiple roles and manage trade-offs between them, while men are expected to specialize in their role as paid worker. The question is whether such role differences, if imposed by social norms, remain satisfactory to individuals of either sex under changing social conditions.

A general framework for approaching this question is offered by social comparison theory (Tajfel 1978*a*, 1978*b*), which continues to exert a considerable influence on social-psychological research on identity. According to this theory, an individual's positive or negative self-image depends in large part on the groups of which she or he is a member, combined with the valuation attached to those groups. At the same time, what constitutes a group with which individuals can identify depends on social recognition of the group as such. Once individuals have located themselves within social groups, their sense of well-being or deprivation depends on comparisons with other groups from which they are excluded. There is a strong tendency for members of majority groups to compare themselves positively with others, while members of minority groups experience feelings of deprivation.

This framework can readily be applied to the feelings of individuals in family-types such as 'male breadwinner', 'two-earner', or 'lone parent'. The suggestion would then be that two-earner families achieve better psychosocial outcomes for their members because such families have become the dominant family form and are associated with the socially applauded values of equal opportunity, while the members of one-earner families experience a kind of social exclusion. There are however contrary viewpoints. For example, gender display theory (Berk 1985), which is enjoying a current revival of interest, suggests that (many) individuals choose or construct roles that permit them to act out their gendered difference (or 'do gender'). In another version of this idea, Brines (1994) argued that the economic subordination of women in the family permitted both men and women to display sexual distinctiveness. Equality was illusory since men retained the main economic power even when women were employed. Indeed, as women took on more of an economic role, men might counter-intuitively reduce their family contribution so as to reassert masculinity. Only where the economic powers of the woman and the man were closely similar could family roles converge and the division of labour at home become more equal. These ideas lead on to the final analysis of this chapter.

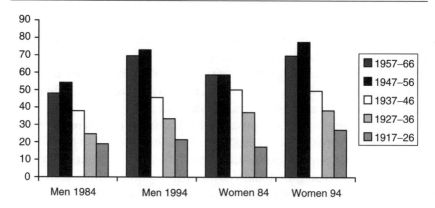

Figure 7.4. Rejection of traditional gender roles by birth cohort, 1984 and 1994: % rejecting traditional work–family roles.

Source: *British Social Attitudes* 1984 and 1994, reported in Scott (1999): Table 3.2 (adapted).

Note: Birth cohorts shown in legend at right of bar chart.

7.5. Employers' Practices and Equal Sharing in the Household

An area where family relationships may benefit from the increased paid work of women is through sharing of household work and childcare with male partners. This in turn links to changing social values about equality between the sexes. There may be special importance in changing attitudes of an egalitarian type towards the roles of women in the family. The crucial question, from our viewpoint, is whether workplace developments help or hinder work-sharing at home. If women's participation in paid work helps towards household equality, could equality even be advanced by long hours and rising work pressures?

Scott (1990, 1999; see also Crompton, Brockmann and Wiggins 2003) has documented large changes between age-groups and over time, in beliefs such as whether women with children should remain at home as carers, and whether home life is as fulfilling as paid work. Younger people (especially younger women) are much more egalitarian in maintaining that women and men should have a similar mix of work and home in their lives. Figure 7.4 rearranges findings from Scott's research in a form that emphasizes the growth of this kind of gender egalitarianism both by cohort and by time-period. This not only shows the age differences in egalitarianism at each date but also reveals that older age-groups have become more egalitarian in successive birth cohorts.

It seems plausible that when women in couples engage in paid work, they themselves spend less time in work in the home while their male partners spend more, either because they are obliged to do so by force of circumstance or because the growing egalitarianism that accompanies women's participation gives men a motivation to help more at home. Time-budget data indicate that some change of this type has taken place, but the fall in women's household work-time is much less than the increase in paid work, and the increase in male household work is small (Gershuny 2000). Gershuny, Godwin, and Jones (1994), using household survey data, estimated that there was only a modest fall in household activity for a full-time employed wife, compared with a non-employed wife.[46] The small size of the change led them to put forward the notion of 'lagged adaptation': couples were adjusting to the increasing participation of women in employment, but rather slowly. This view has also been supported by Layte (1999), who carried out an extended analysis of the same data.

More recently, however, this moderately positive view about gradually growing equality at home has received a battering. Crompton, Brockmann, and Lyonette (2005) showed that while the gently optimistic view held quite well for the 1989–94 period, it failed for Britain in the period from 1994 to 2002. During this recent period, the change achieved during 1989–94 had not been maintained, leading the authors to state that the equalization of household tasks may well have 'stalled' (Crompton, Brockmann, and Lyonette 2005: 219) and the rate of change had become 'glacial' (Crompton, Brockmann, and Lyonette 2005: 228).

The 1992 and 2000 surveys used in the present research deployed a measure of the household sharing of work that was similar to that used by Gershuny, Godwin, and Jones (1994) and Layte (1999). Each respondent with a partner was asked about 'jobs that need to be done to keep a home running, such as shopping, cooking, and cleaning' and answered on a 5-point scale running from 'I do almost all of it' to 'My partner does almost all of it'.[47] The central response was 'We share it half and half'. Comparing the reported housework shares from this question over the two years (Table 7.4), our verdict would be similar to that of Crompton, Brockmann, and Lyonette (2005). Men's replies suggested a 7-percentage-point fall in women doing all the household work, but women's replies suggested a 4-percentage-point increase: averaging over the two, one gets close to no change. Again, men's replies suggest a 4-percentage-point increase in 'we share it half and half', but women's replies suggest no

Table 7.4. Sharing of household work: women's and men's perceptions

	1992			2000		
	Women (%)	Men (%)	All (%)	Women (%)	Men (%)	All (%)
Female partner does almost all	23	16	19	27	9	17
Female partner does most	37	41	39	32	42	37
50/50 share	38	42	40	38	45	42
Male partner does most or almost all	2	1	2	3	5	4
N	1,191	1,238	2,429	693	670	1,363

Note: Table confined to employees in couples.

Sources: EiB (1992); WiB (2000).

change at all. Overall, a stalling of the change process in Britain seems a fair judgement.

Why has this stalling taken place, despite the apparently strong and continuing trends towards gender-egalitarian attitudes? Crompton, Brockmann, and Lyonette (2005) suggest that the pressures in the work-place may provide at least part of the explanation. The pressures they allude to include some that are reminiscent of the argument of Schor (1991) about market power: longer hours are imposed by employers, especially on men, in conditions where competition has increased and unions have become weaker. They also include pressures from within the firm: especially pressures of careers that obstruct personal flexibility between work and family, and pressures of work intensification. The result is a reversion towards primary responsibility for the household falling on the female partner, not by the male partner's choice but by the constraint he faces. These authors, then, are claiming that recent increases in employment pressures reach inside the home to affect the sharing of tasks within couples and, more generally, to obstruct the social movement towards gender equality. This is a claim that can be examined further with the survey data.

7.5.1. *Analysing Homework*

To analyse homework shares, the question displayed in Table 7.4 is used. The further analysis considered how homework sharing was affected by the individual's own hours of work, by the HRM practices that impinged on her or him, and by the employment status of the partner. Because Crompton, Brockmann, and Lyonette (2005) emphasize careers as obstacles to household work-sharing, we also look particularly at the role of social class since this is a useful proxy for career orientation.

The key points from this set of analyses were as follows:

- Consistent with earlier research, the more hours of paid work that a woman did, the more her partner tended to share the housework.

- Men's hours of paid work made no difference to their own contribution to housework.

- The number of HRM practices at the workplace—representing internal pressure—made a significant difference to housework sharing in 2000. Women facing more HRM in their paid work on average got more help in housework from their partners. But men facing more HRM in their paid work on average participated less in housework.

- In 1992, women in higher managerial and professional jobs were very much more likely to have partners who did housework, than women in other classes (consistent with Brines 1994, discussed above). This persisted in 2000, but the class differential narrowed considerably, suggesting that high-career women no longer got such 'special treatment' from their partners.

The results needing most careful unpacking concerned the differences in housework sharing between one-earner and two-earner couples:

- When the woman was the sole earner, male partners tended to take on a larger proportion than if the woman were in a two-earner couple. If the man was the sole earner, he did less of the housework than if his partner also had paid work.

- So women's participation in employment unambiguously shifted housework shares towards equality.

- There are therefore two situations with more sharing: two-earner couples, and one-earner couples where the woman is in paid work. The situation with least sharing is one-earner couples where the man is in paid work.

The results show that pressures from the market and the workplace do indeed make themselves felt inside the home, affecting housework shares between the partners. But their effects are more complex and multifaceted than is inferred by Crompton, Brockmann, and Lyonette (2005). What is most consistent with their interpretation is that HRM practices constrained the participation of men in sharing of household work. However, there was no indication that longer hours affected housework shares differently over the 1992–2000 period, and the influence they exerted continued to be towards greater equality of shares. Even the effect of HRM practices was partly ambiguous because while men were pushed away from sharing in housework by the pressures on themselves, they were pulled forward by pressures from the same source on their partners. An additional change over time is the erosion of the special position of women in higher management and the professions. Even this, though, can be interpreted in contrasting ways. Women's higher careers may be getting less support from men, or alternatively men could be making their support, such as it is, less conditional on the economic status of their partners. Either way, the economic power interpretation of Brines (1994) seems to be weakening over time.

Finally, it is worth briefly noting that these analyses also looked at the same working-time flexibility provisions as were treated in the earlier analyses. The result here is very simple and underlines the limited effectiveness of these provisions:

- Flexibility over hours at work had *no appreciable influence* on the sharing of housework.

Overall, the survey data show that the sharing of housework is substantially affected by working hours and by work practices. In this, it is like the other outcomes considered earlier in this chapter, FRS and satisfaction with childcare. But in the earlier analyses the effects of the market and the workplace were entirely adverse, whereas the effects on work-sharing within the household are more mixed. In particular, women's participation in employment, the hours women work, and the work pressures they consent to continue to be positive drivers towards household equality. The pressures exerted by increasingly intensive HRM practices on men are, however, a current obstacle to their sharing of household roles, as postulated by Crompton, Brockmann, and Lyonette (2005).

7.6. Summary and Conclusions

The theoretical question that motivated Chapters 5 and 6 was why do employees accept or comply with overwork? In the present chapter, that question has been extended: why do employees accept or comply with overwork *that adversely affects their family relations*? The inclusion of the family in the question has then led to further theoretical issues: by what means does overwork affect the family, and what is the nature of the familial relation that is affected?

The preceding chapters indicated that employers obtained employees' compliance with increased requirements for effort by means of increasingly dense systems of control and incentive, and by their use of concerted HRM practices to promote higher performance. This type of explanation continues to hold the centre-ground in the present chapter, but with an enlarged perspective. Through their combined HRM practices, employers put pressure on employees (and hence on family relations). The practices represent the power of the organization to extract progressively more effort from employees through the elaboration of their internal systems. The pervasively negative effects of these practices on family relations indicate the efficacy of this internal power.

Yet this power would evaporate if employees did not respond to incentives. This chapter differs from Chapter 6 in explicitly recognizing that employees' own material aspirations are a necessary condition for the effectiveness of employers' internal systems. Here the chapter has drawn heavily on Schor's (1991) ideas about the role of consumer markets in motivating long working hours for the family. In economic terms, employees' 'choice' of long working hours shows that they prefer more income to more home-time. But the structure of consumer markets (in Britain especially the housing market), along with employers' collective control over the working hours on offer, constrains this choice. The conceptualization can then be extended from its initial focus on working hours to cover employers' internal systems of motivation more generally. In contemporary British employment, the wide earnings differentials, the large and growing emphasis on financial incentives, and the reaffirmation of promotion ladders can all be understood as means of harnessing employees' consumer aspirations to demands for higher effort that are expressed partly through long hours and partly through internal performance management and HRM systems.

It is natural to try to explain the consequences for the family in similar economic or materialist terms. The individual's cost of effort can be equated with the time and personal energy transferred out of the family and into the workplace. The result is a family deficit, expressed most directly in the idea of the 'time squeeze'. Yet this breaks down directly if one looks at FRS. If this corresponded to the time squeeze, then the members of two-earner couples would experience greater strain than those who are sole earners within couples, since two-earner couples on average have 35 hours less family time per week. The British survey evidence shows that the opposite applies, with sole earners much more affected by FRS than those in two-earner couples.

A resolution of this seeming paradox is to accept that family relations are socially constructed, involving identities and roles, and thus attitudes and values. There is no reason to doubt that working time and work effort affect family relations directly, but over and above this there are interactions between job and family of a qualitative type that are not captured by material employment conditions. When, for example, women are in paid work as well as having partners and children, this increases their total job–family workload, and presumably this pressure increases with additional hours of paid work. Yet the same conditions also lead to increased participation by male partners in household work, and so contribute towards gender role equality both through that fact and through further attitude change resulting from altered experience. Since social attitudes have moved strongly in favour of gender role equality, the tendency for women to take on more paid work can reasonably be expected to lead to improved family relations through a sense of socially approved shared roles inside and outside the home, even while it may also place adverse pressures on family relations through a material shortage of time and energy.

Finally, this chapter in its entirety bears upon conventional understandings of the employment relationship. Employment has usually been represented as an initially incomplete contract that is, in effect, completed in the practice of the workplace, in Marx's 'hidden abode'. The evidence of Chapter 6 supported theorists such as Wilhelm Baldamus and Richard Edwards in suggesting that this process of contract completion is, in reality, never complete since there is a continual process of formal or informal negotiation and contestation to stretch the terms of agreement one way or another. With family concerns now accepted as legitimate within the employment sphere, the incompleteness of the employment contract becomes still more apparent. The processes of negotiation and contestation now have to take account of the uncompensated costs that families bear as a result of workplace practice. As the family becomes the main moral resource for society, these costs are becoming increasingly recognized and will tend to reflect back upon and influence the negotiated practice of the workplace.

Notes

1. For example, three in four employees rated their family as 'extremely important' to them, while only one in eight gave this rating to paid work. The questions used were based on the European Values Survey (1990).

2. Source: WiB (2000) survey. The actual figure is 74%.
3. A striking example is pharmacy, where data have been analysed over a forty-year period by Hassell et al. (2002).
4. The estimate from the WiB (2000) survey is 26%, up from 19% in 1992. In 2000, 6% of women worked more than 48 hours per week, up from 4% in 1992.
5. See websites of the Confederation for British Industry, the Work Foundation, and the Department for Trade and Industry.
6. These suites of practices are often referred to as 'high commitment practices' or 'HPWS', although terminology varies greatly.
7. This view can be traced back to 'time preference' studies developed by Best in the 1970s (Best 1980a, 1980b). But many of these studies fail to address the crucial trade-off between hours and earnings (e.g. Clarkberg and Moen 2001), and this is problematic for their argument, for it is too easy for a person to 'prefer' shorter hours when earnings are not in question. Further, some studies that have attempted to deal with the hours–earnings trade-off have perhaps relied too much on their respondents' reasoning capacity. For instance, Horrell, Rubery, and Burchell (1994) asked people whether they would like to have reduced hours, increased hours, or the same hours, given an unchanged hourly wage. This requires an inference that, if say hours are reduced, then so too will earnings since earnings = hours × wage. Some people may find this too subtle.
8. The actual figures were 31% for women and 12% for men, with 27% and 8%, respectively, making requests that were also granted.
9. The actual figures were 25% of those preferring longer hours/more pay, 20% of those wanting shorter hours/less pay, and 14% of those preferring to keep their existing hours and pay.
10. One can also put this in some perspective by considering those who felt their wage or salary was 'on the low side'. Nearly one in three (32%) had this feeling, and of these 27% intended to move on. In all, nearly 9% felt their pay was low *and* were intending to change jobs. More people were on their preferred hours than on a pay level they considered reasonable or better.
11. Some writers (e.g. Rose 2005) continue to argue that there is a real difference between expressions of satisfaction and expressions of dissatisfaction, an idea promoted at an earlier time by Herzberg (1966). This issue was extensively investigated in the past and no evidence was found to justify separate measurement scales (see for instance the review in Smith, Kendall, and Hulin 1969). We follow this latter view and consider that it is legitimate to speak of satisfaction and dissatisfaction interchangeably since they constitute one scale. A decrease in satisfaction is equivalent to an increase in dissatisfaction, and vice versa.
12. This has also been observed in other surveys, notably the British Household Panel survey: see Rose (2005).

13. As Immanuel Kant noted (in his essay of 1784, *What is enlightenment?*), everything changed when Frederick the Great asserted that his people were free to debate whatever they wanted, provided they continued to obey him.

14. A striking recent (2005/6) example was the campaign of British TV chef and celebrity, Jamie Oliver, for schools to provide healthy lunches for children. Previously, the poor quality of British school meals was familiar, but unremarked, to successive generations, but media exposure converted this into a national crisis that evoked the personal intervention of the Prime Minister and substantial additions to school catering budgets.

15. From the *Tractatus Logico-Philosophicus*.

16. For an extensive philosophical analysis of framing in relation to personal evaluations, see Anderson (1993).

17. Information is not available on hours preferences in the 1992 survey. The average satisfaction for all employees in 1992 can be interpreted as an upper bound estimate (Manski 1995) of satisfaction for those off their preferred hours. In other words, those not getting their preferred hours can be assumed to have below-average satisfaction with hours.

18. Schor's book argued that annual hours of paid work had been growing longer in the USA, and this reading of the factual evidence has been contested by others (Coleman and Pencavel 1993; Robinson and Bostrom 1994). Schor's general argument does not however depend on this historical point.

19. From a strictly economic viewpoint, it is hard to see why the time squeeze constitutes a problem for the family. The family can be seen as trading off its time resources against added consumption, a classic formulation of labour supply theory: in such a framework, the trade-off is a reflection of preferences whose rationality cannot be questioned.

20. An earlier analysis along these lines was published in the *British Journal of Industrial Relations* (White et al. 2003). The present analysis has been substantially revised and extended.

21. We also take account in our analysis of any 'moonlighting' hours the individual works in a second job, but we do not add these to the hours in the main job because their meaning is distinct. The hours in the second job really are at the initiative of the individual and cannot be thought of in the same terms as the hours in the primary job.

22. High-performance work systems are a particular configuration of HRM practices that incorporates personal development and participation in decisions as well as the elements included in the present analysis.

23. For the USA, see Osterman (1995); for Britain, see White et al. (2004: 141).

24. In the US literature, what is here called pressure on the family is often referred to more technically as 'negative spillover' from work to home or from work to family. The relatively informal term used here carries the same sense as the more technical one.

25. The measure used here is identical to that in White et al. (2003) where it is called an index of 'negative job-to-home spillover'.

26. According to recent research in the USA, brief episodes in daily life that provoke negative-stress emotional responses are followed by increases in cortisol levels (measured in saliva samples), which can cumulatively have considerable repercussions for cognitive function and for many aspects of health (Adam 2005).

27. In 2000, the correlations were 0.57 with work strain and 0.46 with dissatisfaction with hours/workload. The correlations were lower in 1992 (0.49 and 0.28, respectively).

28. Most people meet other members of their family, even if they have no partner and no child; and most find the questions used in the FRS measure relevant to themselves (White et al. 2003).

29. In this OLS regression model, the coefficients and t-statistics for hours of work were as follows: women, 1992: 0.0216 (4.56); women, 2000: 0.0219 (6.13); men, 1992: 0.024 (6.21); men, 2000: 0.0259 (8.55). These are the increases in FRS for each additional hour.

30. The coefficients and t-statistics were women, 1992: 0.03 (2.25); women, 2000: 0.0516 (4.58); men, 1992: 0.0204 (1.65); men, 2000: 0.0174 (1.71). These are the increases for each additional HRM practice. We interpret the estimates for men as different from zero, since (*a*) they are significant at the 10% level and (*b*) previous research shows that constituent items within the set of HRM practices affect FRS for men to a significant degree (White et al. 2003).

31. The significant coefficients and t-statistics were women, flexible hours system: −0.172 (2.03); men, decide own hours: −0.213 (1.80). Although the latter result is significant only at the 10% level, it differs very significantly from the male estimate for 1992, decide own hours: 0.511 (4.58). These effects are *relative to* having fixed hours of work that go with the job.

32. The *N*s were as follows: women, 1992: 185; women, 2000: 348; men, 1992: 241; men, 2000: 340.

33. In this ordered logit model, the coefficients (multiplicative effects on proportional odds) and t-statistics were women, 2000: 1.104 (2.85); men, 2000: 1.075 (2.01). The corresponding t-statistics for 1992 were less than 1.

34. The coefficient (multiplicative effect on proportional odds) and t-statistic for men in 1992 were 2.972 and 2.53, respectively. Other t-statistics were less than 1.

35. All t-statistics were less than 1.

36. Other possible explanations include that the assistance provided is of variable quality, or that the type or quality of assistance offered lags behind employees' expectations.

37. Childcare assistance was provided, in 2000, only for 5% of the sample with an under-12 child, while career break schemes were available for 10%, and enhanced maternity pay was more widely available, being recognized as a

benefit by 30%. Although enhanced maternity pay applies by definition only to a period when the mother is away from her job, its availability reduces pressure to return early and might have been expected to give more time to set up satisfactory childcare arrangements before resuming paid work.

38. Seven per cent of men worked less than 35 hours per week; the figure was 22% among single people.

39. The quantity being estimated here is the marginal effect or partial effect: the change in the probability of complete satisfaction when increasing the number of HRM practices by one. The calculation is made keeping all other variables at their average values.

40. For instance, as a linear projection or as a positive monotonic function.

41. This is because the analysis model controls for the individual's own working hours, but not the partner's working hours. Models with partner's working hours are considered in the next section.

42. In an analysis confined to couples in 2000, the differences in FRS are given by the coefficients (with t-statistics in brackets) for those in two-earner couples relative to those in one-earner couples: women: -0.243 (2.12) and men: -0.256 (3.41). The estimated differences were smaller in 1992, but in the same direction.

43. An initial rough estimate of partner's earnings can be obtained by imputing the national average hourly wage, for each occupation by sex, from the New Earnings Survey 2000 and multiplying it by the reported weekly hours. These estimates, which are undoubtedly 'noisy', can then be dichotomized into those above and below the median. Dichotomization at the median was shown by Wald (1940) to be a method of reducing the bias from measurement error in a regressor.

44. The coefficients in an OLS regression analysis, with FRS as the dependent variable, were 0.13 for women (t-statistic, 4.02) and 0.04 (t-statistic, 3.04) for men. This is the estimated effect per additional £100 (in year 2000 values) of weekly earnings.

45. Another possible interpretation is suggested by a theoretical model put forward by Gershuny (2000). In essence, he argues that additional income creates a need for additional time for consumption. On this view, the added FRS for high earners may reflect (at least in part) frustrated desire for more time to enjoy family income.

46. The figure they put on this fall was 10 percentage points: this however depended on an arbitrary scaling of ordinal responses.

47. In 1992, the scale was presented with answers running from 'Female partner does nearly all of it' to 'Male partner does nearly all of it'.

8

Unequal jobs: job quality and job satisfaction

Some jobs are better than others. Everyone recognizes this fact, both when they discuss jobs in daily conversation and when they must actually choose among jobs.

Jencks, Perman, and Rainwater (1988: 1323)

A good job is hard to define.

Tilly and Tilly (1998: 162)

8.1. Introduction

In the preceding chapters, we examined recent changes in people's experience of work. In as far as changes have taken place some undoubtedly improve working life while others have a more negative impact. Change has always its upside and its downside: the important question is whether on the average the goods outweigh the bads. What we would really like to know is whether, taking everything into consideration, job quality has on average increased or decreased as a result of these changes. Some aspects of change are rather well documented. Goos and Manning (2003) for instance find that over the last few decades employment growth has been concentrated in both high-wage and low-wage occupations and that to place the emphasis on growth in high-skill sectors is to tell only half the story. If we measure job quality in terms of earnings, the evidence about movements in wage inequality since the 1980s is unequivocal—those at the top of the wage distribution are doing very well and those at the bottom are barely holding their own with most of the growth in inequality happening during the 1980s (Machin 2003). In Chapter 3, we showed that earnings inequalities between broadly defined occupational groups have, in the course of eight years, increased and that in some cases the lowest paid groups may actually have done worse in real terms in 2000 than they did in 1992.

But money, in the sense of wages, is not everything and in this chapter we try to adopt a synoptic view of job quality that allows us to talk of job inequality in general rather than just inequalities in earnings.[1] In doing this, we have to make a sacrifice that gives this chapter a slightly different flavour to those that have preceded it. The difficulty is that we lack suitable data to make synoptic comparisons over time and *faute de mieux* we are restricted to describing the situation in 2000. However, we are able to paint a picture of what British employees on average find desirable and undesirable about the jobs they held in 2000, and we are able to examine how job quality is related to four key aspects of the contractual situation that have been at the centre of the narrative of change developed in the rest of this book: whether there is collective representation in the workplace, part-time versus full-time working hours, open-ended versus fixed-term contracts, and social-class position. The pattern of demographic change with respect to union representation, the prevalence of part-time work and temporary contracts as well as the evolution of the occupational structure are well known and have in part been described above. Although commentators often assume that they know the implications of changes with respect to these variables (normally believing that they are bad), there is actually remarkably little hard evidence about the matter beyond studies of particular cases, anecdotes, and journalistic impressions. In this chapter, we try to provide some hard evidence about the general picture.

Jobs have utilities and disutilities attached to them: those that are inherently unpleasant or that are risky in terms of exposure to unemployment or hazardous to health and personal safety tend to attract higher wages than jobs that are comparable in all other respects. If we want to talk about 'good and bad jobs', and not restrict what this phrase means to differences in wages, then we need to find a way of incorporating other relevant information into the calculus, just as people themselves must do in everyday choice situations. As Jencks and colleagues (hereafter JPR) point out in the quotation that heads this chapter, people seem able to make the distinction between good and bad jobs in everyday conversation and are forced to reveal their understanding of these terms when they make actual job choices. Normally, however, they do not articulate precisely the meaning they give to 'good' or 'bad' or make explicit the relative weight that they give to different job characteristics. They certainly do not try to aggregate the millions of individual weights used by all the employees in the economy in an attempt to define a public ranking of job desirability that summarizes in one number as much information as possible about the community's evaluation of how well someone is doing. In this chapter, we try to estimate what such a ranking would look like if they did.

Trying to say something about what makes a job desirable or undesirable when we do not just mean that it is relatively well or poorly paid involves bringing together insights from several literatures that are rarely brought into conjunction. Sociologists often make use of orderings of occupations generated by various techniques that rank occupational groups in terms of constructs such as prestige, social status, general desirability, and socio-economic status (Goldthorpe and Hope 1974; Stewart, Prandy, and Blackburn 1980; Prandy 1990; Chan and Goldthorpe 2004).[2] The details of how the ranking is made are crucial to defining the meaning of what is actually measured but here we pursue that issue no further than to make two points. First, what is measured is usually said to be more than just earnings, income, or wealth. Second, the rankings arrived at are held to have an objective status in the sense that either they represent the average judgement of the relevant community or they capture the outcome of actual social processes, usually marital or friendship choices, that are influenced by the social status of the choice makers.[3] Within this tradition a good job is simply a job in an occupation that scores highly on the relevant scale.

Setting aside mere observable differences in earnings, economics offers us another way of understanding what might be meant by a good or bad job. There is a sense in which a good job is one in which an individual receives a higher wage than he or she should expect compared to some counterfactual reference point and a bad job is one in which he or she receives a lower wage. Doing better than expectations is sometimes equated with the concept of earning an economic rent—a wage premium in excess of the going market rate for the job—which is resistant to being competed away because of the insider advantages that accrue to job incumbents from tacit job-specific knowledge and the advantages that accrue to employers from not incurring the costs entailed in market search for an equally productive outsider and from the productivity loss incurred while an outsider learns the job.[4] Doing well is beating the market and continuing to be able to do so.

Clearly, there is something complementary about these different ways of looking at the issue. A sociologist might want to say that in terms of the way the community sees things, on average, being a management consultant is more desirable than being a domestic cleaner, whereas an economist might point to the fact that within both of these occupational groups there may be economic rents to be divided between employee and employer and that differences in bargaining strength will lead to variation in job goodness and badness within broad occupational categories.

There is another source of information that we might turn to in order to define job desirability: that is information about levels of job satisfaction. An obvious candidate for the role of measuring relative labour market success is to ask people how satisfied or dissatisfied they are with their job. Indeed, one might claim that such an index is as close as we can get to a direct measure of utility.

A job satisfaction scale explicitly measures individual differences between jobs rather than between occupations, but it suffers from disadvantages that prevent it being entirely suitable as a measure of job desirability mostly because it will be influenced by individual idiosyncrasies of mood and taste. Social survey respondents have information about their satisfaction levels elicited from them in a way that prevents them making an explicit comparison with a fixed and inter-subjectively equivalent anchor point. Without this they can only make assessments relative to their own expectation level. For most people after perhaps the first few years of heady optimism about their career this probably means that they only compare their own situation to others within their feasible set of jobs, including the worst-case scenario they can realistically imagine befalling them. Thus the prodigal son may be quite satisfied to share acorns with pigs—it is better than starving in the gutter—while the investment banker may weep bitter tears because her half a million pound bonus is not quite as large as that of the woman sitting at the next desk.[5] This 'reference group' problem means that data on absolute levels of job satisfaction are unlikely in themselves to be an unambiguous source of information about general labour market advantage. This does not mean that they have no predictive value. What they are likely to contain is information about perceptions of job quality among the jobs in the respondent's current feasible set. Empirical data on job satisfaction invariably shows that the overwhelming majority of respondents to questionnaire surveys are either satisfied or very satisfied with their jobs. Given that the labour market is essentially a gigantic sorting and selecting process this is scarcely surprising. At any one time the population of job holders consists of people who have self-selected themselves into the best job within their feasible set they can get, people who have adjusted the size of their feasible set to be congruent with the offers they actually got and people who feel that they can do better. Job satisfaction data particularly provides valuable information about the latter, who at any one time are, presumably, a relatively small group.[6]

Although job satisfaction ratings will contain relatively weak data about job desirability, it would be odd if job desirability and job satisfaction were completely unrelated. In fact we would expect that measures of desirability that either explicitly or implicitly incorporate information about desirability relative to some reference point or expectation will be relatively good predictors of satisfaction, and in Section 8.9 we examine the effects of earnings and job desirability on satisfaction levels and show that this is the case.

The plan of this chapter is as follows. In Section 8.2, we discuss ways of defining and measuring job quality and explain the logic of the approach that we take. In Section 8.3, we defend ourselves against the claim that there is no need to create a new measure of job quality because adequate conventional measures already exist. In Section 8.4, we show that earnings have a highly non-linear relationship to the way in which people rate their job. In Section 8.5, we discuss the results from estimating a prediction equation for job ratings that includes both monetary and non-monetary aspects of jobs as predictors. The prediction equation leads straightforwardly to an index of job desirability. In Section 8.6, we explore the relationship between the job desirability index and social classifications based on occupations. Particular attention is paid to quantifying the amount of intra-occupational variability in job desirability. This leads in Section 8.7 to a discussion of the desirability of different occupations and the creation of a prediction model that allows the assignment of average job desirability scores to all occupations. In Section 8.8, we consider how indicators of contractual status affect job desirability. In Section 8.9, we explore the relationship between job satisfaction, job desirability, and wages.

8.2. How Would I Know a Good Job If I Saw One?

Right from the outset the reader should take heed of the spirit of Tilly and Tilly's caution about the difficulty of saying something positive about job quality, though in actual fact the problem is not quite as they put it. We can in principle define a good job to be anything we want it to be using any characteristics that seem plausible to us.[7] The real difficulty is in devising a consistent method that captures in a single number as much of the community's agreement as possible about what is to count as good and bad. Inevitably, this will be an exercise in stuffing a quart into a pint pot because a single number cannot summarize complex multidimensional information without sacrificing detail. Neither, as JPR point out, can such an index 'rank jobs in such a way that all workers will prefer all jobs with high scores to all jobs with low scores'. But as they go on to say: 'A good index should, however, rank jobs in such a way as to maximize the proportion of workers who prefer jobs with high scores to jobs with low scores.' If there is no meeting of minds and hence no structure to the community's view about the matter, which seems inherently unlikely, then the single number index will contain no useful information. To the extent that there is a core of commonly understood perceptions, an index can for some purposes be used to summarize them.

It would certainly be convenient if employees perceived the utility they got from employment purely in terms of wages because, on the mild assumption that everyone rates a state of the world in which he or she earns more as preferable to one in which he or she earns less, the relative goodness of a job would be a perfectly predictable function of pay and there would be no difference between the aggregate ordering of jobs and the private orderings. In reality, however, jobs have all sorts of characteristics that people value apart from wages: convenient hours, safe working conditions, long holidays, pleasant colleagues, and so forth all tend to figure in people's calculations. *Ceteris paribus* they may still at the margin prefer higher to lower wages and thus comparing jobs with identical content and identical conditions of service the one paying the higher rate is the better job. However, once we admit that more than just wage rates enter the calculation we can no longer rely on information about what employees choose at the margin to derive a public ranking of job desirability.[8]

In their strangely neglected paper, JPR propose a novel measure of labour market success—the index of job desirability (IJD). This combines both monetary and non-monetary aspects of jobs and weights each element by the impact it has on average on the rating social survey respondents give to the desirability of their own job compared to a notional average job. The beauty of the IJD is that it captures in a single number the outcome of the trade-offs that labour market participants must in fact make when choosing among available jobs. Some people prefer to trade off lower pay against greater job security; others favour more convenient hours over longer holidays. The IJD abstracts from the idiosyncrasies of individual preferences and gives weight only to job characteristics that have, on average, either a net positive or negative effect on ratings of job desirability. It does not capture a consensus about what makes for a good job. No measure can do that because, in the strict sense, there is no societal wide consensus. The IJD is however constructed from the objective aspects of the jobs that people hold and combines these in a single index with weights proportional to the net importance accorded to each aspect, on average, by the working community at large. If it is meaningful to ask what on average do British employees value about their job, an answer can be given by listing the component parts of an IJD along with the weights. In addition, and more important for our purposes, the IJD allows us to rank jobs according to their desirability and gives us scale values that correspond to positions on a one-dimensional continuum. Because of this the IJD is a convenient tool with which to examine both the causes and consequences of inequalities in labour market outcomes. If one needs a single number summary of which jobs are relatively good, bad, or ugly, then the IJD provides it.

8.3. Are You Not Just Reinventing the Wheel?

A reasonable, sounding objection to constructing yet another index of labour market advantage is the entirely understandable one that the research community is already awash with such measures and has no need of one more. The sociologist's alternatives to earnings—social status, socio-economic status, occupational prestige, and various measures of social class—superficially look like they are intended to capture the same information as an IJD. So why do we need another measure? The simple answer is that the existing measures suffer from the disadvantage that they entail the use of aggregated occupational units rather than information about the actual jobs held by individuals. People in similar class positions or of similar social standing can still be heterogeneous with respect to the desirability of the jobs they hold. No matter how good a measure based on occupation is, it can only capture between-occupation variability in job desirability. If, as turns out to be the case, within-occupation variability is about as great as between-occupation variability, and within-occupation variability is not merely noise due to measurement error, then, depending on the purpose of the analysis, occupational status or prestige will be less than perfect substitutes for a measure of job desirability. In most survey investigations we are not in a position to do better than categorize individuals by summary measures of the aggregated occupational category their job belongs to. But this is clearly second best and it would be perverse to continue doing it when we have data that allows us to do much better. Moreover, if one believes that for some purposes the fundamental unit of analysis in the study of labour market success is the job rather than the occupation, then we should measure characteristics of jobs and not the aggregated characteristics of occupations.[9]

8.4. Job Desirability

An index of job desirability should reflect '... how well workers have done in the competition for what other workers regard as desirable jobs' (Jencks et al. 1988: 1324). JPR's solution to the problem is both elegant and simple. First, ask survey respondents to assign a score to their own job reflecting how good they think it is compared to an average job (see row 1 of Table 8.1). In the WiB 2000 interview, each respondent was asked to do just this.[10] After truncating a few absurdly large values the observed range is from 1 to 2,000. The mean rating is 150.0 and the median 130.0. The 25th percentile is 100.0, the 75th 194.0, and the 95th 300.0. The next step is to regress the logarithm of this rating on a set of monetary and non-monetary objective job characteristics that are plausible predictors of job desirability.[11] Then, we take the predicted values from this equation as the index of job desirability. What the third stage does is give to each item in the linear combination an estimated weight that is the average net weight given to it when individuals are asked to make a judgement about which jobs are better than others. Objective features of a job that are of purely idiosyncratic importance will receive zero weight and only those features that individuals give, on average, positive or negative weight to will have any influence. It is crucial to understand that we are not interested in the respondent's rating per se: that will be far too idiosyncratic for our purposes. What matters for us is how these ratings are predicted by objective features of the respondents' jobs.[12]

Clearly, an important part of our story concerns how job ratings are related to earnings and it is important to specify that relationship correctly. Taking the natural logarithm of the reported ratings will simplify interpretation. Likewise it is convenient to be able to interpret the relationship in terms of the percentage change in job rating arising from a percentage change in wage—in other words as an 'elasticity'. To accomplish

Table 8.1. Variables used in constructing the index of job desirability

1. Job rating. 'When most people think of average jobs they think of jobs like car mechanic, electrician, or secretary. Let us give the average job a score of 100. I would like you to compare your job to an average job. If you think your own job is twice as good as an average job, for example, give it 200. If you think your job is half as good as an average job, give it 50. You can give any number you like. Considering everything, if an average job scores 100, what score would you give to your job?'

2. Log (weekly wage/281.65). Split into 3 linear splines with ranges >£4.00 and <£281.65; $\geq$£281.65 and <£626.82; $\geq$£626.82.

3. Respondent has, while in post, personally negotiated with employer about pay and did not receive a pay rise, scored 1. Has not negotiated or successfully negotiated a pay rise, scored 0.

4. Usual weekly hours of work including paid and unpaid overtime.

5. Respondent has, while in post, personally asked for a change in hours of work and request was turned down, scored 1. Has not asked or request granted, scored 0.

6. 'My job requires that I keep learning new things.' Scored: 1, Strongly disagree; 2, Disagree; 3, Agree; and 4, Strongly agree.

7. Respondent has received training in past 2 years paid for by the employer, scored 1. 0 otherwise.

8. Respondent has discretion over work effort. Scored: 1, if respondent mentions his or her own discretion as one of the things that determines how hard he or she works in his or her job; 0, otherwise.

9. Respondent does not control own starting/leaving times. Scored: 1, if starting and/or finishing times checked by a supervisor or management; a time clock; signing on or a similar system; 0, otherwise.

10. 'Suppose there was to be some decision made at your place of work that changed the way you do your job. Do you think that you personally would have any say in the decision about the change or not? How much say or chance to influence the decision do you think you would have?' Scored: 1, No influence; 2, It depends; 3, A little influence; 4, Quite a lot of influence; and 5, A great deal of influence.

11. 'Is yours a job which allows you to design and plan important aspects of your own work or is your work largely defined for you?' Scored: 0, largely defined for respondent; 1, allows respondent to design and plan.

12. Respondent on a career ladder. Scored: 1, if respondent is on a recognized career or promotion ladder within his or her own organization or his or her sort of work has a recognized career or promotion ladder even if it means changing employer to go up it; 0, otherwise.

13. Employer provides free or subsidized meals, scored 1, 0 otherwise.

14. Scored: 1, if management organizes meetings where respondent is informed about what is happening in the organization or where respondent can express his or her views about what is happening in the organization; 0, otherwise.

15. Scored: 0, if no computer use in work, computer used but not at all important, computer used but not very important, computer used and fairly important; 1, if computer use is very important or essential but type of use is simple; 2, if computer use is very important or essential and type of use is moderate; 3, if computer use is very important or essential and type of use is complex; and 4, if computer use is very important or essential and type of use is advanced.

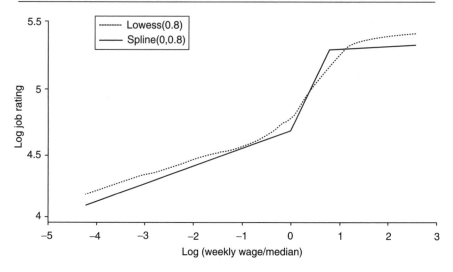

Figure 8.1. Log job rating as a function of log weekly wages. Locally weighted scatterplot smoothing with bandwidth of 0.8 and linear splines with cut points at 0 and 0.8.

this we transform wage by taking its natural logarithm, but before doing this we divide by the median wage (£281.65 per week).[13] The empirical relationship between log job rating and log wage is shown in Figure 8.1 for respondents who have complete data on both rating and wage. Two curves are plotted each giving an estimate of the mean log rating for each value in the range of earnings observed in the data.[14] The curve labelled 'lowess' is arrived at by making minimal assumptions about the nature of this relationship and allows the data to suggest the form of the function that links wages and job rating.[15] We take this to be our best guess as to how rating and wages are related.[16] The curve labelled 'spline' is the approximation to the lowess curve that we will use when we come to consider the joint effect of monetary and non-monetary factors on job ratings.[17]

What Figure 8.1 reveals is that the relationship between log job rating and log wage depends on which of three wage ranges one considers.[18] Between the lowest weekly wage observed in the data and the median wage level (the point on the x-axis corresponding to 0) ratings increase relatively gently—a 1 per cent increase in wages corresponds to a modest 0.13 per cent increase in job rating. Above the median, up to a point which is approximately two and a quarter times the median (£626.82 per week), the effect is much greater—a 1 per cent increase in wages produces

242

a 0.74 per cent increase in job rating. Above this point lies approximately the top 10 per cent of the wage distribution and among the high earners there is essentially no relationship between wage levels and job ratings.[19]

We can make the consequences of these relationships more concrete by comparing two individuals one earning £300 per week (a little above the median) and one earning £140 per week (just under half the median). For the former a 1 per cent increase in wages is £3 and such an increase would, on average, increase their rating of how good their job is by about 0.84 points on the unlogged job rating scale. In order to obtain the same absolute level of increase the person earning £140 per week would have to increase their wage by roughly £5.25 or 3.75 per cent. One per cent of not very much is still not very much and for the lower earners it would seem that it is absolute wage increases that are most significant.

Among the highest earners it is a very different story. They still, of course, on average rate their jobs rather highly, but above the threshold of around £627 wages cease to have any power to predict differences in job ratings. Several explanations of this suggest themselves. Perhaps at a certain wage level a person's instrumental need for earnings to support his or her customary lifestyle and achieve his or her realistic aspirations is satisfied and therefore evaluation of the merits of their job depends only on non-monetary factors that enhance the quality of the working experience itself. Although this interpretation is neat, it seems to us somewhat implausible that at relatively high—but in absolute terms still relatively modest—wage levels people give no weight whatsoever to higher earning and by implication are unable to conceive both more and better wants that require higher wages to fulfil them. It seems more likely that job ratings among higher earners are still a positive function of wages, but that the slope is not very steep and that with the few observations we have in this range, we cannot estimate it with very much precision. It may also be that our method of eliciting job ratings is less effective for the highest earners who will typically have jobs that are both economically and socially distant from those we used as benchmark examples.[20] Higher earners may be unable to calibrate the desirability of their jobs with confidence against jobs that they know little about and that are peopled by types they either rarely come into social contact with or come into contact with only as workplace subordinates. Their ratings may consequently signal nothing more than the certainty that their jobs are better than those they have been invited to make a comparison with but should not be regarded as the outcome of a considered estimation of how much better. If this is the case we would see what in fact we observe, a random scatter of high ratings with no relationship to actual wage levels. Tempting as it is to speculate about what underlies the pattern, there is little we can do to test which, if any, of these accounts hold water.

8.5. What Predicts Job Ratings?

Table 8.1 contains information about the variables in our prediction equation. What we did to produce this equation is involved rather than complex, but rather than try the patience of the general reader we do not describe the details here and instead present them in two appendices, one dealing with model selection (Appendix 1) and the other with the treatment of missing data (Appendix 2). The appendices can be skipped without losing the thread of our argument at the cost of having to trust that what we say in the following sections is based on intellectually respectable foundations rather than magic. The most important thing to understand is that what we do is create a *prediction* model rather than a model that is intended to capture the structure of a causal process. Although below we offer a few casual interpretations of some of the right-hand side variables we caution the reader not to take these too seriously. The reason for this is that the final prediction model is the outcome of a long process of model selection starting with a large number of candidate variables. All of these variables are correlated with each other, some quite strongly. Just because a variable is not named in the final prediction equation does not mean that variation in it is irrelevant to how individuals rate their jobs.[21] It simply means that the effect of variation in it is indistinguishable from the effect of variation of one or more variables with different names. Accordingly, we should be very cautious about building an edifice of interpretation on the precise details of what is included and what is excluded. From the point of view of *prediction* the names of the variables do not matter, from the point of view of *explanation* they do, but we are not primarily interested in explaining why people on average rate some jobs as better than others. We are mostly interested in the outcome of the process—the ranking of jobs. We invite anyone who is upset by our apparent willingness to have our cake and eat it to simply skip the next four paragraphs.

Before looking at the numerical information contained in the prediction equation, a few observations about the variables listed in Table 8.1 are in order. Setting aside wages two types stand out. First, variables that reflect either the employee's control or lack of control over aspects of the work itself or the conditions under which it is performed—effort, working hours, and the way the job is done—and second, indicators of human asset specificity. Three variables in Table 8.1 can be understood as indicative of the importance of human asset specificity for job ratings. Two directly refer to the outcome of an (unsuccessful) negotiation over wages and hours and as can be seen from Table 8.2 decrease the average rating given to a job. The third—employer investment in training—is an indicator of firm-specific training and thus exactly the sort of thing that generates human asset specificity. It has a positive effect on job ratings.

The inclusion of some of the other variables in the prediction equation is unsurprising as is the sign of their effect. Hours of work, usually considered a disutility, are negatively related to job ratings, while holding a job that is a rung on a career ladder has a positive effect. The positive effect of working where the management holds meetings to communicate information downwards or to listen to employee views is readily understandable, either as a job enhancer in itself or as an indicator of the organization's overall HRM style (see Chapters 4 and 5). However, it was not obvious *ex ante* that of all the fringe benefits included in the pool of possible predictors it would be the provision of free or subsidized meals that would be included. Neither was it obvious that the complexity of computer use in work where it is an important or essential part of the job would have such a powerful positive effect.

There is more to be said about the various effects reported in Table 8.2. First, we can say something about the relative predictive power of wage and non-wage variables—wages on their own account for roughly half of the 34 per cent of variance 'explained' by the full job rating equation. The proportion is similar to that reported in JPR's study. Second, we can note that adding the various non-wage factors to the prediction equation has a differential impact on the effect of wages that depends on which wage range is considered. In the bottom half of the wage distribution, a 1 per cent increase in earnings leads to a 12 per cent increase in job rating that hardly differs from the unconditional effect reported above. Between the 50th and the 90th percentile, the elasticity is 45 per cent or roughly 60 per cent of the unconditional effect. Above the 90th percentile, just as in the unconditional case there is essentially no relationship between wages and job rating. The implication is that in those jobs where wages are below the median the correlation between wages and the non-monetary predictors of job ratings is rather weak, whereas between the median and the 90th percentile it is much stronger with 'good' and 'bad' monetary and non-monetary attributes tending to cluster into coherent package deals.

Table 8.2. Regression of logged job rating on job characteristics

	(1)	(2)	(3)	(4)	(5)	(6)	(7)
			Descriptive statistics				
	Mean	SD	Proportion missing	β	t	%	£ per annum
Log (weekly earnings/median) £4–£281.64	-0.076	0.796	0.145	0.116	3.135	—	—
Log (weekly earnings/median) £281.65–£626.81	—	—	—	0.449	7.157	—	—
Log weekly earnings >£626.81	—	—	—	-0.009	-0.092	—	—
Has unsuccessfully bargained over salary	0.098	0.297	0.003	-0.162	-3.049	43	6,351
Usual weekly hours	39.083	13.990	0.004	-0.004	-2.444	1	138
Has unsuccessfully bargained over hours	0.039	0.193	0.003	-0.103	-1.740	26	3,784
Job requires keep learning new things	3.118	0.725	0.001	0.113	5.778	28	4,172
Employer has paid for training in past 2 years	0.518	0.500	9.38e-4	0.073	2.918	18	2,589
Has discretion over own work effort	0.531	0.499	0	0.086	3.559	21	3,092
Does not control own starting/leaving times	0.505	0.500	0	-0.111	-4.213	28	4,126
Can influence job changes	2.819	1.527	0.010	0.035	4.608	8	1,196
Can design/plan own job	0.438	0.496	0.005	0.173	6.541	47	6,861
Job on a career ladder	0.639	0.480	0	0.066	2.343	16	2,310
Employer supplies subsidized or free meals	0.250	0.433	0	0.083	3.450	20	2,959
Management holds meetings	0.782	0.413	0.007	0.088	2.437	22	3,170
Complexity of computer use where use is very important or essential	1.266	1.320	4.69e-4	0.036	3.174	8	1,214
Constant				4.770	48.935		
R^2				0.338			
Sample size			2132				

Notes:

1. The dependent variable is the log of the respondent's rating of their own job compared to an average job. Mean = 4.818, SD = 0.604, Missing = 4.1%.

2. The sampling plan consists of 164 clusters allocated to 41 strata. Data are weighted by the inverse of the selection probability and post-stratified by sex, age, full-time/part-time, and socio-economic group from the Spring 2000 Quarterly Labour Force Survey.

3. Coefficients and t values are averaged over 5 imputations.

Source: WiB 2000.

Column 6 of Table 8.2 quantifies for a job attracting a wage just above the median the effect of a unit change for the worse in each of the non-monetary variables in terms of the percentage increase in wage needed to compensate it. For example, it answers the counterfactual question: on average how much more would you have to earn if you were to give two jobs the same desirability rating but in one you could decide your own starting and leaving time, whereas in the other you could not? The numbers are not straightforward to compare because the metrics of the variables are not the same; however, we can directly compare the effects associated with all of the binary variables where there is a simple switch from one condition to another. To get a better impression of the magnitude of the effects, in column 7 we have translated the percentage increases into absolute increases in annual salary. Some of these effects are surprisingly small—working an extra hour per week can be compensated by earning just an extra £138 per year, which is considerably less than the hourly rate paid to employees earning just above the median weekly wage—while others are so large that they should be treated with scepticism—withdrawing free or subsidized meals would require wages to increase by £2959 per year which is much more than it would cost to buy a decent lunch each working day at market prices. In general adverse changes in variables which tap either control or human asset specificity aspects of job ratings require rather large compensatory wage movements.

One should not take these counterfactual calculations too seriously. It is likely that they capture influences on respondents' job ratings that are related, but not identical, to the label given to a variable. Jobs in the type of organization that provides free meals—say an Oxbridge college—may have other highly positive characteristics that get absorbed into the free meals indicator. In addition, there are institutional facts and psychological mechanisms that make this kind of counterfactual exercise unrealistic. An example of the former would be an institutionalized threshold effect—hours of work for many hourly paid employees are defined in contracts and collective agreements; overtime hours are compensated at pay rates that are higher than the normal hourly rate. This kind of effect is not captured by our prediction equation that simply averages over the effect for all types of employee. An example of a psychological mechanism at work in the way in which people evaluate real gains and losses is that the disutility from losing something tends to be greater than the utility from gaining an equivalent amount (Kahneman and Tversky 1979). Our simple model assumes that a one unit change or a switch in condition in either direction produces changes in job desirability of the same magnitude (but opposite sign). Of course, this would imply that our estimates of amounts of money required to compensate adverse changes in working conditions are actually underestimates!

It would be natural to wonder both how well the IJD predicts other indicators of job quality and whether it does significantly better or worse when compared to simply using information on wage levels. In Table 8.3, we report the estimated percentage of respondents answering 'yes' to a mixed bag of 11 indicators of work attitudes, job attributes, and job rewards evaluated at each of 7 percentiles of the IJD and wage distribution. In all cases, the response patterns have an obvious gradient related to IJD and wage percentiles and in the majority of cases the gradient for the IJD percentiles is steeper than the gradient for wages. For example, the first line of Table 8.3 reports responses to an item asking the respondent to say whether their job is merely a means of earning a living or it means much more to them than that. The difference in the percentage of respondents saying that their job is simply a means of earning a living—measured at the 25th and the 75th percentile—is 25 per cent for the IJD but only 6 per cent for weekly wages. The second item in Table 8.3 is also worthy of comment. Respondents were asked whether they considered their job to be more secure than other jobs requiring similar skill in the same line of work. The question is interesting to us because it explicitly invites respondents to 'control' for aspects of the job that may lead them to rate it favourably. Even so we find that the IJD is still strongly correlated with the likelihood that respondents rate their job as relatively secure (as are wages).[22] On the whole with regard to the indicators examined here we can conclude that the IJD is at least as good a discriminator of differences as wages and in many cases a better discriminator. It thus passes the most elementary test of construct validity.

8.6. Is the IJD Just Social Class in Another Form?

Another natural thought would be to wonder how the IJD is related to the existing measures of labour market position, or social hierarchy, commonly used by sociologists—for example, the standard measures of social class used by sociologists who study 'social stratification'. Almost all of these are based on aggregations of the categories formed when one cross-classifies detailed occupational groups by employment status— distinguishing managerial, supervisory, and other employee roles. We can

Table 8.3. Percentage of respondents answering yes for selected job and employee characteristics by percentiles of the IJD, weekly wage, and hourly wage rate

	Percentiles						
	5	10	25	50	75	90	95
Job is just a means of earning a living							
IJD	62	57	49	37	24	15	12
Weekly wage	43	42	40	38	34	30	26
Job more secure than others of similar skill doing similar work							
IJD	26	26	28	31	34	38	40
Weekly wage	29	29	30	31	32	34	36
Has been made redundant in past 5 years							
IJD	14	13	11	9	7	5	4
Weekly wage	10	10	10	9	9	8	7
Trade union in the workplace							
IJD	26	27	29	31	35	38	40
Weekly wage	31	31	32	33	34	36	38
Limited-term contract							
IJD	13	12	11	10	8	7	7
Wage rate	12	11	10	9	7	6	4
Works up to 16 hours per week							
IJD	18	15	10	5	2	1	1
Wage	37	25	8	1	0	0	0
Wage rate	6	6	6	7	7	8	8
Works 50+ hours per week							
IJD	7	9	11	17	27	40	46
Wage	10	11	13	17	25	36	49
Workplace has more than 100 employees							
IJD	29	31	35	40	48	56	58
Wage	29	31	34	39	47	56	65
28+ days of paid holiday per annum							
IJD	15	16	20	26	35	46	50
Wage	25	25	27	29	33	37	41
Sick pay above the statutory minimum							
IJD	46	50	55	64	73	81	83
Wage	53	55	59	64	71	77	83
Company car or vehicle							
IJD	8	9	12	17	26	38	42
Wage	13	14	15	18	22	28	34

Source: WiB 2000.

get some sense of the likely upper limit of the relationship between the IJD and standard classifications by regressing it on as detailed an occupational classification as is sustainable by the size of the WiB 2000 data-set. To do this we make a crude employment status distinction between managerial occupations (ignoring size of the workplace) and all other employees (including supervisory staff). We then distinguish as many occupational

Table 8.4. Pearson correlations (or multiple correlations) between the IJD and 6 measures of socioeconomic standing

	R^2	Correlation
1. Cambridge scale (linear spline with 2 knots)	.37	.61
2. NS-SEC	.47	.69
3. Socio-economic group	.47	.69
4. EGP classes	.49	.70
5. Shrunken level 2 residual	.58	.76
6. Predicted shrunken level 2 residual (POSAIJD)	.51	.71

Source: WiB 2000.

groups (using the ONS 1990 SOC codes) within these two groups as exist in the data. This gives us a total of 313 distinct occupations. There are various ways to implement the idea of regressing the IJD on this occupational array, the details of which are not important, but the result of carrying out such an exercise is that detailed occupations are estimated to account for between 50 and 60 per cent of the variance in the IJD, depending on the estimation method used.[23] Clearly, there is considerable within-occupation variation in job desirability attributable either to lack of homogeneity among the occupations grouped in the ONS classification or because jobs with similar titles simply differ by organizational context and thus in what they actually entail and in the intrinsic and extrinsic rewards that accrue to them.

If 40–50 per cent of the variance in job desirability is between detailed occupational groups, how well do the standard aggregated categorizations perform? The answer is in the top four rows of Table 8.4 where we compare the predictive performance of the Cambridge scale of social status, Socio-economic Group—fourteen categories, Erikson, Goldthorpe, Portocarero (EGP) class—nine categories and the ONS socio-economic classification (NS-SEC)—twelve categories. The Cambridge scale uses just one degree of freedom in a linear regression and to make a fair comparison between it and the other three schemes that use thirteen, eight, and eleven degrees of freedom respectively, we choose the best fitting linear spline to represent it.[24] The story is straightforward—the Cambridge scale is less closely related to the IJD than any of the other three measures. There is not much to choose between the other three classifications—all share around 50 per cent of their variance with the IJD. In other words, about half of the IJD variance is between the category means and half is within each category around the category means.

One way to interpret this result is as a pleasing example of discriminant validity testing. The Cambridge scale is not designed to measure inequality arising solely from the workplace but is intended to capture more general societal-wide patterns of social acceptance (which we would call social status) indicated by the extent to which members of different occupational groups choose each other as friends and marriage partners. The other occupationally based classifications, with the exception of the more ad hoc SEG, are based, *inter alia*, on the explicit, albeit in some cases informal, consideration of typical workplace conditions and relations and thus are closer to capturing the sort of inequalities that the IJD attends to. However, all of the occupational classifications are less than perfect substitutes for the IJD and this raises the question of how closely the IJD could be approximated at the occupational level?

It might seem perverse given that the central argument for the IJD is the need to capture information at the level of the job to now ask how well that information can be approximated when we aggregate to the occupational level? However, if something like the IJD is to be taken up as a tool of applied research, then the question is of considerable importance. The best way to construct the IJD is to take the weights reported in Appendix 1, Table A1, and combine them with the appropriate variables. But except in exceptional circumstances the variables are unlikely to be included in many data-sets, and this will automatically rule out the adoption of the IJD.[25] Row 5 of Table 8.4 reports the correlation between the IJD and the 313 occupational IJD means that can be distinguished in the WiB data.[26] Although it is reasonably high, over 40 per cent of the variance in the individual level IJD is still around the occupational means. These means can themselves be predicted rather well by aggregate level variables—related to the distribution of earnings, education, and the ability to plan work—measured at the occupational level (see Appendix 3 for details) and this implies that an occupationally based IJD, which we call the Predicted Occupational Shrunken Average Index of Job Desirability (POSAIJD), can be constructed for any occupation defined in the 1990 ONS Classification of Occupations not just for those that have been sampled in the WiB data. Row 6 of Table 8.4 tells us that at best about half of the variance in the IJD will be captured by such a variable in other words about the same proportion as is typically captured by the large aggregated categories of conventional occupational categorizations.

In summary then we can say four things of importance. First, almost as much variability in job desirability is at the level of the job itself as is at the level of the occupation. Second, conventional occupationally based classifications based on information about what people do at work are better at predicting job desirability than a measure like the Cambridge scale that claims to indicate generalized social advantage and disadvantage. Third, job desirability is not just synonymous with social class. Fourth, the average desirability of an occupation is quite accurately predictable from knowledge of the earnings distribution among employees and the proportion in the occupation that have at least one A level. Knowing about occupational desirability is then, quite literally, only half the story, but it is a half that is still worth knowing about and so it is to this that we now turn.

8.7. Good and Bad Occupations

Occupations can be ranked in all sorts of ways, and we would like to know whether ranking them by their average score on the IJD tells us something different from what we would have learned by simply ranking them by average earnings. The Spearman rank correlation between the occupational average IJD scores and occupational median gross weekly earnings (calculated from the Quarterly LFS to ensure large numbers in most occupational groups) is .727 indicating (unsurprisingly) considerable congruence, but important differences in detail. Some of the detail is revealed in Tables 8.5 and 8.6 where we compare the top and bottom twenty occupations as ranked by their IJD score and by median earnings. There is some overlap, but the majority of occupations—twelve and fourteen, respectively—listed in the top/bottom twenty ranked by the IJD do not appear in the top/bottom twenty ranked by earnings. The impression we get from these lists is that scientific, intellectual, and educational occupations are ranked more highly by the IJD than they are by earnings and that labouring, driving, and manufacturing process operatives are ranked less highly by the IJD than by earnings.

League tables like these can be highly misleading and are merely intended to be illustrative. When we construct confidence intervals around the IJD scores, it turns out that the top third of occupations have intervals that overlap substantially, as do the bottom third. We know with more certainty that these occupations differ from those in the middle of the distribution, but it would be a brave person who would bet much on the proposition that secondary school teaching is really more desirable than meteorology or that domestic cleaning is really worse than road sweeping.

Table 8.5. Top 20 occupations in the WiB survey ranked by the IJD and median gross weekly wage

Rank	Occupational title
IJD	
1	*Biological scientists and biochemists E[a]
2	Underwriters, claims assessors, brokers, and investment analysts M[b]
3	Secondary (and middle school deemed secondary) education teaching professionals M
4	Computer system and data processing managers M
5	Treasurers and company financial managers M
6	Actors, entertainers, stage managers, producers, and directors M
7	*Primary school (and primary school deemed primary) and nursery education teaching professionals M
8	Officers in UK armed forces M
9	*University and polytechnic teaching professionals E
10	*Registrars and administrators of educational establishments M
11	*Electronic engineers E
12	*Bank, building society, and post office managers (except self-employed) M
13	*General administrators and national government (HEO to senior principal/grade 6) M
14	Medical practitioners E
15	*Organization and methods and work study officers E
16	Organization and methods and work study managers M
17	*Production, works, and maintenance managers M
18	*Other managers and administrators n.e.c. M
19	*Physicists, geologists, and meteorologists E
20	*Veterinarians E
Median gross weekly earnings[c]	
1	General managers; large companies and organizations M
2	Treasurers and company financial managers M
3	Managers in mining and energy industries M
4	Aircraft flight deck officers E
5	Police officers (inspector and above) M
6	Medical practitioners E
7	Underwriters, claims assessors, brokers, and investment analysts M
8	Officers in UK armed forces M
9	Organization and methods and work study managers M
10	General administrators; national government (assistant secretary/grade 5 and above) M
11	Education officers and school inspectors M
12	Actors, entertainers, stage managers, producers, and directors M
13	Taxation experts M
14	Computer systems and data processing managers M
15	Management consultants and business analysts E
16	Air traffic planners and controllers E
17	Authors, writers, and journalists M
18	Computer analyst/programmers M
19	Secondary (and middle school deemed secondary) education teaching professionals M
20	Medical radiographers E

[a] Employee or supervisor.
[b] Manager.
[c] Ranked by earnings data from the QLFS.
* Occupation is not in the top 20 ranked by earnings.
Source: WiB 2000.

Table 8.6. Bottom 20 occupations in the WiB survey ranked by the IJD and median gross weekly wage

Rank	Occupational title
IJD	
290	*Road sweepers E[a]
291	*Security guards and related occupations E
292	*Other food, drink, and tobacco process operatives n.e.c. E
293	Waiters and waitresses E
294	*Goods porters E
295	*Other building and civil engineering labourers n.e.c. E
296	*Storekeepers and warehousemen/women E
297	*Drivers of road goods vehicles E
298	*Warp preparers, bleachers, dyers, and finishers E
299	*Sewing machinists, menders, darners, and embroiderers E
300	Retail cash desk and check-out operators E
301	*All other labourers and related workers E
302	*Other textile processing operatives E
303	*Bus and coach drivers E
304	*Other chemicals, paper, plastics, and related process operatives n.e.c E
305	Shelf fillers E
306	*Butchers and meat cutters E
307	Kitchen porters and hands E
308	Launderers, dry cleaners, and pressers E
309	Cleaners and domestics E
Median gross weekly earnings[b]	
290	Merchandisers E
291	Other security and protective service occupations n.e.c. E
292	Care assistants and attendants E
293	Library assistants/clerks E
294	Receptionists E
295	Launderers, dry cleaners, and pressers E
296	Petrol pump and forecourt attendants E
297	Educational assistants E
298	Hairdressers and barbers E
299	Waiters and waitresses E
300	Sales assistants E
301	Shelf fillers E
302	Bus conductors E
303	Retail cash desk and check-out operators E
304	Counterhands and catering assistants E
305	Kitchen porters and hands E
306	Playgroup leaders E
307	Cleaners, domestics E
308	Bar staff E
309	Other childcare and related occupations n.e.c. E

[a] Employee or supervisor.
[b] Ranked by earnings data from the QLFS.
* Occupation is not in the bottom 20 ranked by earnings.
Source: WiB 2000.

8.8. Job Desirability and Contractual Status

The point of constructing the IJD was the intuition that it would capture more information about job inequality than any other single measure. The information in Table 8.3 suggests that this might be the case; however, this evidence is less than totally compelling. What we need is a direct comparison with other plausible measures that conditions on the things that are likely to produce workplace inequality. Table 8.7 goes some way towards providing this. Here we report coefficients produced by regressing the IJD and log hourly wages on four variables related to contractual status—coverage by collective bargaining (indicated by trade union membership), hours of work, type of contract, and social class of the occupation (as defined by NS-SEC categories).[27] Part-time hours and non-open-ended contracts are commonly regarded as associated with undesirable working conditions while the presence of a union in the workplace might be taken to indicate that employees have a measure of protection from bad working conditions. In addition to the contract status variables we control for gender, civil status, age, age squared, the highest level of academic qualification, the highest level of vocational qualification, unemployment experience, duration of the current employment episode, number of employees in the workplace, private/public sector, and the interaction between age and semi-routine/routine occupations.[28]

Comparing the IJD and log hourly wages we need to remember that the scales of the variables differ and hence we cannot compare directly the magnitudes of the coefficients, though we can compare their general pattern and signs. Neither equation suggests that there is much impact of union status, the signs for the IJD and wages differ, but the coefficients are insignificant. There is however a difference for working hours. The IJD equation estimates that part-time workers have less desirable jobs while the wage rate equation suggests no significant difference in the wage rate by working hours and it turns out that this difference is not entirely due to the built in dependence of the IJD on gross weekly earnings unadjusted for actual hours. It is generally supposed, at least by sociologists, that jobs with short term as opposed to open-ended contracts are inferior in at least some respects. Certainly, most of the signs both for the IJD and for wages are negative and quite sizeable. However, there are only two significant effects: casual work leads to lower IJD scores and the residual category of 'other type of non-open-ended contract' attracts lower wages. It is surprising given the amount of attention lavished on the growth of fixed-term

Table 8.7. Effects of gender, civil status, and various contract status variables on the IJD and log hourly wages

	IJD		Log hourly wage	
	β	t	β	t
No union in workplace	0	—	0	—
Union in workplace, non-member	−0.092	−1.934	0.012	0.359
Union member	−0.065	−1.386	0.051	1.639
Full-time	0	—	0	—
Part-time 1–15 hours	−0.279	−4.132	−0.001	−0.013
Part-time 16–29 hours	−0.239	−5.595	−0.037	−0.939
Open-ended contract	0	—	0	—
Seasonal work	−0.238	−1.852	−0.200	−1.497
Fixed period/task contract	−0.019	−0.220	0.056	0.880
Agency temping	−0.184	−1.385	−0.039	−0.563
Casual work	−0.518	−2.083	−0.143	−0.616
Other type of non-open-ended contract	−0.103	−1.161	−0.186	−2.868
Higher manager	0	—	0	—
Higher professional I	−0.205	−2.010	−0.168	−2.245
Higher professional II	−0.092	−0.748	0.114	1.011
Lower professional I	−0.517	−6.100	−0.238	−3.695
Lower professional II	−0.311	−1.611	−0.060	−0.381
Lower managerial	−0.356	−3.997	−0.215	−2.760
Higher supervisor	−0.622	−6.058	−0.232	−3.116
Intermediate	−0.906	−10.586	−0.325	−5.046
Lower supervisor	−0.905	−10.272	−0.429	−5.915
Lower technician	−1.068	−10.893	−0.280	−3.649
Semi-routine	−1.174	−13.863	−0.484	−6.525
Routine	−1.454	−16.838	−0.529	−7.271
R^2	0.587	—	0.367	—

Notes:

1. The numbers reported in this table come from OLS regressions that condition on the following variables: gender, civil status, age, age squared, the highest level of academic qualifications, the highest level of vocational qualifications, unemployment experience, log duration of current employment episode, log number of employees in the workplace, private sector; and the interaction of linear age with the semi-routine and routine occupational groups.

2. Standard errors take into account the stratification of and clustering within-sampling units as well as the uncertainty introduced by the multiple imputation of missing values. Values of the IJD are assumed to be known with certainty for the purposes of imputation. This is not, strictly speaking, correct and the reader should be sceptical about *t* values close to those that conventionally indicate significant differences.

Source: WiB 2000.

contracts that the evidence that they offer inferior forms of employment is weak in terms of both desirability and wages (where the coefficient is in fact positive but insignificant). The social class of the occupational group has an unsurprising effect on both measures of inequality—on balance the 'higher' the social class, the greater the desirability and the hourly wage.

We can explore a little further the sources of the detailed differences in the pattern of inequality revealed by the IJD and by hourly wage

Table 8.8. Effects of gender, civil status, and various contract status variables on the IJD_m and the IJD_{nm}

	IJD_m		IJD_{nm}	
	β	t	β	t
No union in workplace	0	—	0	—
Union in workplace, non-member	−0.026	−2.172	−0.066	−1.621
Union member	−0.004	−0.418	−0.061	−1.434
Full-time	0	—	0	—
Part-time 1–15 hours	−0.042	−3.011	−0.237	−3.717
Part-time 16–29 hours	−0.055	−5.837	−0.184	−4.718
Open-ended contract	0	—	0	—
Seasonal work	−0.022	−0.671	−0.216	−1.840
Fixed period/task contract	−0.022	−0.927	0.003	0.047
Agency temping	−0.040	−2.122	−0.144	−1.141
Casual work	−0.028	−0.689	−0.491	−1.992
Other type of non-open-ended contract	−0.031	−1.247	−0.072	−0.887
Higher manager	0	—	0	—
Higher professional I	−0.039	−1.518	−0.166	−1.839
Higher professional II	−0.018	−0.624	−0.074	−0.702
Lower professional I	−0.112	−4.941	−0.405	−5.270
Lower professional II	−0.067	−1.276	−0.244	−1.439
Lower managerial	−0.096	−4.072	−0.260	−3.350
Higher supervisor	−0.124	−5.089	−0.498	−5.361
Intermediate	−0.176	−7.594	−0.731	−9.436
Lower supervisor	−0.159	−6.239	−0.746	−9.304
Lower technician	−0.157	−5.963	−0.911	−10.303
Semi-routine	−0.196	−7.790	−0.979	−12.495
Routine	−0.200	−8.338	−1.254	−15.704
R^2	0.525	—	0.550	—

Notes:

1. The numbers reported in this table come from OLS regressions that condition on the following variables: age, age squared, the highest level of academic qualifications, the highest level of vocational qualifications, unemployment experience, log duration of current employment episode, log number of employees in the workplace, private sector, and the interaction of linear age with semi-routine and routine occupational group.

2. Standard errors take into account the stratification of and clustering within-sampling units as well as the uncertainty introduced by the multiple imputation of missing values. Values of the IJD are assumed to be known with certainty for the purposes of imputation. This is not, strictly speaking, correct and the reader should be sceptical about t values close to those that conventionally indicate significant differences.

Source: WiB 2000.

rates by disaggregating the IJD into two additive components one derived from the weights assigned to the weekly wage splines (IJD_m) and the other derived from the weights assigned to the non-monetary variables. The sum of the two indices so defined is simply the IJD that is the $IJD = IJD_m + IJD_{nm}$. Table 8.8 reports coefficients for the regression of the two components on the same set of variables as in Table 8.7 and is especially revealing in one respect. One might suspect that the difference between the IJD and the hourly wage coefficients with respect to working hours and casual work is purely due to the fact that the wage component of the IJD relates to weekly earnings that are bound to produce low values for those regularly working less than full-time hours or a few hours here and there on a casual basis. In fact, this does not appear to be the explanation because the biggest contribution to the effect of these variables on the IJD does not come from the IJD_m, but from the IJD_{nm}. In other words, part-time jobs and casual jobs are not relatively undesirable just because they pay so little, the major downside relates to all of the negative non-monetary factors that are associated with them.

8.9. Job Satisfaction

In this section, we examine how job desirability is related to job satisfaction. It would be curious if there was no correlation between these constructs as it would mean that having a job that is regarded by the community as relatively good or relatively bad has no bearing on the utility an individual gets from it. Casual introspection suggests that having something that others want or regard as desirable is a source of utility regardless of the primary satisfaction to be derived from the thing itself. Likewise having a job that few others want is likely to contribute to feelings of dissatisfaction independent of whatever other disutilities are attached to it. However, job satisfaction is not the same thing as job desirability.[29]

Nobody would find it curious if a road sweeper were to report that he or she received the same amount of satisfaction from his or her job as reported by a high court judge, though many would raise an eyebrow if one were to claim that on average, in the opinion of the relevant community, the two jobs were equally desirable. Both road sweeper and judge can feel satisfied that they have better jobs than others in their reference group while at the same time acknowledging that most people would find the judge's job superior. It is our contention that considered in isolation job satisfaction scales contain a weak signal about the relative goodness and badness of jobs heavily coloured by the respondent's sense of realistic expectations.

With regard to measures of job satisfaction, there is an embarrassment of riches in WiB. Employees were presented with a battery of fifteen items on various aspects of their job, followed by a question asking them

---

Box 1 JOB SATISFACTION ITEMS

I am going to read out a list of various aspects of jobs and for each one I would like you to tell me … how satisfied or dissatisfied you are with that particular aspect of your own present job.

 1. Your promotion prospects
 2. Your pay
 3. Relations with your supervisor or manager
 4. Your job security
 5. The opportunity to use your abilities
 6. Being able to use your own initiative
 7. The ability and efficiency of management
 8. The hours you work
 9. Fringe benefits
10. The work itself
11. The amount of work
12. The variety in the work
13. The training provided
14. The friendliness of the people you work with
15. The ease of your journey to work

How satisfied are you with the following aspects of the work you do?

 1. The challenge it sets you
 2. The scope for personal responsibility
 3. The chance to help other people
 4. The chance to develop yourself
 5. The opportunity to do something worthwhile
 6. The chance for personal achievement

---

to say 'all in all' how satisfied they were, followed by a further battery of six items mainly concerning satisfaction with the opportunities their job gave them for personal development. In all cases responses were recorded on a 7-point scale with a score of '1' indicating complete satisfaction and a score of '7' complete dissatisfaction. For semantic convenience, we have reversed the scoring so that higher scores indicate greater rather than lesser levels of satisfaction. All items are listed in full in Box 8.1.

With so much information to work with it is necessary to employ some form of data reduction. Our approach is twofold. First, we summarize what is common to all items in the fifteen and six item batteries by calculating scores for each employee based on the first principal component of all twenty-one items. This has the advantage that each item contributes to the final score with a known data-dependent weight that corresponds to the degree to which it shares variation with other items. Thus, for example, the item that invites each respondent to rate his or her satisfaction with 'the ease of your journey to work' is relatively weakly related to all of the other items and contributes rather little to the overall score. Second, we make use of scales that as a matter of convenience can be regarded as measuring more specific sub-dimensions of satisfaction. The technique we use to derive these scales is the so-called Confirmatory Factor Analysis (CFA) and all that it is necessary to appreciate about it here is that it allows us to test whether, by assuming the 'existence' of a small number of 'higher level' constructs we can achieve an adequate simplification of the complex pattern of correlations between the original twenty-one items.

Our simplification is presented in Figure 8.2. It consists of five hypothetical constructs together with one item—satisfaction with ease of journey to work—that cannot be assigned to any of the five constructs. The constructs—represented by the large ovals—and the single item are assumed to be intercorrelated (indicated by the double-headed arrows linking them).[30] We also assume that part of the correlation between the original satisfaction items is not mediated by the higher-level constructs and arises from two sources (both conventionally described as 'error correlation'). The first of these is a methodological artefact. Respondents were not presented with the items in a random sequence; instead, each employee was presented with items in the same order. In this kind of set-up it is likely that there will be 'spill over' in the response scale points chosen for consecutive items that are unrelated to the 'true' underlying positions of the respondent on each item. This must be controlled for. Second, some items will have similar shades of meaning that is not entirely captured by their common dependence on the same hypothetical construct or the correlation between different constructs. Introducing error correlations of this sort can be an entirely ad hoc way of massaging recalcitrant data into shape. To avoid this we have taken care to introduce such correlations only where there is a plausible case for common content and have in fact disregarded apparently quite large error correlations where we can find no prima facie case for them, even though their inclusion would improve the fit of the model.

The CFA model presented in Figure 8.2 fits the data reasonably well.[31] The five satisfaction dimensions it reveals are intrinsic aspects of the job or the work itself (Intrinsic), the extensive and intensive effort the job requires (Effort), the extrinsic financial work motivators (Extrinsic), human relations with superiors and colleagues (Human), and

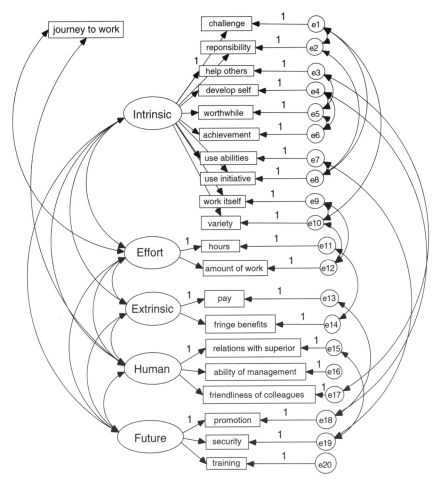

Figure 8.2. Confirmatory factor model of WiB job satisfaction items

future-oriented rewards and concerns (Future). We do not claim that these are the five dimensions that underlie all job satisfaction evaluations or that the dimensions actually exist in any real sense. Our claim is merely that structuring the data in this way gives us a convenient and coherent framework within which to summarize a mass of details. From the five dimensions we construct scales by summing all the items pertaining to a dimension and dividing by the number of items in the scale.[32] Thus, the scales retain the original 1–7 range of their constituent items.[33]

Figure 8.3 shows the relationship between the first principal component of all twenty-one job satisfaction items and four variables that are

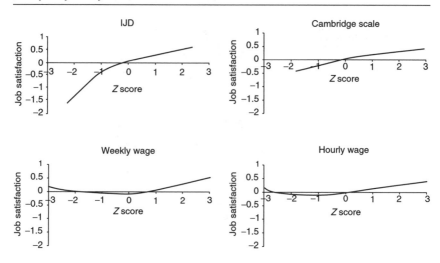

Figure 8.3. The relationship between the first principal component of the 21 job satisfaction items and the IJD, Cambridge scale, weekly wage, and hourly wage.

plausible predictors of it—the IJD, the Cambridge scale of social status, log weekly earnings, and log hourly wage rate.[34] For convenience we have adjusted the horizontal axis so that the predictor variables are on the same standardized scale with mean 0 and unit variance.[35] The two lower panels reveal the weakness of the relationship between money income and absolute satisfaction levels.[36] Both social status and job desirability have a positive relationship with satisfaction throughout their range, but of the two it is the IJD that is most strongly related to satisfaction. The IJD's relationship with satisfaction is non-linear rising steeply to a point roughly one standard deviation below the mean and more slowly thereafter. Those with poor jobs need only slightly better jobs to increase their satisfaction by a given amount while those with good jobs need much better jobs to increase their satisfaction by the same amount. If satisfaction ratings measure utility, then there is declining marginal utility in job 'goodness'.

Table 8.9 reports coefficients for the correlation between satisfaction and a wider set of variables. In each case we allow for non-linearity by retaining higher-order polynomials or fitting dummy variables. Of the seven variables compared, the IJD has by far the strongest relationship with satisfaction. All of the occupation-based measures—socio-economic group, EGP, NSSEC, and the Cambridge scale are correlated with satisfaction to about the same extent. Weekly wages and hourly wage rate trail a long way behind. It would seem that satisfaction levels are scarcely related to absolute earnings levels, weakly related to occupational or social-class

Table 8.9. Pearson correlations (or multiple correlations) between the first principal component of 26 job satisfaction items and 7 measures of socio-economic standing

IJD (cubic)	.38
Cambridge scale (linear)	.20
Log weekly wage (square)	.10
Log hourly wage (linear)	.09
NSSEC	.21
Socio-economic group	.22
EGP classes	.22

Source: WiB 2000.

groupings, and most strongly related to job desirability—combining both monetary and non-monetary job attributes.

It is quite remarkable that wages and satisfaction are so weakly related. However, something important has been omitted. Clark and Oswald (1996) produce empirical evidence for British workers to support the claim that job satisfaction is not in fact a direct function of earnings but of the difference between actual earnings and comparison earnings. Someone earning more than his or her comparators feels he or she is doing relatively well, someone earning less feels he or she is doing relatively poorly whatever the actual level of earnings received. Another way of putting this is to say that how satisfied you feel depends on what you expect and your expectations come from a comparison of how well other people like yourself are doing. Following the strategy of Clark and Oswald we operationalized expected earnings as the predicted values from a regression of weekly wage on a vector of predictor variables.[37] This gave us each individual's comparison point—the average weekly wage for a person with the same characteristics as the individual concerned whose actual wage may be higher or lower than this. When we did this the coefficients from regressing satisfaction on wage and expected wage implied that satisfaction is a positive and *increasing* function of actual wages and a negative function of comparison point. In other words at any given wage-level satisfaction decreases as the comparison wage rises.[38]

Table 8.10 reports the results from the estimation of a random effects regression in which we examine the effects of trade unions, hours of work, contract status, and job desirability on all five sub-dimensions of job satisfaction identified above. The models have a person-specific random intercept that in effect controls for the propensity for individuals to report similar degrees of satisfaction across all five domains and makes it particularly convenient to test whether the effects of the explanatory variables differ across domains. As the metric of the five scales is the same we can directly compare slopes across the columns of Table 8.10 to establish which satisfaction dimensions display the largest group differences.

Being a union member has a clear negative effect on satisfaction levels with the largest effects being on satisfaction in the effort, extrinsic, and human domains. That there should be quite large differences between unionized and non-unionized labour with regard to the components of the work effort bargain—hours, the amount of work, pay, and fringe benefits—is scarcely surprising. Neither is it surprising that unionized and non-unionized employees report different satisfaction levels with regard to relations with supervisors and the ability of management. But it is difficult to interpret the negative signs attached to the differences. It is simply not possible to tell from these data whether the presence of a union in the workplace causes dissatisfaction with contractual conditions or alternatively whether employees join unions in workplaces where satisfaction levels are relatively low. Both mechanisms are possible. What is clear from Table 8.7 is that union members and non-members differ very little with regard to job desirability and wage rates. Union members appear to get little advantage from their membership and experience more dissatisfaction than non-members. In these circumstances why would anyone join a union? The obvious answer is that employees think that they would be worse off if they did not join.

That part-timers express relatively high levels of satisfaction is a standard paradox in the job satisfaction literature. The explanation is usually attributed to the fact that many women prefer short hours that fit in with childcare responsibilities and are thus happy in jobs that allow them the flexibility to both work and care for dependents. The results in Table 8.10 are consistent with the standard story. Employees working for short part-time hours have similar satisfaction levels across all five domains while those working for long part-time hours are especially satisfied on the effort and extrinsic dimensions. In Table 8.7, we saw that part-timers on average had less desirable jobs, but in terms of the reward–effort bargain we find them happy with the deal they have made. Of course, this says nothing about how satisfied they might be with a counterfactual state in which it was easier to combine work and home-life duties.

The negative aspects of having a non-open-ended contract manifest themselves principally in the extrinsic and future domain. Those with

Table 8.10. Slope coefficients from the regression of 5 dimensions of job satisfaction on contract status variables, wage, and job desirability[1]

	Intrinsic		Effort		Extrinsic		Human		Future	
	β^i	t^2	β^{ef}	t^3	β^{ex}	t^3	β^h	t^3	β^f	t^3
No union in workplace	0	—	0	—	0	—	0	—	0	—
Union in workplace, non-member	-0.082	-1.318	-0.005	1.010	-0.003	1.163	-0.075	0.093	0.023	1.527
Union member	-0.090	-1.610	-0.233	-2.338	-0.272	-2.867	-0.233	-2.392	-0.147	-0.963
Full-time	0	—	0	—	0	—	0	—	0	—
Part-time 1–15 hours	0.211	2.110	0.199	-0.115	0.411	1.699	0.385	1.657	0.277	0.610
Part-time 16–29 hours	0.114	1.857	0.247	2.034	0.287	2.639	0.197	1.261	0.130	0.241
Open-ended contract	0	—	0	—	0	—	0	—	0	—
Seasonal work	0.423	1.687	0.008	-1.512	0.526	0.346	0.112	-1.140	0.142	-0.962
Fixed period/task contract	0.143	1.345	-0.040	-1.620	-0.220	-3.157	0.137	-0.056	-0.410	-4.749
Agency temping	-0.056	-0.346	0.015	0.412	-0.430	-2.111	0.149	1.193	-0.671	-3.488
Casual work	0.054	0.208	0.231	0.644	0.097	0.146	0.180	0.456	-0.399	-1.634
Other type of non-open-ended contract	-0.194	-1.361	0.019	1.409	-0.227	-0.215	-0.273	-0.523	-0.996	-5.263
IJD	0.398	10.440	-0.054	-15.574	0.260	-4.682	0.161	-8.146	0.260	-4.736
IJD squared	-0.087	-5.632	-0.087	-5.632	-0.087	-5.632	-0.087	-5.632	-0.087	-5.632
IJD cubed	0.051	4.300	0.051	4.300	0.051	4.300	0.051	4.300	0.051	4.300

Notes:

1. The numbers reported in this table come from a random intercept regression that conditions on the following variables: age, age squared, the highest level of academic qualifications, the highest level of vocational qualifications, unemployment experience, log duration of current employment episode, log number of employees in the workplace, and private sector.

2. The t test is for H_0: $\beta^i = 0$

3. The t test is for H_0: $\beta^i = \beta^{ef}$: H_0: $\beta^i = \beta^{ex}$; H_0: $\beta^i = \beta^h$; H_0: $\beta^i = \beta^f$

Source: WiB 2000.

a fixed period/task contract and those temping for an agency feel less satisfied with their wages, fringe benefits, career prospects, training opportunities, and job security than those with a standard open-ended contract. Those with the residual 'other' type of non-open-ended contract are especially dissatisfied about their future prospects. There is no evidence that employees with non-standard contracts are any more or less satisfied with the intrinsic, effort, or human dimensions of the job than anyone else.

The best-fitting representation of the conditional effect of job desirability on satisfaction is non-linear, in fact it is an S-shaped curve approximated by squared and cubic terms.[39] For four of the five domains, satisfaction increases slowly at low levels of desirability, grows steeply in the middle, and rises less steeply at high levels of desirability. The exception is for the effort dimension where job desirability is positively related to satisfaction at low values of the IJD, negatively related in the middle range, and positively related at very high values. The things that make a job relatively good or relatively bad in the eyes of the working community have their greatest impact on the satisfaction employees derive from the intrinsic qualities of the job itself—the challenge it sets, the responsibilities it entails, and the chances it affords for self-development. The effects on extrinsic and future-oriented satisfaction are somewhat smaller and very similar to each other. The effect on the human dimension is less than half of the effect on the intrinsic dimension. The satisfaction to be had from holding a good job is not just about what you get paid or how likely you are to be promoted, it is principally about the nature of what you do.

8.10. Summary

The starting point for this chapter was an attempt to explore what, apart from money, British employees at the end of the twentieth century gave weight to in deciding whether a job was relatively good or bad. In doing this, we were able to construct a ranking of jobs according to their relative desirability. It turns out that earnings are, of course, an important part of job desirability, but that is not the whole story. The impact of wages on how desirable people perceive their job to be depends on how much or how little they earn and in addition to money the scope a job gives for personal development, the degree to which it involves the employee, the autonomy and discretion it permits, and the strategic advantages it gives in bargaining with the employer are also important. When one looks at the occupations that are on average considered desirable and compares them with the occupations at the top of the salary ladder it is clear that despite doing less well in terms of pay, occupations in the scientific, teaching, and academic sectors are highly rated. Occupations that are felt to be undesirable, but are not among the worst paid, tend to be uninvolving, repetitive, or involve only intermittent direct contact with other people (driving, security, fetching, and carrying).

Despite the amount of attention given in the sociological literature we find that having anything other than the standard open-ended employment contract has only weak negative consequences for job desirability. Where effects exist they are most marked for casual and seasonal work and negligible for those employed on temporary contracts. Our results are somewhat consistent with other studies (see Booth, Francesconi, and Frank 2002) that find an enduring wage penalty is paid by casual and seasonal workers but that this penalty is much smaller for temporary employees and in fact for women disappears following the transition to permanent employment. The mechanism producing this outcome would seem to be the simple fact that a very large proportion of temporary jobs are in fact the probationary precursor of an open-ended appointment. Nevertheless (controlling for how good others judge a job to be) people with fixed-term contracts do appear to be less satisfied with their jobs, both with regard to aspects of the job that concern their future prospects—promotion, training, and security—and with regard to wages and fringe benefits. Obviously, the former has a rational basis: generally people prefer certainty about the future rather than uncertainty, employers invest more in training people they will keep rather than those they are evaluating and promotion may not be possible until an employee has made the transition from a probationary to permanent position. It may be that disquiet about pay also reflects a reality about temporary contracts: Booth, Francesconi, and Frank (2002) show that they do pay less than open-ended contracts, though the magnitude of the difference is too small to be detected reliably in our data.

The situation with regard to part-time jobs is different and rather paradoxical. Jobs involving less than full-time hours have characteristics that the community at large judge to be undesirable. This is not primarily because they pay less well than other jobs; rather, it is because they involve tasks or working conditions that are commonly regarded as relatively uncongenial. Despite this, controlling for job desirability, part-time employees are more satisfied with almost all aspects of their jobs than full-timers. The solution to the puzzle may be that part-timers simply expect less out of the work and are mostly interested in a reward–effort bargain that allows them time for domestic and caring duties. Like Goldthorpe and Lockwood's affluent workers they approach work instrumentally and in as far as employers provide what they are looking for they are, for the moment, satisfied with it (Goldthorpe et al. 1968).

The 'effects' of union membership on job desirability are either weakly negative or broadly neutral. The interpretation of this finding is however not straightforward. It seems unlikely that people would join an organization that delivered a poor outcome for them when they could do better by staying out of the union. It is much more plausible to believe that people organize and unions recruit where working conditions are relatively bad or where there is a genuine threat that they would become worse if the union were not present. It is crucial to keep in mind what the appropriate counterfactual point of reference is when trying to understand the apparent absence of a union wage or job desirability premium.

Union members are more dissatisfied with all dimensions of their jobs than non-members, but they are particularly dissatisfied with the aspects of the job that unions have traditionally been most concerned to bargain about—wages, fringe benefits, the extensiveness and intensiveness of work effort, and relations with management. Clearly, unions raise the saliency of these issues in the minds of employees, indeed this is what unions are for. It is not possible to identify the prime mover with the cross-sectional data at our disposal. We cannot say whether unions encourage employees to look for grievances or they simply focus attention on real grievances. However, it seems perverse to think that employees would be more satisfied with their jobs if they only left the union! The fact that union members are dissatisfied could be read as evidence that unions are still doing their job.

Finally, we come to social class. Although job desirability and social class are not the same thing, we show in this chapter that these are strongly related. In fact, social class is a much better predictor of job desirability than any of the other variables we have considered. In the relentless search for novelty, sociologists have tended to focus on new and emerging lines of division within the world of work and sometimes appear to have convinced themselves that the old lines are no longer of much importance. They could not be more wrong. If you want to know whether a stranger has a relatively good or bad job the best single question to ask him or her is still what he or she does for a living.

Appendix 1: Variable Selection

The key word in the heading of Section 8.5 is *prediction*. Some readers may wonder why we have not used the word *explanation* instead. Ideally we would like to explain judgements about job desirability by the objective features of jobs and the mechanisms that connect these features with the judgements. However, it would be dishonest for us to claim that we can do this with any great confidence. As far as we are aware there is no theory to tell us which variables to use or indicate how individuals combine and weight information about these variables to reach a judgement about their own job. We have prior empirical evidence and common sense to tell us that both monetary and non-monetary factors are important, but not much else. In these circumstances a way forward is to see what more we can learn empirically by using linear regression to summarize the relationship in the data between job rating and its predictors.[40] In doing this we must take precautions to ensure that we minimize the risk of capitalizing on chance associations that are peculiar to the WiB 2000 data. In addition, the reader should appreciate that all of the predictors are intercorrelated. This means that many predictors or combinations of predictors contain more or less the same information as others about job ratings. We should beware of making a fetish out of a name. Simply because a variable called 'trade union membership' is not included in the final prediction equation we are not entitled to claim that trade unions are unimportant in determining how people rate their jobs. Knowing someone is a union member may well help to estimate how he or she rates his or her job, but the information contained in knowledge of union membership may not be unique. If it is shared with another variable or combination of variables, then there will be a degree of arbitrariness as to which variables appear in the final prediction equation and which variable names we attend to and construct interpretations around. If we had an explicit causal model linking trade unionism with more proximate causal factors, then this problem could, at least partially, be addressed, but this is precisely what we do not have.

   The problem we face is one of model selection. Conventional statistical analysis provides well-established methods to quantify and reports the uncertainty involved in estimating the parameters of a model that is assumed correct a priori. There is much less agreement about how to proceed when a major part of our ignorance concerns the structure of the model itself, including the content of the predictors. In what follows we outline the sequence of steps that lies behind our model selection procedure and the numbers reported in Table 8.2.

Step 1

We started with a pool of more than ninety potential predictor variables. These were chosen to replicate as far as possible the variables used in the JPR study. Additional variables with face value plausibility were added according to their availability in the WiB 2000 survey. The only constraint on inclusion was that a variable should relate to an objective feature of the job performed by the individual rather than be a characteristic of the individual performing the job. Thus for example the educational qualifications obtained by an individual are invalid predictors, whereas the educational qualifications needed to obtain the position are valid predictors. It is, of course, true that the dividing line between an objective and subjective characteristic is not clear cut. For example, we measure job security by combining answers to a number of questions that ask the respondent to rate the likelihood of future job loss. This inevitably must contain some subjective element, but the reality it refers to, albeit imperfectly indicated, is not subjective. If we had the data we could in principle estimate for each individual the probability that he or she would lose his or her job in a given time interval and use this estimated probability as a predictor. We do not however have the information with which to construct such estimates so rather than ignore job security entirely, which would be a major omission, we use the data we have on respondent's own perceptions of how things are likely to turn out. In general when we were unsure whether or not to include a variable in the initial sift we erred on the side of inclusiveness.

Some variables have substantial amounts of missing values. For instance, over 14 per cent of cases have no valid weekly earnings data. We solved this problem by multiple imputation (MI), and Appendix 2 explains how it was done. It is however not practical to make MI estimates where there is a very large number of potential predictor variables and substantial model uncertainty. So before we carried out any imputations we reduced the complexity of the problem by selecting a smaller set of predictor variables by backward stepwise regression using all cases for which we had complete information. The criterion for inclusion in the final equation was deliberately set rather generously and all variables with $p < .3$ were retained.

Step 2

The forty-nine predictor variables that survived the first cut along with the logged job rating and plausible predictors of missing values were the raw material for the multiple imputation algorithm. Six complete data-sets were constructed. Five were set aside to be used for estimation once model selection was completed; the sixth was used for model construction. Below we list the forty-nine variables retained for serious consideration under, for convenience, eleven headings:

Earnings: Weekly wages.

Job conditions and perquisites: Enhanced sick pay, free transport to work or other help with travel costs, subsidized or free meals, private health insurance, number of days paid holiday per annum, and number of days paid sick leave without certification.

Hours: Usual number of hours worked per week, respondent works on Sunday, respondent works in the evening, respondent works at night, and respondent has some influence on how working hours are decided.

Training and skill acquisition: Employer has paid for training in the past two years, job involves learning from colleagues, job requires the respondent to keep learning new things, proportion in occupation with lower vocational qualifications, proportion in occupation with medium-level vocational qualifications, proportion in occupation with higher-level vocational qualifications, proportion in occupation with a trade apprenticeship, proportion in occupation with 'O' levels, proportion in occupation with 'A' levels, and proportion in occupation with university degree.

Human resource management regime: Management communicates with staff using electronic media, management holds meetings for upwards and/or downwards communication, union presence in workplace, and formal and regular job performance appraisal.

Task autonomy: Individual has influence on decisions about the way he or she does his or her job, job allows respondent to design and plan important aspects of work, respondent decides the specific tasks he or she carries out from day to day, someone other than respondent decides the amount and pace of work performed, and respondent can decide to introduce a new performance task or work assignment.

Performance monitoring and control: Starting and finishing times are checked, computerized equipment monitors work performance, difficulty of supervisor or manager knowing how much work the respondent does in a week, difficulty of supervisor or manager knowing the quality of work performed, respondent works hard because of production line or machine, respondent can take a 10 minute break without informing a supervisor, and respondent's own discretion influences how hard he or she works.

Job content: Respondent works as part of a team, respondent sometimes performs a different set of tasks to help cope with the pressure of work, importance of computer usage, and complexity of computer usage.

Future prospects: Job is a rung on an internal or an external career ladder, perceived risk of redundancy.

Human asset specificity: Respondent has bargained over salary, respondent has bargained over hours.

Miscellaneous: Job in the private sector, number of employees in the workplace, and temporary contract.

Step 3

The sixth data-set produced by the multiple imputations was divided into two equal-sized random subsets, a training data-set and a testing data-set. The testing data-set was put to one side. The training data-set was divided into $V = 5$ equal-sized partitions for a cross-validation exercise. In each of the five possible

V - 1 partitions, a backward stepwise algorithm was used to choose a subset of predictors. Two criteria, Akaike's information criterion (AIC) (Akaike 1973) and the Bayes's information criterion (BIC) (Schwarz 1978), were used to control selection into the prediction equation. Both exact a penalty for including too many predictors. AIC imposes a smaller penalty than BIC and tends to select a bigger model, which might be considered a virtue for a prediction problem. BIC selects more parsimonious models. For an enlightening discussion of both criteria and model selection in general see Kuha (2004). From each of the $5V$ - 1 partitions we thus had two selection equations, one AIC derived and one BIC derived. Each equation was then fitted to the left over fifth of the data that had not been used to estimate it. The best AIC- and BIC-derived models were chosen by examining the mean square error for predicting the uncontaminated portion of the data. Twenty variables selected by the best performing AIC and BIC models, and the three linear splines representing weekly wages, were retained for further investigation.

Step 4

We now return to the full training sample with the twenty-three variables selected in step 3. In problems such as this it will almost always be the case that many slightly different models will be roughly equivalent in their predictive power. In this circumstance, it makes sense to search not just for the 'best' model but for a set of well-performing models. To do this we use a subset regression algorithm from the *R leaps* library to search over the entire model space for the best predictive models of a given size (for practical details, see Fox 2002). Models with fifteen predictors are roughly halfway between the size of models selected by AIC and BIC in step 3 and for want of any better criterion this is where we concentrated our search. The best twenty models, using BIC as the selection criterion, were retained.

Step 5

We now turned to the test data set aside at the beginning of step 3. Recall that these data played so far no role in model selection. The twenty best models from step 4 were fitted to the test data, and the ten with the smallest mean square error were retained. The best of the ten is our best overall model, but the nine others have scarcely worse predictive power.

Step 6

We now returned to our first five MI data-sets. These were used to calibrate our models and obtain appropriate point estimates incorporating the effects of weighting, clustering, stratification, and missing data uncertainty. In these models we always included the three linear splines representing weekly wages even if one or more of the splines had not been selected in the subset regressions of step 4.

Step 7

The penultimate outcome of this procedure is Table 8.2. In the interests of readability we have chosen in the main text to present OLS parameter estimates only for our 'best' model.

Step 8

The ultimate objective of selecting a model is to use the predicted values as an index of job desirability. However, there is room for argument about which fitted values it is most sensible to use. We considered four possibilities: (a) the predicted values from the OLS regression, (b) the average predicted values from the best ten OLS regressions, (c) the predicted values from a ridge regression using the variables from the best OLS regression, and (d) the predicted values from the lasso regression using the variables from the best OLS regression.[41] The first has the virtue of simplicity, the second is consistent with the idea of acknowledging model uncertainty, but is rather ad hoc. The third and fourth are biased estimators, but penalize over complex models, and are attractive because they make a favourable trade-off between efficiency and bias and thus may increase accuracy. Ridge and lasso regression fall into the class of shrinkage estimators which means in essence

Table A1. Coefficients from Lasso regression

	β
Log (weekly earnings/median) £4–£281.64	0.0021
Log (weekly earnings/median) £281.65–£626.81	0.20706
Log weekly earnings > £626.81	0
Has unsuccessfully bargained over salary	−0.01358
Usual weekly hours	0
Has unsuccessfully bargained over hours	0
Job requires keep learning new things	−0.11672
Employer has paid for training in last 2 years	0.00352
Has discretion over own work effort	0.00142
Doesn't control own starting/leaving times	−0.04226
Can influence job changes	0.03716
Can design/plan own job	0.12472
Job on a career ladder	0.02526
Employer supplies subsidized or free meals	0.00722
Management holds meetings	0.0446
Complexity of computer use where use if very important or essential	0.0488

Notes: The coefficients are averaged across 5 replications. In the estimation all variables are standardized to have a mean of 0 and a variance of 1.

Source: WiB 2000.

that they give less weight to large parameter estimates about which we have relatively little information and 'spread out' the effects of different variables more evenly across the whole set of variables or in the case of the lasso across a subset of variables. This can be given a Bayesian justification. A pragmatic reason for considering shrinkage estimators is that our model selection procedure favours the inclusion of large effects. Some of these will be real; others will be the result of sampling variation. An estimation technique that spreads out the magnitude of effects between all variables or a subset of variables is likely to perform relatively well out of sample. It turns out in our case not to matter too much which method we use to arrive at predicted values. The smallest correlation between a pair of predictions produced by the four methods is .95. Most are correlated at above .98. We chose the predicted values from the lasso regression to form our index.

Appendix 2: Missing Data

Column 4 of Table 8.2 reveals the fact that weekly wage has a significant amount of missing data. Because it was collected on a self-completion schedule, the response variable—the respondent's rating of his or her own job—also has cases with missing values. If we were to work only with cases that have complete data we would have to drop almost 20 per cent of our observations from the estimation of the prediction equation. Although 'list wise deletion' is a common practice, from an estimation point of view it is inefficient. To deal with this problem we use multiple imputation (Rubin 1987, 1996). The basic idea, if not the implementation, is straightforward. First, build an imputation model to predict the missing values. Typically, this model will have a deterministic and a stochastic part reflecting both fundamental and estimation uncertainty. The stochastic portion implies that no two imputations will be exactly the same. Second, use the imputation model to construct M complete data-sets. In these data-sets fully observed variable values are retained and missing values are drawn from a stochastic distribution. Third, analyse each complete data-set with standard complete data methods and then combine the results. Parameter estimates are averaged, and standard errors are calculated so as to reflect both within and between imputation estimation variance. The goals of the procedure are not to predict the missing values with the highest within-sample accuracy. Nor are they to give a causal account of the missing data process. The intention of the procedure is (a) to preserve known features of the distribution of the data and of the relationships between variables and (b) to reflect the uncertainty of the imputation process.

Any imputation procedure must rely on assumptions. We assume that observations are missing at random (MAR) and that the variables in the imputation model are jointly multivariate normal. Both of these assumptions are strong and strictly speaking unwarranted. First, it is plausible to believe that missing values on the wage variable are in fact non-ignorable. In other words, it is likely that the probability of an observation being missing is a function of the true unobserved wage value as well as of the predictor variables in the imputation model. Second, given the presence in the imputation model of several dichotomous and ordinal variables the assumption of multivariate normality can only be a rough approximation. Nevertheless, our multiple imputation approach can scarcely lead to worse inferences than the standard complete case approach. This would have us throw a fifth of the data away and then assume that, conditional on the predictor variables in the analysis model, observations are missing at random—which is precisely what is assumed by our imputation model.

To make the imputations we used the Amelia programme (Honaker et al. 2000). This uses the EM algorithm (Dempster, Laird and Rubin 1977) supplemented with importance sampling (King et al. 2001). Six data-sets were imputed.

Appendix 3: An IJD Based on Occupations

The unique selling point of the IJD is that it measures how good an individual's job is, not how good his occupation, an aggregation of jobs, is. However, to do this requires information that will not be available in many social surveys. For some purposes it may be good enough to know how desirable, on average, the occupation is. We have direct estimates for 313 occupation/employment status combinations, but these are just a sample from the universe of all occupations. We need to be able to predict a score for any occupation and to do this we need a prediction equation. We estimate this in the following way.

Step 1

We estimate a random effects regression where the dependent variable is the IJD value for each individual (in other words the predicted value from the lasso regression). The random effect is formed from the cross-classification of employment status—managerial versus non-managerial (including supervisors)—and the so-called SOC or occupational code from the 1990 Classification of Occupations. This gives us 313 permitted groups that can be considered a sample drawn from a large population of occupations. The random effects model gives us estimates of the between group variance of the IJD means, u_{0j}, and the within-group variance of the individual level residuals, e_{0ij}. These are 0.091 and 0.073, respectively both with standard errors of 0.015. Our interest is in the so-called level 2 residuals. These have a property that is attractive for our purposes. The level 2 residuals for groups with a relatively small number of observations are shrunken towards the overall mean. This makes sense, especially within a prediction framework, because we would like to protect ourselves against ending up with apparently large

275

occupational level means based on few observations that could have an unduly large influence on the outcome of step 2.

Step 2

The inputs into step 2 are the shrunken occupational level IJD residuals from step 1 and aggregate-level information about each occupation mainly calculated from the March–May, June–August, and September–November quarters of the 2000 Quarterly Labour Force Survey (QLFS) excluding all Northern Irish cases and all second and subsequent observations produced by the revolving panel design. This information comprises: the proportion of employees with gross weekly earnings above the median (C50), proportion of employees with gross weekly earnings above the 90th percentile (C90), percentage of employees that have at least one A level (CA), the percentage of employees with at least one A level squared (CA2), the percentage of the employees who say they have considerable scope to plan their work (CPL)—only available in a non-publicly released version of the 1997 March–May QLFS. All explanatory variables are centred around their means. There are 304 occupation/employment status combinations for which we have full covariate information and 309 combinations where we have information just on the earnings and education variables.

Step 3

The best prediction equation, giving each occupation a weight of one is as follows:

$$\hat{Y} = -0.0002 + 0.1870C50 + 0.2716C90 + 0.2006CA + 0.2697CPL$$

with $R^2 = .728$ and $t > 2$ for all coefficients except the constant. Weighting each occupational group by the number of jobs observed in it gives an equation that differs from this principally in two details: first, the coefficient for CPL is about 40 per cent larger and second, the R^2 increases to .865. Because CPL is not likely to be generally available we give a second equation which does almost as well:

$$\hat{Y} = -.0271 + .2583C50 + .2729C90 + .4091CA - .2975CA2$$

with $R^2 = .691$ and $t > 2$ for all coefficients. The weighted version has an R^2 of .855.

With a parsimonious model we can predict occupational IJD scores quite well and very well if we allow the relative size of occupations to influence the prediction equation. In the search for a good specification we experimented with a number of different variables and codings of the variables finally used. We were surprised to find that the proportion of women in an occupation had no predictive power after allowing for earnings, education, and planning.

Notes

1. In this chapter, the terms 'job quality', 'job desirability', and 'good and bad jobs' are used interchangeably.
2. Below we make some explicit comparisons between our measure of job desirability and Stewart et al.'s Cambridge scale of social status. We are unable to make such a comparison with the Hope–Goldthorpe scale of general occupational desirability because there is no straightforward way to map the building blocks of that scale—the 'occupational unit groups' of the 1970 Classification of Occupations—onto the occupational information contained in our data— the 1990 SOC codes.
3. By social status sociologists usually mean the social acceptability of members of one group to members of another as indicated by things such as voluntary association, commensality, connubium, and displays of deference and derogation.
4. For an account of social classes in terms of rent-seeking behaviour, see Sørensen (2000).
5. Stouffer et al. (1949) present empirical evidence on satisfaction with promotion chances in the American military during the Second World War, which illustrates exactly this process.
6. There is good empirical evidence on the predictive validity of job satisfaction scales. For example from the 1987 Household and Community Survey in which a random sample of those interviewed in the 1986 Social Change in Economic Life Survey was interviewed *inter alia* about their labour market behaviour in the intervening twelve months. Analyses of these data show that in a comparison of 5 plausible ways of producing a scale of job dissatisfaction from the 1986 data all of them predict exits from employment within the next year (n = 979, t ranges from 3.248 to 3.752). The magnitude of the effect is non-trivial—in the strongest case the estimated percentage difference at ±1 standard deviation around the mean of the job dissatisfaction scale is approximately 13%, in the weakest about 11%. These figures are estimates for the population of just one of the six geographical locations surveyed (Aberdeen) but the order of magnitude of the effects is the same in all areas. As perhaps one might expect much weaker effects are found for job dissatisfaction in 1986 on obtaining a (self-defined) better job in 1987. In this case none gives a significant result (t ranges from 1.386 to 1.892), though all the signs are in the right direction. The estimated magnitudes of the effects, on the logit scale, are about half those observed for the case of leaving employment. These results are consistent with the following interpretation. Dissatisfaction is predictive of an intention to change one's situation, but obtaining a better job requires more than just the intention, it requires someone to offer it to you.
7. Plausible definition is indeed one of the methods commonly used (see Kalleberg, Reskin, and Hudson 2000; McGovern, Smeaton, and Hill 2004). Criteria

that are to distinguish the good from the bad jobs are chosen on common sense grounds and the presence or absence of these attributes can then simply be empirically ascertained and jobs assigned to the appropriate category. This kind of approach has a long pedigree and is similar to what is done in the vast majority of poverty research where a plausible, but ultimately arbitrary, sheep and goat distinction is made to determine who is to be regarded as poor. In deciding which jobs are to be regarded as bad there is the additional problem of combining information on a number of attributes. None of the available solutions seem entirely satisfactory. Our argument is not that any one of these approaches is wrong; merely that whichever is chosen will lead someone, somewhere, to raise a plausible objection to the arbitrariness of the procedure.

8. We ignore here all considerations relating to the frictional costs involved in moving from one job to another that obviously would enter any real person's assessment at the margin of the relative desirability of two jobs. The simple point being made here is that for the aggregate ranking all other things are, by definition, not equal.

9. In a sense our argument is that for some purposes Grusky's 'small class' programme is not radical enough (Grusky and Sørensen 1998, Weeden and Grusky 2005). Why stop at the level of occupation if there is relevant variation at the level of the individual job? At the same time we have no quarrel with Grusky's main point that for the purpose of understanding collective action the institutional structure of the workplace may make the occupational group the relevant unit of analysis.

10. In what follows, unless we explicitly say otherwise, we always report results estimated from a sample of 2,132 employees.

11. The task we set people was to rate their job on a scale that is explicitly multiplicative. This suggests that taking the natural logarithm of the reported ratings will simplify interpretation. A more technical reason for doing this is that the regression of untransformed job rating on weekly wages produces heteroskedastic residuals and taking the logarithm considerably reduces the seriousness of the problem.

12. There is a possible objection to this procedure. Individuals are not allocated to jobs at random and may either self-select themselves into jobs with the characteristics that they give most weight to or find themselves with only Hobson's choice over the type of job they can get (on the latter point, see Blackburn and Mann 1979). This implies that estimating the weight to be given to different characteristics by a naive regression that does not adjust for self-selection will give the wrong answer about the relative strength of the weights. This is an important argument and one that, for instance, underlies the standard economic objection to placing occupation (a choice variable) on the right-hand side of a wage equation. It is however one thing to point out a possible flaw, another to show that it is in fact the case and a third to figure

out what to do about it. We have some reason to believe that the problem may in fact be less serious than it might seem. Although we were unable to do so ourselves, JPR built into their research design a check on the reliability of the ratings individuals gave to their own jobs by asking the interviewer who elicited the ratings to rate the respondent's job. If respondents were rating jobs in ways that were different to the way in which an external observer would rate the job—giving more weight to characteristics that they personally found important than would be assigned by an individual randomly allocated to that job—then we would expect a relatively weak correlation between the respondent's and the interviewer's rating. In fact, they find a strong correlation between the two ratings.

13. Dividing by the median wage is a device to simplify interpretation, the logarithm of the median wage becoming $\log(1) = 0$.

14. The reader should remember that the lines represent the average rating given to a job with a given wage level. There is, of course, considerable variation around these averages, but we have suppressed the detail contained in the original scatterplot.

15. What are plotted here are the predicted values from a form of smoothing called locally weighted scatterplot smoothing (lowess). The bandwidth (proportion of the sample used to smooth each point) is set at 0.8.

16. It is possible to object that what is of interest is not the marginal relationship between rating and wage but the conditional relationship after controlling for non-monetary factors. This is, of course, true, but we can see no simple alternatives to proceeding as we do. If we knew in advance which non-monetary variables we should condition on, then it would be straightforward to choose the correct functional form for the conditional relationship between rating and wage. However *ex ante* we do not have this information and in fact we have to assume something about the relationship between rating and wage in order to select appropriate variables to condition on. An additional complication is that we wish to impute wage values for individuals whose wages are unknown and to do this in a consistent way requires us to 'correctly' specify the rating–wage relationship in the imputation model before we even begin the business of model selection. The shape of the marginal rating–wage relationship is our best guess about the functional form of the conditional relationship.

17. The spline approximates the lowess curve by assuming that the rating–wage relationship is linear over portions of the wage domain, but that the slope changes at certain knot points. In selecting the number of knot points there is, of course, a trade-off between fit and parsimony. We selected the knot points empirically by dividing up the wage domain into ten equal intervals with nine corresponding knot points and then estimating a sequence of regressions. After each we amalgamated contiguous intervals that appeared to contain similar slopes. After establishing that two knot points seemed

adequate we fine tuned the values of the knots to maximize fit. The R^2 for the regression of the lowess fitted values on the spline fitted values is .99.

18. JPR find in their American data that the relationship between log annual wages and log job rating is best captured by a second degree polynomial. We could find no such simple relationship in our data. The best fitting polynomial was of degree 4, but the fit was still inferior to the linear spline with 2 knot points.

19. Approximately 90% of individuals lie within the range -1.5 to 1.0 on the log (wage/median wage) scale.

20. We have in fact already implicitly assumed this by truncating the highest observed job ratings.

21. A number of variables that we might have expected to be included did not make the final cut. For instance, the availability of private health insurance, company pensions or a company car, the nature and extent of supervision by a superior, whether the employment contract is temporary or permanent, whether the respondent is obliged to work unsociable hours, whether the job is relatively secure.

22. The observant reader of Table 8.3 might object to the inclusion of two measures of working hours on the grounds that hours of work is itself one of the predictors of the job ratings included in Table 8.2. They would however be mistaken because though hours of work is indeed one of the predictors included in the OLS regression reported in Table 8.2, the IJD itself is based on the fitted values from the lasso algorithm (see Appendix 1) and this, as it turns out, gives 0 weight to working hours.

23. Treating occupational group as a fixed effect produces a high end estimate, because a number of occupations have only one observation and their means are thus fitted perfectly. A random effects model of the form $y_{ij} = a + \mu_j + e_{ij}$, where the μ_j are occupation-specific intercepts drawn from a random distribution, gives slightly lower and more plausible estimates.

24. We allow the regression line to bend in two places, but maintain a straight line relationship with the IJD between the knot points.

25. The actual cost of including all the predictors with non-zero coefficients in a social survey is probably less than the cost of coding complex, open-ended responses to questions about occupational titles and job descriptions to produce standard occupational classifications, but social surveys, especially when repeated, are social institutions, and as all sociologists know, social institutions are hard to change.

26. These are not in fact the empirical means, but the so-called level 2 residuals from a random intercepts regression of the IJD on the 313 occupational groups that allows a separate intercept for each occupational group. These residuals are shrunken back towards the mean in proportion to the amount of information they are based on. Thus occupational averages based on a small number of cases are shrunken a long way towards the mean and those averages based on a large number are barely affected. When the aim is to predict outside

of the given sample, this is a sensible way of ensuring that predictions are not unduly influenced by chance features of the sample to hand.

27. The justification for treating the social class of the job as an indicator of contractual status is discussed in Chapter 1 and stems from the arguments made in Goldthorpe (2000a).

28. In Tables 8.7 and 8.8, we ignore the very small effect of the interaction when reporting the social class coefficients.

29. We have presented some of the material in this chapter at a number of seminars and in every one of them somebody has remarked to the effect that 'all you are doing with the IJD is measuring job satisfaction in another way'. We believe that the argument we make below should convince the sceptics that this is not the case. More determined sceptics will need to explain how, if the IJD is a measure of job satisfaction, we can reconcile the following empirical observations. A common finding in the job satisfaction literature is that net of all control variables the relationship between being female and job satisfaction is strongly positive as is the relationship between part-time work and job satisfaction. We find exactly these relationships in the WiB 2000 data. But the relationship between being a woman (regardless of marital status) and job desirability is strongly negative as is the relationship between part-time work and job desirability (on the latter, see Tables 8.7 and 8.8). From this we conclude that empirically the IJD has no construct validity as a measure of job satisfaction.

30. It is implausible to believe that scales purporting to measure different dimensions of job satisfaction will be uncorrelated and any simplification that assumes this seems to us to be of dubious value.

31. The BIC statistic for example suggests that we should prefer our model to the saturated model.

32. This procedure implicitly gives equal weight to each item in the scale. Another approach is to use weights derived from the CFA to scale each item according to the strength of its relationship with the underlying construct. Although this seems a more elegant procedure, it turns out empirically to make no difference of any consequence to any of our substantive findings so we report only results based on the simpler method.

33. It is conventional to report numbers on the reliability (consistency) of scales constructed in this way; in fact, some applied researchers seem to make almost a fetish of it. The estimated alpha coefficients (range 0–1) for our scales are Intrinsic, .93; Effort, .67; Extrinsic, .62; Human, .70; and Future, .63. These numbers for what they are worth seem to us to be comparatively high (usually interpreted as a good thing), though some are below the thresholds that are, without any obvious justification, cited as indicating respectability—why does God love .7 more than .69? We doubt whether there can be any serious reason why those working with social survey data from general population samples should defer to social psychologists' expectations about levels of

scale reliability based on experiences with rather homogeneous populations in highly controlled conditions responding to virtually tautological items.

34. For simplicity we refer to the first principal component throughout this paragraph simply as job satisfaction.

35. The graphs plot the predicted values from locally weighted scatterplot smoothing of data from five multiply imputed data-sets. This explains the apparent lack of smoothness in the earnings and wage rate plots.

36. One should not take the apparent U shape too seriously. It is partly the consequence of a small number of extreme outlying values.

37. The same predictors as were used in Table 8.7. Nothing of importance for our purpose hangs on the fact that we adopt a specification in terms of the logarithm of weekly wages. We do this simply because it gives a marginally better fit to the data than a specification in terms of the untransformed metric.

38. This is in fact true to a varying extent across all the five satisfaction domains represented in Figure 8.2, but the effect is especially strong for intrinsic and extrinsic satisfaction (results not shown).

39. To achieve empirical identifiability we constrain the squared and cubic terms in the regression to be the same across all five satisfaction domains.

40. We, of course, do not claim that the linear model represents the cognitive process that produces the judgements. Our claim is simply that it provides a summary of the outcome of that process.

41. The parameter estimates from an alternative to the ordinary least squares estimator—the so-called *lasso* (least absolute shrinkage and selection operator) estimator—has the useful property of shrinking some coefficients to exactly zero and thus combines parameter estimation and model selection in one algorithm (Tibshirani 1996).

9

Conclusions

One of the most striking developments of the past couple of decades has been the extraordinary resurgence of interest in market forces as a method of economic management. The impact of neoliberal policies of economic deregulation, for instance, has been so far reaching that any attempt to question the perceived new emphasis on market forces may seem strange if not slightly ridiculous. Many scholars have argued that the employment relationship has been profoundly affected, even transformed, by the incorporation of market principles into an area that was traditionally the subject of institutional regulation. We have sought to challenge this argument by focusing on the more theoretically sophisticated conceptions of what we have called the 'marketization' thesis.[1]

This thesis maintains that short-term market relations come to dominate employment just as they increasingly dominate businesses, services, and economies, and in so doing they displace the established form of employment relationship, which we call 'internalized'. Employers withdraw from offers of long-term employment since they cannot maintain them in the face of competitive market imperatives. Accordingly, internal career structures are undermined, as are systems of deferred compensation and rewards for loyalty. Employment becomes contingent on market conditions and market opportunities. Skill and talent are rewarded at their current market value, but employees are exposed to more uncertainty and insecurity, and individualism becomes the order of the day. The breakdown of internal labour markets and differentiated career structures eventually leads to elimination of the 'rents' that employees have been accustomed to enjoy from long-term jobs, and so to a weakening of class differences and a change in the form of inequality. Effort and work pressure are no longer maintained either by feelings of loyalty and obligation or the prospect of future reward, but by the imminent fear of job loss and the general uncertainty of the future: a 'frightened worker' model.

Previous chapters have subjected the ideas and interpretations of the marketization thesis to empirical testing, in a piecemeal manner. The time has now come to draw broader conclusions. There are three main claims, of a general type, within the marketization thesis, and the conclusions will be arranged accordingly. The first general claim is that short-term market pressures have become the dominant influence in the treatment of employees by employers. The second claim is that these developments have led to a displacement or weakening of internalized employment structures (or 'internal labour markets') within workplaces. The third claim is that the distribution of the benefits of employment is being altered, in particular through a reduced role for structural inequality such as, notably, by social class. After assessing each of these claims in turn, the chapter ends with a brief explanation of our central findings.

Before launching into the assessment, it may be useful to recall the nature of the evidence on which it is based. This research has relied chiefly upon evidence from national sample surveys of employees, conducted in 1992 and 2000, supported by material from various other national surveys, both of employees and of employers, conducted between 1984 and 2004 (see Chapter 1, Section 1.6). The inferences that can be based on this type of evidence concern the average circumstances, average effects on those circumstances, and changes over time in those circumstances or effects, for British employees or British workplaces as a whole. Underlying these averages there may well be considerable variation locally, for instance, in special kinds of workplaces or for special groups of people. Our research does not, therefore, deny the value of other kinds of study, such as case studies, which can reveal localized variation within the average picture.

9.1. How Has Market Pressure Affected Employees?

We have accepted the now widely shared assumptions about the competitive, marketized environment in which most organizations operate. While we have some reservations about the public sector, we must acknowledge that substantial parts of the British public sector have been subjected to a range of reforms that have sought to give a greater role to the private sector. So, the relevant questions for our purposes concern the consequences of that assumed market environment on the relations of employment, and how closely those consequences match the predictions of the marketization thesis.

The broad answer comes in two parts. The first is that employees are certainly experiencing some changes in their circumstances that can reasonably be linked to external market pressures. The second is that these changes do not match the predictions of the marketization thesis at all closely, and in a number of respects go completely against those predictions.

Uncertainty is perhaps the aspect of employee experience that comes closest to matching the predictions. Data from our own surveys and from other sources confirm that workforce reductions and redundancies have taken place at many workplaces even in a period of unusual economic prosperity. There is little reason to doubt that the use of redundancies to adjust labour to market demand has become a normal instrument of employer policy in Britain. Moreover, both the experience of past workforce reductions, and the expectation of impending redundancy, stimulate employees towards increased effort, much as the 'frightened worker' model would predict (see Cappelli 1999: 130–2). Not only is the uncertainty of employment a widespread experience or perception, but it also has sufficient force to affect employees' behaviour.

Yet despite these observations, in a number of other respects, the stability of employment has either remained unchanged or has actually increased for British employees. One of the simplest indications of this is that the proportion of employees in permanent (open-ended) employment increased during the 1990s and remains above 90 per cent. Meanwhile temporary (fixed-period or casual) employment, which had increased during the 1980s, once more declined in the subsequent decade. Similarly, the proportion of employees on 'flexible' contracts (self-employed, part-time, and temporary), which increased during the mid-to-late 1980s, fell back in the early 1990s and has remained mostly unchanged since 1994. Any decline in long-term jobs would be, arguably, a still better indicator of a shift towards market solutions yet tenure in jobs of ten years' duration or more has remained roughly unchanged between 1994 and 2004. Employers' policies of cutting jobs and using redundancies are significant, but apparently not sufficient to undermine the existing norm of 'standard' and reasonably stable employment contracts. In sum, the major institutional feature of the employment relationship continues to be the fact that, by and large, employers employ the same workers in the same jobs this year as they did last year. Of course, firms might have occasional lay-offs and employees may change jobs every five or six years but the essential point about the employment relationship is that employers and, in particular, employees are rarely on the market.

Accordingly, claims of a new market-driven era lack credibility because this is obviously where we might expect markets to have a greater role.

When employees construct their careers in the job market (as envisaged in the marketization thesis), this should lead to an increase in the individual negotiation of contractual terms. The indisputable decline of union recognition and union membership should also contribute to such a tendency. There is some evidence that is consonant with this part of the marketization thesis. Substantial minorities of employees reported that they had personally bargained over pay, either on entry to their current job or afterwards. Many employees (especially women) had also requested changes in their hours of work, and the great majority of these requests had been successful. Because these were new questions that had not been asked in previous surveys, we cannot be sure whether these kinds of personal negotiations are an increasing tendency. However, personal pay negotiation becomes more likely in the absence of unions, so that with a falling union presence, growing individualism in bargaining seems plausible.

The marketization thesis suggests, however, that individual bargaining arises not only from the decline of collective bargaining but also from the decline of careers. The individual employee negotiates to maximize the 'spot rate' that she or he can achieve on an open market rather than relying on long-term rewards that are increasingly uncertain. Here, the evidence is far from supportive of the marketization thesis. It is true that the early 1990s witnessed a decline in the prospects offered within many organizations, with some employers publicly reneging on their previous career promises. Yet by the early 2000s, this picture was reversed, with a marked shift in employees' perceptions towards seeing their best future chances as lying within their current workplace rather than on the open job market. Additionally, the proportion of all employees whose jobs belonged to formal career ladders had increased slightly between 1984 and 2000. So any growth of individualized bargaining has not taken the place of careers but is, instead, supplementary.

Another area where the marketization thesis initially appears to have some purchase is in connection with work pressure and effort. In addition to allocating scarce resources, markets can also act as a disciplinary mechanism for firms and workers. For workers, the threat of dismissal is never entirely absent and is likely to increase during periods of high unemployment. Consistent with the logic of market discipline, we found that the frightened worker model does help to explain employees' acceptance of high work demands in contemporary Britain. Where the frightened worker model fails, however, is in its implications for employers' own policies. If employers want to rely on insecurity and fear, they need to have policies that undermine security not only in adverse job markets but also, as in contemporary Britain, under conditions of growth and tight labour supply. For this to happen, employers must direct their labour policies towards a market-driven, hire-and-fire philosophy rather than towards the model of internalized, human resource development. But if employers were relying on this type of motivation, then one would see more jobs on temporary contracts and shorter periods of tenure, and as we have already seen, this has not been taking place. Employers would also have less need for costly internal systems of control, incentives, and development: hire and fire would suffice. The evidence is in general the opposite (this will be detailed in the next section): internalized employment practices, and especially those of a motivational or incentivizing type, were extended over the 1990s. Clearly, employers would not have chosen to invest in costly systems of these types if simple hire-and-fire practices coupled with rapid response to market signals were effective.

For one group of employees, however, the frightened worker model achieves a better fit. This is the routine (generally, the least skilled) occupational class. Employees in this group respond to the experience of job cuts with above-average increases in effort. More importantly, employers appear to be progressively excluding this group from most of the developments in internalized employment systems that will be summarized in the following section, which suggests an increased reliance on hire and fire. Here, then, the frightened worker model appears to be approximated. Even so, not all the evidence is consistent, for employees in the routine class expressed higher confidence in internal advancement in 2000 than in 1992. Possibly jobs at the routine level are being used increasingly as a probationary or 'sorting' area for entry to internalized employment systems.

We can now sum up on the first general claim of the marketization thesis. It offers some useful insights about the effects of competitive market changes on employees, especially in relation to uncertainty and individualism, but its predictions are not supported in regard to contractual forms, stable employment, and careers, and are only partially supported in relation to work effort since employer policies have not changed in the predicted direction, except for routine-level employees. Evidently the marketization thesis underestimates the value of the traditional, internalized employment relationship to employers.

9.2. Have Internalized Employment Structures Been Displaced?

The evidence assembled in previous chapters shows that internalized employment structures have not been displaced or weakened by market pressures. By contrast, they have been changing quite rapidly, and market conditions (along with changing technologies) help to account for this. What we observe is not a decline but a considerable adaptation of internalized employment forms to external pressures.

In Section 9.1, the persistence and indeed resurgence of within-company career expectations among employees was noted. It is important to appreciate that this was not merely a subjective shift of perceptions brought on by improved economic conditions. There is independent evidence, from management informants, that many British employers themselves took deliberate steps to restore career ladders and internal hierarchies around the end of the 1990s. Employers have evidently continued to see value in retaining and developing 'human assets' rather than seeking them on the open market in an ad hoc fashion. The claims of a 'death of careers' and a swing towards expendable jobs seem to have come from misreading the signals from an unusually severe downswing in the economy: short-term turbulence has been too often interpreted as structural change. Having pointed this out, it would be hypocritical not to acknowledge that the more recent findings about buoyant internal careers in part reflect the sustained period of economic growth that many Western economies, and notably Britain, have enjoyed since the mid-1990s. Prospects would doubtlessly once more decline in the face of a new economic crisis. In this respect we are, of course, happy to acknowledge that the employment relationship may be influenced by fluctuations in product markets as firms lay-off employees in response to slack demand. Nevertheless, the essential point is that the internalized structures that generally support the retention and development of employees did not collapse even during the most severe economic setbacks of the post-war era. Once better external conditions emerged, they were able to recover and function effectively within a few years. This resilience of internal career systems constitutes particularly simple and direct evidence against the marketization thesis.

Another strong challenge to the marketization thesis is the growth of what are loosely known as HRM practices. Developed in the USA, these 'best practice' models have emphasized the development of skilled, motivated, and participative employees who would contribute to innovation and flexibility (see, for instance, Beer et al. 1985). Such an approach appears to fit much better with an organization-centred model of the employment relationship, where employers seek to retain and develop firm-specific knowledge and skills, than with one depending on opportunistic actions in the job market. If the market forces were sufficient to govern the employment relationship there would, as Paul Edwards observed, be no requirement for elaborate sets of HRM practices or for all the emerging policies of employee communication and involvement. The market alone should be able to resolve problems of motivation and make decisions about how to respond to changes in the environment (Edwards 1995: 601).

The evidence indicates a continuing adoption by British employers of the canonical HRM practices over the past decade or so. For example, there has been a growing use of systematic communication to employees. Direct participation (that is, participation in decisions relating to an employee's own job) has recently been rising, even while indirect participation through trade unions continues to decline. At the same time, there has been an increase in formally designated work teams, accompanied by a wider development of group-based organizational forms that depend on cooperative and responsible working. Most employees also report policies that support functional flexibility, such as cross-training and taking other roles while colleagues are ill or under pressure. The planning of individual training and development through systems of appraisal emerges as one of the most rapid, recent developments. While such practices are often adopted in a piecemeal or fragmented manner, systemic HRM (in the sense that employees are involved in multiple practices across several domains of workplace organization) has also grown to a significant degree.

The progressive extension of employee voice, through systematic communication and other informal channels, provides an alternative gloss on the decline of unionization and the growth of individualism in the employment relationship. It suggests that employers wish to enhance the employees' sense of membership in an organizational community, involving trust and responsibility. It also suggests that employee voice continues to be valued, and indeed is more valuable under competitive conditions (this was indeed very much part of the original case for HRM). The value of employee voice will however depend on whether employees are retained long enough to become knowledgeable and credible contributors. Accordingly, the extension of employee voice is discordant with the idea of a general shift towards a marketized, short-term employment relationship and more consonant with an open-ended, internalized relationship.

However, the growth of participation and communication does not mean that employees are being progressively freed from regimes of internal control. Rather, methods of control, linked with incentives, are being steadily extended to provide employers with means of extracting additional effort and obtaining employees' compliance with this development. In Britain, the version of HRM that was initially the most widely favoured (variously termed 'performance management' or 'reward management'), pivoted on the use of target-setting, appraisal systems, and an array of pay-for-performance incentives, all of which provide management with the means of wider control (Gallie et al. 1998: 57–86). Increasing proportions of employees became involved in systems of these types in the recent decade, just as they had in the previous one. Indeed, our evidence shows most aspects of performance management being extended. The past decade has also witnessed two developments that should reduce the costs of monitoring employees' performance, so extending the potential for control and incentivization. One of these developments, the use of group- or team-based organization, has been briefly referred to above: here monitoring is provided through team members who are in continuous contact with one another. The other development, the use of online or networked ICT to provide monitoring information, is of recent origin and already covers one half of the workforce. It provides the opportunity for management to control many kinds of administrative, semi-routine and routine work in a particularly detailed way. These developments indicate that the internalized model of employment, with its emphasis on hierarchical control, is growing rather than retreating in the face of competitive market pressures.

Employers would not, we suppose, make the investment in complex systems of control and incentive if they did not yield desired results. It appears, indeed, that appraisal systems, performance incentives, and ICT-based monitoring all tend to increase some aspects of employees' effort at some periods. This is also true of the systemic use of HRM practices, quite apart from their role in developing employee voice. While the links between control-incentive systems and effort have not been entirely stable over time, a weakening of some elements (notably appraisal systems) has been more than balanced by the innovative developments around ICT-based monitoring.

At a purely pragmatic level, then, it is not hard to see why employers continue to develop internalized employment structures and practices.

On the employee side, acceptance of more demanding work regimes and control systems can be at least partly explained in terms of the financial rewards accruing through the personal development, performance pay, promotions, benefits, and deferred compensation that are offered through internalized employment systems. This materialist interpretation is supported and illustrated by the evidence that most British employees reject a trade-off of shorter hours for less pay while a substantial minority is willing to work longer hours for more pay. Employees' consumption aspirations constitute an essential part of the logic of internalized employment systems as they currently operate in Britain. This logic, however, is coming into increasing conflict with employees' non-materialist values, notably those relating to family relations and to gender equality.

9.3. How is Inequality Changing?

The apparently relentless rise of the market as the preferred form of economic organization over the past couple of decades has also been evident in the literature on social stratification. As we indicated in Chapter 3, Aage Sørensen, a prominent scholar of social stratification, claims that the incorporation of market principles into the employment relationship has reduced the influence of social structural positions, such as those associated with employment classes, on the distribution of job rewards. Employers, according to Sørensen, will tend to pay an employee according to the market value of his/her work, and this in turn will tend to reflect individual attributes of ability, effort, and knowledge or know-how, each of which will vary widely within occupations or job types. There will conversely be decreasing opportunities for employees to enter closed systems of progression that guarantee enhanced earnings in the long term. For Sørensen, the overall result is that social inequality is now the product of individual characteristics rather than class location (Sørensen 2000, 2001).

More specific predictions have been directed towards the position of managerial and professional employees, the salariat or service class. The argument is that because of competitive and financial pressures, the salariat is being drawn into performance-based rewards rather like many employees in sales or production. The inference drawn from this is that the special relationship of trust that managers and professionals have tended to enjoy is being eroded, so that classes are converging towards a commodified waged-labour form of employment relationship.

The prediction that class-based differentials are in decline is strongly opposed by our evidence. Indeed, class differentials in earnings increased rather than decreased over the period 1992–2000. The increase in class-based earnings inequality reflected both very large real increases in the median earnings of higher managers (with a somewhat lower, but still substantial, gain for lower managers) and a rather static or even declining situation for those in the semi-routine and routine occupations. There was also a particularly large increase in the variation of earnings within the managerial groups, especially the higher managerial: most were doing well, but some were doing exceedingly well.

The analysis of class differences also covered employees' access to a range of fringe benefits, including for example occupational pensions, occupational sickness pay, and paid holiday entitlement. In both 1992 and 2000, there was a marked 'class gradient' in the receipt of benefits, with higher managerial and higher professional groups most likely to have access and those in semi-routine and routine groups least likely. We also investigated whether that gradient had shrunk, grown, or remained constant during the 1990s. The conclusion here is that in all domains except one, class differences have either remained stable or have actually increased. The exception is days of self-certified sickness absence, and the movement towards equalization of contractual conditions here is due primarily to changes in employment law that impose standards.

Like many other findings in social research, these results may not come as a surprise once they are pointed out. Even so, they are significant because they contradict the received wisdom in the employment relations literature on the decline of 'status divide' type inequalities (e.g. Russell 1998). Specifically, we find no evidence to suggest that the growth of non-manual employment has eliminated inequalities in employment conditions, because these are also present within white-collar employment (e.g. between the higher and lower service classes). Furthermore, the idea that new management rubrics, such as HRM, have accelerated a general trend towards the harmonization of conditions is not supported by our analysis. Instead, we find that inequality in employment conditions has either remained stable or, in some cases, even increased across the 1990s.[2]

While inequality is usually examined in terms of economic returns to work, individuals often find jobs attractive or unattractive for non-pecuniary reasons. We therefore adopted and validated an Index of Job Desirability (IJD) (see Jencks et al. 1988) as part of the present research; it takes account of both material and non-material attributes of jobs insofar as they affect individual assessments of job desirability. This measure was only available for the year 2000, so change over time could not be analysed. However, a strong class gradient was found in that year both for the overall IJD and for its material and non-material components considered separately. In fact social class emerges as a much better predictor of job desirability than any of the other variables considered, accounting for about one-half of all the job-level variability in the IJD.

Again, we can conclude that inequality in employment continues to be distributed largely in accordance with class, that is, with positions in the productive structure of employment. There are however some changes taking place in the treatment of particular classes.

Most notably, our evidence is consistent with previous reports of performance incentive and control systems being increasingly applied to managers and professionals. The salariat now emerges as having both the highest involvement of any class in these systems, and also a particularly rapid rate of increase. This involvement in performance incentive and control systems is not, in general, of a token or symbolic form. It appears to be a significant development in the treatment of the salariat, as those managers and professionals taking part generally obtain substantial increases in their overall earnings while also working for longer hours than what we would otherwise expect. Furthermore, these repercussions are similar to the corresponding effects of performance incentives on employees in the combined class of semi-routine and routine occupations. Speculatively, one might link this change in the treatment of managers and professionals with greater priority being given to narrowly financial or quantitative performance criteria, both by financial markets and by governments. Performance incentives are then used by employers to signal these priorities and to focus individual attention on them.

It is not, however, correct to infer from this development either that the overall employment situation of the salariat is being marketized, or that there is a convergence in conditions between the salariat and other classes. The growth of managerial and professional participation in incentive-control systems is taking place within a general expansion of HRM practices, in which managers and professionals are themselves more involved than other classes. As noted in Section 9.2 of this chapter, there is little sense in implementing elaborate HRM policies and practices except as part of a long-term relationship. Nor is the use of incentives necessarily at odds with the growth of HRM. Incentives have been considered an essential element in some influential versions of HRM that emphasize higher performance through participation, team-building, and personal development. The growth in incentives, controls, and HRM practices should be seen as a whole, and are then better interpreted as a rebalancing of the internalized employment relationship for managers and professionals than as a move towards a marketized or commodified relationship.

Moreover, at the same time, there have been changes in the treatment of lower administrative, semi-routine and routine classes that further differentiate them from the salariat. The long-established methods of incentive and control are becoming less central to the work situation of these subordinate classes even as they are becoming more central to the work situation of managers and professionals. The application of ICT-based monitoring systems to performance checking and control has diffused quite rapidly in recent years, and the consequences of this development include a major impact on levels of effort extracted from employees in the subordinate positions. The technology, however, has had no measurable impact on the work effort of managers and professionals. Dissimilarity in the means of control therefore persists by class. Moreover, while the salariat gains financially by its participation in performance incentives, no financial gains have yet been reaped by those in the lower administrative, semi-routine and routine classes from their participation in ICT-based monitoring systems.

Overall, then, even though there are significant changes in the treatment of particular classes, these changes considered together do not point towards class convergence, and they may even contribute to the widening financial inequality between classes.

9.4. Towards an Explanation

The central empirical conclusion of this research is that the marketization thesis fails in each of its three major claims, when applied to the contemporary British experience. First, while it is correct to draw attention to growing uncertainty in employment conditions, the predicted declines in stable, open-ended, long-term employment and in internal careers have not taken place, and employers have not come to rely on the fear of job loss to motivate employees. Secondly, employers have maintained and, in most respects, extended internalized practices that both presume and support a long-term relationship with employees. These include internal progression and career ladders, performance incentive and control systems, and systemic HRM practices. Thirdly, inequality in terms of material rewards and benefits, overall job quality, and control of work, have remained strongly differentiated by class.

Why, then, do the proponents of the marketization thesis appear to have got it so wrong? Certainly, the marketization thesis suffers from some conceptual confusion as changes at the organizational level are often conflated with change at the level of the individual employee (see Chapter 2). But the fundamental problem, we believe, is that those proclaiming the arrival of a new market-mediated era have made a basic theoretical mistake by assuming that labour is, or will become, simply another market commodity. Sociologists, both Marxist and non-Marxist, would maintain that labour is a 'fictitious' commodity, one that differs from conventional commodities in its variability and plasticity (Offe 1985: 56–7; Polanyi 1944: 76). Furthermore, as Marx pointed out some time ago, the employer hires only *labour power* (or the employees' capacity to work) rather than actual *labour* (or the product of their work). A further complication is that labour cannot be physically separated from the employees who provide it. The implication of these points is that employers can never be sure about the quantity and quality of any employee's work over the long term, partly because the interests of the parties are not identical. This challenge invariably requires control over employees with regard to the tasks that they do, the way they are coordinated with other workers and, indeed, their motivation and behaviour generally. In other words, it inevitably requires some form of hierarchy or complex organization.[3]

Having recognized the need for hierarchy, we must subsequently acknowledge what Jacoby has termed 'the organizational realities of managing a workforce' (Jacoby 1999a: 136; see also Chapter 2). Such realities mean that any attempt to reallocate risk between employers and employees must take place within a well-established set of organizational constraints. Most managers, according to Jacoby, recognize that tacit skills and knowledge are important, new employees have to be trained and employees' commitment and loyalty have to be nurtured. Indeed, we would also argue that such tasks become all the more important in an age of knowledge-intensive forms of work, better-educated employees, and rapidly changing markets.

Following on from these observations, the second major failing of the marketization thesis is its inability to distinguish between different kinds of employees, the work that they do and the skills that they possess. We believe this failing stems from the overwhelming tendency of the management change literature to focus on organizations rather than groups of employees or even occupations. Consequently, much of what we have undertaken in this study can be interpreted as an attempt to bring the employment relationship back into contemporary analyses of economic restructuring. More specifically, we have sought to distinguish between the experiences of those employed in different kinds of employment relationships by drawing on a well-established social class schema.

It is for this reason that we have found Goldthorpe's adaptation of a rational choice model of employment contracts to be particularly valuable. As indicated in the second part of Chapter 1 (Sections 1.4 and 1.5), the model assumes that moral hazard and asymmetric information are inherent to the employment relationship. From the employer's perspective, the two major dimensions of contractual hazard are the difficulty of monitoring the work of employees and the degree to which the employee's skills are specific to her employer. The resulting two-dimensional typology distinguishes between *labour-* and *service-type* employment relationships, as well as those that are a mixture of both. What this tells us is that the labour contract is inclined towards a 'money for effort' bargain, as the work is easy to monitor and requires limited firm-specific knowledge, while the service contract implies a more diffuse and open-ended effort–reward bargain that provides salary increments, promotion, and security in exchange for loyal service. Within the present research, we have provided some empirical validation for this model by showing that employment practices map into classes in the predicted ways (Chapter 3).

Given that the service and labour contracts are based on such different logics of social and economic exchange, we would not expect both to be equally vulnerable to processes of market exposure. By contrast, those who proclaim the arrival of market-driven employment relationships fail to make any such distinctions, possibly because they assume that managerial employees, for instance, are as likely to be laid-off as their blue-collar counterparts (see also Jacoby 1999*b*). We would argue that those employed in service-class positions are relatively unlikely to be subjected to any significant processes of market exposure. Indeed, the evidence on job tenure and long-term employment that we presented in Chapter 2 supports this point. The reason, as Breen suggests, is contained in the fundamental asymmetry in the service relationship between the employer and employee (Breen 1997). The employer depends on these employees to exercise their discretion in the organization's interests because the employer is unable to monitor their day-to-day performance. Indeed, attempting to do so would probably require such an elaborate form of supervision that it would quickly become prohibitive in economic terms. Accordingly, we would argue that firms are unlikely to move towards the commodification of service-class jobs because they recognize the importance of trust, discretion, and judgement in such roles.

Rather it is those employed in labour contract type arrangements who may be most vulnerable to processes of commodification because their relationship most resembles that of a spot contract (see also, Breen 1997: 480). Here, we have to admit that such an interpretation would be consistent with the results of the 'frightened worker' hypothesis that we described earlier: workers in this category respond to the experience of job cuts with above-average increases in effort. However, the market-mediation argument cannot account for another important finding: the increase in the proportion of those in semi-routine and routine working-class position who claim that their jobs belong to formally recognized career ladders. This is significant because it means that the marketization thesis cannot explain all that has been happening to that section of the labour force where it may be considered most appropriate.

One of the pay-offs of Goldthorpe's model is that it explains a number of the most important findings of our research that cannot be accounted for by marketization arguments. In particular, it shows how variations in the specificity of human capital and the organization of work can lead to a substantial degree of differentiation within internalized employment relationships. For instance, it explains why those in service-class positions continue to enjoy higher levels of pay and a greater range of fringe benefits than those in intermediate or routine working-class positions. Put simply, the basic strategy of the service relationship is to provide high levels of reward to encourage appropriate levels of performance when this is not possible through direct supervision. It also offers a possible explanation for why those in service-class positions are best placed to engage in individual pay bargaining. In the latter case, for example, employees may be simply able to take advantage of high levels of organization-specific knowledge, skills, and contacts. Turning to the less privileged end of the labour market, relatively low amounts of such skill combined with routine or prescribed work roles probably explains why those in working-class occupations, specifically semi-routine and routine employees believe that they have little, or no, influence on changes affecting their jobs when compared to higher professional and managerial employees (Chapter 4). Finally, the relative ease with which those in *labour contracts* can be monitored might explain why ICT-based forms of performance monitoring have had a significant impact on the effort levels of those in working-class jobs.

We would not wish, however, to argue that internalized employment systems provide an 'optimal' solution to the needs of employers and employees, or even that they are tending towards such a solution. In the first place, there is a far from perfect correspondence between those features of employer practice that yield increased effort and those that yield an increase in financial reward for employees. Disjunctions of this type suggest that effort–reward bargains tend to remain incomplete and under pressure for renegotiation. Furthermore, internalized systems have both internal tensions and social costs, which provide scope for criticism and opposition. For instance, the growth of employee participation aims to evoke reciprocity and 'organizational citizenship', but this often takes place in organizations that make use of periodic downsizing, develop stronger hierarchical controls, or make insistent demands for increased effort. Again, while employees generally comply with a regime of long hours and intensified effort, there are extensive indications of adverse repercussions on families, for which no convincing remedy has as yet been found. Accordingly, our interpretation of internalized systems includes an emphasis on the essentially contestable nature of employment bargains.

Yet, if internalized employment systems are imperfect and under pressure, they also appear to have more flexibility and capacity for innovation than has generally been credited. There is perhaps a tendency to view internalized employment systems as part of rigid, top-heavy bureaucracies that are ignorant of the marketplace. This may be one of the reasons for believing that they will be supplanted by market-based employment systems. This perception is doubtlessly correct in the case of certain organizations, but is grossly incorrect as a generalization. There are indeed numerous innovative developments within the internalized employment systems described in previous chapters, showing that these systems are being actively adapted to changing market conditions and technological opportunities. Examples include the wider diffusion of HRM practices that were thought to be 'leading edge' as recently as the mid-1990s; the refocusing of performance incentives on managers and professionals; and the intensification of control over subordinate employees through ICT-based monitoring. There is nothing in our evidence, nor in our interpretations, to suggest that internalized employment systems are divorced from the market or unaffected by its pressures. As currently developed by British employers, internalized systems redirect external financial and market pressures into additional demands on employees. Their effectiveness is indicated in part by the commitment of employers to continue investing in them, and by the strains experienced by employees in consequence.

Finally, we would like to conclude by noting that one of the central aims of this research has been to identify where change has, and has not, affected the employment relationship. The most influential contemporary account of change is one that gives a substantial role to market forces in the organization of employment arrangements. However, our analysis of the marketization argument shows that it has led researchers to look for change in the wrong places. Instead, we would argue that the most profound changes over the past decade or so relate to the extension of hierarchies rather than the incorporation of markets within organizations. Here we would highlight the growing use of individualized performance incentives, the dramatic rise of ICT-based performance monitoring systems, and the continued growth of various forms of work organization that promote greater employee involvement. Each of these deserves much greater research though we suspect that, like many other aspects of the employment relationship, they will remain fundamentally differentiated by social class.

Notes

1. We are aware that markets are widely acknowledged to be a driving factor in the literature on the transformation of industrial relations systems (see, for instance, Kuruvilla and Erickson 2002: 172). However, we have not engaged directly with that literature because it is concerned only with trade unions and collective bargaining.
2. We acknowledge that some of the more visible manifestations of the status divide, notably segregated changing, dining, and toilet facilities, may have disappeared. We suspect that this may contribute to the widespread perception that few significant differences remain in the distribution of fringe benefits and other employment conditions.
3. Accordingly, we would agree with Goldthorpe that the kind of spot market contracts that we have associated with marketized employment relationships need not be, and are often not, the most efficient form of employment contract (Goldthorpe 2000*b*: 1579).

References

Abraham, K. G. (1990). 'Restructuring the Employment Relationship: The Growth of Market-Mediated Work Arrangements', in K. G. Abraham and R. B. McKersie (eds.), *New Developments in the Labour Market: Toward a New Institutional Paradigm*. Cambridge, MA.: MIT Press.

Ackroyd, S. and Procter, S. (1998). 'British Manufacturing Organization and Workplace Industrial Relations: Some Attributes of the New Flexible Firm', *British Journal of Industrial Relations*, 36: 164–83.

Adam, E. K. (2005). 'Momentary Emotion and Cortisol Levels in the Everyday Lives of Working Parents', in B. Schneider and L. J. Waite (eds.), *Being Together, Working Apart: Dual-Career Families and the Work-Life Balance*. Cambridge: Cambridge University Press.

Akaike, H. (1973). 'Information Theory as an Extension of the Maximum Likelihood Principle', in B. N. Petrov and F. Csaksi (eds.), *2nd International Symposium on Information Theory*. Budapest: Akademiai Kiado.

Althauser, R. P. and Kalleberg, A. L. (1981). 'Firms, Occupations and the Structure of Labour Markets: A Conceptual Analysis', in I. Berg (ed.), *Sociological Perspectives on Labour Markets*. New York: Academic Press.

Anderson, E. (1993). *Value in Ethics and Economics*. London: Harvard University Press.

Anderson, J. A. (1984). 'Regression and Ordered Categorical Variables', *Journal of the Royal Statistical Society B*, 46: 1–30.

Appay, B. (1998). 'Economic Concentration and the Externalization of Labour', *Economic and Industrial Democracy*, 19: 161–84.

Appelbaum, E., Bailey, T., Berg, P., and Kalleberg, A. L. (2000). *Manufacturing Advantage: Why High-Performance Work Systems Pay Off*. Ithaca, NY: Cornell University Press.

Armstrong, P., Glyn, A., and Harrison, J. (1984). *Capitalism Since World War II*. London: Fontana.

Arthur, M. B. and Rousseau, D. M. (1996). *Boundaryless Career: A New Employment Principle for a New Organizational Era*. New York: Oxford University Press.

Arthurs, A. (1985). 'Towards Single Status?', *Journal of General Management*, 11: 1–12.

Atkinson, J. (1985). *Flexibility, Uncertainty and Manpower Management*. Brighton: IMS, University of Sussex.

Auer, P. and Cazes, S. (2000). 'The Resilience of the Long-Term Employment Relationship', *International Labour Review*, 139: 379–408.

Babcock, L. and Laschever, S. (2003). *Women Don't Ask: Negotiation and the Gender Divide*. Princeton, NJ: Princeton University Press.

Bacon, N. and Storey, J. (1995). 'Individualism and Collectivism and the Changing Role of Trade Unionism', in P. Ackers, C. Smith, and P. Smith (eds.), *The New Workplace and Trade Unionism*. London: Routledge.

Bain, G. S. (1970). *The Growth of White-Collar Unionism*. Oxford: Clarendon Press.

—— and Elias, P. (1985). 'Trade Union Membership in Great Britain: An Individual Level Analysis', *British Journal of Industrial Relations*, 23: 71–92.

—— and Elsheikh, F. (1979). 'An Inter-Industry Analysis of Unionization in Britain', *British Journal of Industrial Relations*, 17: 137–57.

—— and Price, R. (1983). 'Union Growth in Britain: Retrospect and Prospect', *British Journal of Industrial Relations*, 21: 46–68.

Bain, P. and Taylor, P. (2000). 'Entrapped by the "Electronic Panopticon"? Worker Resistance in the Call Centre', *New Technology, Work and Employment*, 15: 2–18.

—— Watson, A., Mulvey, G., Taylor, P., and Gall, G. (2002). 'Taylorism, Targets and the Pursuit of Quantity and Quality by Call Centre Management', *New Technology, Work and Employment*, 17: 170–85.

Baldamus, W. (1961). *Efficiency & Effort: An Analysis of Industrial Administration*. London: Tavistock Publications.

Barker, J. R. (1993). 'Tightening the Iron Cage: Concertive Control in Self-Managing Teams', *Administrative Science Quarterly*, 38: 408–37.

Barnett, R. C. (1999). 'A New Work-Life Model for the Twenty-First Century,' *Annals of the American Academy of Political and Social Science*, 562: 143–58.

Baron, J. N. (2000). 'Comment on Cappelli's "Market-Mediated Employment: The Historical Context"', in M. M. Blair and T. A. Kochan (eds.), *The New Relationship: Human Capital in the American Corporation.*, Washington DC: Brookings Institution Press.

—— and Kreps, D. M. (1999). *Strategic Human Resources: Frameworks for General Managers*. New York: John Wiley.

Batt, R. and Valcour, P. M. (2003). 'Human Resource Practices as Predictors of Work-Family Outcomes and Employee Turnover', *Industrial Relations*, 42: 189–220.

Beck, U. (1992). *Risk Society: Towards a New Modernity*. London: Sage.

—— (2000). *The Brave New World of Work*. Cambridge: Polity Press.

Beer, M., Spector, B., Lawrence, P. R., Mills, Q. D., and Walton, R. E. (1984). *Managing Human Assets*. New York: Free Press.

—— Spector, B., Lawrence, P. R., Mills, Q. D., and Walton, R. E. (1985). *Human Resource Management: A General Manager's Perspective*. New York: Free Press.

Behrend, H. (1957). 'The Effort Bargain', *Industrial and Labour Relations Review*, 10: 503–15.

References

Bell, D. (1960). 'The Racket-Ridden Longshoremen: The Web of Economics and Politics', in D. Bell (ed.), *The End of Ideology*. New York: Free Press.

Bell, D. (1974). *The Coming of Post-Industrial Society*. London: Heinemann Educational Books.

Belt, V. (2002). 'A Female Ghetto? Women's Careers in Call Centres', *Human Resource Management Journal*, 12: 51–67.

Bender, K. A. and Sloane, P. J. (1998). 'Job Satisfaction, Trade Unions, and Exit-Voice Revisited', *Industrial and Labour Relations Review*, 51: 222–40.

Berk, S. F. (1985). *The Gender Factory: The Apportionment of Work in American Households*. New York: Plenum.

Best, F. (1980*a*). *Exchanging Earnings for Leisure: Findings of an Exploratory National Survey on Work Time Preferences*. Research and Development Monograph No. 79, Washington DC: Department of Labour.

—— (1980*b*). *Flexible Life Scheduling*. New York: Frederick A. Praeger.

Bevan, A. (1952). *In Place of Fear*. London: Heinemann.

Beveridge, W. (1942). *Social Insurance and Allied Services (Beveridge Report)*. London: HMSO.

—— (1944). *Full Employment in a Free Society*. London: George Allen & Unwin.

Beynon, H., Grimshaw, D., Rubery, J., and Ward, K. (2002). *Managing Employment Change: The New Realities at Work*. Oxford: Oxford University Press.

Bielby, W. T. and Bielby, D. D. (1989). 'Family Ties: Balancing Commitments to Work and Family in Dual Earner Households', *American Sociological Review*, 54: 776–89.

Blackburn, R. and Mann, M. (1979). *The Working Class in the Labour Market*. London: Macmillan.

Blanchflower, D. and Oswald, A. (1990). 'Self Employment and Mrs Thatcher's Enterprise Culture', in R. Jowell, S. Witherspoon, and L. Brook (eds.), *British Social Attitudes: The 1990 Report*. Aldershot: Gower Press.

Bluestone, B. and Rose, S. (1997). 'Overworked and Underemployed: Unravelling an Economic Enigma', *The American Prospect*, 31: 58–69.

Bolger, A. (1998). 'Insecurity at Work on the Increase Says CBI', p. 9 in *Financial Times*. London.

Booth, A. L., Francesconi, M., and Frank, J. (2002). *Labour as a Buffer: Do Temporary Workers Suffer?* IZA Discussion Paper 205, Bonn: Institute for the Study of Labour (IZA).

—— and Frank, J. (1999). 'Earnings, Productivity, and Performance-Related Pay', *Journal of Labour Economics*, 17: 447–63.

Bowles, H. R., Babcock, L., and McGinn, K. L. (2005). 'Constraints and Triggers: Situational Mechanics of Gender in Negotiation', *Journal of Personality and Social Psychology*, 89: 951–65.

Bowles, S. and Gintis, H. (1993). 'The Revenge of Homo Economicus: Contested Exchange and the Revival of Political Economy', *Journal of Economic Perspectives*, 7: 83–102.

302

Brannen, J. and Moss, P. (1991). *Managing Mothers: Dual Earner Households After Maternity Leave*. London: Unwin Hyman.

Breen, R. (1997). 'Risk, Recommodification and Stratification', *Sociology*, 31: 473–89.

Bresnahan, T. F. (1999). 'Computerisation and Wage Dispersion: An Analytical Reinterpretation', *Economic Journal*, 109: F390–F415.

Brines, J. (1994). 'Economic Dependency, Gender, and the Division of Labour at Home', *American Journal of Sociology*, 100: 652–88.

Brook, K. (2002). 'Trade Union Membership: An Analysis of Data from Autumn 2001', *Labour Market Trends*, 110: 343–54.

Brown, P. (1995). 'Cultural Capital and Social Exclusion: Some Observations on Recent Trends in Education, Employment and the Labour Market', *Work, Employment and Society*, 9: 29–51.

—— and Scase, R. (1994). *Higher Education and Corporate Realities: Class, Culture and the Decline of Graduate Careers*. London: UCL Press.

Brown, W. (1986). 'The Changing Role of Trade Unions in the Management of Labour', *British Journal of Industrial Relations*, 24: 161–8.

—— (1993). 'The Contraction of Collective Bargaining in Britain', *British Journal of Industrial Relations*, 31: 189–201.

—— Deakin, S., Hudson, M., Pratten, C., and Ryan, P. (1998). *The Individualization of Employment Contracts in Britain*. London: Department of Trade and Industry.

Buckingham, L. (1998). 'The Only Certainty is Uncertainty', p. 17 in *The Guardian*. Manchester.

Buckle, M. and Thompson, J. (2004). *The UK Financial System*. 4th edn. Manchester: Manchester University Press.

Bugler, J. (1965). 'Shopfloor Struggle for Status', *New Society*, 25 November.

Burchell, B. (2002). 'The Prevalence and Redistribution of Job Insecurity and Work Intensification', in B. Burchell, D. Ladipo, and F. Wilkinson (eds.), *Job Insecurity and Work Intensification*. London: Routledge.

—— Day, D., Hudson, M., Ladipo, D., Mankelow, R., Reed, H., Wichert, I., and Wilkinson, F. (1999). *Job Insecurity and Work Intensification: Flexibility and the Changing Boundaries of Work*. York: Joseph Rowntree Foundation.

—— Ladipo, D., and Wilkinson, F. (eds.) (2002). *Job Insecurity and Work Intensification*. London: Routledge.

Butler, T. and Savage, M. (eds.) (1995). *Social Change and the Middle Classes*. London: UCL Press.

Callender, C., Millward, N., Lissenburgh, S., and Forth, J. (1997). *Maternity Rights and Benefits in Britain 1996*. DSS Research Report No. 67, London: Stationery Office.

Cappelli, P. (1995). 'Rethinking Employment', *British Journal of Industrial Relations*, 33: 563–602.

—— (1999*a*). *The New Deal at Work: Managing the Market-Driven Workforce*. Boston, MA: Harvard University Press.

References

Cappelli, P. (1999*b*). 'Career Jobs are Dead', *California Management Review*, 42: 146–66.

—— (2001). 'Assessing the Decline of Internal Labour Markets', in I. Berg and A. L. Kalleberg (eds.), *Sourcebook of Labour Markets: Evolving Structures and Processes*. New York: Kluwer Academic/Plenum Publishers.

—— Bossi, L., Katz, H., Knoke, D., Osterman, P., and Useem, M. (1997). *Change at Work*. New York: Oxford University Press.

Casey, B., Metcalf, H., and Millward, N. (1997). *Employers' Use of Flexible Labour*. London: Policy Studies Institute.

Cassy, J. and O'Hara, M. (2000). *The End of C&A: Fashion Wars Kill High Street Chain*. p. 3 in *The Guardian*. Manchester.

Castells, M. (1996). *The Rise of the Network Society*. Cambridge, MA: Blackwell.

—— (2000). *The Rise of the Network Society*, 2nd edn. Cambridge, MA: Blackwell.

Chan, T. W. and Goldthorpe, J. H. (2004). 'Is There a Status Order in Contemporary British Society? Evidence from the Occupational Structure of Friendship', *European Sociological Review*, 20: 383–401.

Clark, A. E. and Oswald, A. J. (1996). 'Satisfaction and Comparison Income', *Journal of Public Economics*, 61: 359–81.

Clark, R. (1979). *The Japanese Company*. New Haven, CT: Yale University Press.

Clark, T. N. and Lipset, S. M. (1991). 'Are Social Classes Dying?', *International Sociology*, 6: 397–410.

Clarkberg, M. and Moen, P. (2001). 'Understanding the Time-Squeeze: Married Couples' Preferred and Actual Work-Hour Strategies', *American Behavioural Scientist*, 44: 1115–35.

Claydon, T. (2004). 'Human Resource Management and the Labour Market', in I. Beardwell, L. Holden, and T. Claydon (eds.), *Human Resource Management: A Contemporary Approach*. London: FT Prentice Hall.

Coleman, M. and Pencavel, J. (1993). 'Changes in Work Hours of Male Employees, 1940–1988', *Industrial and Labour Relations Review*, 46: 262–83.

Craig, C. (1969). *Men in Manufacturing Industry*. Cambridge: Department of Applied Economics, University of Cambridge.

Crompton, R. (1999). 'Restructuring Gender Relations and Employment: The Decline of the Male Breadwinner', in R. Crompton (ed.), *Restructuring Gender Relations and Employment*. Oxford: Oxford University Press.

—— Brockmann, M., and Wiggins, R. D. (2003). 'A Woman's Place . . . Employment and Family Life for Men and Women', in A. Park, J. Curtice, K. Thomson, L. Jarvis, and C. Bromley (eds.), *British Social Attitudes: The 20th Report*, London: Sage.

—— Brockmann, M., and Lyonette, C. (2005). 'Attitudes, Women's Employment and the Domestic Division of Labour: A Cross-National Analysis in Two Waves', *Work, Employment and Society*, 19: 213–34.

Crouch, C. (1977). *Class Conflict and the Industrial Relations Crisis*. London: Heinemann.

—— (1999). *Social Change in Western Europe*. Oxford: Oxford University Press.

Cully, M., Woodland, S., O'Reilly, A., and Dix, G. (1999). *Britain at Work: As Depicted by the 1998 Workplace Employee Relations Survey*. London: Routledge.

Danford, A. (1998). 'Teamworking and Labour Regulation in the Autocomponents Industry', *Work, Employment and Society*, 12: 409–31.

Daniel, W. W. (1980). *Maternity Rights: The Experience of Women*. PSI Report No. 588, London: Policy Studies Institute.

—— (1987). *Workplace Industrial Relations and Technical Change*. London: Frances Pinter.

de Tocqueville, A. (1835, 1840/1966). *Democracy in America*. (G. Lawrence, tran.) J. P. Mayer and M. Learner (eds.). New York: Harper and Row.

Deakin, S. and Wilkinson, F. (2005). *The Law of the Labour Market: Industrialization, Employment, and Legal Evolution*. Oxford: Oxford University Press.

Deery, S., Iverson, R., and Walsh, J. (2002). 'Work Relationships in Telephone Centres: Understanding Emotional Exhaustion and Employee Withdrawal', *Journal of Management Studies*, 39: 471–96.

—— and Walsh, J. (1999). 'The Decline of Collectivism? A comparative Study of White-Collar Employees in Britain and Australia', *British Journal of Industrial Relations*, 37: 245–69.

Delaney, J. T. (1996). 'Unions, Human Resource Innovations, and Organizational Outcomes', *Advances in Industrial and Labour Relations*, 7: 207–45.

Delery, J. E. and Doty, D. H. (1996). 'Modes of Theorizing in Strategic Human Resource Management: Tests of Universalistic, Contingency, and Configurational Performance Predictions', *Academy of Management Journal*, 39: 802–35.

Dempster, A. P., Laird, N. M., and Rubin, D. (1977). 'Maximum Likelihood from Incomplete Data via the Em Algorithm (with Discussion)', *Journal of the Royal Statistical Society B*, 39: 1–38.

Department of Trade and Industry (2002). *High Performance Workplaces: The Role of Employee Involvement in a Modern Economy*, Discussion paper, July 2002, DTI website document

Dex, S. and McCulloch, A. (1995). *Flexible Employment in Britain: A Statistical Analysis*. Manchester: Equal Opportunities Commission.

—— and McCulloch, A. (1997). *Flexible Employment: The Future of Britain's Jobs*. Basingstoke: Macmillan.

DiNardo, J. and Lemieux, T. (1997). 'Diverging Male Wage Inequality in the United States and Canada, 1981–1988: Do Institutions Explain the Difference?', *Industrial and Labour Relations Review*, 50: 629–51.

—— and Pischke, J.-S. (1997). 'The Return to Computer Use Revisited: Have Pencils Changed the Wage Structure Too?', *Quarterly Journal of Economics*, 112: 291–303.

—— Fortin, N. M., and Lemieux, T. (1996). 'Labour Market Institutions and the Distribution of Wages, 1973–1992: A Semiparametric Approach', *Econometrica*, 65: 1001–46.

Dipboye, R. L. (1985). 'Some Neglected Variables in Research on Discrimination in Appraisal', *Academy of Management Review*, 10: 116–27.

DiPrete, T. A. (1990). 'Adding Covariates to Loglinear Models for the Analysis of Social Mobility Tables', *American Journal of Sociology*, 84: 804–19.

Disney, R. (1999). 'Why Have Older Men Stopped Working?', in P. Gregg and J. Wadsworth (eds.), *The State of Working Britain*. Manchester: Manchester University Press.

—— Gosling, A., and Machin, S. (1994). 'British Unions in Decline: An Examination of the 1980s Fall in Trade Union Recognition', *Industrial and Labour Relations Review*, 48: 403–19.

Doeringer, P. B. and Piore, M. J. (1971). *Internal Labour Markets and Manpower Analysis*. Lexington, MA: Heath.

Donovan, L. (1968). *Report of the Royal Commission on Trade Unions and Employers' Associations*. London: HMSO.

Doogan, K. (2001). 'Insecurity and Long-Term Employment', *Work, Employment and Society*, 15: 419–41.

Dore, R. (1973). *British Factory—Japanese Factory: The Origins of National Diversity in Industrial Relations*. London: Allen and Unwin.

—— (1989). 'Where We Are Now: Musings of an Evolutionist', *Work, Employment and Society*, 3: 425–46.

Drazin, R. and Auster, E. R. (1987). 'Wage Differences Between Men and Women: Performance Appraisal Ratings vs Salary Allocation as the Locus Of Bias', *Human Resource Management*, 26: 157–68.

Ebbinghaus, B. and Visser, J. (1999). 'When Institutions Matter: Union Growth and Decline in Western Europe, 1950–1995', *European Sociological Review*, 15: 135–58.

Edwards, P. (1995). 'Assessment: Markets and Managerialism', in P. Edwards (ed.), *Industrial Relations: Theory and Practice in Britain*. Oxford: Blackwell.

—— and Wajcman, J. (2005). *The Politics of Working Life*. Oxford: Oxford University Press.

—— and Wright, M. (2001). 'High-Involvement Work Systems and Performance Outcomes: The Strength of Variable, Contingent and Context-Bound Relationships', *International Journal of Human Resource Management*, 12: 568–85.

Edwards, R. C. (1979). *Contested Terrain: The Transformation of the Workforce in the Twentieth Century*. New York: Basic Books.

Elliott, L. and Atkinson, D. (1998). *The Age of Insecurity*. London: Verso.

Erikson, R. and Goldthorpe. J. H. (1993). *The Constant Flux: A Study of Class Mobility in Industrial Societies*. Oxford: Clarendon Press.

Etzioni, A. (1975). *A Comparative Analysis of Complex Organizations*, revised and enlarged edition. New York: Free Press.

Evans, G. (1992). 'Testing the Validity of the Goldthorpe Class Schema', *European Sociological Review*, 8: 211–32.

—— and Mills, C. (1998). 'A Latent Class Analysis of the Criterion-Related and Construct Validity of the Goldthorpe Class Schema', *European Sociological Review*, 14: 87–106.

—— —— (2000). 'In Search of the Wage-Labour/Service Contract: New Evidence on the Validity of the Goldthorpe Class Schema', *British Journal of Sociology*, 51: 641–61.

Faggio, G. and Nickell, S. (2003). 'The Rise in Inactivity Among Adult Men', in R. Dickens, P. Gregg, and J. Wadsworth (eds.), *The Labour Market Under New Labour*. Basingstoke: Macmillan.

Felstead, A., Burchell, B., and Green, F. (1998). 'Insecurity at Work: Is Job Security Really Much Worse Than Before?', *New Economy*, 5: 180–4.

Fernie, S. and Metcalf, D. (2005). *Trade Unions: Resurgence or Demise?* New York: Routledge.

Flanders, A. and Clegg, H. A. (1954). *The System of Industrial Relations in Great Britain: Its History, Law and Institutions*. Oxford: Blackwell.

Forth, J. and Millward, N. (2004). 'High-Involvement Management and Pay in Britain', *Industrial Relations*, 43: 98–119.

Fourastié, J. (1979). *Les Trentes Glorieuses, ou la révolution invisible de 1946 à 1975*. Paris: Fayard.

Fox, A. (1974). *Beyond Contract: Work, Power and Trust Relations*. London: Faber and Faber.

—— (1985). *History and Heritage: The Social Origins of the British Industrial Relations System*. London: Allen and Unwin.

Fox, J. (2002). *An R and S-Plus Companion to Applied Regression*. London: Sage.

Friedmann, G. (1954). *Industrial Society: The Emergence of the Human Problems of Automation*. Glencoe, IL: Free Press.

Gallie, D. (1996). 'Trade Union Allegiance and Decline in British Urban Labour Markets', in D. Gallie, R. Penn, and M. Rose (eds.), *Trade Unionism in Recession*. Oxford: Oxford University Press.

—— Penn, R., and Rose, M. (1996*a*). *Trade Unionism in Recession*. Oxford: Oxford University Press.

—— Rose, M., and Penn, R. (1996*b*). 'The British Debate on Trade Unionism: Crisis and Continuity', in D. Gallie, R. Penn, and M. Rose (eds.), *Trade Unionism in Recession*. Oxford: Oxford University Press.

—— White, M., Tomlinson, M., and Cheng, Y. (1998). *Restructuring the Employment Relationship*. Oxford: Oxford University Press.

Geary, J. (2003). 'New Forms of Work Organization: Still Limited, Still Controlled but Still Welcome?', in P. Edwards (ed.), *Industrial Relations: Theory and Practice*, 2nd edn. Oxford: Basil Blackwell.

Gershuny, J. (2000). *Changing Times: Work and Leisure in Postindustrial Society*. Oxford: Oxford University Press.

—— Godwin, M., and Jones, S. (1994). 'The Domestic Labour Revolution: A Process of Lagged Adaptation?', in M. Anderson, F. Bechhofer, and J. Gershuny (eds.),

The Social and Political Economy of the Household. Oxford: Oxford University Press.

Godard, J. (2001). 'High-Performance and the Transformation of Work? The Implications of Alternative Work Practices for the Experience and Outcomes of Work', *Industrial and Labour Relations Review*, 54: 776–805.

Goldthorpe, J. H. (1982). 'On the Service Class, Its Formation and Future', in A. Giddens and G. Mckenzie (eds.), *Social Class and the Division of Labour*, Cambridge: Cambridge University Press: 162–85.

—— (with C. Llewellyn and C. Payne) (1987). *Social Mobility and Class Structure in Modern Britain* (2nd edn.). Oxford: Clarendon Press.

—— (1995). 'The Service Class Revisited', in T. Butler and M. Savage (eds.), *Social Change and the Middle Classes*. London: UCL Press:

—— (1998). 'Rational Action Theory for Sociology', *British Journal of Sociology*, 49: 167–92.

—— (2000*a*). *On Sociology: Numbers, Narratives, and the Integration of Research and Theory*. Oxford: Oxford University Press.

—— (2000*b*). 'Rent, Class Conflict, and Class Structure: A Commentary on Sørensen', *American Journal of Sociology*, 105: 1572–82.

—— and Hope, K. (1974). *The Social Grading of Occupations*. Oxford: Clarendon.

—— and McKnight, A. (2004). *The Economic Basis of Social Class*. CASE paper 80, London: Centre for Analysis of Social Exclusion, London School of Economics.

—— Lockwood, D., Bechhofer, F., and Platt, J. (1968). *The Affluent Worker: Industrial Attitudes and Behaviour*. Cambridge: Cambridge University Press.

Goos, M. and Manning, A. (2003). 'McJobs and MacJobs: The Growing Polarization of Work in Britain', in R. Dickens, P. Gregg, and J. Wadsworth (eds.), *The State of Working Britain*. Basingstoke: Palgrave Macmillan.

Gordon, M. E. and Denisi, A. S. (1995). 'A Re-Examination of the Relationship Between Union Membership and Job Satisfaction', *Industrial and Labour Relations Review*, 48: 222–36.

Gorz, A. (1999). *Reclaiming Work: Beyond the Wage-Based Society*. Cambridge: Polity Press.

Gosling, A. and Lemieux, T. (2001). *Labour Market Reforms and Changes in Wage Inequality in the United Kingdom and the United States*, NBER Working Paper 8413.

Gospel, H. F. (1992). *Markets, Firms, and the Management of Labour in Modern Britain*. Cambridge: Cambridge University Press.

—— and Willman, P. (2005). 'Changing Patterns of Employee Voice', in J. Storey (ed.), *Adding Value through Information and Consultation*. Basingstoke: Palgrave Macmillan.

—— and Wood, S. (2003). *Representing Workers: Trade Union Recognition and Membership in Britain*. London: Routledge.

Grainger, H. (2006). *Trade Union Membership 2005*. London: Department of Trade and Industry.

Gray, J. (1998). *False Dawn: The Illusions of Global Capitalism*. London: Granta.

Green, F. (2001). 'It's been a Hard Day's Night: The Concentration and Intensification of Work in Late 20th Century Britain', *British Journal of Industrial Relations*, 39: 53–80.

—— (2006). *Demanding Work: The Paradox of Job Quality in the Affluent Economy*. Woodstock: Princeton University Press.

Gregg, P. and Wadsworth, J. (1996). 'A Short History of Labour Turnover, Job Tenure and Job Security, 1975–93', *Oxford Review of Economic Policy*, 11: 73–90.

—— and Wadsworth, J. (1999). 'Job Tenure, 1975–98', in P. Gregg and J. Wadsworth (eds.), *The State of Working Britain*. Manchester: Manchester University Press.

—— Knight, G., and Wadsworth, J. (2000). 'Heaven Knows I'm Miserable Now: Job Insecurity in the British Labour Market', in E. Heery and J. Salmon (eds.), *The Insecure Workforce*. London: Routledge.

Grimshaw, D. and Rubery, J. (1998). 'Integrating the Internal and External Labour Markets', *Cambridge Journal of Economics*, 22: 199–220.

—— Ward, K. G., Rubery, J., and Beynon, H. (2001). 'Organizations and the Transformation of the Internal Labour Market', *Work, Employment and Society*, 15: 25–54.

Grusky, D. B. and Sørensen, J. B. (1998). 'Can Class Analysis be Salvaged?', *American Journal of Sociology*, 103: 1187–234.

Guest, D. (1989). 'Human Resource Management: Its Implications for Industrial Relations and Trade Unions', in J. Storey (ed.), *New Perspectives on Human Resource Management*. London: Routledge.

Guveli, A. (2006). *New Social Classes Within the Service Class in the Netherlands and Britain. Adjusting the AGP Class Schema for the Technocrats and the Social and Cultural Specialists*. Nijmegen: ICS-Dissertation.

—— and De Graaf, N. D. (2007). 'Career Class (Im)mobility of Social-Cultural Specialists and Technocrats in the Netherlands', *European Sociological Review*, 23: 185–201.

—— Need, A., and De Graaf, N. D. (2007). 'The Rise of 'New' Social Classes Within the Service Class in the Netherlands. Political Orientation of Social and Cultural Specialists and Technocrats Between 1970 and 2003', *Acta Sociologica*, 50: 129–146.

Hakim, C. (1990). 'Core and Periphery in Employers' Workforce Strategies: Evidence from the 1987 E.L.U.S. Survey', *Work, Employment and Society*, 4: 157–88.

—— (2004). *Key Issues in Women's Work: Female Diversity and the Polarisation of Women's Employment*. London: Glasshouse.

Hales, C. (2000). 'Management and Empowerment Programmes', *Work, Employment and Society*, 14: 501–19.

Hall, P. A. and Soskice, D. (2001). *Varieties of Capitalism: The Institutional Foundations of Comparative Advantage*. Oxford: Oxford University Press.

Handy, C. (1996). *Beyond Certainty: The Changing World of Organizations*. London: Arrow Books.

Harley, B. (2001). 'Team Membership and the Experience of Work in Britain: An Analysis of the WERS98 Data', *Work, Employment and Society*, 15: 721–42.

Harrison, B. (1997). *Lean and Mean: Why Large Corporations Will Continue to Dominate the Global Economy*. New York: The Guildford Press.

—— and Bluestone, B. (1988). *The Great U-turn: Corporate Restructuring and the Polarizing of America*. New York: Basic Books.

Hassell, K., Fisher, R., Nichols, L., and Shann, P. (2002). 'Contemporary Workforce Patterns and Historical Trends: The Pharmacy Labour Market Over the Past 40 Years', *The Pharmaceutical Journal*, 269(August): 291–6.

Heckscher, C. (1995). *White-Collar Blues: Management Loyalties in an Age of Corporate Restructuring*. New York: Basic Books.

Hedges, B. (1994). 'Work in a Changing Climate', in R. Jowell, J. Curtice, L. Brook, D. Ahrendt, and A. Park (eds.), *British Social Attitudes: The 11th Report*. Aldershot: Dartmouth.

Heery, E. and Salmon, J. (2000*a*). 'The Insecurity Thesis', in E. Heery and J. Salmon (eds.), *The Insecure Workforce*. London: Routledge.

—— —— (eds.) (2000*b*). *The Insecure Workforce*. London: Routledge.

Hendrickx, J. (1999). 'Using Categorical Variables in Stata', *Stata Technical Bulletin STB-52*.

Herzberg, F. (1966). *Work and the Nature of Man*. New York: World.

Hill, S. (1991). 'Why Quality Circles Failed but Total Quality Management Might Succeed', *British Journal of Industrial Relations*, 29: 543–68.

—— and Wilkinson, A. (1995). 'In Search of TQM', *Employee Relations*, 17: 8–25.

—— Martin, R., and Harris, M. (2000). 'Decentralization, Integration, and the Post-Bureaucratic Organization: The Case of R&D', *Journal of Management Studies*, 37: 563–85.

Hirschhorn, L. (1984). *Beyond Mechanization: Work and Technology in a Post-Industrial Age*. Cambridge, MA: MIT Press.

—— (1985). 'Information Technology and the New Services Game', in M. Castells (ed.), *High Technology, Space and Society*. Beverly Hills, CA: Sage.

Hochschild, A. R. (1983). *The Managed Heart: Commercialization of Human Feeling*. Berkeley, CA: University of California Press.

Hodgson, G. M. (1999). *Economics and Utopia: Why the Learning Economy is not the End of History*. London: Routledge.

Honaker, A., Joseph, A., King, G., and Scheve, K. (2000). *Amelia: A Programme for Missing Data*. Harvard University (http://GKing.Harvard.edu).

Horrell, S., Rubery, J., and Burchell, B. (1994). 'Working Time Patterns, Constraints and Preferences', in M. Anderson, F. Bechhofer, and J. Gershuny (eds.), *The Social and Political Economy of the Household*. Oxford: Oxford University Press.

Howell, C. (2005). *Trade Unions and the State: The Construction of Industrial Relations Institutions in Britain, 1890–2000*. Princeton, NJ: Princeton University Press.

Hudson, M. (2002). 'Disappearing Pathways and the Struggle for a Fair Day's Pay', in B. Burchell, D. Ladipo, and F. Wilkinson (eds.), *Job Insecurity and Work Intensification*. London: Routledge.

—— Lissenburgh, S., and Sahin-Dikmen, M. (2004). *Maternity and Paternity Rights in Britain 2002: Survey of Parents*. Department of Work and Pensions Report No. 131, London: HMSO.

Huselid, M. A. and Becker, B. E. (1996). 'Methodological Issues in Cross-Sectional and Panel Estimates of the Human Resource-Firm Performance Link', *Industrial Relations*, 35: 400–22.

—— Jackson, S. E., and Schuler, R. S. (1997). 'Technical and Strategic Human Resource Management Effectiveness as Determinants of Firm Performance', *Academy of Management Journal*, 40: 171–88.

Hutton, W. (1995). *The State We're In*. London: Jonathan Cape.

Ichniowski, C., Shaw, K., and Prennushi, G. (1997). 'The Effects of Human Resource Management Practices on Productivity: A Study of Steel Finishing Lines', *American Economic Review*, 83: 291–313.

Incomes Data Services (1992). *Performance Management*, IDS Study 518, November.

—— (1997). *Performance Management*, IDS Study 626, May.

Industrial Relations Review and Report (1989). 'Harmonization: A Single Status Surge', *IRS Employment Trends*, 445: 5–10.

—— (1993). 'Sweet Harmony? A Single Status Survey', *IRS Employment Trends*, 548: 7–12.

Jacoby, S. M. (1999*a*). 'Are Career Jobs Headed for Extinction?', *California Management Review*, 42: 123–45.

—— (1999*b*). 'Reply: Premature Reports of Demise', *California Management Review*, 42: 168–79.

Jencks, C., Perman, L. and Rainwater, L. (1988). 'What is a Good Job? A New Measure of Labour-Market Success', *American Journal of Sociology*, 93: 1322–57.

Kahneman, D. and Tversky, A. (1979). 'Prospect Theory: An Analysis of Decision Under Risk', *Econometrica*, 47: 263–92.

Kalleberg, A. (2003). 'Flexible Firms and Labour Market Segmentation: Effect of Workplace Restructuring on Jobs and Workers', *Work and Occupations*, 30: 154–75.

—— Reskin, B. K., and Hudson, K. (2000). 'Bad Jobs in America: Standard and Nonstandard Employment Relations and Job Quality in the United States'. *American Sociological Review*, 65: 256–78.

Kanter, R. M. (1989). *When Giants Learn to Dance: Mastering the Challenge of Strategy, Management, and Careers in the 1990s*. New York: Routledge.

—— (1991). 'Future of Bureaucracy and Hierarchy in Organizational Theory: A Report from the Field', in P. Bourdieu and J. S. Coleman (eds.), *Social Theory for a Changing Society*. Boulder, CO: Westview Press.

Katz, L. and Autor, D. H. (1999). 'Changes in the Wage Structure and Earnings Inequality', in O. C. Ashenfelter and D. Card (eds.), *Handbook of Labour Economics*, vol. 3A. Amsterdam: Elsevier.

Kaur, H. (2004). *Employment Attitudes: Main Findings from the British Social Attitudes Survey 2003*. Employment Relations Research Series. London: Department of Trade and Industry.

Kersley, B., Alpin, C., Forth, J., Bryson, A., Bewley, H., Dix, G., and Oxenbridge, S. (2005). *Inside the Workplace: First Findings from the 2004 Workplace Employment Relations Survey (WERS 2004)*. London: Department of Trade and Industry.

—— —— —— —— —— —— —— (2006). *Inside the Workplace: Findings from the 2004 Workplace Employment Relations Survey*. London: Routledge.

Kerr, C. (1950). 'Labour Markets: Their Character and Consequences', *American Economic Review*, 40: 278–91.

—— (1954). 'The Balkanization of Labour Markets', in E. Wight Bakke (ed.), *Labour Mobility and Economic Opportunity*. New York: Wiley.

Kessler, I. and Purcell, J. (1995). 'Individualism and Collectivism in Theory and Practice: Management Style and the Design of Pay Systems', in P. Edwards (ed.), *Industrial Relations: Theory and Practice in Britain*. Oxford: Blackwell.

King, G., Honaker, J., Joseph, A., and Scheve, K. (2001). 'Analyzing Incomplete Political Science Data: An Alternative Algorithm for Multiple Imputations', *American Political Science Review*, 95: 49–69.

Kochan, T. A. and Osterman, P. (1994). *The Mutual Gains Enterprise*. Boston, MA: Harvard Business School Press.

Korczynski, M. (2002). *Human Resource Management in Service Work*. Basingstoke: Palgrave Macmillan.

Krueger, A. B. (1993). 'How Computers Have Changed the Wage Structure—Evidence from Microdata, 1984–1989', *Quarterly Journal of Economics*, 108: 33–60.

Kuha, J. (2004). 'AIC and BIC: Comparisons of Assumptions and Performance', *Sociological Methods and Research*, 33: 188–229.

Kuruvilla, S. and Erikson, C. L. (2002). 'Change and Transformation in Asian Industrial Relations', *Industrial Relations*, 41: 171–227.

Ladipo, D. and Wilkinson, F. (2002*a*). 'More Pressure, Less Protection', in B. Burchell, D. Ladipo, and F. Wilkinson (eds.), *Job Insecurity and Work Intensification*, London: Routledge.

—— —— (2002*b*). 'What Can Governments Do?', in B. Burchell, D. Ladipo, and F. Wilkinson (eds.), *Job Insecurity and Work Intensification*. London: Routledge.

Lane, R. (1991). *The Market Experience*. Cambridge: Cambridge University Press.

Lawler, Edward E. (1986). *High-Involvement Management*. San Francisco, CA: Jossey-Bass.

Layte, R. (1999). *Divided Time: Gender, Paid Employment, and Domestic Labour*. Aldershot: Ashgate.

Lazear, E. P. (1981). 'Agency, Earnings Profiles, Productivity, and Hours Restrictions', *American Economic Review*, 71: 606–20.

—— (1995). *Personnel Economics*. Cambridge MA.: MIT Press.

—— (1998). *Personnel Economics for Managers*. New York: John Wiley.

Lee, Y.-S. (2005). 'Measuring the Gender Gap in Household Labour: Accurately Estimating Wives' and Husbands' Contributions', in B. Schneider and L. J. Waite (eds.), *Being Together, Working Apart: Dual-Career Families and the Work-Life Balance*. Cambridge: Cambridge University Press.

Levitt, T. (1972). 'Production Line Approach to Service', *Harvard Business Review*, 72 (5): 41–52.

Lewin, D. (1994). 'Explicit Individual Contracting in the Labour Market', in C. Kerr and P. D. Staudohar (eds.), *Labour Economics and Industrial Relations*. Cambridge, MA: Harvard University Press.

Lindbeck, A. and Snower, D. (1988). *The Insider-Outsider Theory of Employment and Unemployment*. Cambridge, MA: MIT Press.

Locke, E. A. (1976). 'The Nature and Causes of Job Satisfaction', in M. D. Dunnette (ed.), *Handbook of Industrial and Organizational Psychology*. Chicago: Rand McNally.

Lockwood, D. (1958). *The Blackcoated Worker: A Study in Class Consciousness*. London: Allen and Unwin.

—— (1989). *The Blackcoated Worker: A Study in Class Consciousness*, 2nd edn. London: Allen and Unwin.

Lupton, T. (1963). *On the Shop Floor*. Oxford: Pergamon.

—— (ed.) (1972). *Payment Systems*. Harmondsworth: Penguin Books.

Machin, S. (1999). 'Wage Inequality in the 1970s, 1980s and 1990s', in P. Gregg and J. Wadsworth (eds.), *The State of Working Britain*. Manchester: Manchester University Press.

—— (2000). 'Union Decline in Britain', *British Journal of Industrial Relations*, 38: 631–45.

—— (2003). 'Skill-Biased Technical Change in the New Economy', in D. Jones (ed.), *New Economy Handbook*. Amsterdam: Elsevier.

—— and van Reenen, J. (1998). 'Technology and Changes in Skill Structure: Evidence from Seven OECD Countries', *Quarterly Journal of Economics*, 113: 1215–44.

MacInnes, J. (1987). *Thatcherism at Work: Industrial Relations and Economic Change*. Milton Keynes: Open University Press.

McGovern, P. (1998). *HRM, Technical Workers and the Multinational Corporation*. London: Routledge.

—— Hailey, V. H., and Stiles, P. (1998). 'The Managerial Career After Downsizing: Case Studies from the Leading Edge', *Work, Employment and Society*, 12: 457–78.

—— Smeaton, D., and Hill, S. (2004). 'Bad Jobs in Britain', *Work and Occupations*, 31: 225–49.

McRae, S. (1991). 'Occupational Change Over Childbirth: Evidence from a National Survey', *Sociology*, 25: 589–605.

Manski, C. F. (1995). *Identification Problems in the Social Sciences*. Cambridge, MA: Harvard University Press.

Marchington, M., Goodman, J., Wilkinson, A., and Ackers, P. (1992). *New Developments in Employee Involvement*. Sheffield: Employment Department.

Marks, S. R. and MacDermid, S. M. (1996). 'Multiple Roles and the Self: A Theory of Role Balance', *Journal of Marriage and the Family*, 58: 417–32.

Marmot, M. (2004). *Status Syndrome: How Your Social Standing Directly Affects Your Health and Life Expectancy*. London: Bloomsbury.

Marmot, M. G., Davey, S. G., Stansfeld, S., Patel, C., North, F., Head, J., White, I., Brunner, E., and Feeney, A. (1991). 'Health Inequalities Among British Civil Servants; the Whitehall II Study', *The Lancet*, 337: 1387–93.

Marsden, D. (1999). *A Theory of Employment Systems: Micro-Foundations of Societal Diversity*. Oxford: Oxford University Press.

Marshall, G., Newby, H., Rose, D., and Vogler, C. (1988). *Social Class in Modern Britain*. London: Hutchinson.

Marshall, T. H. (1965). 'Citizenship and Social Class', in T. H. Marshall (ed.), *Class, Citizenship and Social Development*. New York: Anchor Books.

Martell, R. F. (1991). 'Sex Bias at Work: The Effects of Attentional and Memory Demands on Performance Ratings of Men and Women', *Journal of Applied Social Psychology*, 21: 1939–60.

Marx, K. (1976). *Capital*. Harmondsworth: Penguin. (Originally published in German in 1867.)

—— (1979). *Wages, Price and Profit*. London: Central Books. (Originally published in German in 1865.)

Milgrom, P. and Roberts, D. J. (1992). *Economics, Organization, and Management*. Englewood Cliffs, NJ: Prentice Hall.

Milkie, M. A. and Peltola, P. (1999). Playing All the Roles: Gender and the Work-Family Balancing Act', *Journal of Marriage and the Family*, 61: 476–90.

Mills, C. W. (1951). *White Collar: The American Middle Classes*. New York: Oxford University Press.

Millward, N. (1994). *The New Industrial Relations*? London: Policy Studies Institute.

—— Bryson, A., and Forth, J. (2000). *All Change at Work? British Employment Relations 1980–98, as Portrayed by the Workplace Industrial Relations Survey Series*. London: Routledge.

Morgan, P., Allington, N., and Heery, E. (2000). 'Employment Insecurity in the Public Services', in E. Heery and J. Salmon (eds.), *The Insecure Workforce*. London: Routledge.

Neathey, F., Dench, S., and Thomson, L. (2003). *Monitoring Progress Towards Pay Equality*. EOC Research Discussion Series. Manchester: Equal Opportunities Commission.

Nichols, T. (1991). 'Labour Intensification, Work Injuries and the Measurement of the Percentage Utilization of Labour (PUL)', *British Journal of Industrial Relations*, 29: 569–601.

Nielsen, F. and Alderson, A. S. (2001). 'Trends in Income Inequality in the United States', in I. Berg and A. L. Kalleberg (eds.), *Sourcebook of Labour*

Markets: Evolving Structures and Processes. New York: Kluwer Academic/Plenum Press.

Nivea, V. F. and Gutek, B. A. (1980). 'Sex Effects of Evaluation', *Academy of Management Review*, 5: 267–76.

O'Connell Davidson, J. (1993). *Privatization and Employment Relations: The Case of the Water Industry*. London: Mansell.

OECD (1997). *Employment Outlook*. Paris: OECD Publications.

Offe, C. (1985). *Disorganized Capitalism*. Cambridge: Polity Press.

Oliver, N. and Wilkinson, B. (1992). *The Japanization of British Industry: New Developments in the 1990s*. Oxford: Blackwell.

Osterman, P. (1995). 'Work/Family Programmes and the Employment Relationship', *Administrative Science Quarterly*, 40: 681–700.

Padavic, I. and Reskin, B. (2002). *Women and Men at Work*. Thousand Oaks: Pine Forge.

Pakulski, J. and Waters, M. (1996). *The Death of Class*. London: Sage.

Perry-Jenkins, M., Repetti, R. L., and Crouter, A. C. (2000). 'Work and Family in the 1990s', *Journal of Marriage and the Family*, 62: 981–98.

Piore, M. J. (1975). 'Notes for a Theory of Labour Market Stratification', in R. C. Edwards, M. Reich, and D. M. Gordon (eds.), *Labour Market Segmentation*. Lexington MA: Heath.

Polanyi, K. [(1944) 1957]. *The Great Transformation*. Boston: Beacon.

Prandy, K. (1990). 'The Revised Cambridge Scale of Occupations', *Sociology*, 24: 629–55.

Price, L. and Price, R. (1994). 'Change and Continuity in the Status Divide', in K. Sisson (ed.), *Personnel Management: A Comprehensive Guide to Theory and Practice*, 2nd edn. Oxford: Blackwell.

Price, R. (1989). 'The Decline and Fall of the Status Divide?', in K. Sisson (ed.), *Personnel Management in Britain*. Oxford: Blackwell.

Purcell, J. (1993). 'The End of Institutional Industrial Relations', *Political Quarterly*, 64: 6–23.

Purcell, K. and Purcell, J. (1998). 'In-sourcing, Outsourcing, and Growth of Contingent Labour as Evidence of Flexible Employment Strategies', *European Journal of Work and Organizational Psychology*, 7: 39–59.

Ramsey, H., Scholarios, D., and Harley, B. (2000). 'Employees and High-Performance Work Systems: Testing Inside the Black Box', *British Journal of Industrial Relations*, 38: 501–32.

Robinson, J. P. and Bostrom, A. (1994). 'The Overestimated Workweek? What Time Diary Measures Suggest', *Monthly Labour Review*, 111(August): 11–23.

Robinson, P. (1995). 'Evolution Not Revolution: Have UK Labour Market Changes Been Vastly Overstated?', *New Economy*, 167–72.

Robinson, T. (1972). *Staff Status for Manual Workers*. London: Kogan Page.

Roche, W. K. (2001). 'The Individualization of Irish Industrial Relations?', *British Journal of Industrial Relations*, 39: 183–206.

Rose, D. and Pevalin, D. J. (2003). *A Researcher's Guide to the National Statistics Socio-Economic Classification*. London: Sage Publications.

Rose, M. J. (2005). 'Job Satisfaction in Britain: Coping with Complexity', *British Journal of Industrial Relations*, 43: 455–67.

Rosenthal, P., Hill, S., and Peccei, R. (1997). 'Checking Out Service: Evaluating Excellence, HRM and TQM in Retailing', *Work, Employment and Society*, 11: 481–503.

Rousseau, D. M. (1995). *Psychological Contracts in Organizations: Understanding Written and Unwritten Agreements*. Thousand Oaks, CA: Sage.

Roy, D. P. (1952). 'Quota Restriction and Goldbricking in a Machine Shop', *American Journal of Sociology*, 57: 427–42.

Rubery, J., Earnshaw, J., Marchington, M., Cooke, F. L., and Vincent, S. (2002). 'Changing Organizational Forms and the Employment Relationship', *Journal of Management Studies*, 39: 645–72.

Rubin, D. (1987). *Multiple Imputation for Nonresponse in Surveys*. New York: Wiley.

—— (1996). 'Multiple Imputation after 18+ Years', *Journal of the American Statistical Association*, 91: 473–89.

Russell, A. (1991). *The Growth of Occupational Welfare in Britain: Evolution and Harmonization of Modern Personnel Practice*. Aldershot: Avebury.

—— (1998). *The Harmonization of Employment Conditions in Britain: The Changing Workplace Divide Since 1950 and the Implications for Social Structure*. Basingstoke: Macmillan.

Savage, M. (2000). *Class Analysis and Social Transformation*. Buckingham: Open University Press.

Sayer, A. (1997). 'Contractualisation, Work and the Anxious Classes', in J. Holmer and J. C. Karlsson (eds.), *Work - Quo Vadis? Re-Thinking the Question of Work*. Aldershot: Avebury.

Scase, R. (1999). *Britain Towards 2010: The Changing Business Environment*. London: ESRC/DTI—Foresight.

Schneider, B. and Waite, L. J. (2005). 'Why Study Working Families?', in B. Schneider and L. J. Waite (eds.), *Being Together, Working Apart: Dual-Career Families and the Work-Life Balance*. Cambridge: Cambridge University Press.

Schor, J. (1991). *The Overworked American: The Unexpected Decline of Leisure*. New York: Basic Books.

Schwarz, G. (1978). 'Estimating the Dimension of a Model', *Annals of Statistics*, 6: 461–4.

Scott, J. (1990). 'Women and the Family', in R. Jowell, S. Witherspoon, and L. Brook (eds.), *British Social Attitudes: The 7th Report*. Aldershot: Gower.

—— (1999). 'Family Change: Revolution or Backlash in Attitudes?', in S. McRae (ed.), *Changing Britain: Families and Households in the 1990s*. Oxford: Oxford University Press.

Selznick, P. with Nonet, P., and Vollmer, H. M. (1969). *Law, Society, and Industrial Justice*. New York: Russell Sage Foundation.

Sennett, R. (1998). *The Corrosion of Character: The Personal Consequences of Work in the New Capitalism*. New York: W.W. Norton.

—— (2006). *The Culture of the New Capitalism*. New Haven, CT: Yale University Press.

Siebert, W. S and Addison, J. T. (1991). 'Internal Labour Markets: Causes and Consequences', *Oxford Review of Economic Policy*, 7: 76–92.

Sinclair, D. M. (1995). 'The Importance of Sex for the Propensity to Unionize', *British Journal of Industrial Relations*, 33: 173–90.

Skinner, C., Stuttard, N., Beissel-Durrant, G., and Jenkins, J. (2002). 'The Measurement of Low Pay in the UK Labour Force Survey', *Oxford Bulletin of Economics and Statistics*, 64: 653–76.

Smeaton, D. (2006). 'Work Return Rates After Childbirth in the UK—Trends, Determinants and Implications: A Comparison of Cohorts Born in 1958 and 1970', *Work, Employment and Society*, 20: 5–25.

Smith, A. (2001). 'Perceptions of Stress at Work', *Human Resource Management Journal*, 11: 74–86.

Smith, I. (1992). 'Reward Management and HRM', in P. Blyton and P. Turnbull (eds.), *Reassessing Human Resource Management*. London: Sage.

Smith, P. C., Kendall, L. M., and Hulin, C. L. (1969). *The Measurement of Satisfaction in Work and Retirement*. Chicago: Rand McNally.

Sørensen, A. B. (1996). 'The Structural Basis of Inequality', *American Journal of Sociology*, 101: 1333–65.

—— (2000). 'Toward a Sounder Basis for Class Analysis', *American Journal of Sociology*, 105: 1523–58.

—— (2001). 'Careers and Employment Relations', in I. Berg and A. L. Kalleberg (eds.), *Sourcebook of Labour Markets: Evolving Structures and Processes*. New York: Kluwer Academic/Plenum Press.

Stedman Jones, G. (1971). *Outcast London: A Study in the Relationship Between Classes in Victorian Society*. Oxford: Oxford University Press.

Stewart, A., Prandy, K., and Blackburn, R. M. (1980). *Social Stratification and Occupations*. London: Macmillan.

Storey, J. (1992) *Developments in the Management of Human Resources*. Oxford: Blackwell.

—— and Bacon, N. (1993). 'Individualism and Collectivism: Into the 1990s', *International Journal of Human Resource Management*, 4: 665–84.

Stouffer, S. A., Suchman, E. A., DeVinney, L. C., Star, S. A., and Williams, R. M. Jnr (1949). *The American Soldier: Adjustment During Army Life*. Princeton: Princeton University Press.

Streeck, W. (1987). 'The Uncertainties of Management in the Management of Uncertainty: Employers, Labour Relations and Industrial Adjustment in the 1980s', *Work, Employment and Society*, 1: 281–308.

Tåhlin, M. (2007). 'Class Clues', *European Sociological Review*. Forthcoming.

References

Tajfel, H. (1979*a*). 'Interindividual Behaviour and Intergroup Behaviour', in H. Tajfel (ed.), *Differentiation Between Social Groups: Studies in the Social Psychology of Intergroup Relations*. London: Academic.

Tajfel, H. (1979*b*). 'Social Categorization, Social Identity and Social Comparison', in H. Tajfel (ed.), *Differentiation Between Social Groups: Studies in the Social Psychology of Intergroup Relations*. London: Academic.

Taylor, P. and Bain, P. (2005). 'India Calling to the Far Away Towns: The Call Centre Labour Process and Globalization', *Work, Employment and Society*, 19: 261–82.

Tibshirani, R. (1996). 'Regression Shrinkage and Selection via the Lasso', *Journal of the Royal Statistical Society B*, 58: 267–88.

Tilly, C. and Tilly, C. (1998). *Work Under Capitalism*. Boulder, CO: Westview.

Towers, B. (1997). *The Representation Gap: Change and Reform in the British and American Workplace*. Oxford: Oxford University Press.

Townsend, P. (1979). *Poverty in the United Kingdom*. London: Allen Lane.

Turnbull, P. and Wass, V. (2000). 'Redundancy and the Paradox of Job Insecurity', in E. Heery and J. Salmon (eds.), *The Insecure Workforce*. London: Routledge.

Vernon, H. M. (1977). *Industrial Fatigue and Efficiency*. Salem, New Hampshire: Ayer.

Waddington, J. (2003). 'Trade Union Organization', in P. Edwards (ed.), *Industrial Relations: Theory and Practice*, 2nd edn. Oxford: Blackwell.

Wald, A. (1940). 'The Fitting of Straight Lines if Both Variables are Subject to Error', *Annals of Mathematical Statistics*, 11: 284–300.

Walters, S. (2002). 'Female Part-Time Workers' Attitudes to Trade Unions in Britain', *British Journal of Industrial Relations*, 40: 49–68.

Walton, R. E. (1972). 'How to Counter Alienation in the Plant', *Harvard Business Review*, 72 (6): 70–81.

—— (1985). 'From Control to Commitment in the Workplace', *Harvard Business Review*, 85 (2): 77–84.

—— (1987). *Innovating to Compete*. London: Jossey-Bass.

Warr, P. B. (1990). 'The Measurement of Well-Being and Other Aspects of Mental Health', *Journal of Occupational Psychology*, 55: 297–312.

Waterman, R. H. Jr., Waterman, J. A., and Collard, B. A. (1994). 'Toward a Career-Resilient Workforce', *Harvard Business Review*, 94 (4): 87–95.

Webb, S. and Webb, B. (1894). *The History of Trade Unionism*. London: Longmans.

Weber, M. (1947). *The Theory of Social and Economic Organization* [A. M. Henderson (trans.) and T. Parsons (trans. & ed.)]. New York: Free Press.

—— (1968). G. Roth and C. Wittich (eds.), *Economy and Society*. New York: Bedminster Press.

Wedderburn, D. and Craig, C. (1974). 'Relative Deprivation in Work', in D. Wedderburn (ed.), *Poverty, Inequality and the Class Structure*. Cambridge: Cambridge University Press.

Weeden, K. A. and Grusky, D. B. (2005). 'The Case for a New Class Map', *American Journal of Sociology*, 111: 141–212.

318

Weitzman, M. L. (1985). 'Profit Sharing as Macroeconomic Policy', *American Economic Review*, 75: 937–53.

Western, B. (1997). *Between Class and Market: Postwar Unionization in the Capitalist Democracies*. Princeton, NJ: Princeton University Press.

White, M., Hill, S., McGovern, P., Mills, C., and Smeaton, D. (2003). ' "High-Performance" Management Practices, Working Hours and Work-Life Balance', *British Journal of Industrial Relations*, 41: 175–96.

White, M., Hill, S., Mills, C., and Smeaton, D. (2004). *Managing to Change? British Workplaces and the Future of Work*. Basingstoke: Palgrave Macmillan.

Wickens, P. (1987). *The Road to Nissan: Flexibility, Quality, Teamwork*. Basingstoke: Macmillan.

Williamson, O. E. (1981). 'The Economics of Organization: The Transaction Cost Approach', *American Journal of Sociology*, 87: 548–77.

—— (1985). *The Economic Institutions of Capitalism*. New York: The Free Press.

Wood, S. (1996) 'High Commitment Management and Payment Systems', *Journal of Management Studies*, 33: 53–77.

—— (1999). 'Human Resource Management and Performance', *International Journal of Management Reviews*, 1: 367–413.

—— and de Menezes, L. (1998). 'High Commitment Management in the UK: Evidence from the Workplace Industrial Relations Survey and the Employers' Manpower and Skills Practices Survey', *Human Relations*, 51: 485–515.

—— —— and Lasaosa, A. (2003). 'Family-Friendly Management in Great Britain: Testing Various Perspectives', *Industrial Relations*, 42: 221–50.

Worrall, L. and Cooper, C. (2001). *The Quality of Working Life: 2000 Survey of Managers' Changing Experiences*. London: The Institute of Management.

Yeuk-Mui, M. T. (2001). 'Information Technology in Frontline Service Work Organization', *Journal of Sociology*, 37: 177–206.

Author Index

Subject Index